THE GREAT ROMAN DRAMATISTS

PLAUTUS, *ca.* 255–184 B.C., was born into a lower-class family and began writing plays to save himself from a life of drudgery. He was so successful that he became one of the most widely imitated playwrights of the ancient world.

TERENCE, 185–159 B.C., was brought to Rome from North Africa as a slave by a freethinking master who educated him and freed him. As a playwright, he is notable for his deep understanding of human nature. As he said in one of his works: "I am a human being: whatever is human concerns me."

SENECA, *ca.* 4 B.C.–A.D. 65, was a philosopher, a writer, and a Roman senator. He is also famous as the tutor of Nero, who accused him of conspiracy and forced him to commit suicide.

THE LIBRARY OF WORLD DRAMA

JOHN GASSNER

*Sterling Professor of
Dramatic Literature
Yale University*

GENERAL EDITOR

also available in this series

SPANISH DRAMA
edited by Angel Flores

CLASSICAL FRENCH DRAMA
edited and translated by Wallace Fowlie

CLASSICAL GERMAN DRAMA
translated by Theodore H. Lustig
with an introduction by Victor Lange

19TH CENTURY RUSSIAN DRAMA
translated by Andrew MacAndrew
with an introduction by Marc Slonim

20TH CENTURY RUSSIAN DRAMA
translated and introduced by Andrew MacAndrew

MEDIEVAL AND TUDOR DRAMA
edited, with introductions and modernizations by John Gassner

ROMAN DRAMA

TRANSLATED BY
SAMUEL LIEBERMAN
and
FRANK JUSTUS MILLER

WITH AN INTRODUCTION BY
SAMUEL LIEBERMAN
QUEENS COLLEGE

BANTAM BOOKS / NEW YORK

ROMAN DRAMA

A Bantam Classic / published August 1964

Library of Congress Catalog Card Number: 64-20908

Medea, Hippolytus and Oedipus from SENECA'S TRAGEDIES, *Volume I,*
translated by Frank Justus Miller, 1960. Reprinted by permission of
Harvard University Press and the Loeb Classical Library.

Contents

The Legacy of Rome

BY JOHN GASSNER

It is not too much to say that without legacies from classical Rome the European and American theatre would have followed a different course of development. Whether or not we hold the remains of Roman dramatic literature in a high esteem today, and it was once held in the *highest* esteem, Rome gave impetus to the emergence of modern drama out of the religious folk drama of the Middle Ages. Familiarity with dramatic craftsmanship and characterization since the Renaissance requires some knowledge of both classical comedy and tragedy, and the history of the postmedieval European stage cannot be written without reference to the Roman theatre.

Two ways of appreciating this influence have been apparent; one way has been to regard Rome as a primary transmission belt for Greek culture, and the other to credit the Roman authors with originality of treatment. In either case, the absence of virtually all the Greek plays upon which Plautus and Terence based their comedies, the liberties of adaptation taken by the authors, and the marked differences between the Latin language and the Greek compel us to focus attention on the extant plays as if they were independent creations. These adaptations have given pleasure to many generations of Western man, and have multiplied delight both by inspiring adaptations themselves and by setting writers of European comedy an example. And if there is decidedly less to be said for Roman tragedy, almost entirely represented by nine plays written by Seneca and an additional one attributed to him, its literary interest was by no means negligible and its effect on the theatre of the Renaissance considerable.

Rome is said to have been founded in the year 753 B.C., but Latin literature as we know it virtually starts five centuries later with the advent of Plautus (*ca.* 255–184 B.C.), the first of the Roman master playwrights. Comedy had been written successfully before his time. But the extravagant type of political play

1

associated with the Athenian comic poet Aristophanes came to an end with the close of the fifth century, and the work of the later Greek playwrights which Plautus and Terence imitated has survived only fragmentarily. The most substantial fragments (by Menander) were discovered only in our own time and could not directly affect the course of the postclassic theatre. It is evident, moreover, that Plautus infused classic comedy with his own theatrical flair and his own boisterous sense of humor, replete with worldly wisdom or folksy philosophy. Although the exuberance of a social and political critic like Aristophanes could no longer arise in the classic theatre, Plautus proved that domestic comedy based upon fairly familiar types of people and situations could be invigorated and enlivened by a playwright able to draw upon native resources of humor. Plautus, in brief, possessed in considerable measure the exuberance that had gone into Aristophanic comedy and that vanished with the political decline of Athens. With characteristic Roman vigor, and with the buoyancy of a natural comedian and strolling player, Plautus gave the European theatre a new lease on the comic energy, the *vis comica,* that has kept it a going concern, with and without literary distinction, for well over two thousand years.

His contribution, moreover, came not so much from the content of the comedies that have come down to us (even the plot of mistaken identities had been well exploited before him), but through the varied vivacity of his dialogue and lyric passages and through the characters who sustain the action. It is these attributes that made Plautus a master of comedy and not merely of farce. He did not, it is true, invent these characters; and the frequency of their appearance in comedy and the recurrence of the traits by which they are recognized make us refer to them as "character types" or even stereotypes. But they are rich with *theatrical* life; and their liveliness, along with the diversity of characters within each type, accounts for a good deal of their long life in the theatre, which has been further assured by the universality of the traits they embody. We would not be able to recognize a considerable portion of the world's dramatic literature without the lovelorn young men (*adulescentes*), old men (*senes*), or intractable fathers, designing courtesans, pretentious military persons (the *miles gloriosus,* or "braggart soldier" type), cunning servants or slaves (*servi*), panders, parasites, and other types that provide the comic élan of a countless number of plays. They constitute the familiar world with which the playwrights of Europe were most rewardingly concerned whenever they left the majestic heights of tragedy and the fairy land of romantic adventures and pastoral pleasures.

Terence, born some seventy years after Plautus, contributed the grace (rather than the vigor) and the literary finesse (rather than the theatrical adroitness) indispensable to *high* comedy; by comparison, the art of Plautus is *low* or broad comedy. "Where Plautus descends to farce," wrote Moses Hadas (*A History of Latin Literature,* 1952), "Terence rises to the true comedy of manners." The six plays of Terence are models of distinguished writing originally intended for a cultivated rather than a popular public. His treatment of sex, for instance, was not farcical, and he was somewhat salacious in his extant plays only once, in the *Eunuchus,* in which a young man gains access to a girl by disguising himself as a eunuch. Instead of hearty Plautine laughter, Terence (185–159 B.C.) offers his admirers a knowing smile; and the urbane intellectualism that guided his youthful and short career is also exemplified by his argumentative prologues in which he defends himself against detractors and pleads for unbiased attention. It is plain that he took liberties with the original Greek plays. One scholar (W. Beare, *The Roman Stage,* 1951, p. 971) goes so far as to say that Terence "was, in a limited sense, an original dramatist forced by circumstances to pose as a mere translator."

If Terence, with his generally subdued language and action, could not become a popular dramatist in his own lifetime, he nevertheless became an influence and inspiration in later times— and much sooner than Plautus; it was possible to tolerate his refined humor in the medieval age of faith, and the tenth-century Saxon nun Hrotsvitha, while rejecting his worldly morality, tried to use his plays as models for her morally unimpeachable "high comedies." His command of characterization and of contrasts of character, so apparent, for instance, in his masterpiece, *The Brothers,* could indeed not fail to be appreciated in the period of Renaissance humanism; an entire school of stage production, utilizing shallow arcadelike stages, was inspired by the vogue of his plays in educated circles. His elegantly written plays, free from topical allusions, also made clear and pleasurable reading; few writers of Latin needed less explication.

Habent sua fata libelli, the Latin saying that books have their own destiny, applies equally to the plays of the two playwrights who divided the world of comedy between them. Among their debtors have been the greatest modern playwrights, too, from Molière to Bernard Shaw; and, in encountering in their work a

frequent blending of Plautine joviality with Terentian intel-
lectuality, one would be hard put to it to decide to whom they
were more indebted, the bluff Roman soldier of fortune or his
successor, the young fastidious darling of the Roman aristocracy.

Edith Hamilton (in *The Roman Way,* 1932) stresses another
distinction between Plautus and Terence, regarding the former
as the virtual originator of the type of comedy that relies on
comic irony (the plot is summarized in advance, so that the
public knows everything that the character on the stage does not
yet know) and the latter as the master of "the method of suspense and surprise, depending upon plot or upon the reaction
of character to character, or to situation." Plautus, evidently trying to hold the attention of a festive crowd, provides a synopsis
in his prologues; Terence, addressing himself to a more sophisticated public, supplies no advance information, and he even uses
double plots and unexpected turns of action. Molière depends
upon comic irony in his *Amphitryon* and in a famous scene in
The Miser in which the elderly miser is talking about his money
—and the young man about his lady-love, while each supposes
the other has the same object in mind. Shakespeare employs
comic irony in *Much Ado About Nothing,* in which much of the
humor arises from the spectators' knowledge of the plot to bring
Beatrice and Benedick together. A judicious mixture of comic
irony and interest in the development of plot and character is
about as far as playwrights have been able to go in aiming at
effectiveness.

The amplitude of humor in the robust and varied work of
Plautus justifies his being regarded by the great classical scholar,
J. W. Mackail (*The Legacy of Rome,* 1923) as "the parent and
source of all modern comedy in its many varieties, the master
and literary ancestor of Shakespeare and Molière no less than of
a thousand dramatists of inferior achievement and less established
fame." And the fine finish of Terence, also apparent in distinguished European plays by Molière, Marivaux, Beaumarchais,
Goldoni, Musset, Schnitzler, and others, is an especially treasured
quality of English comedy of manners since the Restoration
period. Such celebrated practitioners as Congreve, Sheridan,
Wilde, Maugham, Van Druten, Philip Barry and S. N. Behrman
could justifiably claim descent from Terence.* The genre of so-

---

* Molière's *The School for Husbands* (*L'École des Maris*) derives from
Terence's *The Brothers* (*Adelphoe*), and *The Miser* (*L'Avare*) is a close adapta-
tion of Plautus' *Aulularia* (*The Pot of Gold*). Molière imitated Terence's
Phormio closely in the famous light comedy *Les Fourberies de Scapin* (*The
Deceits of Scapin*). Shakespeare's *Comedy of Errors* is based, in part, on the
Menaechmi, and Ben Jonson's *The Case Is Altered* combines the action of the

called comedy of ideas we associate with a number of Bernard Shaw's plays has a worthy ancestor in the provocative laughter of *The Brothers,* in which Terence deals with the problem of bringing up the young; and the English theatre's greatest comedy of manners, Congreve's *The Way of the World,* is also the most completely Terentian comedy in the language.

Although the history of literary comedy virtually ends with the death of Terence in 159 B.C., the Roman theatre did not cease to pour comic style and matter into the common store of European humor for many centuries. Plays with Italian backgrounds and characters wearing the traditional Roman toga (*fabulae togatae*) succeeded the *fabulae palliatae,* the plays with Greek backgrounds and *dramatis personae* wearing the Greek palliata written by Plautus and Terence. Early improvisatory plays, the *fabulae Atellanae* or Atellan farces, acquired a relatively fixed form in the second and first centuries before Christ, and *mimes,* specializing in gesticulation and acrobatics, proliferated and even passed into wordless pantomime. Since these entertainments have not come down to us as more than titles and fragments, we have no way of estimating their merit beyond concluding that whatever merits they possessed were subliterary. They left their mark primarily on the nonliterary, largely improvisatory art of the strolling players of the Middle Ages and the Renaissance, indirectly influencing the purveyors of popular entertainment in continental Europe after 1550. These players who acquired the name of *commedia dell'arte* for their professionalism, used mere scenarios or outlines of plots instead of fully written plays.

When we encounter literary drama in Rome after the death of Terence it is in the form of plays intended for reading and recitation in private halls rather than for public performance. All but one of the surviving examples dealt with the materials of Greek tragedy (already between four and five hundred years old) and were written by the Spanish-born courtier, statesman and philoso-

---

Aulularia and *Captivi* (*The Captives*). Plautus' *Miles Gloriosus* (*The Braggart Soldier*) is imitated in the best pre-Shakespearean comedy, *Ralph Roister Doister* (*ca.* 1533), by the schoolmaster Nicholas Udall, who also borrowed somewhat from Terence's *The Eunuch.* Gilbert Highet in *The Classical Tradition* (Oxford, 1949) lists many other imitations, starting with one made in Italian in the late fifteenth century for the Duke of Ferrara, about half a century after twelve of the lost plays of Plautus were discovered and brought to Rome in 1429. The play was the *Menaechmi,* which was also adapted in Spain. The roundabout nature of the dispersion of Roman comedy is illustrated by Ariosto's *Gli Suppositi,* which the Italian poet based on *The Captives* of Plautus and *The Eunuch* of Terence in 1502-1503. It was then adapted in England by George Gascoyne in 1566 under the title of *The Supposes* for production at Oxford and London.

pher, Seneca (*ca.* 4 B.C.–A.D. 65). Seneca combined stoic moraliza-
tion with an almost ghoulish taste for melodrama that would have
qualified him as the poet laureate of Parisian *grand guignol*. Displays of extreme emotional intensity expressed with high-voltage
rhetoric but ill-suited for the stage, his tragedies could have
easily disappeared from world literature. Instead, these "closet
dramas" set the fashion for Renaissance tragedy, contributing
the conventional figure of the ghost to Elizabethan drama and
the grandeur of characters who display their sense of worth with
ringing affirmativeness or sum up the dramatic action with high-
sounding, epigrammatic statements known as *sententiae*. As the
classical scholar George E. Duckworth noted, "Seneca portrays
human life as dignified and meaningful," attributing freedom of
will to men and enabling them to rise above misfortune or to face
death with fortitude. It was well said by T. S. Eliot that "when
an Elizabethan hero or villain dies, he usually dies in the odour
of Seneca"—that is, with "a quotation from Seneca, or a thought
or figure ultimately derived from Seneca." And with good reason,
since Seneca was a master of ethical postures and of dramatic
emphasis: "In the verbal *coup de théâtre* no one has ever ex-
celled him" (Eliot, *Selected Essays,* 1950), and rhetoric or de-
clamatory speech was indeed an important element, the great
virtue as well as the great defect, in the plays of Marlowe,
Shakespeare, and their contemporaries.

The vogue of treachery, the revenge motive, the appearance of
ruthless tyrants on the stage, the examples of stoic hardihood, the
explosions of passion, the fascination with torture and murder,
the sense of life being lived and death being suffered at the highest pitch, the self-regard of individuals and their concern with
their posture before the world, and the prevalence of strong
language ranging from sheer bombast to memorable expression—
these qualities, which the English-speaking world associates especially with the Elizabethan and Jacobean theatre, had their origin
chiefly in the work of a Roman man of letters who did not even
write for the theatre. But Seneca possessed such an overflowing
feeling for dramatic situations oddly at variance with his profes-
sions of philosophical detachment that the course of the sixteenth-
and early-seventeenth-century theatre is almost unthinkable without him. Through his vehement declamations, Rome fathered
European tragedy, while the superior achievements of fifth-century Athenian tragedy remained in the limbo of ignorance or at
most led a shadowy existence for all but a small circle of scholars.

Seneca's influence on the English theatre after his great vogue
in Italy and France, which is to be found in the work of Kyd,

Marlowe, Chapman, Marston, Ben Jonson, and other Elizabethan writers, is discussed in several important studies, such as John W. Cunliffe's *The Influence of Seneca on Elizabethan Tragedy* (London, 1893; New York, 1907) and F. L. Lucas' *Seneca and Elizabethan Tragedy* (Cambridge University Press, 1922). Especially influential, in view of the popularity of revenge tragedy and melodrama started by Thomas Kyd's *The Spanish Tragedy* about 1586, was Seneca's *Thyestes*. But the Senecan tone or style of expression was a stronger influence than Senecan plot. Although Shakespeare apparently never quoted Seneca in the original except in his frenetic melodrama *Titus Andronicus*, he knew the plays quite well. According to Gilbert Highet (*The Classical Tradition*) his conception of tragedy and some of his memorable speeches were inspired by Seneca: "For the English playwrights of the Renaissance, Seneca was the master of Tragedy." Professor Highet calls attention to an interesting parallel between Hercules' speech in Seneca's *Hercules Furens*:

> Why this my soul should linger in the world
> there's now no reason. Lost are all my goods,
> mind, weapons, glory, wife, children, strength,
> even my madness

and Macbeth's

> I have lived long enough; my way of life
> Is fallen into the sere, the yellow leaf;
> And that which should accompany old age,
> As honour, love, obedience, troops of friends,
> I must not look to have.

But these parallels do not have to be insisted upon when it is possible to find numerous close quotations throughout the dramatic literature of the age, and when his style set so early an example to English playwrights that Sir Philip Sidney could salute *Gorboduc,* produced in 1561, as "full of stately speeches and well sounding phrases, climbing to the height of Seneca his style, and as full of notable morality which it doth most delightfully teach and so obtain the very end of Poesie. . . ." It is not surprising, considering the admiration implied in this tribute, that after Sidney's death his sister, the Countess of Pembroke, should have gathered around her a number of writers of "Senecal" plays. And it is to be noted that Seneca, whose Latin text was accessible to educated gentlemen and whose plays were produced in Latin at Cambridge and Oxford, could have made his considerable impression on the first Elizabeth's subjects even without being translated into English. A number of imitations in Latin were also produced at the universities and the Inns of Court. But translations began to appear by 1559, when Jasper Heywood's version of *Troades* (*Trojan Women*) was published; his versions of *Thyestes* and *Hercules Furens* appeared in 1560 and 1561 respectively; and by 1581, about half a decade before the production of that enormously popular, more or less Senecan, melodrama, *The Spanish Tragedy* (its author, Thomas Kyd, may have also written the first *Hamlet*), all nine plays by Seneca, along with an *Octavia* wrongly attributed to him, were printed in English under the title of *Seneca: His Tenne Tragedies,* edited by Thomas Newton. The compilation constitutes one of the great Tudor translations. A reprint in two volumes published in 1927 contains a long and illuminating introduction by T. S. Eliot, which also appears in his *Selected Essays* (1950). According to him, "Not only the evolution of the dramatic structure, but the evolution of the blank verse cadence, took place under the shadow of Seneca." If this claim should seem extravagant, it is made by a master of prosody whose opinion cannot be lightly dismissed. And it is especially correct to say that Elizabethan drama was lifted to its familiar heights by a ferment consisting of literary Senecan and popular theatrical elements.

Rome, we should note in conclusion, also contributed an influence to the development of the Renaissance and modern stage because of the Roman tendency toward specific representation. This was apparent in the multiplication of masks for the comic character types (each type had its prescribed costume, wig, and mask) and in the increasing illusionism and spectacularity of the Roman theatre. Plautus relies heavily on theatricality, strong gesture and stage movement, mime, and interlarded songs (the so-called *cantica*), but his speech is so colloquial that an austerely formalistic style of stage production is almost unthinkable in his case; apparently he even dispensed with masks. Roman actors performed on a raised stage against a back-scene pierced by three doors that could represent three different houses, with the area in front of the houses serving as a street. This was the basic pattern of the Renaissance stage first developed in Italy as a result of the survival of information, illustrated with diagrams, on the architecture of the Roman theatre in a first-century B.C. treatise, *De Architectura,* by Vitruvius, discovered in 1419, printed in 1511, and translated into Italian in 1521. Perfect illusion was not aimed at, of course, since the use of the mask is a formal device and since women's parts were played by men; Plautus also achieved comic effects by having an actor violate illusion in stepping out of his part and addressing the audience. Interior scenes could not be represented on the Roman stage so that the dramatic action, including banquets, took place in front of the stage houses—in the street, as it were. But revolving stands or prisms (*periaktoi*), with scenery painted on them, added illusion to the stage productions, and certain conventions facilitated it too; an imaginary street ran behind the houses, and the side-exits on the street to the spectator's right and left were supposed to lead to the city Forum or to the harbor and the country respectively. Temporary wooden structures were used at first. They were supplanted by permanent theatres (with a roof over the stage area) during the first century B.C. (the first stone theatre was erected in 55 B.C.) and became increasingly elaborate in décor; they were also supplied with drop curtains for concealing and revealing scenery.

It was not long before there were excellent open-air theatres throughout the Roman Empire. These became the scene of spectacles of all sorts, gladiatorial and even nautical, that were equaled only when the Renaissance and Baroque theatres of Europe became the home of opera fifteen centuries later. It is unfortunate, however, that the drama declined while the spectacles grew more lavish. When the hostility of the early Christian Church became strong enough to curtail the theatre in the fifth century A.D. and to close its doors in the sixth century, there was nothing left that could not be carried away by itinerant mimes in the form of remembered character types and comic situations.

Introduction

BY SAMUEL LIEBERMAN

The reading public is more familiar with Greek drama than with Roman drama, and when people think of ancient comedy it is generally Aristophanes who comes to mind. Yet there is a whole area of ancient comedy—New Comedy—that was largely unknown until the last decade, except for fragments and references to the names of Greek playwrights who worked in this medium and, happily, for the plays of the Romans Plautus and Terence. While this situation has been remedied somewhat by the recent discovery, publication, and translation of *Dyskolos* (*The Curmudgeon,* or *The Grouch*), a complete play by Menander, the most esteemed of the New Comedy writers, the plays of Plautus and Terence, though in Latin, are still the best indicators of the range and quality of this type of drama. For the modern reader and audience however, these Roman plays are of interest not only from the point of view of the history of drama, but also because they are entertaining and moving in themselves if properly translated and effectively staged.

Roman drama has been called Greek drama Romanized, but this is an oversimplification, especially in the case of comedy. One might with equal, or as little, justice say that much of Shakespeare is Plutarch Anglicized, or that Molière is a French version of Plautus and Terence. Such oversimplifications lose sight of individual genius, and of the special qualities of the national cultures which these writers express in their works. True, Plautus and Terence adapted Greek comedies, but they did not merely translate; they creatively adapted the Greek material into something a Roman audience could respond to and appreciate, and the result was usually masterly. Seneca coming at the end of a 300-year tradition of tragedy, tried, like his predecessors, to do similarly with this form of drama, but does not seem to have been as successful, at least by today's tastes. Yet the sixteenth- and seventeenth-century European dramatists admired him greatly, took him as their master, and imitated him extensively. His long rhetorical speeches and melodramatic action were perfectly to the taste of the time, and Shakespeare, Racine, and the Italian and Spanish dramatists found him an important source and model.

The Romans and their Italic kinsmen had, before their contact with the Greeks, their own native proto-dramatic forms which, though rude and primitive, might well have developed into genuine theatre. These were the Satura, a medley of improvisations performed with song, dance, and pantomime, but having no plot; the Fescennines, exchanges of amusing vituperation, but not dramatic; and Atellan Farces with stock characters and bawdy humor. These receded into the background about the third century B.C., when the Greek influence began to profoundly affect Roman civilization in general, and the highly developed Greek comedy and tragedy was eagerly translated, imitated, and adapted. Among the pioneers in this endeavor were Ennius (best known as the founder of Latin epic), Accius, and Pacuvius, whose works have not survived except in fragments. In some of the Roman playwrights, notably Plautus, the lusty native Italic elements maintained a strong influence, so that his plays, though Greek in origin, locale, and characters, are unmistakably Roman in spirit and tone. On the other hand, Terence's more elegant and restrained comedies, though written in a Latin so pure that it became a model of style, have a thoroughly Greek feeling.

The Greek plays that Plautus and Terence adapted were not, then, the fifth-century Old Comedy of writers like Aristophanes with their outspoken political satire, but were rather the quieter apolitical, social comedies of men like Menander, Diphilus, and Philemon, who wrote in the fourth and early third centuries B.C. when a new spirit was in the air in Greece. This was the period when the Greek city-state had passed its prime, and the conquests of Alexander and the subsequent establishment of Hellenistic empires limited the political independence of the Greek cities, making political satire unattractive and impossible. It was also a period in which the emphasis was more on individual problems than on the community and its political life. The New Comedy is thus bourgeois comedy with average, middle-class characters and everyday problems heightened and dramatized, and they were as popular with Greek audiences as they were later in Latin adaptation with the Romans. (For the political satire which flourished among them, Roman writers developed a separate and distinct form: verse satire.)

Such comedies accordingly dealt with family problems—problems of father-and-son relationships, conflicts between husband

and wife, love between young people, separation of families by war or other disasters. Like many modern movies designed for mass audiences, the plots were frequently "boy-meets-girl," with the complication of parental objection to their union—the girl in the case, though pretty and accomplished, is not a suitable match, but is a slave girl or even an apparent courtesan. After much maneuvering, attended by comic incidents, misunderstandings, deceptions involving parasites, clever slaves, friends, and other standard characters, there is a happy ending in which the girl turns out to be the long-lost daughter of a respectable citizen, and all is well. Such plots appealed to audiences (as they do even now) and did not appear too far-fetched for many reasons. First, in the numerous wars and upheavals of the Hellenistic period, enough such separations and reunions had actually occurred in the Mediterranean world to make the incidents believable. Second, the materials were handled with enough variation and verve to keep the spectators interested. Finally, in a playwright like Plautus, the humor, wit, and high spirits make the plot as such less important, and in a Terence the development of character, the style, the poet's humanity similarly rise far above the variations of the same old story.

While the materials that Plautus and Terence worked on were similar their finished products were different, as were their lives and personalities. Plautus, the earlier of the two (*ca.* 255–184 B.C.), wrote at a time when Rome, dominant in Italy, was engaged in a life struggle with Carthage for control of the western Mediterranean and almost simultaneously half-unwillingly found herself involved in a series of wars and diplomatic maneuverings to keep order among the Greek states and Macedonia. By the middle of the second century, Rome found herself with a world empire, changing social, economic, and political conditions, and an overwhelming tide of Greek culture to be absorbed. The audiences which Plautus' comedies played to were the same Roman people who had served in the armies and had acquired a taste for and some familiarity with things Greek, although Roman leaders were at odds about the advisability of diluting Roman traditions with Greek culture. Some, like the conservative Cato the Elder, resisted almost to the end; others, like the broad-minded Scipios, also eminent leaders, welcomed it and became the center of Hellenizing tendencies in Rome. By the time Terence was writing, these tendencies were in the ascendant and he enjoyed the patronage of this family of philhellenes.

Titus Maccius Plautus, like many a Roman writer, was not a

native Roman. Born into a lower-class family in northern Italy, he came to Rome as a young man to seek his fortune. There he seems to have done both manual work and some acting in the temporary wooden theatres of the time. For a period thereafter he was engaged in business, and when this failed he supported himself by hard work in a mill. He eventually liberated himself from this toil by writing plays, and he became so successful that imitators passed off their work as his, so that 130 works, more than he actually wrote, were attributed to him. Of his many works twenty-one complete plays have come down to us, of which twenty are considered genuine. The larger number claimed for him by ancient sources is also due to the fact that he helped other playwrights revise their plays, a not uncommon practice then as now. Somewhere in his long life he learned Greek and perfected his Latin, for his native dialect was Umbrian.

The life of Publius Terentius Afer, or Terence, too, is unusual for one who became a classic of drama and Latin style, and shows the assimilative power of Roman and Greek culture. He was not even an Italian like Plautus, but a North African, as his cognomen, Afer (the African), and ancient sources indicate. Born in 195 B.C. in Carthage, though not a Carthaginian, and dark in complexion, he came to Rome as the young slave of the senator Terentius Lucanus, from whom he got part of his name. His master, attracted by his good looks and good mind, educated him and set him free. Soon thereafter this handsome and intelligent ex-slave became a friend of the younger Scipio and Laelius, leaders of the cultured circle who were making Greek thought and literature fashionable at Rome and who encouraged him in his efforts at writing plays. What is especially noteworthy is that this foreigner learned Latin so well that his language was of the purest quality and beauty. He wrote so well, in fact, that not only was he held up as a model of Latinity by later generations, but in his own day his enemies charged that his aristocratic friends must have collaborated with him if they had not, in fact, done the job themselves. Before his premature death on a voyage to Greece in 159 B.C., this gifted man produced six plays, all extant, which though they did not have the robustness of Plautus (which he did not aim at), are most effective and even moving in their quiet way, and more true to life. Terence is deservedly admired for his depiction of character, which rises above mere types, his humanity, his language, and his epigrams, some of which now circulate almost as proverbs. One of his sayings, widely quoted as expressing the essence of true humanism, is from *Heauton Timoroumenos* (*The Self-Tormentor*): *Homo sum: humani nihil a me alienum puto*—"I am a human being: whatever is human concerns me."

The plays of Plautus selected for translation in this volume are three of his best and they show his wide range. *The Menaechmi Twins* (*Menaechmi*), the basis of many later comedies, particularly Shakespeare's *Comedy of Errors*, is a farce turning on mistaken identities. The action is fast and furious, abounding in hilarious situations and humorous repartee, puns and other plays on language. Its aim is the "belly laugh" and it is still very funny today. *Prisoners of War* (*Captivi*), a quieter comedy, has a more serious intent, which Plautus emphasizes in the play's final speech to the audience: "This play was composed on good moral principles and nothing improper was put into it. There is no illicit love affair, no substitution of children, and no young man secretly in love buys the freedom of a prostitute without his father's knowledge. Writers produce few comedies of this kind, in which the good become better." The play turns on the mutual loyalty and love between a slave and his young master, both prisoners of war. The slave here is not the standard rascal typical of ancient comedy but a man as good as his master. While part of the plot does involve an exchange of identities between the two, the stress is rather on character, on the human being and his reactions to the misfortunes of war, whether captor or captive. *The Rope* (*Rudens*) is in turn quite different from the first two in that, though it has its share of standard characters, nature too is in a sense a character. The play takes place on a rocky North African coast, and the action is set in motion by a violent storm at sea, resulting in a shipwreck which, though dangerous at its height, ultimately brings happiness to those who deserve it and humane punishment to those who deserve that. In addition, the young man in love is vigorous and energetic instead of a weakling to be extricated from his troubles by a clever slave, and the girl he loves has character and personality and takes an active part in the development of the action. Through it all smiles the Goddess of Love whose temple is part of the scenery of that rocky shore.

The three plays by Terence here translated, though much more similar in plot to one another than the three of Plautus, are yet also different in a subtler way. All involve the problem of young men in love with or secretly married to young girls against the wishes of their fathers, but the treatment and themes are quite varied. In *The Brothers* (*Adelphoe*) the theme deals with the best way of bringing up sons—strictness or enlightened leniency. As Micio, the sophisticated father who advocates leniency, says early in the play: "I believe it is better to control children by developing in them a moral sense and a sense of honor rather than by fear." Referring to his brother Demea, who is of the opposite conviction, he says: ". . . he is making a big mistake if he believes control is greater and more effective if it is imposed by force than if it is exercised by friendliness." Of course, both extremes produce problems, and it is worth noting that the same debate is still going on today. In the *Phormio,* the play is given a certain poignancy when the elderly father of one of the two young men in trouble turns out himself to be in trouble because of a secret love affair conducted years before in another town while he was away on business, an affair whose results have an important bearing on the action of the play. Also, the Phormio of the title is a parasite, usually a comic role, but here the chief agent in tangling and disentangling the plot complications. In *The Woman of Andros (Andria),* which is the basis of Thornton Wilder's novelette of the same name, a father's pleasure at his son's retention of good character in spite of his acquaintance with gay companions and a lady of ill repute turns to dismay when he realizes he has been looking in the wrong direction. It is not the courtesan, recently dead, who had roused his son's emotions but her young, lovely, and apparently pure ward. Involved also are the helplessness of a young woman alone in a hard world and the close friendship of two elderly men strained to the breaking point by impossible demands on the claims of friendship to save a son from what is thought to be corruption. Here a faithful slave risks his own neck to bring things to a happy conclusion.

While these translations are in prose, the reader is reminded that Roman, like Greek, comedy was written in unrhymed verse. The dialogue was in a six- or seven-beat iambic meter, and numerous lyrical passages were interposed in the form of solos, duets, and even trios. These lyrical passages with musical accompaniment were sung either by the actor or actors in the role or by a special member of the cast called *cantor,* or singer, while the actor played the role in dance or pantomime. This *cantor* was also the one who, in the plays of Terence, was assigned the task of calling for applause at the end.

Another characteristic of New Comedy as seen in the works of Plautus and Terence (as well as in the newly discovered *Dyskolos*) was the prologue, which was not used to summarize the plot, but to give the background to the action of the play. In Plautus the prologue is also used to put the audience in a

pleasant, receptive mood, often giving opportunity for direct
banter with them, as in *The Menaechmi Twins* and *Prisoners of
War*, or for a bit of good-natured, homely moralizing relevant
to the story, as in *The Rope*. Terence, however, used his prologues for a different purpose and was an innovator in this
respect. The antecedent action in his plays is presented quite
naturally, much as in a modern drama, in the opening scenes by
two characters who present the exposition in dialogue. The prologues proper are used by Terence for literary manifestoes to
present his ideas on dramatic composition, or more specifically
to defend himself against his critics and detractors, the chief
of whom was the dramatist Luscius Lanuvinus, the "older writer"
whom he refers to, none of whose works have come down to
us. The main charges against him, besides the already mentioned canard that his noble friends helped him do the writing,
were *contaminatio*, or fusing two Greek plays into one Latin
play, and *furtum*, or plagiarism, which in those days meant that
he had used Greek plays that had already been utilized by other
Roman writers and were therefore not rightfully to be used by
him. He was also accused of the artistic failing of thin dialogue
and a trivial style. All these charges, which were most unjust,
he refutes effectively, as can be seen in reading his prologues
and the plays themselves. As for style, Roman writers after
him extolled him for his *puri sermonis*, or fine style.

In the field of tragedy, though many Roman writers from
the beginning of Roman literature worked in this branch of
drama, the only examples that have survived are the nine plays
by Seneca, together with a tragedy on a contemporary Roman
subject, the *Octavia*, which though included in the corpus of
his work, was probably written by someone else in the same
period who was influenced by him. Seneca's literary reputation is
based not on his plays, but on his essays, which are notable for
their pithy epigrammatic style and their expression of Stoic
philosophical ideas tempered to suit the tastes and inclinations
of the cultured, worldly Roman gentleman of his day. The
tragedies themselves, though ultimately based on Euripides and
Sophocles, are a far cry from the work of these great Greek
dramatists. They were surely not written to be presented on
the stage, but in an age—the first century A.D.—when declama-
tion was a favorite method of literary presentation and rhetoric
the chief study of the educated, these plays, abounding in long
passages of florid rhetoric, must surely have been intended as
closet dramas to be recited to the literati.

Seneca's plays, three of which—*Medea, Hippolytus* (or *Phae-*

dra), and *Oedipus*—are included in this volume, are ultimately based on the Greek tragedy of Sophocles and Euripides, but the spirit that pervades them and the manner of their writing are quite different. While the Greek plays are truly tragic and deal with the buffeting of a truly noble character by fate, Seneca's plays are essentially melodramatic and deal with the lengths to which a highly emotional person will go when driven by the devils within him or her. This difference is the result partly of the taste of his age which enjoyed sensationalism in entertainment, and partly of Seneca's personality whose neuroticism is reflected in that of his characters. It was also the result of the Roman delight in rhetoric, of which Seneca's long vivid speeches are masterly examples.

Thus, his Hippolytus is motivated not so much by chastity and laudable refusal to violate his father's marriage bed as by his unnatural hatred of all women. Phaedra is not a basically good woman overpowered by forces against which she, a mere mortal, cannot fight, but an unnatural creature motivated by out-and-out lust for her handsome stepson. Medea is not so much the wronged woman of basic nobility and intelligence, but the personification of blind revenge, willing in her fury to smash the whole world to gain her bloody end. And where, in Euripides, her skill in magic is taken for granted, in Seneca we are exposed to a long scene in which she calls on all the powers of darkness and witchcraft to aid her.

Horrors, ghoulish and grotesque, abound. In Seneca's *Oedipus*, instead of a gradual and restrained unfolding, bit by bit, of the evidence of the King's guilt, events and emotions move at fever pitch, and the son's sin is revealed by the gory ghost of the father in a violent, macabre scene of necromancy. This scene, in turn, is preceded by one equally harrowing in which the blind seer Tiresias interprets the awful omens, as they are described to him, of an ill-fated sacrifice. Sometimes the horrors may strike the modern reader as somewhat grotesquely comic. At the end of the *Hippolytus*, when the pieces of his son's mangled body are being collected and fitted together, Theseus, holding a bloody chunk of flesh and blood, says in effect, as if doing a jig-saw puzzle, "I don't know where this fits, but here is a vacant space and I'll put it in anyway." A second instance, a scene which the playwright surely intended as a brutally ironic climax, occurs when Medea flees to the safety of the palace roof holding one slain child in her arm and the still living one by the hand. Jason pleads with her to spare him at least one son, but in a final burst of revenge, she stabs this one too. Then throwing the two bodies down to the feet of her husband, she shrieks, "Here, take your sons!" Sheer melodrama and quite grotesque!

Nothing is spared the reader. Violence mounts and mounts. Emotions, high to begin with, rise higher and higher. The characters declaim and rage in long rhetorical speeches, able even in their fury to punctuate their tirades with epigrams, like the dying tenors who can expire on grace notes. Operatic is perhaps the word for Seneca's plays. Their action is highly melodramatic, their emotion strong and violent, their characters larger than life, towering in their rages and passions. But that is what the writer aimed at. He was not writing tragedies about man's fate. Rather he was interested in showing heroic characters in the grip of intense emotions and in so doing also dramatized certain principles of the Stoicism he professed. Thus his *Oedipus* involves free will, sin and retribution, and *Medea* and *Phaedra* show the results of the excess of passion. Yet it is really the passions themselves that concern him rather than the lessons.

And these passions, violent as they are, and these heroes and heroines, beserk and bereft of restraint as they are, become strangely fascinating as we read. They were especially fascinating to the playwrights of the dawn of modern drama in the sixteenth and seventeenth centuries. And if truth must be told, the modern novel and drama is again presenting such characters and emotions in modern dress and language. Seneca's heroic neuroses are in fashion again.

Lucius Annaeus Seneca, unlike our other two playwrights, was by birth both a Roman citizen and a member of the upper classes. Born in Spain about the year 1 of the Christian era, son of an influential Roman rhetorician, or teacher of oratory and style, he was brought to Rome in early infancy where he received the best education of his day. Close to the imperial family in adulthood, he was a senator under Caligula and Claudius and later became teacher to the young Nero, over whom he exerted considerable influence for several years during which he was, in effect, the youthful emperor's prime minister, and tried to guide him along the proper path. His high position brought him great wealth, so that his preaching of simplicity in his philosophical essays while living in a palace strikes some readers as hypocritical. Others, however, may see this as an intelligent man's realization that high position and wealth are dangerous in an autocracy, for he ultimately suffered and died because of it. In the reign of Claudius he was exiled to Corsica, but returned after the emperor's death to take up his post with the new emperor, Nero, and wrote a bitter lampoon against the deceased *princeps,* the *Apocolocyntosis,* or *Pumpkinification of the Divine Claudius.* After several successful years with his young disciple, he finally met disfavor with Nero, who accused Seneca of complicity in a conspiracy, but actually coveted his wealth. He was forced to commit suicide in 65 A.D.

Our three playwrights, then, exemplify three different kinds of Romans: Plautus, the man of the people, who understood their feelings, their lives, and their idiom, and set out to entertain them, but who as an artist used their language in a manner that lives and laughs robustly to this day; Terence, the foreigner and former slave (perhaps through accident of war), who learned the language of his captors in its every nuance, and whose sensitivity to and understanding of human nature were such that his dramas appealed more to the discriminating than to the folk; and Seneca, the highly cultured philosopher and man of affairs, who wrote at a time when true drama was no longer in demand in places of entertainment and whose carefully wrought and elegantly phrased, though sensational and melodramatic, plays reflected some of the brutality that lurked even in the cultured circle of upper-class Roman society.

Frank Justus Miller's prose translations of Seneca's plays, three of which have been included here with minor revisions, are excellent. His rhythmical prose is as close as possible in sense to the original Latin and yet effectively reproduces much of the effect and tone of Seneca's verse. The only changes I have made in his translations are of two kinds: to remove expressions that seem excessively archaic as well as certain "poetic" contractions that are not in accord with modern taste and are not really necessary; and to reduce the number of notes, which Seneca's many allusions to obscure myths make necessary, by modifying the translation wherever possible so as to avoid the necessity of a note. This principle I have violated on occasion when I have felt it necessary to add a note. But on the whole there has been a reduction in explanations. I hope my changes have not affected the rhythm or beauty of the translation. If they have, I pray forgiveness of the *manes* of Frank Justus Miller and the indulgence of the reader for whom I strove.

As for my own translations of the six comedies, I have endeavored to produce an accurate, readable, and even actable version in as good colloquial English as the colloquial Latin of the original, and have avoided slang, which tends to sound anachronistic and loses its savor in a short time. My aim has been to give the reader the same effect of the plays in English as the Roman audience or reader received in the Latin of the original.

While the translator of verse into prose is relieved of the difficult burden of rendering good verse into equally good verse in his own language, yet, if he is translating comedy and wishes his reader or audience to laugh where the ancient audience laughed, his task is still no laughing matter. There are puns and other plays on words to reproduce, jokes with topical or local allusions to handle, rapid exchanges of conversation with parts left unexpressed in words but clarified in gesture, exclamations of distress, sorrow, and joy to be rendered into normal English, which is frequently less demonstrative than Latin and its daughter languages, and so on. But most important is to reproduce the tone of the two comedic writers, the verve, bravura, brashness, and folk quality of Plautus, and the quieter liveliness and charm of Terence. To paraphrase the prologue to *The Menaechmi Twins:* I bring you Plautus and Terence—and I hope you enjoy them as much as their Roman audiences did, and as much as I have enjoyed bringing them to you.

The Menaechmi Twins
(Menaechmi)

A COMEDY

by
PLAUTUS

❖ ❖ ❖

translated by
Samuel Lieberman

DRAMATIS PERSONAE

PENICULUS (Brush), a parasite, a man in his late thirties.
MENAECHMUS OF EPIDAMNUS (Menaechmus I), a man in his early thirties.
MENAECHMUS OF SYRACUSE, originally called Sosicles (Menaechmus II), his twin.
EROTIUM, a courtesan.
CYLINDRUS, her cook, a man in his forties.
MESSENIO, slave of Menaechmus of Syracuse, about thirty.
MAID of Erotium.
WIFE of Menaechmus of Epidamnus.
FATHER-IN-LAW of Menaechmus of Epidamnus, an old man.
DOCTOR, about forty or fifty.

Scene: Epidamnus, a Greek city on the coast of Illyria, on the Adriatic, north of Greece proper. All the action takes place on the street, in front of the houses of Menaechmus I and Erotium, which are next to one another, separated by a narrow alleyway into which characters slip when the occasion demands, to be temporarily unseen or to eavesdrop. On the audience's left is the way to the harbor; on their right, the way to the forum, the center of town.

Prologue

Let me begin at the beginning, gentlemen of the audience, with a friendly hello to you—and to me.

I bring you Plautus—in a play, not in person. Please receive him with kindly attention. And now give *me* your attention so that I can give you the background to our story. I'll do it in as few words as possible.

You know the kind of things writers do in their comedies. They like to say that all the action takes place in Athens, so that it may seem more truly Greek to you. *I* will not say that it takes place anywhere but where it's supposed to take place. Now actually our story starts in Greece, though it isn't Attic Greece, but Sicilian Greece.

That was the introduction to the prologue. Now I'll give you the prologue and plenty of it, not just a peck full or a bushel full, but a whole barn full. That's how generous I am with prologues.

There was once a merchant living in Syracuse, a man in his forties, and he had two sons, twins. The boys were so alike in appearance that not even the nurse who suckled them could tell them apart, nor even their own mother who had borne them— as indeed a man told me who had seen them. I myself never saw them, just in case you should think so.

When the boys were seven years old, the father loaded a large ship with a sizable cargo of goods, took one of the twins with him on board, and sailed off with him to Tarentum on a business trip. The other twin he left at home with his mother.

Now it happened that public games were being held at Tarentum when they got there, and crowds of people had gathered, as is usual at games. The boy wandered off from his father and got lost in the crowd. A merchant from the city of Epidamnus happened to be there. He picked up the boy and sailed away with him to Epidamnus. When the boy's father realized the boy was lost and he could not find him, he went to pieces with grief and became so ill that a few days later he died in Tarentum.

23

When news of this got back to Syracuse to the grandfather of
the boys—that one of the boys had disappeared and his father
had died in Tarentum—the grandfather changed the name of
the remaining twin. He loved him so much—the boy who had
disappeared—that he gave his name, Menaechmus, to the boy
who had stayed at home. And the grandfather himself was also
called by the same name. The reason I remember the grandfather's name so well is that I've heard it shouted very often
—by his creditors.

In order that you don't go wrong, I'm repeating what I said:
the twin brothers have the same name.

Now, let me retrace my steps to Epidamnus, so that I can
explain this thing to you exactly. If any of you wants me to take
care of anything for him in Epidamnus, let him speak up boldly
and give me an order. But make sure to give me the means to
take care of it for you. For anyone who gives me an order without
giving me any money is just being a fool, and anyone who gives
me money is an even bigger fool!

All right, now I'm back where I came from without moving
from my place.

That Epidamnian that I've been speaking about, the one
who took away the other twin boy, had no children of his own.
In fact, the only thing he had, and plenty, was money. So he
adopted the lost boy as his son, got him a wife with a good dowry
when he grew up, and when the old man died the boy inherited
all his wealth.

You might be interested to know how the old man died. Well,
he happened to be going to the country one day after a heavy
rain when he stepped into a rapid stream not far from the city.
The rushing stream grabbed him by the feet, the way he had
grabbed the boy, and actually dragged him all the way down
to hell. His great wealth fell to the young man.

The twin who was lost, then, lives here in Epidamnus. Now,
the twin who lives in Syracuse has just come to Epidamnus with
his slave to search for his twin brother. This, here (*pointing to
stage*), is the city of Epidamnus while the play is being acted.
When another play is presented, it will be another city, just as
the actors also change their parts. Sometimes a pimp lives here
(*pointing to the houses*), sometimes a young man, sometimes
an old man, or a poor beggar, or a patron, a parasite, or a
fortuneteller, and so on. Now, on with the play.   (*Exit.*)

Act I

(*Enter Peniculus.*)

PENICULUS (*to audience*). The young men around here call me Peniculus, or Brush, for the reason that when I eat I sweep the table clean.

Speaking of eating, it is my opinion that people who tie up prisoners in chains and who clamp leg irons on runaway slaves are making a foolish mistake. For if you take a poor miserable wretch who is already in plenty of trouble and heap more trouble on him, he has an even greater desire to run away and do something desperate. Chains they can always get free of somehow or other. They file through the leg irons with a rasp or they smash the lock with a heavy stone. So treating them like that is just a joke!

If you really want to keep someone from running away, you have to use food and drink to chain him up. Clamp the fellow's ugly mouth to a full table. As long as you keep giving him something to eat and drink, as much as he wants, all he can eat, daily, by Pollux, he'll never try to escape, even if he has committed a capital crime! You will easily keep him a prisoner as long as you make food the tie that binds him. That's the kind of hold food has on a person. The freer you are with it the tighter it holds.

Now, me, I'm on my way to see Menaechmus here. I've sort of assigned myself to his custody, you might say. I am going voluntarily, so that he can get me all tied up in food. For he doesn't just feed a fellow, he stuffs him, he rebuilds him. In that kind of medicine nobody can beat him!

That's the kind of man he is—he's just all food—and he gives dinners worthy of the Feast of the Goddess Ceres. He heaps up the tables so high, he composes such a harmonious symphony of piled-up platters, that you've got to stand up on your dining couch if you want to get something from the top.

But I haven't seen him for several days now. I've been all tied up at home with my dear ones. Dear, did I say? There's nothing I eat or buy these days that isn't dear! And here's

25

another thing. Those dear things—one day you have them around you, next thing you know they're gone—the deserters!

Now I'm going to visit him. But the door is opening. There I see Menaechmus himself! He's coming out.

(MENAECHMUS I *comes out of his house, scolding his wife who stands at the door silently and sullenly.*)

MENAECHMUS I. Behave yourself! No more of your foolishness! No more losing your temper! If there is something your husband hates, you'd better hate it too! And furthermore, from now on if you act the way you did today, I'll act: out you go, back to your father with a divorce!

Every time I want to go out, you hold me back, you call me back! You keep asking, where am I going? What am I doing? What business do I have? What am I after? What am I carrying? What did I do outside? I've married a regular intelligence agent, the way I have to report on every single thing that I've done or am doing!

I've been spoiling you. Now I'll tell you how it's going to be from now on: since I provide you with maids, food, wool, gold, clothes, and expensive dyes, and there is nothing you lack, you'll stay out of trouble if you're smart! You'll stop spying on your husband! And now, just so your spying won't be a total loss, just for spite, today I'm taking a courtesan out to dinner and I'm making reservations somewhere in town.

PENICULUS (*in the alleyway between the two houses*). He acts like he's scolding his wife, but he's really hurting me with his words. For if he dines out, he is surely punishing me, not her.

(*Wife goes in and slams the door.*)

MENAECHMUS I (*gleefully*). It's worked, by Hercules! I've finally driven my wife from the door with my scolding. Where are the husbands who are keeping women on the side? Why don't they rush out and shower me with gifts and congratulations for having put up a good fight? (*Holding up a cloak.*) I've just stolen this cloak from my wife. I'm bringing it to the courtesan. That's the only way to treat them. You've got to be clever to cheat a crafty female custodian!

Isn't this a beautiful job! Isn't it skillful! It's neat! A masterpiece! In stealing this from my wife, I've really stolen from myself, and now I'll just throw it away on a courtesan.

I've captured loot from the enemy and got away without losing a single man!

PENICULUS (*from alleyway*). Hey, young fellow, is there any share in that loot for me?

MENAECHMUS I (*scared, turning in the direction of the voice*). Just my luck! I've fallen into a trap!

PENICULUS (*still in alleyway*). No, you're safe! Don't be scared.

MENAECHMUS I. Who's that?

PENICULUS (*coming out, smiling*). It's me!

MENAECHMUS I. Oh, my friend in need, my friend indeed! Hello!

PENICULUS. Hello!

MENAECHMUS I. How are you?

PENICULUS (*shaking his hand*). Fine, now that I'm shaking my guardian spirit's hand.

MENAECHMUS I. You couldn't have met me at a more opportune time!

PENICULUS. That's exactly the way I am. I've made a science of being at the right place at the right time.

MENAECHMUS I. You want to take a look at a brilliant job?

PENICULUS. Who cooked it? Who's the chef? I'll know soon enough whether he's made a mistake somewhere when I've tasted the leftovers.

MENAECHMUS I. Tell me, did you ever see a mural painting in which an eagle is carrying off Ganymede, or where Venus and Adonis ———?

PENICULUS. Many times. But what have those pictures to do with me?

MENAECHMUS I (*draping the cloak around himself effeminately*). Look at me! Do I remind you of anything?

PENICULUS. What kind of get-up is that?

MENAECHMUS I (*still posturing*). Say I'm a very charming man.

PENICULUS. When do we eat?

MENAECHMUS I. Just say what I told you to!

PENICULUS. All right. You're a very charming man.

MENAECHMUS I. Wouldn't you like to add something on your own?

PENICULUS. And lots of fun.

MENAECHMUS I. Continue.

PENICULUS (*annoyed*). By Hercules, I'm not continuing unless I know what for!

You've been having a quarrel with your wife, so I'd better watch my step with you.

MENAECHMUS I. Never mind her. My wife hasn't the remotest idea of where we're going for a good time today, where we're going to make this day a real hot one!

PENICULUS. Well then, now you're talking! How soon do we light a fire under it? Because, you know, the day is already half gone—right down to the belly-button.

MENAECHMUS I. Don't be in such a hurry to interrupt me!

PENICULUS. You can knock my eye right through the sole of my foot if I ever utter another word except what you order me to say!

MENAECHMUS I. Come over here, away from the door.

PENICULUS (*comes closer to* MENAECHMUS). Very well.

MENAECHMUS I. A little further away.

PENICULUS (*closer*). All right.

MENAECHMUS I. Now still further, and boldly, away from the lion's den.

PENICULUS. By Pollux, fellow, you'd make an excellent charioteer, I'd say.

MENAECHMUS I. Why?

PENICULUS. Because you keep looking back all the time to see if your wife is gaining on you!

MENAECHMUS I (*showing him the cloak*). Well, what do you say?

PENICULUS. Me? Whatever you wish, I'll say it or not say it.

MENAECHMUS I. If you happen to smell something, can you guess from the odor what it is?

PENICULUS. At smelling I'm an expert.

MENAECHMUS I. Well, then, smell this cloak that I have here. What does it smell of? (PENICULUS *turns away in disgust.*) Why do you turn away?

PENICULUS. A woman's garment has to be smelled from the top. For when you smell from the bottom the nose is defiled by an unwashable odor.

MENAECHMUS I (*pointing to top*). So smell from here, Peniculus. (PENICULUS *turns up his nose.*) How delicately you turn up your nose!

PENICULUS. It's the only thing to do!

MENAECHMUS I. Why? What does it smell of? Tell me.

PENICULUS (*starts statement disgustedly, ends brightly*). Thievery, adultery, cookery!

MENAECHMUS I. May the gods bless you with everything you wish me! By Pollux, you're exactly right! I stole this from my wife. Now I'm going to take it to my girl friend, the courtesan Erotium. Then I'll order a dinner to be prepared for you and me and her.

PENICULUS. Wonderful!

MENAECHMUS I. And we'll keep on drinking till tomorrow morning!

PENICULUS. Now you're talking! Should I knock at the door?

MENAECHMUS I. Knock—or rather, wait a second!

PENICULUS. I can't wait so long for a drink.

MENAECHMUS I. Knock gently.

PENICULUS. Are you afraid the doors are made of china?

MENAECHMUS I. Wait, wait, please, by Hercules! There! She's coming out herself! Oh, do you see how the sun itself is dimmed by the shining beauty of her body!

(EROTIUM *comes out of her house, sees* MENAECHMUS I, *and stretches out her arms lovingly toward him.*)

EROTIUM. Menaechmus, darling! Hello! (*She kisses him.*)

PENICULUS. How about me?

EROTIUM. You don't count.

PENICULUS. Just like the army! If you're in the auxiliaries and not in the front lines, all you get is a good-conduct medal.

MENAECHMUS I (*to* EROTIUM). Today at your house I'm ordering——

PENICULUS (*interrupting*). A battle! It will take place today. The weapons will be drinking cups around the table. The winner will be decided by the wine cup! You are our commander. Decide with which of us you will spend the night.

MENAECHMUS I (*to* EROTIUM, *affectionately, paying no attention to* PENICULUS). My darling! How the mere sight of you makes me hate my wife!

PENICULUS (*to* EROTIUM). He's brought you something to wear.

EROTIUM (*eagerly*). What is it?

MENAECHMUS I. A stole for you that I stole from my wife, my sweet rose!

EROTIUM. You're the winner! You easily win over any of the men who have been with me!

PENICULUS (*aside*). A courtesan is nice to you only as long as she can get something out of you. For if she really loved you, she would devour you with kisses, nose and all!

MENAECHMUS I (*unfolding the cloak*). Hold this up, Peniculus. I wish to dedicate properly the booty which I have vowed to this goddess.

PENICULUS. Here! (*Helps* MENAECHMUS I *with cloak.*) But do me a favor, by Hercules. Dance with the cloak now.

MENAECHMUS I. I dance? Are you crazy or something?

PENICULUS. I'm not, you are! If you're not going to dance, take that thing off!

MENAECHMUS I. After all the trouble I had stealing it!

PENICULUS. Come to think of it, Hercules didn't have as much trouble stealing the girdle from Hippolyta.

MENAECHMUS I (*to* EROTIUM, *offering the cloak*). Take this. It's for you! Since you're the only one alive who understands and appreciates me.

EROTIUM. That's how we should feel toward lovers who treat us right.

PENICULUS (*aside*). And who in so doing rush to ruin themselves into beggary!

MENAECHMUS I. That cloak cost me four minas¹ when I bought it this year for my wife!

PENICULUS (*aside*). Four minas clearly wasted, as I reckon it.

MENAECHMUS I (*to* EROTIUM). Now, do you know what I want you to arrange?

EROTIUM (*alluringly*). I know. I'll arrange whatever you wish.

MENAECHMUS I. Have a dinner prepared for the three of us at your home.

PENICULUS. And buy something really special in the market. Let's see—some nice cuts of fresh pork, some delicious ham, half a pig's head, and other delicacies along those lines. Have them cooked in such a way that when they are set before me on the table, they'll give me the appetite of a ravenous hawk.

MENAECHMUS I. And get started on it at once.

EROTIUM. Certainly, by Castor!

MENAECHMUS I. We're going to the forum, but we'll be back soon. Then, while it's cooking, we'll have a few drinks.

EROTIUM. Come back whenever you wish. It will be ready.

MENAECHMUS I. But waste no time. (*to* PENICULUS.) You come along with me.

PENICULUS. By Hercules, I certainly will, and I'll keep my eyes glued to you. I wouldn't lose you today for all the wealth of the gods!
(*They go off.*)

¹ Two kinds of money were in use in the Greek cities of the period of the plays. One kind actually existed in physical form as coins in circulation, the other existed only as money of account, used in calculating prices or expressing the weights of precious metals. Of the former, the basic coins were the *obol* and the *drachma*. While expressing their values in modern terms is difficult because of fluctuating purchasing power then as now, an approximation may be made. The *obol*, a bronze coin, was worth between 3¢ and 6¢, and the *drachma*, in silver, was equivalent to six obols, or from 18¢ to 36¢. Some times double-drachma or four-drachma pieces were issued, and some Hellenistic kings issued coins that were called by their names, such as *philippics*, which are mentioned in some of the plays. The money of account consisted of the *mina*, equivalent to 100 drachmas and therefore worth between $18 and $36, and the *talent*, equivalent to 6000 drachmas, or $1,080 to $2,160. A cloak costing four minas is therefore a garment of substantial value, and a slave girl costing thirty minas is an expensive proposition.

EROTIUM (*to slaves inside*). You in there, tell Cylindrus the cook I want to see him out here right away!

(*Enter* CYLINDRUS, *in an apron, from the house.*)

EROTIUM. Take the basket and some money. Here are three silver pieces.

CYLINDRUS. Got 'em.

EROTIUM. Go and get some provisions, enough for three people, no more and no less.

CYLINDRUS. Who are the three?

EROTIUM. I and Menaechmus and his parasite.

CYLINDRUS. That makes ten, for the parasite can easily eat enough for eight!

EROTIUM. I've told you the number of guests. You take care of the rest.

CYLINDRUS. Very well. It's practically cooked. Tell them to come and sit down.

EROTIUM. Return quickly.

CYLINDRUS. I'll be here soon.

(*Exit* CYLINDRUS *in direction of forum;* EROTIUM *enters her house.*)

Act II

(*Enter Menaechmus II and Messenio on the audience's left, from the harbor. They are accompanied by two sailors, slaves, carrying luggage; Messenio is carrying a leather purse, and, perhaps, a small bag.*)

MENAECHMUS II. You know, Messenio, when you're on a ship at sea, there's no greater pleasure than catching sight of land from a distance.

MESSENIO. It's even greater if the land you see as you come to it is your own. But tell me, why are we stopping in Epidamnus? Or are we just going around all the islands as if we were the sea?

MENAECHMUS II. I'm searching for my twin brother.

MESSENIO. Isn't there any limit to your search? This is the sixth year that we've been at it. Istria, Spain, southern France, the whole Adriatic, Sicily, all the coasts of Italy, wherever the sea approaches we've circumnavigated. If you were looking for a needle in a haystack, I'm sure you would have found it by this time if it were findable. I'm telling you, we're searching for a dead man! We would have found him by now if he were alive.

MENAECHMUS II. That's exactly what I want to make sure of. I've got to find someone who will say that he knows he is dead. Then I'll give up my search. But if not, as long as I live, I'll never stop looking. He's so dear to my heart!

MESSENIO. You're just wasting your time! Why don't we just go home. Unless we're going to write a travel book?

MENAECHMUS II (*annoyed*). Just do what you're told, eat what you're given, and stay out of trouble! Don't be a nuisance! I'm not going to do things to suit you!

MESSENIO (*aside, disgruntled*). Hm! In case I forget it, those words remind me that I'm a slave! He couldn't possibly have put it more plainly. (*Stresses the p's.*) But, anyway, I have to speak up. I can't keep it in! (*To* MENAECHMUS.) You know, Menaechmus, when I look into our purse, by Hercules, we are rather thinly provided for. And I think, by Hercules (*Looking into purse.*), yes, if you don't turn back, you'll be sorry when you have nothing left while you're still looking for your brother.

For you've got to watch out for the kind of people they have here. Among the Epidamnians there are some real big voluptuaries and heavy drinkers. Then, too, many crooks and confidence men live in this town. And they say that nowhere in the world are the courtesans more enticing and persistent. That's why this town is called Epidamnus, because hardly anyone ever gets out of here without damage!

MENAECHMUS II. I'll take care of that. Hand over the purse!

MESSENIO. What do you want with it?

MENAECHMUS II. From what you said, I'd better not trust you with it.

MESSENIO. What are you afraid of?

MENAECHUS II. That you'll do me some damage in Epidamnus! You are a great lover of women, Messino, and I'm a man that's quick to anger and with a very short temper. So, if I have the money, I'll prevent two things: *you* won't do something wrong, and *I* won't get angry with you.

MESSENIO. Take it and keep it. Whatever you do is all right with me.

(*Enter* CYLINDRUS *from the center of town with a full market basket. At first he doesn't see* MENAECHMUS II *and* MESSENIO *who are still at the other end of the stage.*)

CYLINDRUS. I've shopped well and got exactly what I wanted. I shall prepare an excellent dinner. (*Notices* MENAECHMUS II.) But there's Menaechmus! Oh, my back! The guests are coming to the door before I've returned from shopping! I'll go over and speak to them. (*Approaches.*) Hello, Menaechmus!

MENAECHMUS II. The gods love you, whoever you are!

CYLINDRUS. Whoever I am? Don't you know who I am, Menaechmus?

MENAECHMUS II. No, by Hercules, certainly not!

CYLINDRUS. Where is the other guest?

MENAECHMUS II. What guest are you talking about?

CYLINDRUS. Your parasite.

MENAECHMUS II. My parasite? This fellow is surely mad!

MESSENIO. Didn't I tell you there were lots of crooks here?

MENAECHMUS II. What parasite of mine do you mean, my good fellow?

CYLINDRUS. Peniculus, the Brush.

MESSENIO. That I have safe in my bag.

CYLINDRUS. Menaechmus, you've come back too early for dinner. I've just returned from shopping.

MENAECHMUS II. Tell me, my good man, how much do pigs cost here? I mean ritually pure ones, for sacrificing.

CYLINDRUS. Two drachmas a piece. Why?

MENAECHMUS II. Here, take this two-drachma piece. Have yourself purified and prayed over at the temple. For I'm pretty sure you're insane if you bother a man whom you don't know, whoever you are!

CYLINDRUS. I'm Cylindrus. Don't you know my name?

MENAECHMUS II. Whether you're Cylinder or Collander, you can go to hell! *I* don't know you, and furthermore, I don't want to know you!

CYLINDRUS. Your name is Menaechmus?

MENAECHMUS II. As far as I know. You sound sane when you call me by name. But where do you know me from?

CYLINDRUS. Where do I know you from? You who have as a mistress my mistress Erotium!

MENAECHMUS II. By Hercules, I don't have a mistress, nor do I know who you are!

CYLINDRUS. You don't know who I *am?* Why, I've often poured wine for you when you drank at our house!

MESSENIO. Too bad I don't have something with which to smash this guy's head in!

MENAECHMUS II. You used to pour wine for me? Why, this is the first time I ever saw or was in Epidamnus!

CYLINDRUS. You deny it?

MENAECHMUS II. Certainly, I deny it, by Hercules!

CYLINDRUS (*pointing to* MENAECHMUS I's *house*). You don't live in that house over there?

MENAECHMUS II. May the gods damn those who live in that house!

CYLINDRUS (*aside*). He's really crazy, to curse himself. (*To* MENAECHMUS II.) Listen, Menaechmus.

MENAECHMUS II. What do you want?

CYLINDRUS. The money that you just promised to give me— for you're the one that's crazy, I'm sure, Menaechmus, when you curse yourself—you'd better, if you'll take my advice, spend it on a cure for yourself!

MENAECHMUS II. By god, I can't stand this man much longer!

CYLINDRUS (*aside, suddenly getting a bright idea*). He must be joking with me, as he usually does. What a sense of humor he has when his wife isn't around! (*To* MENAECHMUS, *as if all joking aside*.) Well, what do you say?

MENAECHMUS II. I say: What do you want?

CYLINDRUS. Do you think I've bought enough food here (*Showing the basket*.) for the three of you, or should I get more for you, the parasite, and the lady?

MENAECHMUS II. What lady and what parasite are you talking about?

MESSENIO (*to* CYLINDRUS). What villainy drives you to annoy this man?

CYLINDRUS (*to* MESSENIO). What business do I have with you? I don't know you. I'm talking to him, whom I know.

MESSENIO. By Pollux, you're not sane, of that I'm sure!

CYLINDRUS (*to* MENAECHMUS II, *trying to get back to business*). So now I'll have these cooked. There will be no delay. Don't go too far away from the house. Anything else you wish?

MENAECHMUS II. Yes. Just go to hell!

CYLINDRUS. By Hercules, *you'd* better go——and sit down while I (*Getting "literary."*) set these on Vulcan's violent flames. I'll go and tell Erotium you're here, so she can invite you in rather than have you stand here outside. (*Enters* EROTIUM's *house*.)

MENAECHMUS II. Has he gone? He's gone! By Pollux, I realize now your words were not false.

MESSENIO. Just watch out! I believe a courtesan lives here, as indeed that madman said who left us.

MENAECHMUS II. But I wonder how he knew my name.

MESSENIO. Not surprising at all, by Hercules! It's the standard procedure with courtesans. They send slave boys or slave girls to the harbor when a foreign ship comes in. They ask where she's from, what the passengers' names are. Then they immediately attach themselves to a man and stick to him like glue. If they get their clutches on him, they send him home broke.

Now, in that harbor (*Pointing to* EROTIUM'*s house.*) stands a pirate ship of which we've got to beware! I mean it!

MENAECHMUS II. By Hercules, you've certainly warned me properly!

MESSENIO. I'll know if I've warned you properly if you'll follow my warning and be careful.

MENAECHMUS II. Keep quiet a moment. I hear the door opening. Let's see who's coming out.

MESSENIO. I'll put this bag down meanwhile. (*To sailors.*) Watch this, will you, sea legs!

(EROTIUM *comes out, speaking to her slaves through the open door.*)

EROTIUM. Leave the door the way it is, and go. I don't want it closed. Get ready inside, get everything arranged, do whatever is necessary! Put covers on the couches, burn some incense! A romantic atmosphere stimulates a lover's passions. In a pleasant setting a lover lets himself go and we profit by it.

But where is he? The cook said he was in front of the house. (*Sees* MENAECHMUS II.) Ah, there he is, the man who is of great advantage and profit to me! And that's why it is that, as he deserves, he is such a favorite in my house. Now I'll go up and say something nice to him. (*Approaches.*)

Sweetheart, I'm surprised that you stand here outside when the door is open for you! This is more your home than your own home. Everything is ready as you ordered and as you wished, and they're waiting inside. (*He pays no attention.*) The dinner you ordered is ready to be served. You may come in and sit down whenever you like.

MENAECHMUS II. Who is this woman talking to?

EROTIUM. To you.

MENAECHMUS II. What business have I ever had with you, before or now?

EROTIUM. Why, you above all, by Pollux, Venus has wished me to magnify! And you certainly deserve it. For, by Castor, you alone are making me flourish by your benefactions.

MENAECHMUS II (*ignoring her*). This woman is certainly either insane or drunk, Messenio. She addresses me, a stranger to her, so familiarly!

MESSENIO. Didn't I tell you that this is what usually happens here? Now only leaves are falling on you. But if we stay here two or three days, whole trees will fall on you. That's the way the courtesans are here: all gold-diggers! (*To* EROTIUM.) Hey, woman, I want to say something to you.

EROTIUM. What is it?

MESSENIO. Where did you meet this man?

EROTIUM. The same place he met me, in Epidamnus some time ago.

MESSENIO. In Epidamnus? But he never set foot in this city before today!

EROTIUM. Ha ha! You're joking! (*To* MENAECHMUS.) My dear Menaechmus, please, why don't you go in? You'll be more comfortable there.

MENAECHMUS II. By Pollux, she calls me by my right name, this woman! I wonder what this is all about!

MESSENIO. She got a sniff of that purse you're holding.

MENAECHMUS II. Yes, by Pollux, you were right when you warned me. Here, take it. I'll soon know whether she loves me or my purse more.

EROTIUM. Let's go in so we can have dinner.

MENAECHMUS II (*sarcastically, assuming it is going to cost him money*). Very good of you to invite me. Thank you very much.

EROTIUM. But you ordered me to have dinner cooked for you.

MENAECHMUS II. *I* ordered you to have it cooked?

EROTIUM. Certainly! For you and your parasite.

MENAECHMUS II. What damned parasite? This woman is certainly not in her senses!

EROTIUM. Peniculus, the Brush!

MENAECHMUS II. Who is this Brush you keep talking about? Something to clean shoes with?

EROTIUM. Why, the one who came with you before, when you brought me the cloak that you stole from your wife.

MENAECHMUS II. What are you talking about? *I* gave *you* a cloak that I stole from my wife? Are you in your right mind? Surely this woman is asleep on her feet like an old horse!

EROTIUM. What pleasure do you get out of making fun of me and denying what you did?

MENAECHMUS II. Tell me, what is it that I've done which I deny doing?

EROTIUM. That you gave me your wife's cloak today.

MENAECHMUS II. I still deny it. I don't have a wife, and I've never had a wife, and furthermore, since the day I was born I've never set foot inside your door. I ate on the ship; then I came here and met you.

EROTIUM. Ceres help me in my troubles! What *ship* are you talking about now?

MENAECHMUS II. A wooden one, often scraped, often fixed, often hit with a hammer to tighten the pegs, like a furrier's stretching board with one peg next to another.

EROTIUM. Now, please, stop making jokes and come in with me.

MENAECHMUS II. Woman, you're expecting some other man, not me.

EROTIUM. I don't know you, Menaechmus, son of your father Moschus? You were born, they say, in Syracuse, in Sicily, when Agathocles was king there; after him Phintias reigned, then Liparo who at his death handed over the throne to Hiero, and Hiero is now king.

MENAECHMUS II. What you say is not false, woman.

MESSENIO. By Jupiter, is it possible she comes from there that she knows you so well?

MENAECHMUS II (*to* MESSENIO). By Hercules, I suppose she can't be denied further!

MESSENIO. Don't do it! You're finished if you cross the threshold!

MENAECHMUS II (*quietly to* MESSENIO). Why don't you keep quiet? I'm on to a good thing. I'll agree to whatever she says if I can get—hospitality. (*Aside to* EROTIUM, *as if not wanting* MESSENIO *to hear.*) Lady, all this time I've been opposing you out of prudence. I was afraid of this fellow (*Pointing to* MESSENIO.) that he might report to my wife about the cloak and the dinner. Now, whenever you wish, let us go in.

EROTIUM. And the parasite, are you waiting for him?

MENAECHMUS II. Him? I am neither waiting for him nor do I give a hang about him! And if he comes, I don't want him to be let in!

EROTIUM. By Castor, I'm with you on that! But do you know what I'd like you to do?

MENAECHMUS II. Your wish is my command.

EROTIUM. That cloak that you brought me, I'd like you to take it to the embroiderer to have it repaired and have some trimmings added that I want.

MENAECHMUS II (*playing along*). Why, Hercules, you're right! That way it won't be recognized, and my wife will not know you have it when she sees you in the street!

EROTIUM. So take it with you later (*Smiling enticingly.*) when you leave.

MENAECHMUS II. Certainly!

EROTIUM. Let's go in.

MENAECHMUS II. I'll follow you in a moment. I want to say something to him.   (EROTIUM *goes into the house.*)

(*In great glee to* MESSENIO.) Hey, Messenio!

MESSENIO. What's up?

MENAECHMUS II. Leap for joy!

MESSENIO (*dourly*). Why should I?

MENAECHMUS II. You should! I know what you'll think of me! (*Proud of himself.*)

MESSENIO (*still dour*). So much the worse for you!

MENAECHMUS II (*gleefully*). I've got loot! And I've only just begun! Go as fast as you can, take these fellows (*Pointing to sailors.*) to an inn right away. And make sure you come for me before sunset.

MESSENIO (*worried*). You don't know those courtesans, Master.

MENAECHMUS II. Keep quiet, I say, and do your job! I'll be sorry, not you, if I act foolishly. This woman is stupid and unsuspecting. As far as I can see, there's loot here for us.

(*Exit into* EROTIUM's *house.*)

MESSENIO. Damn! Are you gone already? He's finished, for sure! The pirate ship is leading the pleasure yacht to its ruin. But I don't know how I can expect to control my master. He bought me to obey *his* orders, not to give *him* orders. (*To sailors.*) Follow me, so that, as he ordered, I can meet him on time.

(*Exeunt in direction of harbor.*)

Act III

(*Enter Peniculus, tired and annoyed with himself. He is alone.*)

PENICULUS. In all the more than thirty years that I've lived, I've never committed a more stupid or criminal act than today when I had the misfortune to get myself involved in a meeting of the city assembly! While I stood there gaping, Menaechmus slipped away from me, and went off to his mistress, without, I suppose, wanting to take me along.

May all the gods damn the man who first thought up the idea of assembly meetings to keep busy people busy! Wouldn't it be more fitting to choose men of leisure for this purpose? And then if they didn't attend when they were summoned, let them be fined on the spot. There are plenty of people who eat only one meal a day, who are therefore not busy, and who are neither invited out to eat nor invite others. They are the ones who ought to devote themselves to the discussion and business meetings of the assembly.

If we ran things that way, I wouldn't have missed a dinner today which, as sure as I'm alive, he wanted me to have with him. I'll go anyway. Surely there will be some leftovers, I hope. (*Brightening.*) Even that will be a pleasure.

But what do I see? Menaechmus is coming out, wearing a garland! The party is over! (*Ironically.*) By Pollux, I've certainly come on time! I'll watch and see what he does. Then I'll go over and speak to him. (*Hides in alleyway, but is visible to audience.*)

(MENAECHMUS II *comes out of* EROTIUM's *door, carrying the cloak, with a garland on his head, slightly drunk. He is speaking to* EROTIUM *who stands at the door inside, holding it half open.*)

MENAECHMUS II. You can rest assured. I'll bring this back to you today in good time, excellently and beautifully retrimmed. I promise you, you won't think it's the same, it will be so changed.

PENICULUS (*aside*). He's taking the cloak to the embroiderer. The dinner is finished, the wine is drunk up, and the poor parasite is locked out! No, by Hercules, I'm not the man I am if I don't avenge myself properly for the wrong he's done me! Watch what I'll do!

(EROTIUM *goes in; door closes.*)

MENAECHMUS II (*gleefully*). Oh, immortal gods, to what man have you given more good when he hoped for less! I dined, I drank, I made love! I've made off with this cloak and nobody around here will fall heir to it after today!

PENICULUS (*straining to hear from the alleyway*). I can't hear what he is saying from my hiding place. Stuffed as he is, he's now talking about me and my share!

MENAECHMUS II (*as before*). She says I gave this to her and stole it from my wife. (*Holds out cloak.*) Since I knew she was

mixed up—right away—as if we were really acquainted, I began
to play along with her. Whatever she said, I said the same. Need
I tell you more? I've never enjoyed myself at less expense!

PENICULUS. I'll go over to him, for I'm just dying to make a
row. (*Starts to approach.*)

MENAECHMUS II. Who is this coming up to me?

PENICULUS. Well, what have you got to say for yourself, you
feather-weight character, you lowest of the low, you no-account,
you disgrace of a man, sneak, cheapskate! What have I done to
deserve the harm you did me? You sneaked away from me in the
forum a while ago, and while I was absent, killed off and buried
a dinner! How could you dare to do it when I had as much right
to it as you?

MENAECHMUS II (*baffled*). Tell me, my good man, what have
I ever done to *you?* I don't know you, you don't know me. Why
do you insult me? Or do you want some serious injury in return
for your insults?

PENICULUS. That, dammit, you have already given me!

MENAECHMUS II. Tell me, my good fellow, if you don't mind,
what is your name?

PENICULUS. You make fun of me too, as if you don't know
my name!

MENAECHMUS II. No, by Pollux, as far as I know, I've never
seen you or met you before today! But really, whoever you are,
be a decent fellow and don't bother me.

PENICULUS. Menaechmus, wake up!

MENAECHMUS II. I'm awake all right, by Hercules, as far as
I know!

PENICULUS. You don't know *me?*

MENAECHMUS II. I wouldn't deny it if I did!

PENICULUS. You don't know your own parasite?

MENAECHMUS II. Your head isn't on right, fellow, as I can
see.

PENICULUS. Tell me, did you steal that cloak from your wife
today and give it to Erotium?

MENAECHMUS II. By Hercules, I don't have a wife, and I
didn't steal a cloak and give it to Erotium! Are you crazy or
something?

PENICULUS. That finishes it! I didn't see you going out wearing the cloak?

MENAECHMUS II. I'll knock your block off! You think everybody is a fairy because you are? You have the nerve to say I
was wearing a woman's cloak!?

PENICULUS. Yes, by Hercules, I do!

MENAECHMUS II. You'd better go down (*Pointing toward hell.*) where you belong! Or have your head examined and your madness exorcized in the temple!

PENICULUS. No one, by Pollux, is ever going to exorcize me from telling your wife everything, exactly as it happened! All your curses will fall right back on you! I'll fix you so that you'll be sorry you ever ate up that dinner!

(*Exit into* MENAECHMUS I's *house.*)

MENAECHMUS II. What is this all about? It's more than I can stand that whenever I see somebody, they start playing games with me! But I hear the door.

(EROTIUM's *maid comes out of the courtesan's house, holding a bracelet.*)

MAID (*sweetly and pertly*). Menaechmus, Erotium would love you very much if at the same time you would take this to the jeweler and have an ounce of gold added to it. Tell him to remodel this bracelet completely.

MENAECHMUS II (*taking bracelet*). Add an ounce of gold, remodel the bracelet, whatever she wants. Tell her I'll do whatever she wants.

MAID. Do you know which bracelet this is?

MENAECHMUS II. I don't know, except that it's gold.

MAID. This is the one you said you secretly stole from your wife's jewel box.

MENAECHMUS II (*doubtfully, and for the moment not on his guard*). I didn't!

MAID. You don't remember? Then give me back the bracelet if you don't remember.

MENAECHMUS II (*takes a look at it*). Wait! Why, of course, I remember! This is the one which I gave her, the very one! (*Greedily taking a shot in the dark*). Where are the armlets which I gave her at the same time?

MAID. You never gave her any armlets!

MENAECHMUS II. Of course, by Pollux, I just gave her this one piece.

MAID. Shall I tell her you'll attend to it?

MENAECHMUS II. Tell her, it will be taken care of. The cloak and the bracelet, I'll have them back at the same time.

MAID (*sweetly*). And please, dear Menaechmus, have some earrings made for me, heavy ones, drop earrings, so that I'll be happy to see you when you come to our house.

MENAECHMUS II. Gladly! Give me the gold, I'll pay for the labor.

MAID. Please lay out the money. I'll repay you later.

MENAECHMUS II. No, you lay out the money and I'll repay you double.

MAID. I don't have it.

MENAECHMUS II. Well, give it to me whenever you have it.

MAID (*getting ready to leave*). Anything else?

MENAECHMUS II. Tell her I'll take care of these things—(MAID *goes in.*)—in such a way that as soon as possible, for whatever I can get, they'll be sold!

Has she gone in already? She has. She's closed the door. The way all the gods are helping me, enriching me, loving me! But why do I wait while I have the chance and the time, to get away from the lion's den? Hurry, Menaechmus! Shake a leg! Step out!

I'll take off this garland and throw it to my left in the direction of the forum, so that if they try to follow me they'll think I went that way. (*Throws down garland*). I'll go and meet my slave, ahead of time if I can, so I can tell him the good things the gods are giving me.

(*Hurries off to audience's left, in direction of harbor.*)

Act IV

(*Wife of Menaechmus I comes out of house with Peniculus. She is angry and shouting.*)

WIFE. Should I let my husband deceive me while he secretly steals whatever is in the house and takes it to his kept woman?

PENICULUS. Quiet down! I'll show you how to catch him in the act. Just follow him in this direction. (*Points toward audience's right.*) He was drunk, with a garland on his head, and was on his way to the embroiderer with the cloak which he stole today from your house.

See, there's the garland he was wearing! (*Points to it.*) Was I lying? Yes, he went this way (*Pointing toward forum.*) if you want to track him down. (*At this moment enter* MENAECHMUS I *at the end of the stage, walking from the direction of the forum, tired and annoyed.*) By Pollux, wonderful! There he is coming back, but he is not carrying the cloak!

WIFE. What should I do to him now?

PENICULUS. What you always do, scold him! That's my advice. Let's go in here; we'll take him from ambush. (*They go into alleyway.*)

MENAECHMUS I (*stops near his house and gives vent to his feelings*). What an utterly foolish and tiresome custom we have here, and how the leading citizens particularly are burdened with it! They all want to have clients.[2] Whether the clients are honest or not, they don't give a hoot! They are more concerned about their clients' riches than about their reputations. If a man is poor but of good character, he is considered a good-for-nothing, but if he is rich and a scoundrel, he is considered an excellent client. People who always violate the law, and never deal honestly, get themselves patrons to look out for their interests. They are greedy, grasping men, who are always being sued and deny that they received what was given them. They get their cases won by bribery and perjury, and they are always in trouble with the law.

When a day is set for trial for them, it is set for their patrons too, since we have to plead for them on the crooked deals which they have perpetrated, whether the case goes before a public tribunal or before a city official or before a judge. That's the way a client of mine delayed me and detained me all day today so that I couldn't do what I wished nor with whom I liked.

Before the city commissioners I pleaded his case for his many and completely dishonest acts. I proposed many complicated and difficult terms. Speaking sometimes more sometimes less than I had to, I defended him so well that I finally got him off with a settlement. And what did *he* do? He almost didn't want to pay! Never did I see a man more clearly guilty! For each of his crooked deals there were three excellent witnesses!

May all the gods damn him for ruining my day, especially today! Damn me too for even poking my nose inside the forum today! I've ruined what was to have been a wonderful day! I ordered a dinner, my mistress is waiting, I know. As soon as I possibly could I rushed to get out of the forum. Now she's angry

[2] This is one of the many examples of the mingling of Roman and Greek institutions and customs by Plautus. In Rome, especially during the Republic, the more well-to-do and politically powerful acted as patrons to less-favored citizens, their clients, whom the patrons aided with hand-outs of food, money, or jobs and by representing them in court. In return the clients supported their patrons politically and in other ways. In Greek cities like Athens the position of the *metics,* or resident aliens, was somewhat similar in their need to be legally represented in the courts, but otherwise their position was quite different, for *metics,* not being citizens, had no political rights, and in addition many of them were quite wealthy.

at me, I suppose. Maybe the cloak that I gave her will soothe her, the one I stole from my wife and brought to Erotium.

PENICULUS (*to* WIFE, *triumphant*). Well? What do you say?

WIFE (*unhappily, and perhaps getting tearful*). That it's too bad I'm married to a husband that bad!

PENICULUS. Have you heard enough?

WIFE (*disgustedly*). Enough!

MENAECHMUS I (*still unaware of their presence, and continuing as before*). If I'm smart, I'll get away from here and go where things will be better.

PENICULUS (*coming out of hiding*). Wait, it will be the worse for you!

WIFE (*following him*). Yes, I'll give it to you with interest, for stealing that cloak!

PENICULUS. That's it! Give it to him!

WIFE. You thought you could do such disgraceful things without my knowing it?

MENAECHMUS I. What's this all about, dear wife?

WIFE. You're asking me?

MENAECHMUS I. Do you want me to ask him? (*Tries to caress her.*)

WIFE. Take your hands off me!

PENICULUS. (*to* WIFE). That's the way! Keep it up!

MENAECHMUS I. (*to* WIFE). Why are you angry with me?

WIFE (*angrily*). You ought to know!

PENICULUS. He knows, but he pretends he doesn't, the rat!

MENAECHMUS I. What is it all about?

WIFE. My cloak——

MENAECHMUS I. Your cloak?

WIFE (*getting tearful*). The cloak—someone—

PENICULUS (*to* MENAECHMUS I). Why are you pale?

MENAECHMUS I. I'm not at all pale!

PENICULUS. Except for one thing, when she said: "Cloak," you suddenly looked like you would croak! And you shouldn't have eaten a dinner in secret without me! (*To* WIFE.) Go on! Attack your husband some more!

MENAECHMUS I (*quietly, to* PENICULUS). Won't you keep quiet?

PENICULUS (*quietly*). No, by Hercules, I certainly won't keep quiet! (*Aloud to* WIFE.) He motioned to me not to speak!

MENAECHMUS I. By Hercules, I absolutely did not motion or wink at you at all!

PENICULUS. There's nothing more brazen than this man who keeps denying what you can see with your own eyes!

MENAECHMUS I. By Jupiter and all the gods; I swear, dear Wife—is that good enough for you?—that I did not motion to him!

PENICULUS. All right. She believes you about that. Get back to the main point.

MENAECHMUS I. What main point?

PENICULUS. Why, the embroiderer, I'd say. Go bring the cloak back!

MENAECHMUS I. What cloak are you talking about?

PENICULUS. I'm keeping quiet now, since she doesn't mention the matter herself.

WIFE (*tearfully*). Yes, by Castor, I'm an unhappy woman!

MENAECHMUS I. Why are you unhappy? Explain it to me. Did one of the slaves do something wrong? Have the servants answered back? Tell me. They won't get away with it.

WIFE (*sarcastically*). You're kidding!

MENAECHMUS I. Surely it's one of the house slaves you're angry at?

WIFE. You're kidding!

MENAECHMUS I. Then you're angry at *me?*

WIFE. Now you're not kidding!

MENAECHMUS I. *I* haven't done anything wrong!

WIFE. Now you're kidding again!

MENAECHMUS I. Tell me, my wife, what's bothering you?

PENICULUS (*sarcastically*). The fine gentleman is so considerate of you!

MENAECHMUS I (*to* PENICULUS). Can't you stop annoying me? Am I speaking to you? (*Caresses* WIFE *again.*)

WIFE. Take your hands off me!

PENICULUS. Give it to him! That'll fix you for eating a dinner without me, and then making fun of me in front of the house, drunk, with a garland on your head!

MENAECHMUS I. By Pollux, I didn't! I haven't dined or set foot in there today!

PENICULUS. You deny it?

MENAECHMUS I. I certainly do deny it, by Hercules!

PENICULUS. There's nothing more brazen than this man! You mean to say that I didn't see you a while ago standing in front of the house with a crown of flowers on your head, when you said my head wasn't on straight, and you said you didn't know me and that you were a stranger?

MENAECHMUS I. Why, this is the first time I've been back since I left you!

PENICULUS. I'm on to you! You didn't think I was the kind of person who would take revenge on you. But, by Hercules, I've told her everything!

MENAECHMUS I. What did you tell her?

PENICULUS. I don't know. Ask her yourself.

MENAECHMUS I. What's this, Wife, what did he tell you?

WIFE. As if you don't know!

MENAECHMUS I. By Pollux, would I be asking you if I knew?

PENICULUS. By Pollux, what a wicked man! How he pretends! You can't hide it! She knows all about it, in detail. I told her everything, by Hercules!

MENAECHMUS I (*to* WIFE). What *is* it?

WIFE. Since you are not ashamed and you don't want to confess of your own free will, listen and pay attention, and I'll make you understand why I am angry and what he has told me. My cloak was stolen from the house!

MENAECHMUS I. A cloak stolen from me?

PENICULUS. See how the rascal is trying to catch you! It was stolen from her, not you! For surely if it were stolen from you, you couldn't get it back.

MENAECHMUS I (*to* PENICULUS). I've got nothing to do with you. (*To* WIFE.) But what are you saying, dear?

WIFE. The cloak, I'm saying, is gone from the house.

MENAECHMUS I. Who stole it?

WIFE. By Pollux, the man who stole it knows that!

MENAECHMUS I. And who is the man?

WIFE (*mockingly*). A certain Menaechmus.

MENAECHMUS I. By Pollux, what a dirty trick! Who is this Menaechmus?

WIFE. You, I say!

MENAECHMUS I. Who, me?

WIFE. Yes, you!

MENAECHMUS I. Who's got proof?

WIFE. *I* do!

PENICULUS. And I. And you took it to that girl friend of yours, Erotium!

MENAECHMUS I. I gave it to her?

WIFE. You, you, I tell you!

PENICULUS (*to* MENAECHMUS I). Do you want me to get an owl to keep saying, "You! You!" all the time? We're getting tired!

MENAECHMUS I. By Jupiter and all the gods, I swear to you, Wife (are you satisfied?) I did not give it to her!

PENICULUS. By Hercules! We swear we are not telling lies!

MENAECHMUS I. But I didn't give it to her to keep! I just lent it to her!

WIFE. By Castor, do I ever lend out your tunic or your cloak to anyone? If any lending is to be done, a woman should lend women's clothing and a man men's! Bring my cloak back home!

MENAECHMUS I. I'll do it. I'll get it back.

WIFE. You'd better! For I'm telling you, you'll never enter this house unless you bring the cloak back! (*Turns to go.*) I'm going home.

PENICULUS (*hopefully*). What about me, who helped you in this matter?

WIFE (*sardonically*). I'll return the favor when something is stolen from your house. (*Enters her house and closes door with an air of finality.*)

PENICULUS. That, by Pollux, will never happen, for there's nothing to steal in my house.

May the gods damn both of you, husband *and* wife! I'll hurry over to the forum, for I can plainly see that this family is finished with me. (*Exit.*)

MENAECHMUS I (*alone and nursing his wounds*). My wife thinks she's hurting me when she shuts me out. As if I didn't have another better place where I'll be made welcome! If I displease you, I must bear it. But I'll please Erotium here who will not lock me out, but will lock me in her house and heart.

Now I'll go and ask her to return the cloak which I gave her. I'll buy her another better one. (*Approaches* EROTIUM'S *door.*) Hello! Is the gatekeeper here? Open up and call Erotium to the door, somebody!

EROTIUM (*coming out*). Who's calling for me?

MENAECHMUS I (*lovingly*). Someone who loves you more than himself!

EROTIUM (*affectionately, and surprised*). My Menaechmus! Why are you standing in front of the house? Come inside!

MENAECHMUS I. Wait! Do you know what I've come to you for?

EROTIUM (*caressingly*). I know—so that we should make a little love.

MENAECHMUS I. No, by Pollux! The cloak, which I gave you. Please, dear, return it to me. My wife found out everything, exactly as it happened, in detail. I'll buy you another cloak, twice as expensive, whatever you want.

EROTIUM. But I already gave it to you, to take to the embroiderer, and also the bracelet, to take to the jeweler!

MENAECHMUS I. You gave me the cloak and the bracelet?! Surely you're mistaken! I haven't been back here or seen you since the time I gave it to you and left for the forum.

EROTIUM (*getting angry*). I see what you're trying to do! I trusted you and you're trying to cheat me! That's the kind of game you're playing!

MENAECHMUS I. I am not, by Pollux, asking for it to cheat you! Didn't I tell you my wife found out?

EROTIUM. I didn't *ask* you to give it to me. You brought it to me on your own. You gave it to me as a gift. Now you want it back. All right! Keep it! Take it, wear it, you or your wife, or lock it up in your safe! But as for you, from today on, you won't set foot in here, don't fool yourself! Since you hold me, who deserved well of you, in contempt, you won't be able to make love to me for free! You'll have to bring money like everyone else! From now on find another girl to cheat!

(*Exit, slams door.*)

MENAECHMUS I. Hercules, is she angry with me! (*To the closed door.*) Hey, dear, I want to say something! Wait! Come back! (*Waits a moment.*) Are you there? Won't you please come back, for my sake?

She's gone in. She's locked the door. Now I'm completely shut out. Nobody believes me, not my wife, not my mistress. I'd better talk this over with my friends and see what they think I ought to do.

(*Walks off toward forum.*)

Act V

(*Menaechmus II carrying the cloak enters from the direction of the harbor, where he has been searching for Messenio. He is worried and annoyed.*)

MENAECHMUS II. That was a very foolish thing I did when I entrusted Messenio with the purse containing money. I suppose he's sunk himself in some dive.

WIFE OF MENAECHMUS I (*opening her door*). I'll look out and see when my husband returns home. (*Sees* MENAECHMUS II.) Why, there he is! I'm saved! He's bringing home the cloak!

MENAECHMUS II (*not noticing her*). I wonder where Messenio is now?

WIFE. I'll go over and welcome him with the words he deserves. (*To* MENAECHMUS II.) Aren't you ashamed to come into my sight with that garment, you disgrace of a man?!

MENAECHMUS II (*bewildered*). What is it? What's troubling you, woman?

WIFE. You still have the impudence to dare to utter a single word or speak to me?

MENAECHMUS II. What have I done that I should not dare to speak?

WIFE. You're asking me, you shameless, brazen man?

MENAECHMUS II. Do you know, lady, why the Greeks used to say that Hecuba [3] was a bitch?

WIFE (*highly indignant*). I certainly don't!

MENAECHMUS II. Because she did the same thing that you are now doing. She kept heaping curses at everyone she saw. And that's why she rightly began to be called a bitch!

WIFE. I can't bear these insults! I'd rather be divorced the rest of my life than endure such insults from you!

MENAECHMUS II. What do I care whether you stay married or leave your husband! Is it the custom here to tell your hard-luck stories to any passing stranger?

WIFE. What stories? I tell you, I won't stand it any longer! I'll get a divorce rather than endure your behavior!

MENAECHMUS II. As far as I'm concerned, by Hercules, you can stay divorced as long as Jupiter holds the heavens!

WIFE. But you kept saying you hadn't stolen this (*Pointing to cloak.*) and now you're holding it right before my very eyes! Aren't you ashamed?

MENAECHMUS II (*angry*). By Hercules, you've got a lot of nerve! You dare to say this was stolen from you when another woman gave it to me to have it repaired?

WIFE. Yes, that does it, so help me Castor! I'm going to call my father and tell him all the disgraceful things you've done! (*To slave, who has come out during the argument.*) Go, Decio, find my father and bring him back with you! Tell him everything that's happened. I'll show him the terrible things you've done!

---

[3] The tragic queen of Troy, together with a surviving son and daughter, was made a slave of the Greeks when they destroyed her city. After the daughter was sacrificed and her son murdered, she finally went mad and, baying like a dog and reviling her captors, killed her son's murderer, who in his last moments prophesied she would turn into a bitch.

MENAECHMUS II. Are you sane? What terrible things?

WIFE. You rob your wife of a cloak and jewelry and take them to your mistress. Is that right enough, the way I tell it?

MENAECHMUS II (*sarcastic*). Please, lady, by Hercules, if you know, show me what medicine to take so that I'll be able to bear your impudence! What man you take me for, I don't know. But I don't know you from Hercules' grandfather!

WIFE. You may make fun of me, but, by Pollux, you won't be able to do it to my father! (FATHER-IN-LAW *appears in the distance from the direction of forum, coming very slowly.*) There he comes! Take a look at him. Do you know him?

MENAECHMUS II. I don't know him from Calchas, the pre-historic prophet!

WIFE. You say you don't know me and you say you don't know my father?

MENAECHMUS II. I'd say the same thing if you brought over your grandfather!

WIFE. By Castor, you're acting exactly the way you always do! (*Enter* FATHER-IN-LAW, *still at some distance, leaning on a staff, shuffling and tottering with difficulty, an old man.*)

FATHER-IN-LAW (*wearily*). I'll move my legs and hurry ahead as fast as my age permits and the occasion demands. But if I'd say that it's easy for me, I'd be lying. My spryness has left me! I'm just planted all over with old age! My body is a burden. (*Groans.*) My strength is gone. What a bad bargain is age, bad indeed! For when it comes, it brings many miseries. (*Groans.*) To list them would make a long story.

But what really is on my mind and worries me is: what in the world is it that has suddenly caused my daughter to frantically call for me? She didn't make it clear *what* it is, *what* she wants, *why* she summoned me. But I know what it is just the same. I'm sure she's been having an argument with her husband.

That's how they are, these women who insist that their husbands be subservient to them! Very headstrong and independent they are because of their dowries. And the husbands, too, are often not free from blame! But there's a limit as to how much a husband should take from a wife! Yet, by Pollux, a daughter never calls for her father unless something serious or some quarrel is the cause. But whatever it is, I'll soon know.

Ah, there she is before the house, and her husband looks peeved. It's what I suspected. I'll speak to her.

WIFE. I'll go and meet him. (*Approaches, kisses him.*) How are you, Father?

FATHER-IN-LAW. How are you? I'm here. Is everything all

right? Why are you so downcast? Why is he standing away from you, looking angry? You've been having a bit of a spat, the two of you! Tell me, in a few words, not in long speeches, which of you is to blame.

WIFE. I've done nothing wrong. I can relieve you of that first, Father. (*Getting tearful.*) But I cannot live here or bear it any longer! So take me away from here!

FATHER-IN-LAW. But what is it?

WIFE. I've been made into a laughingstock, Father!

FATHER-IN-LAW. By whom?

WIFE. By the man whom you married me to, my husband!

FATHER-IN-LAW. So it *is* an argument! How often have I told you, both of you, not to come to me with your quarrels?

WIFE. How can I avoid it, Father?

FATHER-IN-LAW. You're asking me?

WIFE. Unless you don't want me to!

FATHER-IN-LAW. How often have I explained to you to put up with your husband, whatever he does, and not to keep spying on where he is going and what he is doing!

WIFE. But he has been having an affair next door with a courtesan!

FATHER-IN-LAW. He's got good taste! And because of your meddling, I suppose, he'll love her all the more!

WIFE. And he gets drunk there!

FATHER-IN-LAW. Is it any of your business whether he drinks more or less, there or somewhere else, if he likes? What damned impudence is this? Next thing you know you'll be trying to stop him from accepting an invitation to dinner, or from inviting someone to his own house!

Do you women expect husbands to be your slaves? Next thing you know you'll be expecting him to do housework! You'll give him a supply of wool and you'll order him to sit among the housemaids and card wool!

WIFE. It looks as though I've brought you here not to defend me, Father, but to defend my husband! You stand on my side, but you plead his case!

FATHER-IN-LAW. If he has done anything wrong, I'll blame him even more than I've blamed you. Since he keeps you well provided with clothes and jewelry, and furnishes you with enough maids and food, it is better to be sensible, woman.

WIFE. But he steals jewelry and cloaks out of my closets! He robs me and takes my best clothing to prostitutes!

FATHER-IN-LAW. He does wrong if he does that. If he doesn't do it, you do wrong to accuse an innocent man.

WIFE. Why, even now he is holding the cloak, Father, and the bracelet which he had taken to her! Now that I've found out, he is bringing them back!

FATHER-IN-LAW (*aside*). Now I'll find out his side of the story. I'll go over and speak to him. (*To* MENAECHMUS II.) Tell me, Menaechmus, what you two were arguing about, so that I may know. Why are you cross? Why is she angry and standing apart from you?

MENAECHMUS II. Whoever you are, whatever your name is, old man, I call Jove on high and all the gods as witnesses——

FATHER-IN-LAW. To what—to what in the world?

MENAECHMUS II. That I've never done any harm to this woman, who accuses me of stealing this (*Pointing to cloak or holding it up.*) and taking it from her house!

WIFE. He perjures himself!

MENAECHMUS II. If I've ever set foot in her house, where she lives, I wish that I should be the most wretched of all wretched men!

FATHER-IN-LAW. Are you in your right senses, to wish for that and to deny that you ever set foot in the house where you live, you utter madman?

MENAECHMUS II. Do you, old man, say that I live in that house? (*Points to* MENAECHMUS I's *house.*)

FATHER-IN-LAW. Do you deny it?

MENAECHMUS II. Of course I deny it, by Hercules!

FATHER-IN-LAW. Then your denial is untrue! Unless you moved out during the night! Daughter, come here! (*She approaches.*) Tell me, you people haven't moved out of here, have you?

WIFE. Where to, or for what reason, tell me?

FATHER-IN-LAW. I don't know, by Pollux!

WIFE. He's making fun of you, don't you see?

FATHER-IN-LAW (*to* MENAECHMUS II). Now, really, Menaechmus, enough of your joking. Now be serious about this matter!

MENAECHMUS II. Please, what have I to do with you? Where did *you* come from, or who are you? What do I owe you or her, who is a nuisance to me in every way?

WIFE (*in some alarm, to her father*). Do you notice that his eyes are getting green, how a greenish color is rising on his temples and his forehead? Look how his eyes glitter!

MENAECHMUS II (*aside*). What's better for me than that, since they say I'm crazy, I may as well pretend to be crazy to scare them away! (*Starts to make faces.*)

WIFE (*really alarmed this time*). Look how his face is getting twisted and gaping! What should I do now, Father?

FATHER-IN-LAW (*protectively*). Come over here, my daughter, as far away from him as you can! (*She comes close to him.*)

MENAECHMUS II (*feigning madness, in a parody of tragic style, as if listening to a god calling him from above*). Evoe! Evoe! O Bacchus, where in the forest do you call me to hunt? I hear, but I cannot get away from these regions! That rabid bitch guards me on the left, and behind me is that garlic-smelling old goat who has often ruined innocent citizens with his false testimony!

FATHER-IN-LAW (*pityingly*). Oh, you poor, poor man!

MENAECHMUS II (*in the same manner as before*). Behold, Apollo commands me by his oracle to burn out her eyes with lighted torches!

WIFE (*frantic*). Help me, Father! He's threatening to burn out my eyes!

MENAECHMUS II (*aside*). They say I'm crazy when they are the crazy ones!

FATHER-IN-LAW (*quietly*). Daughter, psst!

WIFE (*quietly*). What is it?

FATHER-IN-LAW (*quietly*). What shall we do? What if I call the slaves here? I'll go tell them to carry him away from here and tie him up in the house before he makes any more disturbance.

MENAECHMUS II (*aside, having overheard*). Then I'm caught! Unless I figure out a plan, they'll carry me to their house! (*Aloud, again as if to a god.*) You forbid me to hold back my fists from any part of her face, unless she gets right out of my sight? I'll do what you order, Apollo!

FATHER-IN-LAW (*to his daughter*). Run home, as fast as you can, so he won't beat you!

WIFE (*going*). I'm running! Please watch him, Father, so that he doesn't get away. What an unhappy woman I am to hear such things! (*Runs into her house.*)

MENAECHMUS II (*aside*). I didn't do such a bad job of getting rid of her! Now for this filthy, bearded, tremulous, ill-begotten, shrunken Tithonus! (*Aloud, as before.*) So you command me to smash his body and his bones and his limbs with that staff that he is holding? (*Makes a threatening gesture toward the old man.*)

FATHER-IN-LAW (*unsteadily brandishing his staff*). You'll get it if you so much as touch me or come closer!

MENAECHMUS II (*again as if to Apollo*). I'll do whatever you order! I'll take a double-bladed axe and hack this old man's insides bit by bit right down to the bone!

FATHER-IN-LAW (*fearful*). I'd really better be careful to watch out for myself. I'm truly afraid, the way he threatens me, that he may do me some harm!

MENAECHMUS II (*still pretending*). Many are your commands to me, Apollo! Now you bid me get a team of horses, untamed, fierce, and to get on the chariot so that I may run over this smelly, toothless, overaged lion! Now I'm standing in the chariot; now I'm holding the reins! The whip is in my hands! (*Acts all this out.*) Git-ye-up, horses! Let's hear the sound of your hoofs! (*In epic style.*) Bend your fleet legs in swift pursuit! (*Prances around as if driving a chariot.*)

FATHER-IN-LAW (*tremulously protecting himself with staff*). You threaten me with a team of horses?!

MENAECHMUS II (*threatening the old man*). Behold, Apollo, again you bid me make an attack on him who stands there and kill him! (*Jerks his head.*) But who is it who pulls me by the hair from the chariot? He alters the command and edict of Apollo! (*As if another god has intervened, he stops.*)

FATHER-IN-LAW. Alas, what a terrible and sudden illness! O gods, I depend on your help! Look at him who has gone mad! How well he was just a while ago! So great an illness has suddenly fallen upon him! I'll get a doctor as fast as possible.
(*Exit, tottering, in direction of forum*)

MENAECHMUS II (*looking around*). Have they gone from my sight, I ask you, these people who absolutely forced me, a sane man, to be insane? I'd better get back to the ship while I can safely do it.

(*To audience.*) All of you, I beg of you, if the old man gets back, don't tell him down which street I've escaped.
(*Exit toward the harbor.*)

(*The* FATHER-IN-LAW *has left a message at the office of the busy* DOCTOR, *and is now impatiently waiting for him in front of* MENAECHMUS I's *house.*)

FATHER-IN-LAW. My buttocks hurt from sitting, and my eyes from looking and waiting for the doctor till he gets back from a visit! Finally, at long last, the great doctor gets back from his patients and he says he has put splints on Aesculapius' fractured leg or Apollo's arm. So now I wonder whether I'm getting a doctor or a carpenter!

(*Catching sight of him.*) Here he comes! Walking so deliberately! Get a move on, Doctor!

(*Enter* DOCTOR, *very medical and officious.*)

DOCTOR. What kind of sickness does he have? Tell me, sir,

is he possessed or touched in the head? I'd like to know. Is he in a coma or does he have dropsy?

FATHER-IN-LAW. Why, that's why I sent for you, so you can tell me and make him well!

DOCTOR (*confidently*). That's easily done! He'll be well, I give you my word on that!

FATHER-IN-LAW. I want you to give him the best treatment.

DOCTOR. I'll give him my best bedside manner, with six hundred "hm's" and "hah's" a day. In that way I'll cure him for you with the best treatment.

(*Enter* MENAECHMUS I, *from the forum. He looks unhappy.*)

FATHER-IN-LAW. Why, there he is himself! Let's see what he does! (FATHER-IN-LAW *and* DOCTOR *slip into alleyway.*)

MENAECHMUS I. By Pollux, this day has sure turned out perverse and adverse for me! All the things I thought I was doing secretly, that parasite has brought right out into the open and has filled me with disgrace and fear! My clever Ulysses, who has stirred up so much trouble for his patron! That man! As sure as I'm alive I'll strip him of his life! But it's foolish of me to say "his life" when it really belongs to me. It's my food and my expense that he lives on. No more! I'll cut off his livelihood!

And that courtesan! She acted true to form, exactly what you would expect of a courtesan! Just because I ask that the cloak be returned to my wife, she says I gave it to her to keep. Ah, by Pollux, I'm in a terrible mess! (*Waves his arm in distress.*)

FATHER-IN-LAW. Do you hear what he says?

DOCTOR. He says he's in a terrible mess.

FATHER-IN-LAW. I'd like you to go over to him.

(*The two approach* MENAECHMUS I, *the* FATHER-IN-LAW *a little behind the* DOCTOR.)

DOCTOR. Hello, and the best of health to you, Menaechmus. But why do you uncover your arm? Don't you realize that in your condition you can do yourself harm?

MENAECHMUS I. Why don't you hang yourself?

FATHER-IN-LAW (*to* DOCTOR). You see?!

DOCTOR (*to* FATHER-IN-LAW). I see all right. He's so far gone that whole acres of medicine won't help him! (*To* MENAECHMUS I.) But tell me, Menaechmus——

MENAECHMUS I. What do you want?

DOCTOR. Answer this question, please: Do you drink red wine or white wine?

MENAECHMUS I. Why don't you go to hell!

DOCTOR. By Hercules! The first symptoms of insanity are really beginning to show themselves! Why don't you answer the questions I asked?

MENAECHMUS I. Why don't you ask me whether I eat purple bread, or red or yellow bread? Or whether I eat chicken with the scales on or fish with feathers?

FATHER-IN-LAW. Oh ho! Do you hear, Doctor, how he is getting delirious? Hurry up! Give him some medicine before insanity really gets a hold on him!

DOCTOR. Now just wait a minute. My examination isn't over. I've got a few more questions to ask him.

FATHER-IN-LAW. You'll kill him with all your questions and chatter!

DOCTOR (to MENAECHMUS I). Now tell me, do your eyes ever get fixed or staring, you know—pop-eyed?

MENAECHMUS I. What do you think I am, a lobster, you rascally quack?

DOCTOR. Tell me, do your insides ever—gurgle, as far as you can tell?

MENAECHMUS I. When I've had a full meal, there's no gurgling; when I'm hungry they gurgle.

DOCTOR. Now, by Pollux, that's a pretty sane answer for a man who's supposed to be crazy! (Deliberates a moment.) Do you sleep through the night? Fall asleep easily when you go to bed?

MENAECHMUS I. I sleep all right if I've paid all my bills—may Jupiter and all the gods damn you!

DOCTOR (to FATHER-IN-LAW). That last statement is a symptom of an insane seizure, so watch out!

FATHER-IN-LAW. Why, no! From those last words I'd say he is sanity and wisdom personified compared to before! For he was saying that his wife was a rabid bitch!

MENAECHMUS I (indignant). I said that?

FATHER-IN-LAW (forgivingly). You were insane, I suppose.

MENAECHMUS. Me?!

FATHER-IN-LAW. Yes, you! And you threatened to run over me with a four-horse chariot. I saw you do it. I can prove it to you!

MENAECHMUS I (excitedly). And I can prove to you that you broke into a temple and stole Jupiter's sacred crown, and for that you were thrown into prison in chains! And I know that when you were let out you were stuck in the stocks and beaten with whips! And I know that you killed your father and sold your mother, and I can prove it! How's *that* for matching insulting slander with insulting slander? Do I seem sane enough now?

FATHER-IN-LAW. Oh, Heaven help us, Doctor! Hurry, do what you're going to do! Don't you see the man is stark staring mad?

DOCTOR (*to* FATHER-IN-LAW). Do you know what you should do? Have him brought to my office right away.

FATHER-IN-LAW. Is that your best opinion?

DOCTOR. Yes. There under my personal attention I'll be able to cure him.

FATHER-IN-LAW. Well, you're the doctor!

DOCTOR (*to* MENAECHMUS I). I'll see to it that you take laxatives and medicines for twenty days straight!

MENAECHMUS I (*to* DOCTOR). And I'll string you up and stab you with goads for thirty days straight!

DOCTOR (*to* FATHER-IN-LAW). Go, summon some men to bring him to me!

FATHER-IN-LAW. How many will we need?

DOCTOR. Considering his insanity, four—no less!

FATHER-IN-LAW. They'll be here at once. You hold on to him, Doctor!

DOCTOR. Uh—no! I'll go home and make all the necessary preparations. You tell your servants to bring him to me.

FATHER-IN-LAW. I'll get him there soon.

DOCTOR. I'm going.

(*Exit briskly, if not hurriedly, toward forum.*)

FATHER-IN-LAW. Good-bye.

(*Exit a few moments later, tottering in same direction.*)

MENAECHMUS I (*sighs with relief*). My father-in-law has gone! The doctor has gone! I'm alone!

O Jupiter, why is it that these people say I'm insane? Since the day I was born I've never been sick a day in my life! I'm neither insane nor do I start fights and quarrels. I'm as sane as anybody else I see! I recognize people, I speak to them. Are they falsely accusing me of insanity or are they themselves insane?

What am I to do now? I want to go home; my wife won't let me in. There (*Pointing to* EROTIUM's *house, or motioning to it with his head.*) nobody considers me welcome. Things have turned out pretty badly! I'll just stay right here. At night, at least, I hope, I'll be let into the house. (*Stands around moping for a while.*)

(*Enter* MESSENIO, *from the direction of the harbor, well*

satisfied with himself. He stops at his end of the stage, not seeing MENAECHMUS I.)

MESSENIO. This is the perfect picture of a good slave: a person who takes care of his master's property and watches it, keeps it in order, and keeps his mind on it, so that when the master is away he guards it diligently, as if it were his own, or better. His back must be stronger than his gullet, and his legs than his stomach, if he has the right attitude.

Let them remember, those who are worthless, the kind of reward lazy, wicked slaves get from their masters. Whips, leg-irons, hard labor at the mill, fatigue, hunger, and bitter cold: these are the rewards for laziness. This kind of punishment I'm badly afraid of! Therefore I've made up my mind to be good rather than bad. For I can much more easily bear tongue-lashings than whiplashings. I'm much happier to eat what the mill grinds than to grind it myself! Therefore I follow my master's command and obey it well and to the letter! So let others act the way they think is best for them, I'll act the way I have to.

Let me have a healthy sense of fear, let me be free of blame, so that I may be helpful to my master on every occasion. Slaves who are free from blame, who have a healthy sense of fear, are usually helpful to their masters. Those who don't fear their masters, *they've* got something to really be afraid about when they've done something to deserve punishment!

I will not have to keep my fears much longer. The time is near when my master will reward me for my services. So, it's with this in mind that I serve, as long as I think it's to the advantage of my back.

Now that I've settled the luggage and the slaves at an inn, as he ordered, I'm returning to meet my master. I'll knock at the door, so he will know I'm here, and so that I may lead him out of this den of damnation. (*Approaches* EROTIUM'S *door*). But I'm afraid that I've come too late, and the battle is over!

(FATHER-IN-LAW *comes in from the other end of stage, followed by four husky, strong-armed slaves.*)

FATHER-IN-LAW (*to slaves*). By the gods and men, I'm telling you to be careful to carry out without mistake every command that I've commanded! Get that man (*Pointing.*) lifted on your shoulders and into the doctor's office, unless you don't mind the whip on your legs and backs! Don't let any of you fear any threat he may make. (*They hesitate.*)

Go on! Why are you standing around? What are you hesitating about? You should have grabbed him and lifted him up by now! I'm going to the doctor. I'll be waiting for you there when you arrive. (*Exit toward forum.*)

(*Slaves approach* MENAECHMUS I *menacingly.*)

MENAECHMUS I (*frightened*). I'm done for! What's this all about? Why are those men running toward me? (*They are right next to him, looking for the best way to grab hold of him.*) What do you want? What are you looking for? Why do you surround me? (*They seize him.*) Where are you grabbing me? Where are you carrying me to? Help! Citizens of Epidamnus, I beg of you, help, rescue me! (*To slaves.*) Why don't you let me go? (*Struggling.*)

MESSENIO (*rushing up*). Oh immortal gods! What do I see with my eyes? My master, these people are carrying him away! What an outrage!

MENAECHMUS I (*desperately*). Won't someone please help me?!

MESSENIO. I, Master, most boldly! Oh what a shameful terrible crime! Citizens of Epidamnus, my master, here, is being kidnaped on the street in a peaceful city in broad daylight! He came here a free man! (*To slaves, punching.*) Let him go!

MENAECHMUS I. I beg of you, whoever you are, give me a hand! Don't let them do such a thing to me! It's outrageous!

MESSENIO. Certainly, I'll give you a hand, and I'll defend you and help you with all my might! I'll never let you die! I'd rather die myself!

(*Flailing and tearing at the abductors.*) Tear his eye out, the fellow who has you on his shoulder, Master, go on! I'll plough into their faces and plant them with my fists! By Hercules, you'll be sorry you carried him off today! Let him go! (*Punching.*)

MENAECHMUS I (*fighting*). I've got this fellow's eye!

MESSENIO. Pull it out of his head so only the socket shows! You scoundrels, you crooks, you thugs! (*Keeps punching, shoving, and pulling at them.*)

SLAVES (*giving way*). Murder! We give up! Please!

MENAECHMUS I (*pushing or kicking one of the slaves*). Why are you touching me! (*To* MESSENIO.) Flatten him with your fists!

MESSENIO (*punching this one and then another*). Go on! Get out of here! Get away from here! (*Kicks another slave.*) Here's one for you! Since you're the last to leave, here's a present for you! (*All the assailants flee.*)

(*To* MENAECHMUS I.) By Pollux, Master, I came to your aid in the nick of time!

MENAECHMUS I. May the gods always bless you, young man, whoever you are! For without you I certainly wouldn't be seeing the sun set today!

MESSENIO. Then, by Pollux, if you want to do right by me, Master, set me free.

MENAECHMUS I (surprised). I free you!

MESSENIO. Certainly, Master, since I saved your life!

MENAECHMUS I. I'm afraid, young man, you're making a mistake.

MESSENIO. What? A mistake?

MENAECHMUS I. By Father Jupiter, I swear—I'm not your master!

MESSENIO. Don't say that!

MENAECHMUS I. I mean it! No slave of mine ever did what you did for me!

MESSENIO. So, even if you say I don't belong to you, send me away a free man, anyway.

MENAECHMUS I. By Hercules, as far as I'm concerned (Pronouncing a standard formula of manumission.) you are hereby a free man and free to go wherever you wish!

MESSENIO. Is that an order?

MENAECHMUS I (smiling). It's my order, if I have any jurisdiction over you.

MESSENIO. Good-bye, Master, hello, Patron! Now I'll say the words of the witness: "Since you are a free man, Messenio, congratulations!" And I say: "Very much obliged to you both!"

But, Patron, I want you to realize it, I am yours to command no less than when I was your slave. I'll live at your house, and when you go home, I'll go with you.

MENAECHMUS I (aside). Oh no!

MESSENIO. Now I'll go to the inn and bring back your luggage and your money. The purse with your money has been properly sealed in the trunk. I'll bring it to you now.

MENAECHMUS I (eagerly). Bring it, by all means!

MESSENIO. I'll return it to you safe and sound, exactly as you gave it to me. Wait here for me. (Exit toward harbor.)

MENAECHMUS I (with an air of bewilderment). All kinds of strange things have happened to me today in a remarkable fashion! Some say I'm not myself and lock me out. And now this slave whom I've set free says he is mine! (Shakes his head.)

He says he is going to bring me a purse with money. If he brings it, I'll tell him he's free to leave me to go wherever he wishes, so that when he recovers his senses, he won't ask me for the money. (Grins.)

My father-in-law and the doctor (*Frowns.*) say I'm crazy. I wonder what it's all about! It all seems like a dream, nothing less!

Now I'll go to the courtesan's house, even though she's angry with me, to see if I can induce her to return the cloak so I can take it back home. (*Enters* EROTIUM's *house.*)

(*Enter* MENAECHMUS II *and* MESSENIO *from the harbor side,* MENAECHMUS II *scolding.*)

MENAECHMUS II. Do you have the nerve to say that you met me anywhere today after I ordered you to meet me here?

MESSENIO. Why, I just rescued you from four men who were trying to carry you off to this house! (*Points to* MENAECHMUS I's *house.*) You kept calling on all the gods and men for help, when I ran over and rescued you by violent fighting against their will! That's the reason you set me free, because I saved you.

When I said I was going to get the money and the luggage, you must have run on ahead as fast as possible so you could deny it as you have! (*Looks hurt.*)

MENAECHMUS II. I ordered you to go free?

MESSENIO. Certainly!

MENAECHMUS II. Well, I can assure you that I'd rather become a slave myself than ever set you free!

(*Enter* MENAECHMUS I, *leaving* EROTIUM's *house, angrily uttering his final words to those inside.*)

MENAECHMUS I. Even if you people were to swear by your eyes, you still wouldn't make it more true that I took away the cloak and bracelet, you disreputable women!

MESSENIO (*notices* MENAECHMUS I). Oh immortal gods! What am I seeing!

MENAECHMUS II. What do you see?

MESSENIO (*excitedly*). Your reflection!

MENAECHMUS II. What are you talking about?

MESSENIO (*excitedly*). Your image! As like as you as possible!

MENAECHMUS II (*taking a look*). By Pollux, he's not at all dissimilar, now that I consider my own face!

MENAECHMUS I (*noticing* MESSENIO). Oh, young man, hello, you who saved me, whoever you are!

MESSENIO. Sir, please, by Hercules, if you don't mind, tell me your name!

MENAECHMUS I (*genially*). After what you did for me, by Pollux, I wouldn't mind doing anything for you that you wish. My name is Menaechmus.

MENAECHMUS II (*surprised*). By Pollux, so is mine!

MENAECHMUS I. I'm a Sicilian, from Syracuse.

MENAECHMUS II. The same city and country as mine!

MENAECHMUS I (*also surprised now*). What did you say?

MENAECHMUS II. Nothing but the truth!

MESSENIO (*pointing to* MENAECHMUS I *in confusion*). This man I know. He is my master, and I am his slave. But I believed I belonged to (*Pointing to* MENAECHMUS II.) that one. (*To* ME-NAECHMUS II, *still confused.*) Please forgive me if I spoke somewhat foolishly or imprudently to you.

MENAECHMUS II. You seem to me to be delirious! Don't you remember you disembarked from the ship with me today?

MESSENIO (*recovering from his confusion*). You're certainly asking a fair question. (*To* MENAECHMUS II.) *You* are my master. (*To* MENAECHMUS I.) *You* go look for your own slave. (*To* MENAECHMUS II.) *You*, hello! (*To* MENAECHMUS I.) *You*, good-bye! I say that *he* (*Points to* MENAECHMUS II.) is Menaechmus!

MENAECHMUS I. And I say that I am!

MENAECHMUS II. What kind of a story is this? You're Menaechmus?

MENAECHMUS I. I say I am. My father was Moschus.

MENAECHMUS II. You are my father's son?

MENAECHMUS I. Not at all, sir! *My* father's son! I'm not trying to take or make off with yours!

MESSENIO (*aside*). O immortal gods, grant me the unhoped-for hope that I suspect! Unless my mind is betraying me, these are the twin brothers! For they both mention the same father and the same country as being theirs. I'll call my master aside. (*Aloud.*) Menaechmus!

BOTH MENAECHMI. What do you want?

MESSENIO. I don't want both of you, but whichever one of you sailed on the ship with me?

MENAECHMUS I. Not I!

MENAECHMUS II. I did!

MESSENIO. Then I want you. Come over here.

MENAECHMUS II. Here I am. What is it?

MESSENIO (*quietly*). That man is either a sharper or he is your twin brother! For I never saw two men more alike. Water is no more like water, or milk like milk than you look like him and he like you. Besides, he claims the same country and father. We had better go over and ask him a few questions.

MENAECHMUS II (*quietly*). By Hercules, how good your advice is! I'm really grateful. Continue your efforts, please, by Hercules. You'll be a free man if you really find he is my brother!

MESSENIO (*quietly*). I hope so!

MENAECHMUS II (*quietly*). And I hope so too!

MESSENIO (*to* MENAECHMUS I). Tell me, I think you said you are called Menaechmus?

MENAECHMUS I. That's true!

MESSENIO (*pointing to* MENAECHMUS II). His name is also Menaechmus. You said you were born in Sicily, in Syracuse. He was born there too! Now you can both give some help to me and yourselves too at the same time.

MENAECHMUS I. No matter what you ask, you deserve to get what you want. I, a free man, am at your service as if you bought me for money!

MESSENIO. It is my hope that I will prove that you two are twin brothers, born from one mother and one father on one day.

MENAECHMUS I. What you say is marvelous! If you can only accomplish what you promise!

MESSENIO. I can. But come now, both of you, answer what I ask.

MENAECHMUS I. Begin asking what you please. I will not keep back anything I know.

MESSENIO (*to* MENAECHMUS I). Is your name Menaechmus?

MENAECHMUS I. Yes.

MESSENIO (*to* MENAECHMUS II). Is yours the same?

MENAECHMUS II. It is.

MESSENIO (*to* MENAECHMUS I). Your father was Moschus, you say?

MENAECHMUS I. That's right.

MENAECHMUS II. So was mine.

MESSENIO (to MENAECHMUS I). Are you from Syracuse?

MENAECHMUS I. Certainly!

MESSENIO (*to* MENAECHMUS II). What about you?

MENAECHMUS II. Of course!

MESSENIO. So far all the signs point in the same direction. Now give me your attention a little further. (*To* MENAECHMUS I.) What is the furthest back you remember in your country, tell me.

MENAECHMUS I. When I went away to Tarentum with my father on a business trip, and then wandered off from my father in a crowd, and was taken away from there.

MENAECHMUS II (*excitedly*). Great Jupiter help me!

MESSENIO (*to* MENAECHMUS II). Why do you cry out? Why don't you keep quiet? (*To* MENAECHMUS I.) How old were you when your father took you away from home?

MENAECHMUS I. Seven years old. My teeth were just then beginning to fall out. And I never saw my father again after that.

MESSENIO (*to* MENAECHMUS I.) Something else: how many sons were you?

MENAECHMUS I. To the best of my recollection, two.

MESSENIO. Which was the elder, you or your brother?

MENAECHMUS I. We were both the same age.

MESSENIO. How can this be?

MENAECHMUS I. We were twins!

MENAECHMUS II. The gods are answering my prayers!

MESSENIO (*to* MENAECHMUS II). If you interrupt, I'll keep quiet!

MENAECHMUS II. All right. I'll keep quiet!

MESSENIO (*to* MENAECHMUS I). Tell me, did you both have the same name?

MENAECHMUS I. Not at all! I had the name I now have. They called my brother, Sosicles.

MENAECHMUS II. I accept the identification. I can't keep from embracing him! My own twin brother! I am Sosicles! (*Tries to embrace* MENAECHMUS I.)

MENAECHMUS I (*somewhat skeptical*). How then did you later get the name Menaechmus?

MENAECHMUS II. After it was reported to us that you had wandered off from Father and had been carried off by an unknown man, and that Father had died, our grandfather changed it. He gave me the name you had.

MENAECHMUS I. I believe that it happened as you say. But I have one question.

MENAECHMUS II. Ask it!

MENAECHMUS I. What was our mother's name?

MENAECHMUS II. Teuximarcha.

MENAECHMUS I. That's right! (*Embraces him.*) Oh, it's good to see you! I had given up all hope, and now I see you after all these years!

MENAECHMUS II. And you too, Brother, after all the trouble and difficulty I've had looking for you! How happy I am to have found you at last!

MESSENIO. That's why the courtesan called you by his name! She thought you were he, I suppose, when she called you in to dinner.

MENAECHMUS I. Why, of course, by Pollux! I ordered dinner to be prepared for me at her house today without the knowledge of my wife, from whom I took a cloak and gave to her! (*Points to* EROTIUM'S *house.*)

MENAECHMUS II. Is this the cloak you mean? (*Holds it up.*)

MENAECHMUS I. That's it! How did it get to you?

MENAECHMUS II. The courtesan! She led me in to dinner, she said I had given it to her! I had an excellent meal, I drank well, I made love to her. Then I got the cloak and the jewelry from her.

MENAECHMUS I. I'm very happy if any good came to you because of me! Of course! When she called you in, she thought it was me!

MESSENIO (*amiably to* MENAECHMUS II). Is there any reason to delay freeing me as you said you would?

MENAECHMUS I. His request is most fair, and he's right, Brother. Do it for my sake.

MENAECHMUS II (*to* MESSENIO, *using a formula of manumission*). I bid you be free from henceforth!

MENAECHMUS I (*acting as witness*). Since you are free, Messenio, my congratulations!

MESSENIO (*hinting at money*). But I'll need better auspices for the future in order to be permanently free.

MENAECHMUS II. Brother, since things have turned out to our liking, let's both go back to our own country.

MENAECHMUS I. Brother, I'll do as you wish. I'll hold an auction here and sell everything. Meanwhile let's go in, Brother.

MENAECHMUS II. All right!

MESSENIO (*to* MENAECHMUS I). Do you know what I'd like to ask of you?

MENAECHMUS I. What?

MESSENIO. That you give me the job of auctioneer.

MENAECHMUS I. It's yours!

MESSENIO. Then do you want me to announce the auction?

MENAECHMUS I. Yes. Tell them it will take place in seven days.

MESSENIO (*to audience, like an announcer*). Menaechmus will hold an auction seven days from today! On sale will be slaves, furniture, farms, the town house, everything! They will be sold for whatever they bring, spot cash! On sale will also be—his wife, if a buyer turns up!

I don't suppose the proceeds will come to more than (*Exaggerating.*) five million. (*Pauses.*)

And now, members of the audience, good-bye, and give us your loud applause!

Prisoners of War
(Captivi)

A COMEDY

by

PLAUTUS

❧ ❧ ❧

translated by
Samuel Lieberman

DRAMATIS PERSONAE

ERGASILUS, a parasite
HEGIO, a wealthy citizen of Aetolia
PHILOCRATES, a young officer from Elis } The Prisoners of War
TYNDARUS, his slave, about the same age }
ARISTOPHONTES, a young officer from Elis
PHILOPOLEMUS, a young officer from Aetolia, a son of Hegio
STALAGMUS, a runaway slave of Hegio's
Varied Overseers and Slaves

Time: Acts I, II, III—the morning.
       Acts IV, V—several hours later, in the afternoon.
Place: The street in front of Hegio's house in the city of
       Pleuron in Aetolia, Greece.

Prologue

*At the side of the stage stand two Elean prisoners of war,
heavily fettered, one in officer's dress, one in slave's dress.
Enter Prologue.*

PROLOGUE. These two prisoners of war you see standing here,
they're standing, not sitting because those people in the back
(*Gesturing with his head toward the spectators in the rear.*) have
no seats. You people who are standing can testify to that. (*Waits
for a laugh.*)

The old man who lives here, Hegio (*Points to Hegio's house.*)
is this man's father (*Points to Tyndarus.*) but, if you will give
me your attention, I'll tell you in the prologue how he came to
be his own father's slave.

This old man had two sons. One of the boys, at the age of
four years, was kidnaped by a runaway slave who sold him to
this man's father. (*Points to Philocrates.*) Do you understand
so far? Very good.

That man in the back (*Gesturing toward back of theater.*)
says he doesn't. Will you come forward, sir? (*Indignantly.*) If
you don't have a place to sit, there is a place where you can
take a walk. (*Pointing to the exit.*) What are you trying to do,
force an actor to go begging? You're making a big mistake if you
think I'm going to shout myself hoarse just for you!

You others who are voting citizens because you have the means,
here is the rest of the story. I don't want to have to owe anybody
anything.

That runaway slave, as I said before, sold his young master
whom he had kidnaped on running away from home to this
man's father. (*Pointing to Philocrates.*) After Philocrates'
father had bought the boy (*Pointing to Tyndarus.*) he gave him to his
son Philocrates as a personal slave because they were about the
same age. At present he is a slave in his own father's house, but
his father doesn't realize it. The gods certainly treat us human
beings like playthings!

There you have the account of how Hegio lost one son. Now

after the recent war between the Aetolians and the Eleans, as
frequently happens in wars, the second son was taken prisoner.
A doctor named Menarchus bought him, right there in Elis.

He (*Pointing to Hegio's house.*) has begun to buy up Elean
prisoners of war in an attempt to find one whom he could exchange for his son—the one who is a prisoner. He doesn't know
that the one who is in his house is his other son. And since he
heard yesterday that there is a captured Elean cavalry officer of
highest rank and excellent family, he has spared no expense provided he could spare his son. In order to recover his son he has
bought these two from the questors [1] in charge of the war booty.

Both of them, however, have cooked up a cunning scheme by
which the slave will get his master sent back home. So they have
exchanged clothing and names with one another. He (*Pointing
to Tyndarus.*) is calling himself Philocrates, and he (*Pointing to
Philocrates.*), Tyndarus. Today this one (*Pointing.*) is pretending
to be that one, and that one (*Pointing.*) is pretending to be this
one. And today this one (*Pointing to Tyndarus.*) will cleverly
carry out the deception and put his master in full possession of
his freedom, and in so doing will save his own brother and without intending to will bring him back free to his own country and
father. This is exactly the way things often happen. In many in-
stances a person accomplishes more good unintentionally than in-
tentionally.

But without intending to, they have prepared their deceptions
and devised their plots and contrived things in such a way
through their own planning that he (*Pointing to Tyndarus.*) will
remain in slavery with his own father. So now without knowing it
he is in bondage to his own father. Come to think of it, how
insignificant is mere man after all!

This is the story that will be acted out as if real by us—a play
for you. But there is still something which I would like to point
out to you. It will certainly be worth your while to give this play
your close attention. It does not have a hackneyed theme and it
is not at all like other plays. It has no indecent lines that are not
repeatable. Here there is no perjuring pimp, no callous courtesan,
no bragging soldier.

And don't be afraid because I said there was a war between
Aetolia and Elis. The battles will take place offstage there. For it
would be quite inappropriate for us with our comic costumes and
decor to suddenly try to play tragedy. So if anyone is looking for
a battle, let him start a fight of his own. If he gets himself a

[1] The Roman term for civil or military officials in charge of finance, supplies,
procurement, etc.

good strong opponent, I promise him he'll get such a good battle that he'll never want to see another for the rest of his life.

I'm leaving now. Good-bye, most just judges at home and most excellent warriors in war. (*Bows, exit.*)

Act I

(*Enter Ergasilus, a parasite, very lean and unhappy.*)

ERGASILUS. The young men have nicknamed me "Call Girl" because I'm always called on when there is a party. I know that comics say that this is not much of a joke, but I say that it is well put. For when a fellow is at a party with a girl he has picked up and he is throwing the dice, he usually calls on his girl friend's name for luck. So is a call girl called on or not? Obviously! But, by Hercules, it is less obvious that we parasites are called on these days. No one ever calls on us or invites us.

We are like mice—always eating other people's food. But when vacation time comes and people are away in the country, then our teeth get a vacation too. It's the same with snails. When it gets hot, they hide in their shady holes and live on their own juices if no dew falls. In the same way, when vacation time comes, parasites, poor fellows, hide in their holes and try to live on their own juices while the people from whom they might have got a nibble are off in the country relaxing.

In the vacation period we parasites are hunting hounds, and by the time they return we are man-eating Molossian mastiffs, hungry wolfhounds, and brazen boarhounds. And here in this town, unless a parasite can take a few slaps in the face and bear having wine jars broken on his head, he'd better go out beyond the city gate and carry a porter's sack for a living.

There is some danger that this is what is going to happen to me. For ever since my patron was captured by the enemy. . . . (*Sighs.*) You see, there is a war on now between Aetolia and Elis. This is Aetolia, you know, and Philopolemus, the son of Hegio who lives here (*Pointing to Hegio's house.*), was captured in Elis. How sad this house has become for me. I'm in tears whenever I look at it. (*Gets tearful.*)

Now he has gone into this business for his son's sake, not a
very respectable business and most disagreeable to a man of his
character. He buys up prisoners of war in the hope of being able
to find one he can exchange for his son. How I hope he succeeds!
I've got nothing to hope for from the other young men around
here. They all love themselves. But he was a young man of the
old school, and when I smoothed the cares from his face and
made him laugh, it was not for nothing in return. His father is
just like him in character. Now I'll visit him. But the door,
through which I often came out brimming over with food and
drink, is opening.

(*Enter* HEGIO *from the house with* OVERSEER *of slaves.* HEGIO
doesn't notice ERGASILUS *at first.* OVERSEER *holds two sets of
light chains.*)

HEGIO (*to* OVERSEER). Now listen carefully. Put the light
chains on those two prisoners that I bought yesterday out of the
war booty from the questors. Take off those heavy ones with
which they are tied. You can let them walk around, outside if
they wish, or inside. But make sure they are carefully guarded.
For a free prisoner is like a wild bird. Once he is given a chance
to escape, that's enough. You can never catch him again.

OVERSEER. All of us would surely rather be free than slaves.

HEGIO. You don't look like that to me.

OVERSEER. If I can't get the money to buy my freedom, what
do you want me to do, tell my feet to go bye-bye?

HEGIO. If you do, I'll give you a bye-bye you'll never forget!

OVERSEER. I'll make myself into a bird, just as you said.

HEGIO. Just try it! And if you do, I'll clap you into a cage.
But enough of this chatter. Attend to what I ordered and hurry.
(*Exit* OVERSEER *into house.*)

I'll go to my brother's to see if my other prisoners have caused
any trouble during the night. Then I'll return home at once.
(*He begins to go off.*)

ERGASILUS. It really hurts me to see this poor old gentleman
working as a jailer because of his son's troubles. But if his son can
be brought home again, I would be able to bear doing any work;
I would even take a job as a hangman.

HEGIO (*turning around*). Who is speaking?

ERGASILUS. I, who am wasting away because of your worries.
I am growing lean, I pine away, I am skin and bones with miserable malnutrition. And nothing that I eat at home helps me.
(*Aside.*) Any little thing that I even taste on the outside does me
lots of good.

HEGIO. Hello, Ergasilus!

ERGASILUS (*starts to sob*). May the gods love you well, Hegio.

HEGIO. Don't cry.

ERGASILUS. Why shouldn't I cry? Shouldn't I shed tears over such a fine young man?

HEGIO. I always realized you were a friend to my son and I knew he was to you.

ERGASILUS. We only appreciate the good things in our lives when we have lost those we had. Now that your son has been captured by the enemy, I realize how much he meant to me, and I miss him.

HEGIO. When you, an outsider, are so unhappy at his misfortune, what can a father feel about his only son?

ERGASILUS (*reproachfully*). An outsider? I an outsider to him? Ah, Hegio, don't ever say or think that! He is an only son to you, but to me he is more only than only.

HEGIO. I have nothing but praise for the way you consider your friend's misfortune your misfortune. But take heart!

ERGASILUS. Alas, here's where it really hurts (*Patting his stomach.*)—because my eating army has been dismissed from service.

HEGIO (*smiling*). Haven't you meanwhile found somebody to reactivate the army which, as you say, has been dismissed?

ERGASILUS. Would you believe it? Everyone avoids this branch of the service ever since your son Philopolemus who was in charge of it has been captured.

HEGIO (*archly*). By Pollux! It's no wonder they shun the responsibility. You need many and various types of troops.[2] (*Counting on his fingers.*) First of all you need the flower [flour] of the Florentines, and there are several types of flours. Then you need Pisans [pizzans], and you need Paeonians [pie-ownians], and you need Bolognians and Sardinians, to say nothing of the marines for your fresh fish.

ERGASILUS (*aside, with enthusiasm*). How often the greatest talent fails to get a chance to express itself! What a general he would make—and he's only a civilian!

---

[2] Hegio's humorous listing of the troops in Ergasilus' "eating army" in the passage that follows consists of a volley of puns on foods and nationalities which are impossible to reproduce exactly into English. I have therefore had to make what are I hope adequate substitutions. Hegio lists: *Pistorenses*, from *pistor*, miller, and *Pistoria*, an Etruscan town; *Panici*, from *panis*, bread, and *Punici*, Carthaginians; *Placentini*, from *placenta*, cake, and *Placentia*, a town in northern Italy; *Turdetani*, from *turdus*, thrush, and *Turdetani*, a Spanish tribe; and *Ficedulenses*, an imaginary nationality composed of the Latin *ficedula*, a small bird esteemed by ancient epicures. In my translation I have purposely avoided the obvious hamburgers and frankfurters because the cities from which they are derived did not exist in Plautus' day.

HEGIO. Just keep up your courage. I'm confident I'll get him home in a few days. You see this young Elean prisoner? (*Pointing to* TYNDARUS.) He is from a family of highest rank and great wealth. I'm exchanging him for my son.

ERGASILUS. I'm confident you'll do it. May the gods and goddesses bring it to pass! By the way—have you been invited out to dinner anywhere?

HEGIO. Nowhere that I know of. Why do you ask?

ERGASILUS. Because today is my birthday and I would like to invite—myself to your house for dinner.

HEGIO. Cleverly put! All right, if you can be satisfied with little.

ERGASILUS. As long as it's not *very* little. Because I enjoy that kind of meal at home. (*Pretending to play hard to get.*) Well, then, make me an offer. And I'll say, "I'll take it if no one makes me a better offer, the terms of which will satisfy me and (*Patting his stomach.*) my friends." Just as if I'm selling a couple of acres, I'll state my terms.

HEGIO. You look as though you're selling a belly-acher, not a couple of acres! But if you come, come early.

ERGASILUS. Well, I've got plenty of free time.

HEGIO. Just come, but bring your own steak. All you'll get from me are spareribs. For the way my meals go these days, they are pretty rough going.

ERGASILUS. You'll never scare me with that, Hegio. Don't expect to. I'll come with my teeth well shod.

HEGIO. My food is really rough.

ERGASILUS. Do you eat thorns?

HEGIO. My suppers are earthy.

ERGASILUS. Well, pork comes from an earthy animal.

HEGIO. I eat vegetables mostly.

ERGASILUS. You should open up a health farm. Anything else?

HEGIO. Come on time.

ERGASILUS. No need to remind me. I have it well in mind.

(*Exit* ERGASILUS.)

HEGIO. I'll go in and figure up my accounts, to see how little I have left at my banker's. Then I'll go on to my brother where I said I was going. (*Goes off toward the Town Square.*)

Act II

(*Overseers enter from the house, followed by some slaves. They change the prisoners' chains.*)

OVERSEER (*while fetters are being changed*). If the immortal gods have wished you to suffer this hardship, you've got to bear it patiently. If you do, your suffering will be less severe. You were free men at home, I believe. Now slavery happens to be your lot. It's a good idea to make the best of it and of your master's orders. Use your brains and make things easier for yourselves. What's wrong is right if your master does it. That's the attitude to take.

TYNDARUS AND PHILOCRATES. Oh—oh—oh!

OVERSEER. There is no need for wailing. Your eyes already express your many miseries. When things are going badly, it helps to take them as they come.

TYNDARUS. But we are ashamed to be in chains.

OVERSEER. And the master will be sorry later if he releases you from chains and lets you be unfettered when he paid good money for you.

TYNDARUS. What has he got to fear from us? We know what our duty is if he allows us to be unchained.

OVERSEER. But you're planning to escape. I realize what you're up to.

TYNDARUS. We? Escape? Where to?

OVERSEER. To your country.

TYNDARUS. Go on! That wouldn't be decent—for us to imitate runaway slaves!

OVERSEER. By Pollux, I'm not saying you shouldn't if you get the chance.

TYNDARUS. Please, grant us one request.

OVERSEER. What is it?

TYNDARUS. Give us a chance to talk without them (*Pointing to slaves.*) and you fellows hanging around us.

OVERSEER. Very well! (*To slaves.*) Get away from here. (*To overseers.*) Let us go over here. (*To TYNDARUS and PHILOCRATES.*) But make your talk brief.

TYNDARUS. Of that you can be sure. (*To* PHILOCRATES.) Come over here.

OVERSEER (*To slaves*). Go away from them.

TYNDARUS (*with dignity*). We are much obliged to you for giving us the chance we want.

PHILOCRATES (*going with* TYNDARUS *to the other side of stage*). Come over here, far away from them so that no one can overhear our plans, and our scheme will not leak out. Plots are not plots if you don't guard them carefully, but they become the greatest disaster if they come out in the open. If we are pretending that you are my master and I am your slave, we must watch out and be careful so that this is handled prudently, cleverly, effectively without eavesdroppers. It's got to be letter perfect. It's a big undertaking and it mustn't be done half asleep.

TYNDARUS. I'll be the way you want me to.

PHILOCRATES. I should hope so!

TYNDARUS. You realize, of course, that I am offering my life for your dear life, cheaply.

PHILOCRATES. I know.

TYNDARUS. But remember to know it when you get what you want. For this is usually the way with most people. When they are trying to get what they want, they are fine and good. But when they have it in their possession, they turn from having been fine and good into the worst and the most deceitful people.

PHILOCRATES. Now I'll tell you what I want you to do. What I would urge on you I would even urge on my own father. By Pollux, I could even call you my father if I wanted to, for you're the nearest thing to a father I have, next to my father.

TYNDARUS. I understand.

PHILOCRATES. Therefore, I can't remind you often enough to remember: I am not your master but your slave.

Now I beg this one thing of you. Since the immortal gods have shown us that they no longer wish me to be your master but your fellow slave—what I once used to order you by right, I now beg of you as a favor. By the uncertainty of Fortune and by the kindness of my father toward you, by our common servitude, which has come by the hand of the enemy, don't deal with me less honorably than when you were a slave, and remember to keep in mind what you are no longer and what you are now.

TYNDARUS. I know full well that I am you and you are me.

PHILOCRATES. Well, if you can remember that, there is hope for us in this scheme.

HEGIO (*coming out of the house and speaking to an overseer inside*). I'll be back soon. I want to ask them a few questions.

(*Looking about.*) Where are they? I gave orders that they be brought here in front of the house.

PHILOCRATES. By Pollux, I'm sure you don't have to worry about finding us, we're so barricaded with chains and guards.

HEGIO (*sententiously*). The man who is cautious not to be taken in is hardly cautious even when he is cautious. Even when he thinks he has been cautious, the cautious man is often caught and cheated. Don't I have a good reason to guard you securely when I paid so much money for you?

PHILOCRATES. By Pollux, it's not fair for us to blame you for guarding us nor for you to blame us for running away if we had the chance.

HEGIO (*with feeling*). Just as you are here, my son is being guarded the same way among your people.

PHILOCRATES. Is he a prisoner?

HEGIO. Yes.

PHILOCRATES. So we are not the only cowards!

HEGIO. Come over here, for there are things I want to know from you alone. And I don't want you to lie to me about these things.

PHILOCRATES. I won't. I'll tell you what I know. If there is anything I don't know, I'll tell you I don't know. (*Goes with HEGIO to other end of stage.*)

TYNDARUS (*aside, watching them*). Now the old man is in the barber shop! Now he'll get clipped! He hasn't even asked for a towel to be put over him so he won't get his clothes dirty. But whether he gets a complete clipping or just a trimming, I don't know. But if Philocrates does his job properly, he'll leave him without a hair on his head.

HEGIO. Now then, would you rather be a slave or free? Tell me.

PHILOCRATES. The nearest to what is good and the farthest from what is bad, that's what I want. My slavery has not been very burdensome, for I was treated practically as if I were a son of the family.

TYNDARUS (*aside*). Hah! I wouldn't exchange him for Thales the philosopher of Miletus, if you gave me a mint of money! Compared to this man's wisdom, the philosopher was an utter fool! How cleverly he discourses on philosophy!

HEGIO. From what family does Philocrates come?

PHILOCRATES. The Polyplusius family, which is one of the most powerful and influential families there.

HEGIO. What about himself? What is his position?

PHILOCRATES. The highest. He is one of the top men there.

HEGIO. Then, since he has so much influence, as you say, what about his wealth? Are they rich?

PHILOCRATES. So rich his old man is just dripping with it.

HEGIO. What about his father? Is he alive?

PHILOCRATES. He was alive when we left there. Whether he is living now or not, only Hades knows.

TYNDARUS (aside). It's going beautifully! He is not only a liar but a philosopher too.

HEGIO. What is his father's name?

PHILOCRATES. Tons-of-gold-and-moneybags-ides.[3]

HEGIO. It looks as though he got his name from his wealth.

PHILOCRATES. No, by Pollux, from his avarice and nerve.

TYNDARUS (aside). His name is really Theodoromedes.

HEGIO. You don't say! You say his father is grasping?

PHILOCRATES. Just to give you a better idea—when he sacrifices to his guardian spirit,[4] he uses cheap earthenware dishes, for the utensils necessary for the religious service so that the guardian spirit won't steal them. So you can see how much he trusts others.

HEGIO. Come this way with me. There are a few questions I want to ask him, too. (Approaches TYNDARUS.) Philocrates, this fellow has done what an honest man must do. I have found out from him what family you come from. He has told me. If you want to confirm his statements you may do so by your own account, though I know them already from him.

TYNDARUS (with dignified resignation). It was his duty to tell you the truth, Hegio, though I wanted very much to keep my high rank as well as my family and wealth a secret. Since I have now lost my country and my freedom, I don't think it is right for him to fear me more than you. The power of the enemy has made my fortunes equal to his. I remember when he didn't dare to hurt me by so much as a word, now he can hurt me by deed. But you see, Fortune fashions and molds human affairs as she pleases. She has made me, who was free, a slave, the lowest from the highest. I, who was accustomed to command, now

---

[3] The false name which Philocrates gives for his father in the Latin is *Thensaurochrysonicochrysides*, which is one of Plautus' or his source's ludicrous Greek compounds and means "son of gold, surpassing treasuries of gold." In my translation I have tried to produce a similarly shaped mouthful which retained the initial *T* and the final patronymic *-ides*, and had about the same meaning. The result is not brilliant, but neither is the original.

[4] Each Roman male had a guardian spirit, *genius*, like a guardian angel, who was both the personification of the best qualities of the individual and the spiritual or divine force which, like our conscience, was supposed to guide him to express his better qualities. In some contexts the phrase may be translated as one's "better self." Religious services were regularly held for the *genius*. Women had a similar guardian spirit.

obey the command of someone else. And indeed, just as I myself once gave commands to my slaves, now that I have a
master over me, I will not object when his commands to me
are unjust or severe. (*Hesitating.*) But Hegio, there is something
I wanted to warn you about unless perhaps you don't want me to.

HEGIO. Speak up boldly.

TYNDARUS (*with great earnestness*). I was once free like your
son. The hand of the enemy took away my freedom as from him.
He is a slave among us there the way I am a slave with you
here. There is surely a god who hears and sees what we do. He
has seen to it that, just as you hold me here, so they hold him
there. If a man deserves well, things go well with him. If not,
things go badly. As you now miss your son, so my father misses
me.

HEGIO. I realize that. But do you admit to what Tyndarus has
told me?

TYNDARUS. I admit that my father has great wealth and that
I come of a family of the highest rank. But I appeal to you,
Hegio. Don't let my wealth make you greedy, or my father, even
though I am his only son, may think it better for me to be a slave,
well taken care of at your expense and in your clothing, than
have me live there as a beggar where it is least honorable.

HEGIO. Thanks to the gods and my ancestors, I am rich enough.
I don't think that wealth is always entirely advantageous to a
man. I know that money has spoiled many people. There are
even cases where it is better to suffer a loss of money than to
make a gain. I hate gold. Too much of it often leads many people
astray.

Now keep this in mind, so that you may know exactly what
I think. My son is held a prisoner there among you in Elis. If
you can get him back to me, you won't have to give me one cent,
and I will send you and him (*Pointing to* PHILOCRATES.) back
home. On no other terms do you leave here.

TYNDARUS (*relieved*). An excellent and very fair proposal!
And you are the best of men. But is he—your son—owned by
a private citizen or by the state?

HEGIO. He is in private slavery, with a doctor, Menarchus.

TYNDARUS (*aside*). By Pollux, *he's* a client of my master's!
(*Aloud.*) That's as easy as rain rolling off a roof.

HEGIO. Arrange to have him ransomed.

TYNDARUS. I will. But this I ask you, Hegio——

HEGIO. I'll do anything as long as you don't ask anything to
my disadvantage.

TYNDARUS. Listen, then you'll know. I don't demand that I

be released until your son returns here, but I do ask that you let me have *him* (*Pointing to* Philocrates.) to send back to my father under a forfeit to arrange for the exchange of prisoners.

Hegio. I'd much rather send someone else from here, when there is a truce, to meet with your father, someone who would carry out your orders exactly as you wish.

Tyndarus. But it would be worthless to send him someone he doesn't know. You would be wasting your time. Send him. (*Pointing to* Philocrates.) He'll get the whole transaction completed once he gets there.

You could not send my father anyone more dependable, nor one he would trust more, nor one who is more a slave after his own heart, nor one to whom he would more confidently entrust his son. Don't be afraid. At my own risk I'll take a chance on his trustworthiness. I'll put my reliance on his good character because he knows I am kind to him.

Hegio. Very well, I'll send him on forfeit, on your word, if you wish.

Tyndarus. I wish it very much. I want this to be done as quickly as possible.

Hegio. And you have no objections, if he doesn't return, to paying me twenty minas for him?

Tyndarus. No objections whatsoever.

Hegio (*to overseers, pointing to* Philocrates). Untie that fellow; better still—untie both of them.

Tyndarus (*with emotion*). May the gods give you everything you have wished, for treating me so honorably and releasing me from my chains!

(*Aside.*) This isn't at all bad, now that I've got my neck free of the neck ring.

Hegio. Do a good deed to a good man, and the kindness will bring a crop of good. Now, if you are going to send him there, tell him, show him, explain to him what message you want him to give your father. Do you wish me to call him to you?

Tyndarus. Please do.

Hegio (*approaching* Philocrates). Your new master—may things turn out well for me, my son and both of you—wishes you to obey your old master's wishes faithfully. I've given you to him under a forfeit of twenty minas. He wishes to send you to his father, who can then return my son and thus an exchange of our sons may be effected.

Philocrates. My heart turns and moves in two directions, toward you and toward him. You may use me as a wheel. I'll turn here or there, whichever way you command me.

HEGIO. Your good disposition is of great advantage to you, since you bear your servitude as it ought to be borne. Follow me. (*Goes with* PHILOCRATES *toward* TYNDARUS.) Well, here is your man.

TYNDARUS. I thank you very much, for giving me the opportunity of making it possible to send him back as a messenger to my parents. (*To* PHILOCRATES.) Tell them how I'm getting along here and report in detail to my father everything that I wish done. Now, Tyndarus, this is what has been agreed between me and this gentleman. I am going to send you under forfeit to my father in Elis. If you don't come back here, I am to pay twenty minas for you.

PHILOCRATES. An excellent agreement, I think. For your father expects me or some other messenger to come to him from here.

TYNDARUS. Therefore I want you to pay strict attention to the message you are to give my father at home.

PHILOCRATES. Philocrates, as I've done so far, I'll do my best to act to your best advantage. I'll work toward that with all my heart and soul and ears.

TYNDARUS. You act the way you have to act. Now here's what I want you to do. First of all, greet my father and mother for me, and my relatives and any other well-wisher you see. Tell them I'm well here and that I'm serving as a prisoner with this excellent gentleman, who treats me and has always treated me with the honor due my rank.

PHILOCRATES. You don't have to give me those kinds of instructions. I'm fully aware of them anyway.

TYNDARUS. Tell them that, except for the fact that I am guarded, I would think I were a free man. Tell my father the terms of agreement between me and this gentleman about his son——

PHILOCRATES (*interrupting*). It's really a waste of time to remind me about things I am so well aware of.

TYNDARUS. ——that he should release him and return him in exchange for the two of us.

PHILOCRATES. I understand clearly.

HEGIO. And as soon as possible—that is most advantageous for both of us.

PHILOCRATES. You are not more anxious to see your son than he is to see his.

HEGIO. My son is dear to me and each man's son is dear to him.

PHILOCRATES (*turning to go*). Is there anything else you wish me to tell your father?

TYNDARUS (*detaining him*). That I am well here—and you

can speak without hesitation, Tyndarus—tell him we've got along very amicably together, and that you have done nothing to be blamed for, nor I toward you, and that you have been most loyal and obedient to your master in our many trials and tribulations; that you never deserted me nor failed me in deed or trust in our precarious circumstances. When my father knows what your attitude has been toward his son and himself, it is certain, Tyndarus, he will free you without payment. And if I return home, I'll make every effort to see to it that he does it more than willingly. For through your efforts and companionship, and your good character and wisdom, when you admitted to this man the facts about my family and wealth, you will have made it possible for me to be permitted to return to my parents again. In that way you will have released your master from chains by your wisdom.

PHILOCRATES. I have done as you have said, and I am pleased that you remember. But you deserved to have me do these things. (*Hinting to stop delay.*) For if I were also to recall the many good things *you've* done for me, Philocrates, night would overtake the day. You couldn't have been more indulgent toward me than if you had been my slave.

HEGIO (*wiping his eyes*). The gods help me! What noble characters these men have! How they squeeze tears out of me. You can see they love one another with all their hearts. What praise the slave has heaped on his master!

PHILOCRATES. By Pollux, he hasn't praised me one hundredth as much as he deserves to be praised.

HEGIO (*to* PHILOCRATES). Therefore, since you've done excellently, now is your chance to add to your store of good deeds by carrying out this matter faithfully toward him.

PHILOCRATES. I can not wish to do more than try to succeed in my efforts. That you may know this, I call on Jupiter on high as witness that I will not be unfaithful to Philocrates——

HEGIO. You are a fine man.

PHILOCRATES. ——and that I will never do to him otherwise than I would do to myself.

TYNDARUS. I want you to accomplish what you have just said in deed and action and to give your attention to what I have said I wanted of you.

And don't become angry at what I say next, but I beg of you, keep in mind you are being sent home as forfeit, on *my* promise, and that it is my life that has been placed as pledge for you. So don't forget me as soon as you've left my sight. When you leave me here as a slave in servitude in your place and consider yourself as free, don't forfeit the pledge, and don't fail to work toward returning this man's son in exchange for me. Keep in mind that you are being sent off under a forfeit of twenty minas. Work faithfully at being faithful, don't wear your faithfulness loosely. Keep me your friend forever and keep this new-found friend (*Pointing to* HEGIO.) as a friend. (*Taking* PHILOCRATES' *hand*.) This I beg of you, as I hold your right hand in mine: don't be more unfaithful to me than I to you. Attend to the matter. You are now my master, you are my protector, you are my father—to you I entrust all my hopes and resources.

PHILOCRATES. You have given me orders enough. Will you be satisfied if I come back with your orders carried out?

TYNDARUS. Satisfied.

PHILOCRATES. I'll come back bringing what you wish and (*To* HEGIO.) what you wish. Anything else?

TYNDARUS. Return as soon as possible.

PHILOCRATES. That's what the situation demands.

HEGIO (*to* PHILOCRATES). Follow me, so that I can have my banker give you travel money and at the same time get you a passport from the praetor's [5] office.

TYNDARUS. What passport?

HEGIO. The one he is to take with him to the legion on the frontier, so that he may be permitted to return home. (*To* TYNDARUS.) You. Go inside.

TYNDARUS (*to* PHILOCRATES). Have a good trip!

PHILOCRATES. Thank you and keep well yourself!

(TYNDARUS *goes inside*.)

HEGIO. By Pollux, I certainly set my affairs in order when I bought those prisoners from the praetors. I will have released my son from slavery, if the gods are willing. And to think I even hesitated for some time before deciding whether to buy these men or not!

(*To those inside*.) Guard him in there, will you, slaves, and see that he doesn't set foot anywhere without a guard. I'll return home at once. I'm just going to my brother's to have a look at my other prisoners. While I'm at it I'll ask whether anyone knows this young man. (*To* PHILOCRATES.) You follow me, so that I can send you on your way. I want to attend to this first.

[5] The Roman term for officials in charge of judicial and legal matters.

Act III

(Enter Ergasilus, returning from the Town Square.)

ERGASILUS. Unfortunate is the one who looks for something to eat and has trouble finding it. But even worse off is he who has trouble finding it and finds nothing, and worst off is he who when he wants to eat has nothing to eat. By Hercules! What a day! I'd gladly knock its eyes out if I could. It's a day in which everybody has borne ill-will toward me. I've never seen a hungrier day, nor one more stuffed with starvation, nor one which was less successful in whatever it started out to accomplish! It has given my belly and my gullet a real holiday from eating.

The way the young men have kept themselves aloof from us indigent jokesters has just about sent the parasite's trade to hell. The frugal Spartans with their hard wooden benches have nothing on us. We are just members of the guild of Slap-in-the-Face. We make our jokes without food or a penny in return. They invite for dinner only those who will gladly return the invitation. They go marketing themselves—that used to be the parasites' job! And they are not ashamed to go openly by themselves to the procurers' quarters to make their own—arrangements, as if, for all the world to see, they were in the public assembly openly pronouncing sentence on a guilty defendant! They don't give a damn about jesters. They just love themselves, all of them!

Just to give you an example: when I left here some time ago, I went over to the young men in the Square. "Greetings," I say. "Where are we going today, you and I?" They keep quiet. "Who says, 'to my house' or who makes me an offer?" I say. They shake their heads. I tell a little joke, one of my better ones, the kind with which I used to provide myself with feasts for a month. No one laughs. I know right away they are acting in cahoots. No one is even willing to imitate an angry dog. If they won't laugh, let them at least show their teeth—a smile at least. I leave them when I see they are making a fool of me. I go on to some others, then to others, then to others. The same thing! They are all doing it by agreement, like the olive-oil merchants in Velabrum [6] when they raise their prices.

So now I've come back, since I see I'm being made a fool of there. It's the same with the other parasites. They are wandering around in the Square in vain. I've finally decided to enforce one of those Roman laws forbidding conspiracy. I'll get a summons issued against anyone who enters into a conspiracy to deprive us of food and livelihood, and I'll demand as a fine that he should give me ten dinners, of my own choice, when the price of grain and food is high! That's what I'll do. Now I'll go off to the harbor. That's the only place left where I can hope for a dinner. If that last hope trickles away, I'll come back here to the old man and his horrible meal.

(*Makes a face, and exit.*)

(*Enter* HEGIO, *with* ARISTOPHONTES, *an Elean prisoner and friend of* PHILOCRATES.)

HEGIO. What is sweeter than to manage one's affairs to one's own advantage and for the public good at the same time! As I did today when I bought those men. Everybody who sees me comes up to me and congratulates me for what I've done. They've made me so tired from stopping me and so weary from detaining me that it was with the greatest difficulty that I finally extricated myself from all those congratulations. Finally I went to the praetor's office. I didn't get any rest there either. I asked for a passport. I got it on the spot. I gave it to Tyndarus. He has gone to his own country.

Then, as soon as that was over I went off to my brother's, where my other prisoners are. I asked whether anyone among them knows Philocrates from Elis. Finally this fellow called out that *he* does, and is a close friend of his. I told him he was at my house. Right away he begged and beseeched me to let him see Philocrates. On the spot I ordered him to be released from his chains. (*To* ARISTOPHONTES.) Now follow me, so you can meet the man. (*Enter* TYNDARUS *from the house. On seeing* HEGIO *and* ARISTOPHONTES, *he runs to the side of the house.*)

TYNDARUS (*aside, in great agitation*). Now is the time when I really wish I didn't exist! Now all hope, help, and aid abandon and desert me. This is the day when there is no hope of saving my life, and there's no way out of the disaster which faces me. I don't even have a hope which may drive away this fear from me. I have nothing, anywhere, to cover up my crafty lies. I have

---

[6] A section in Rome where the oil-merchants had their shops.

nothing to protect myself against informers or tattletales. There is no way of asking pardon for my perfidies and no escape from my wrongdoings. There is no safe harbor for my impudence, no refuge for my schemings. Whatever was undercover is uncovered. My trickery is transparent, and everything is out in the open. Now, there is nothing that can stop me from dying like a dog, from suffering destruction in place of my master—my destruction.

This Aristophontes is going to be the ruin of me! He knows me, he is a relative and a close friend of Philocrates. Not even Safety herself, in person, even if she wished, could save me now, nor is there a chance, unless I put my heart in it and dream up some clever scheme. What scheme, damn it? What can I dream up? What can I can come up with? I'm stuck!

(*Runs into alleyway.*)

HEGIO (*looking around*). I wonder where that fellow rushed to out of the house?

TYNDARUS (*aside*). Now I'm a goner for sure! The enemy are coming at you, Tyndarus. What can I say? What story can I make up? What can I deny and what can I admit? Everything is up in the air. I've lost confidence in myself. If only the gods had destroyed you, Aristophontes, before you got out of your country! It's all up with me unless I can play a really clever trick.

HEGIO (*to* ARISTOPHONTES). Follow me. There's your man. Go and speak to him.

TYNDARUS (*aside*). Who in the world is more miserable than I?

ARISTOPHONTES. Why do you avoid my eyes, Tyndarus, and ignore me as if you didn't know me? After all, *I'm* as much a slave now as you even though *I* was free at home, and *you* from boyhood served as a slave in Elis.

HEGIO (*with a laugh*). By Pollux, I'm not surprised that he avoids your eyes and hates you, when you call him Tyndarus instead of Philocrates.

TYNDARUS (*pulling* HEGIO *away*). Hegio, this man is considered raving mad in Elis. Don't listen to anything he tells you. At home he's been known to chase after his mother and father with javelins! And sometimes he gets attacks of the disease that makes him foam at the mouth and spit. So you'd better move away from him.

HEGIO (*to slaves in attendance*). Keep him away from me.

ARISTOPHONTES. What, you rascal? You say I'm raving mad and chased my father with javelins and that I have the disease that makes me want to spit?

HEGIO (*soothingly*). That's all right. There are many people suffering from that disease. Spitting relieves them. It's good for them.

ARISTOPHONTES (*to* HEGIO, *angrily*). What do you mean? You actually believe him?

HEGIO. About what do I believe him?

ARISTOPHONTES. That I am insane?

TYNDARUS (*pretending terror*). Do you see with what a hostile expression he looks at you? You'd better withdraw. (*With a shriek.*) Hegio! It's happening—just as I told you! The madness is starting to grow! Watch out for yourself!

HEGIO. I thought he was crazy the moment he called you Tyndarus.

TYNDARUS. Why, sometimes he doesn't know his own name or who he is.

HEGIO. Yet he said you were a good friend of his.

TYNDARUS (*ironically*). Sure! Those proverbial madmen Alcmaeon, Orestes, and Lycurgus [7] are as much friends of mine as he is!

ARISTOPHONTES. You still dare to speak badly of me, you jailbird? I don't know you?

HEGIO (*with a laugh*). By Pollux, it's certainly clear that you don't know him when you call him Tyndarus instead of Philocrates. The man you see you don't know, the man you name you don't see.

ARISTOPHONTES. On the contrary, *he* is not the man he says he is. And he denies who he really is.

TYNDARUS (*with dignity and sarcasm*). And you, of course, tell the truth and I don't.

ARISTOPHONTES. By Pollux, the way *I* see it you are the kind of person who tries to prove you're telling the truth by lying! But, by Hercules, come on, look at me.

TYNDARUS (*looking at him*). There!

ARISTOPHONTES. Just tell me. Do you deny you are Tyndarus?

TYNDARUS (*boldly*). I deny it, I tell you.

ARISTOPHONTES. Do you say you are Philocrates?

TYNDARUS. I am, I tell you.

ARISTOPHONTES (*to* HEGIO). Do you believe him?

HEGIO (*with some hesitation*). More than I believe you—or myself. For today the man who you say he is went to Elis to *his* father.

---

[7] All of these characters of myth and tragedy were driven mad, the first two by the Furies for killing their mothers, and the last by the god Dionysus for attacking him.

ARISTOPHONTES (*sarcastically*). What father? A man who is a slave?

TYNDARUS. You're also a slave! You're no longer a free man. But I'm confident that I will be if I get this gentleman's son back here a free man.

ARISTOPHONTES. What are you saying, jailbird? You call yourself freeman?

TYNDARUS. I don't call myself Freeman, I call myself Philocrates.

ARISTOPHONTES (*turning to* HEGIO). What is this? Like the rascal he is, Hegio, he is making a fool of you now! He's *only* a slave himself and he has never had a slave.

TYNDARUS. Just because you were poor in your country and didn't have a home to live in, do you want everyone to prove to be like you? I'm not surprised. It's the nature of the poor to be jealous and envious of the well-off.

ARISTOPHONTES (*earnestly*). Hegio, don't heedlessly persist in believing him. As I can clearly see, he has already scored a couple of hits here. What he says about restoring your son to you doesn't please me at all.

TYNDARUS. I know you don't want that to happen but I'll accomplish it anyway if the gods help me. I'll restore his son to him, and furthermore he will restore me to my father in Elis. That's why I sent Tyndarus off to my father.

ARISTOPHONTES. But that's *you*, and there *is* no other slave in Elis with your name!

TYNDARUS. Do you persist in throwing up to me that I am a slave, a thing that happened to me by force of war?

ARISTOPHONTES. I can't control myself any longer!

TYNDARUS. Aha! Do you hear what he says? Quick, get away from him! If you don't order him seized, he'll be chasing us with stones!

ARISTOPHONTES. I can't stand it any longer!

TYNDARUS. His eyes are burning! He can't help it, Hegio. Do you see how his whole body is getting spotted with ghastly spots? The black bile is working on him.

ARISTOPHONTES. By Pollux, if this old man were smart, you would be worked on by hot black tar, and the executioner would make your whole body blaze up.

TYNDARUS. He's already talking deliriously. The evil spirits are driving him, Hegio.

HEGIO. What if I should order him seized?

TYNDARUS. You would be very wise.

ARISTOPHONTES. It enrages me that I don't have a stone to

smash in that scoundrel's skull. He is driving me insane with his words!

TYNDARUS. Do you hear him asking for a stone?

ARISTOPHONTES. I'd like a word with you in private, Hegio.

HEGIO (*alarmed*). If you want to say something, speak from there—at a distance!

TYNDARUS. By Pollux, if you go any closer, he'll take your nose off with one bite.

ARISTOPHONTES (*trying to speak calmly*). By Pollux, Hegio, don't believe I am insane or ever was. And I don't have the disease he says. But if you have any fear of me, have me bound up. I'm willing, provided he is bound up too.

TYNDARUS (*embarrassed*). Not me, Hegio. He is the one who wants to be bound up.

ARISTOPHONTES (*contemptuously*). Just shut up, you false Philocrates! I'll show you up as a true Tyndarus today. (TYNDARUS *makes signs to him behind* HEGIO's *back.*) Why are you shaking your head and signaling to me?

TYNDARUS. I'm shaking my head at you?

ARISTOPHONTES (*to* HEGIO). What would he be doing if you were further away?

TYNDARUS (*hastily*). Nonsense! He'll make a fool of you. He'll gabble something you won't be able to make head or tail of. All that's missing is the get-up—otherwise when you look at him you can see mad Ajax [8] himself!

HEGIO. I don't care. I'll approach him anyway. (*Walks toward* ARISTOPHONTES.)

TYNDARUS (*aside*). Now I'm completely finished. Now I'm between the altar stone and the sacrificial knife. And I don't know what to do!

HEGIO (*to* ARISTOPHONTES). I'm giving you a chance, Aristophontes, if there is anything you want of me.

ARISTOPHONTES. From me you'll hear the truth, though you now think it's false, Hegio. But first of all, I wish to clear this point up for you: I am not insane and I suffer no illness—except for the fact that I am now a slave. But may the King of Gods and Men help to restore me to my country, that fellow is no more Philocrates than I am or you are.

HEGIO. Oho! Then tell me, who *is* he?

ARISTOPHONTES. What I've been telling you from the beginning. If you find it otherwise I have no objection to remaining in your possession, deprived of my parents and my freedom.

[8] A Greek hero of the Trojan War who went mad after the arms of the dead Achilles were awarded to Odysseus instead of to him.

HEGIO (*to* TYNDARUS). What have you to say?

TYNDARUS. That I am your slave and you are my master.

HEGIO (*sharply*). That's not what I asked you. Were you born free?

TYNDARUS. I was.

ARISTOPHONTES. He certainly wasn't. He's talking nonsense.

TYNDARUS. How do you know? Were you perhaps my mother's midwife that you dare speak so boldly?

ARISTOPHONTES. I saw you when we were both children.

TYNDARUS. And I see you when we are both grown up. So there! You wouldn't interfere in my affairs if you acted properly. I don't interfere in yours, do I?

HEGIO. Was his father Tons-of-gold-and-moneybags-ides?

ARISTOPHONTES. He was not, and I've never heard of that name before today. Philocrates' father was Theodoromedes.

TYNDARUS (*aside*). I'm finished for certain! Keep quiet, go hang yourself, my heart! You keep leaping up, when I can hardly stand for fear.

HEGIO. Then the correct answer to my inquiries is that this fellow was a slave in Elis and that he is not Philocrates? Is that correct?

ARISTOPHONTES. So correct that you will never find it otherwise. But where is Philocrates now?

HEGIO. The last place I want him to be and the very place where he most wants to be. To my misfortune, I have been cut down to size and torn apart by the machinations of this rascal who has led me on by his deceptions. But are you sure?

ARISTOPHONTES. This is a fact that I could have told you from the beginning.

HEGIO. You're certain?

ARISTOPHONTES. I tell you, you will find nothing more certain than this. Philocrates has been a friend of mine from boyhood on.

HEGIO (*brightening with a sudden thought*). But wait. What does your friend Philocrates look like?

ARISTOPHONTES. He has a thin face, sharp nose, fair skin, black eyes, reddish hair, curly locks in ringlets——

HEGIO (*sadly, interrupting*). The description fits.

TYNDARUS (*aside*). —so well, by Hercules, that I'm in a terrible spot! Woe to the poor whipping rods that will die on my back today!

HEGIO. I see that I have been fooled.

TYNDARUS (*aside*). Oh shackles, why don't you hasten and embrace my legs so that I may guard you?

HEGIO. Those rascally captives have certainly caught me in their snares today! The other one pretended to be the slave while this one said he was the free one. I've let go the meat of the nut, and all I have left is the empty shell! How stupid I've been! At least this fellow will never laugh at me again. (*Calls to overseers.*) Hey, Puncher, Paddler, Knocker! Come out of there, bring thongs!

PUNCHER. Are we going for wood?

HEGIO. Put your biggest handcuffs on that scoundrel.

TYNDARUS. What's the matter? What crime have I committed?

HEGIO. You ask, you master sower and hoer of mischief? You'll be a reaper too!

TYNDARUS. Wouldn't you like to mention harrower first? For farmers always harrow before they hoe.

HEGIO. So! How confidently he stands up to me!

TYNDARUS. An innocent and guiltless slave *ought* to be confident before his master who is so powerful.

HEGIO. Tie up his hands tightly!

TYNDARUS. I am your property. You could even order them to be cut off. But what is the reason you are angry at me?

HEGIO. Because when I and all my happiness depended on you alone, you by your dastardly lying deceptions have torn it to shreds and smashed all my hopes! You've put an end to everything, all my plans, when you got Philocrates out of my possession with your deception. I believed *he* was the slave and *you* the free man. That's what you both said and that's why you exchanged names with one another.

TYNDARUS (*boldly*). I admit that everything happened as you say and that he got away from you by a deception worked out by my cleverness. I ask you, by Hercules, is that why you are angry with me?

HEGIO. And you will get the severest punishment for doing it.

TYNDARUS. As long as it is not because of wrongdoings that I die, I care little. If he doesn't return as he said he would, and I do die, this will be a deed to be remembered after my death, that I sent my master back to his country and his father a free man, and that I preferred to place my own life in danger rather than that he should perish.

HEGIO. Then enjoy the glory of your fame in Hades!

TYNDARUS. He who dies for valor does not wholly die!

HEGIO (*bitterly*). When I have punished you with the worst torments and have sent you to death for your intricate schemes, let them say you died partly or completely. As long as you die, I won't stop them from saying you're alive.

TYNDARUS. By Pollux, if you do that you won't get away with it if he returns here, as I'm confident he will.

ARISTOPHONTES (*aside. He has shown great surprise during this conversation*). Oh immortal gods! Now I understand it! Now I see what this is all about! My good friend Philocrates is now at liberty with his father in his native land. That's good, and there's nobody to whom I would rather have it happen. But I can't forgive myself that I've done Tyndarus a bad turn and now—because of me and my words—he is in chains.

HEGIO (*to* TYNDARUS). Didn't I forbid you today to say anything false to me?

TYNDARUS. You did.

HEGIO. Why did you dare to lie to me?

TYNDARUS. Because the truth hampered the man I was helping. Lies have helped him.

HEGIO. But they have harmed *you*.

TYNDARUS. Very well! But I've saved my master whom I'm happy to have saved and to whom my older master assigned me as a guardian. Do you think I did wrong in that?

HEGIO. Very wrong.

TYNDARUS. But I say I did right and I differ with you completely. For consider how grateful you would feel, if some slave of yours had done this for your son. Would you free this slave or not? Wouldn't such a slave be most welcome in your sight? (HEGIO *remains silent.*) Answer me.

HEGIO (*reluctantly*). I suppose so.

TYNDARUS. Then why are you angry at me?

HEGIO. Because you were more faithful to him than to me.

TYNDARUS. What? Did you expect, in one night and one day, to teach me, a recent captive—just arrived, newly enslaved—to be more interested in you than a man with whom I've lived from childhood on?

HEGIO (*impatiently*). So ask *him* to thank you. (*To overseers.*) Take him to where he gets heavy thick leg irons. From there go with him to the stone quarries. There, when others dig out eight stones apiece, unless you do half as much again you'll be called Six-Hundred Lashes.

ARISTOPHONTES (*coming forward*). By the gods and men, I beg you, Hegio, don't harm this man.

HEGIO (*sarcastically*). He'll be taken care of! By night he will be tied up and guarded securely. I'll punish him for a long time. I will not let him off for one day.

ARISTOPHONTES (*appealingly*). Are you sure you want to do that?

HEGIO (*angrily*). Death is no more sure. (*To overseers.*) Take him away at once to Hippolytus, the smith. Order thick shackles clamped on him. Then have him taken outside the gate to my freedman, Cordalus the Killer, in the stone quarries, and tell him I want this fellow taken care of in such a way that he gets worse treatment than whoever is getting the worst.

TYNDARUS. Why should I ask to be spared against your will? Any danger to my life is at your own risk. Once I am dead there is no evil for me to fear in death itself. Even if I survive to the end of my normal life span, it is a short time to endure what you threaten me with. So, good-bye and be well, even though you deserve to have me say otherwise. Farewell, to you, Aristophontes, as well as you deserve from me. For it is because of you that this has happened to me.

HEGIO (*in a rage*). Take him away!

TYNDARUS (*as overseers are removing him*). There is only one thing I ask of you. Give me a chance of meeting Philocrates if he comes back.

HEGIO (*to overseers*). Damn it! Get him out of my sight at once!

(*They drag* TYNDARUS *off the stage.*)

TYNDARUS (*impudently*). By Hercules, you are really getting rough—dragging and pushing me at the same time! (*Exit.*)

HEGIO. He has been taken to do hard labor as he deserves. I'll make him an example for the other prisoners, so that no one will dare to try a thing like that again. If it were not for this man (*Indicating* ARISTOPHONTES.) who discovered it for me, they would still be deceiving me with their schemes. Now I'm determined not to believe anybody about anything from now on. I've been fooled once and that's enough!

(*With a sigh.*) Ah, how I had hoped to free my son from slavery! But that hope has slipped away. I had already lost one son, the four-year-old boy whom a slave stole from me, and I never found the slave or my son. My elder son is a captive in the hands of the enemy. What an awful thing this is! It seems I produced children only to lose them! (*To* ARISTOPHONTES.) Follow me this way. I'll take you back to where you were. (*Bitterly.*) No one is going to get any pity from me!

ARISTOPHONTES. I've had the good fortune to get out of my chains for a while. As I read the omens now, I must return to them again.

Act IV

(*Ergasilus hurries in from the harbor, greatly excited.*)

ERGASILUS. Oh Supreme Jupiter, you have saved me and increased my resources! And you offer me the greatest and most sumptuous abundance: glory, gain and gladness, fun, feasts and festivity, parades, provisions and potations, satiety, joy! And I won't have to go begging from anyone from now on! For I can bless my friend and even blast my enemy. With what delightful delight has this delightful day filled me! I've come into a very rich inheritance with no strings attached!

Now I'll rush over to old man Hegio, to whom I'm bringing as much as he himself wishes from the gods and more. I'd better do what the slaves in comedies do. I'll throw the ends of my cloak around my neck, so I can run faster, and be the first to tell him the good news. And I hope because of this news (*Smacking his lips.*) that I'll get meals for life. (*Throws the ends of his cloak around his neck and shoulders and runs.*)

(HEGIO *comes out of his house without seeing him at first.*)

HEGIO (*sadly*). The more I turn this over in my mind, the greater is the regret in my heart. That they should have made such a monkey out of me today! And that I should not have realized that when it becomes known, I'll be a laughingstock all over the city! As soon as I come to the Town Square everyone will say, "This is the clever old man who was fooled." (*Sees* ERGASILUS.) But is that Ergasilus whom I see at a distance? He's got the ends of his cloak around his neck. What in the world is he trying to do?

ERGASILUS (*to himself, without seeing* HEGIO). Cut out the delay, Ergasilus, and get on with it! (*Holds up fists.*) Anyone who stands in my way had better watch out, unless he thinks he has lived long enough. For, whoever stands in my way will find himself flat on his face!

HEGIO. He's starting a fist fight!

ERGASILUS (*continuing*). And I *mean* it! So let everybody stay where they are, and let nobody bring any of his business on this street (*Shaking his fist and making other appropriate gestures.*) for my fist is a war engine for shooting punches, my elbow is a catapult, my shoulder is a battering-ram. Then if I use my knee on anybody, I'll knock him to the ground. And I'll make anybody I hit count his teeth!

HEGIO (*aside*). I can't stop wondering what the meaning is of all this threatening.

ERGASILUS. I'll see to it that this day and this place will always be remembered. Whoever stands in my way will stand in the way of his own life!

HEGIO (*aside*). What is he trying to do with all those threats?

ERGASILUS. First I decree, let no one be caught through his own fault. Stay home, keep my power away from you!

HEGIO (*aside*). I wonder if his confidence comes from something he ate. Woe to the poor fellow by whose food he has become so imperious!

ERGASILUS. Then those pig-pasturing millers, who feed their hogs on bran and whose odor is so bad that no one can go past the mill. If I see any of their pigs in public I'll beat the bran out of the masters themselves with my fists.

HEGIO. He issues royal and imperious edicts. He must be full. He has surely stuffed his stomach with confidence.

ERGASILUS. Then the fishermen who furnish stinking fish to the public, that are brought on a four-footed tormented nag and the smell of those fish drives all the loungers in the arcade into the Square. I'll beat their faces with their fish baskets so they'll know what it means to offend other people's noses. Then the butchers will get theirs, who bereave the ewes of their young, who are in the business of slaughtering lambs and selling the meat at twice the right price, who call the ram that leads them to slaughter Rocky. If I see that Rocky on the public street, I'll make Rocky and his master a couple of most unhappy people.

HEGIO (*aside*). Listen to him! He issues orders like a Highways and Markets Commissioner. I'm surprised our people of Aetolia haven't made him Market Director!

ERGASILUS. Now I'm no longer a parasite, but a king more royal than kings, so great is the amount of food I have in the harbor ready to enter my stomach! But why do I delay filling old Hegio with joy? There is no man alive today who is more fortunate than he.

HEGIO (*aside, with surprise*). What joy is this which he is so joyously lavishing upon me?

ERGASILUS (*knocking at* HEGIO's *door*). Hey, where are you people? Anybody here? Is anybody opening this door?

HEGIO (*aside*). He's come to have dinner with me.

ERGASILUS (*wildly*). Open both these doors before I bring destruction on them by beating them to pieces.

HEGIO. I'd certainly like a word with him. (*Going forward.*) Ergasilus!

ERGASILUS (*not turning around*). Who is calling Ergasilus?

HEGIO. Turn toward me.

ERGASILUS. What Fortune never does or will, do you order me to? But who is it?

HEGIO. Turn around and look at me. It's Hegio.

ERGASILUS. Oh, you best of best men, you've come just in the nick of time.

HEGIO (*smiling*). You must have found somebody at the harbor with whom to dine, you're so haughty.

ERGASILUS (*excitedly*). Give me your hand.

HEGIO. My hand?

ERGASILUS. Your hand, I say. Give it to me at once.

HEGIO. Here you are. (*Gives him his hand.*)

ERGASILUS (*shaking* HEGIO's *hand*). Rejoice!

HEGIO. Why should I rejoice?

ERGASILUS. Because I order you to. (*Shaking it again.*) Come on, rejoice!

HEGIO (*reproachfully*). I have more to grieve about than to rejoice about.

ERGASILUS. Don't get angry. I'll soon drive every shred of grief out of your body. (*Shaking his hand again.*) Rejoice with a will!

HEGIO. I'm rejoicing even though I don't know what I'm rejoicing about.

ERGASILUS. Good. Now order . . . (*Stops to think.*)

HEGIO. What should I order?

ERGASILUS. . . . a fire to be lighted.

HEGIO. A big fire?

ERGASILUS. That's what I say, a big one.

HEGIO. What, you vulture? Do you think I'll burn my house down just for you?

ERGASILUS. Don't get angry. Will you or will you not order the pots to be made ready, the pans to be washed, the fat and the feast to be heated on the fiery hearth? Send someone to buy fish——

HEGIO. He's dreaming with his eyes open!

ERGASILUS. Send someone else to buy pork, and lamb and chicken——

HEGIO. You know how to eat well if you had the means.

ERGASILUS. ——ham, and eel, pickled fish, mackerel, sting-ray, tuna, and soft cheese.

HEGIO. You will have a better chance of naming them than eating them here in my house, Ergasilus.

ERGASILUS. You think I'm saying it for my sake?

HEGIO. You'll not get *nothing* to eat here today, but not much more, make no mistake. So just bring me a stomach that expects your normal daily meal.

ERGASILUS. Why, I'll have you wanting to make a big spread even if I forbid you.

HEGIO. Me?

ERGASILUS. Yes, you!

HEGIO. Then you are my master.

ERGASILUS. No, your well-wisher. Do you want me to make you fortunate?

HEGIO. Better than to make me unfortunate.

ERGASILUS. Give me your hand.

HEGIO. There's my hand.

ERGASILUS (*solemnly*). All the gods are aiding you.

HEGIO. I don't think so at all!

ERGASILUS. You're thick—with that grass you eat. That's why you don't think so. But quickly order ritually pure vessels to be prepared for the divine feast and the appropriate fat lamb to be brought.

HEGIO. Why?

ERGASILUS. So you may sacrifice.

HEGIO. To which of the gods?

ERGASILUS. To me, by Hercules! For to you I am now Supreme Jupiter, and I am also the deities Safety, Fortune, Light, Happiness, Joy. Therefore pacify this god with satiety.

HEGIO. I seem to feel pangs of hunger around here.

ERGASILUS. I'm the one that's hungry, not you.

HEGIO. May Jupiter and the gods damn you!

ERGASILUS. You, by Hercules—should thank me for bringing the news. I bring you so much good from the harbor! (*Smiling.*) Now the thought of a dinner with you appeals to me.

HEGIO. Go away! You're foolish, you come too late!

ERGASILUS. If I had come earlier, then you would be more justified in saying that. Now receive from me this happiness which I bring you. (*Excitedly.*) Your son—I have just seen him in the harbor—Philopolemus, alive, safe and sound! He arrived in a government express ship and with him that young man from Elis—and also your slave Stalagmus, who ran away from home and kidnaped the four-year-old boy, your little son!

HEGIO. To Hades with you, you're fooling me!

ERGASILUS (*earnestly*). So help me holy Satiety, Hegio, and may she always honor me with her name! I swear I saw them.

HEGIO (*in great amazement*). My son?

ERGASILUS. Your son and my guardian spirit.

HEGIO. And the prisoner from Elis?

ERGASILUS. Yes, by Apollo!

HEGIO. And my slave Stalagmus, who kidnaped my younger son?

ERGASILUS. Yes, by the Holy Maiden!

HEGIO. They have already——

ERGASILUS. Yes, by Praeneste!

HEGIO. ——arrived?

ERGASILUS. Yes, by Signia!

HEGIO. You're sure?

ERGASILUS. Yes, by Frusino!

HEGIO. You're certain?

ERGASILUS. Yes, by Alatrium!

HEGIO. Why do you swear by those foreign towns? [9]

ERGASILUS. Because they sound as harsh as you said your food was.

HEGIO. Oh, go to hell!

ERGASILUS. You go, since you believe nothing that I tell you in all seriousness. Stalagmus—what nationality was he when he left here?

HEGIO. A Sicilian.

ERGASILUS. Well, he's no longer a Sicilian. He's a Teuton [10] now. He's covered with two tons of thongs.

HEGIO. Tell me, what you just told me, were you speaking in good faith?

ERGASILUS. In good faith.

HEGIO. Immortal gods! I feel I'm born again if what you say is true.

ERGASILUS. Say? You still have doubts when I swear to you by all that's holy? Then, Hegio, if you have little faith in my oath, go to the harbor and see for yourself.

HEGIO. That's exactly what I *am* doing! Go inside and arrange what is necessary. Take, demand, open up whatever you wish. I make you my butler.

---

[9] Praeneste, Signia, Frusino, Alatrium are Italian towns, hence foreign to the Greek characters in the play.

[10] In the original Ergasilus says: *Boius est, boiam terit*, i.e., "He's a Boian (a type of Gaul), he rubs against the *cowhide thongs* (in which he is tied)." To retain a pun I have changed Boian to Teuton.

ERGASILUS. By Hercules, if I haven't foretold correctly, you can give me a trimming with your staff.

HEGIO. I'll dine you for life if what you say is true.

ERGASILUS. At whose expense?

HEGIO. At mine and my son's.

ERGASILUS. Is that a promise?

HEGIO. I promise.

ERGASILUS. And I promise you in turn that your son has arrived.

HEGIO. Arrange for the very best dinner you can.

ERGASILUS. Have a good trip to the harbor and back.

(*Exit* HEGIO.)

ERGASILUS (*smacking his lips and rubbing his stomach*). He's gone. He's put me in full charge of his food supply! Ye gods! Will I now make a slaughter of sides of meat! What a holocaust will fall on hams! What a battle against bacon! What a savagery against sows! What a slitting of skins! What a weariness for butchers and pork sellers! (*Heaves a sigh, as if tired himself.*) If I mention anything else which makes good food for the stomach, I'll be wasting time.

Now I'll go and, by the powers vested in my office, I'll pass sentence on the bacon, and any hams that hang around unsentenced, I'll help end their suspense. (*Goes into the house. After a moment a clatter of pans and dishes is heard within. Soon one of* HEGIO's *slaves rushes out in great agitation.*)

SLAVE. May Jupiter and the gods destroy you, Ergasilus, and your stomach, and all the parasites, and all who give parasites dinner from now on! Catastrophe, calamity, and fury has just come into our house! (*To audience.*) Like a hungry wolf he was. I thought he would take a bite out of me! I got so scared of him, by Hercules, the way he was gnashing his teeth! He came in and pulled down the meat, frame and all. He grabbed a sword and slashed choice bits from sides of meat. He broke all the jars and dishes, unless they were ten-gallon size. He kept asking the cook whether the vats could take the heat. He broke into all the storerooms and opened up the food closet. (*Calling through the door.*) Watch him, will you, slaves! I'll get the old master. I'll tell him to stock up another supply of provisions if he wants to use any himself. This fellow has made such a mess of it, there's already nothing left—or there soon will be. (*Runs toward the harbor.*)

Act V

(Enter Hegio, very happy, with his elder son, Philopolemus, accompanied by Philocrates. Stalagmus, the slave who had kidnaped Hegio's younger son, follows in custody.)

HEGIO. To Jupiter and all the gods I give the great thanks they deserve for having brought you back to your father and for freeing me from the great unhappiness which I suffered while you were away! I thank the gods too that I finally see *him (Nodding toward* STALAGMUS.) in our hands and that *his* promise *(Nodding toward* PHILOCRATES.) has been kept.

PHILOPOLEMUS *(somewhat impatiently)*. I have been unhappy enough myself and have been torn enough by tears with worry for you. I've already heard enough about your troubles when you spoke about them at the harbor. Let's get on with it! *(Looking toward* PHILOCRATES.)

PHILOCRATES. What now, since I kept my promise to you and brought your son back in freedom?

HEGIO. After what you've done, Philocrates, my son and I can never thank you sufficiently the way you deserve.

PHILOPOLEMUS. You surely can, Father. You and I will find a way, and the gods will show you the way to repay our benefactor for his kindness as he deserves. Just as you can give this one *(Indicating* STALAGMUS.) what he richly deserves.

HEGIO. What's the use of talking? I can say nothing against anything you ask.

PHILOCRATES. I ask that you return the slave I left here as a pledge for me—a man who has always been better to me than to himself—so that I may reward him for his kind deeds.

HEGIO. Because of the kindness you have done me, I am happy to give you what you ask for. This and anything else you ask of me is yours. *(Hesitating.)* But I hope you won't get angry at me for treating him badly when I lost my temper.

PHILOCRATES *(in anxiety)*. What did you do?

HEGIO *(somewhat abashed)*. I threw him into the stone quarries when I found out I had been deceived.

PHILOCRATES. Oh, my god! That such a fine man should have got into trouble for my sake!

HEGIO. Because of this you don't have to pay me a penny for him. You may have him back—he is a free man.

PHILOCRATES. By Pollux, Hegio, that's very kind of you. But please have him brought here.

HEGIO. Of course. (*Goes to door of his house and calls to slaves inside.*) Where are you people? Go right away, bring Tyndarus here!

(*To the young officers.*) You two, go inside.

Meanwhile I want to ask this whipping block here what he has done with my younger son. Go in and wash yourselves.

PHILOPOLEMUS. This way, Philocrates. Let's go in.

PHILOCRATES. After you.

HEGIO (*with bitter irony to* STALAGMUS). Get over there, my good man, my charming slave!

STALAGMUS (*surlily*). What am I supposed to do when a man like you speaks falsely? I was handsome and charming, but never a good man or a very honest one, and I never will be. Don't set your hopes on my being honest.

HEGIO. You know very well where your fortunes lie. If you are truthful, you will make things a little better for yourself. Speak honestly and truly. But you have never acted honestly or truly so far.

STALAGMUS. Do you believe I feel any shame when you state what I admit?

HEGIO. I'll *make* you feel ashamed; I'll make you blush red all over!

STALAGMUS. Huh! I believe you. I've had a lot of experience with the lashes that you threaten me with. But enough of that. State what you want, so that you can find out what you want to know.

HEGIO. You speak well enough, but I want to cut short the talk. Let's get to the point. Now give me your attention and answer my questions. If you are truthful, you will make things a little better for yourself.

STALAGMUS. That's a lot of nonsense! Don't you think I know what is in store for me?

HEGIO. You can escape some of it if not all.

STALAGMUS (*bitterly*). I'll escape little enough, I know. For there is much coming to me and I deserve it, because I ran away, and stole your son and sold him.

HEGIO. To whom?

STALAGMUS. To Theodoromedes in Elis, of the Polyplusius family, for six minas.

HEGIO (*with a shout*). Oh, immortal gods! That's *his* father! (*Running to the door.*) Philocrates!

STALAGMUS. Oh, I know that, better than you, and I saw him quite often.

HEGIO (*impatiently*). Help me, Jupiter Supreme, help me and my son! Philocrates, by your guardian spirit, I beg you, come out. I want you.

(PHILOCRATES *hurries out.*)

PHILOCRATES. Hegio, here I am. If there is anything you wish, just command me.

HEGIO (*excitedly*). He says—my son—he says he sold my son to your father—for six minas in Elis!

PHILOCRATES. How long ago was this?

STALAGMUS. It was twenty years ago.

PHILOCRATES. He's lying.

STALAGMUS. Either I am or you are. He was a little four-year-old when your father gave him to you as your personal slave.

PHILOCRATES. What was his name?

STALAGMUS. He was called Paegnium. Later you people gave him the name of Tyndarus.

PHILOCRATES. Why don't I know you?

STALAGMUS. Because it's characteristic of people to forget and not to know those whose good-will goes for nothing.

PHILOCRATES. Tell me, is he the one whom you sold to my father, the one who was given to me as my personal slave?

STALAGMUS. *His* son. (*Nodding toward* HEGIO.)

HEGIO. Is he still alive?

STALAGMUS. I got my money, I did not worry about anything else.

HEGIO (*to* PHILOCRATES). What do you say?

PHILOCRATES (*with sudden comprehension*). Why, that *is* Tyndarus himself, your son, according to the proofs this fellow presents. For he was brought up with me well and properly from childhood, until we reached manhood.

HEGIO. And I am both wretched and fortunate if you two are telling the truth. I am wretched because I treated him badly if he is my son. Alas that I did more and less than I should have. That I treated him badly, I cannot forgive myself. If only it could be undone (*Looking to door.*) There he comes, but not decorated the way his fine qualities deserve.

(*Enter* TYNDARUS, *in heavy chains, sweaty, exhausted, carrying a crowbar.*)

TYNDARUS. I've often seen many paintings of the torments of Hell, but Hell is nothing compared to where I've been, in the stone quarries. There finally is the place where every last ounce of strength is drained out of your body and you drop from exhaustion. When I got there . . . (*pause for breath*) . . . you know the way children of the upper classes are given birds to play with, jackdaws, ducks, or quails—well, when I got there, I was given a crow (*Holds up his crowbar.*), that is, a crowbar, to enjoy myself with. (*Seeing* HEGIO.) But there is my master before the door—and (*With excitement.*) there's my other master, back from Elis!

HEGIO (*unable to keep silent any longer*). Welcome, my long-awaited son!

TYNDARUS (*surprised*). Huh? What is this "my son"? Aha! I know why you pretend you are my father and I am your son. Because, just like parents, you give me the chance of seeing the light.

PHILOCRATES. Hello, Tyndarus.

TYNDARUS. And hello to you for whose sake I suffer this misery.

PHILOCRATES. But now, I assure you, you'll be a free man and will come into wealth. For this man (*Pointing to* HEGIO.) is your father. (*Pointing to* STALAGMUS.) This is the slave who stole you from him when you were four years old and sold you to my father for six minas. My father gave you to me as my personal slave when we were both small boys. This fellow has just proved it. We brought him here from Elis.

TYNDARUS. What? *His* son?

PHILOCRATES. Yes, and inside there is your own brother.

TYNDARUS. You really mean it? You brought him with you, his captive son?

PHILOCRATES. I told you he is inside.

TYNDARUS. Well and honorably done!

PHILOCRATES. And this (*Pointing to* HEGIO.) is your father. This (*Pointing to* STALAGMUS.) is the thief who stole you away from here when you were small.

TYNDARUS. And now that he and I are both grown up, I'll have him hanged as a thief.

PHILOCRATES. He deserves it.

TYNDARUS. Then, by Pollux, I'll give him what he deserves. (*Turning to* HEGIO.) But tell me, I beg you, are you really my father?

HEGIO (*slowly with emotion*). I am, my son.

TYNDARUS. Now at last I begin to recall, when I think it over.

Now, by Pollux, the memory comes back to me, as if through a mist, of hearing my father being called Hegio.

HEGIO. I am he——

PHILOCRATES (*interrupting*). Please have these heavy chains removed from your son and put them on this slave.

HEGIO. That is certainly the first thing I have to attend to. Let's go in, so that I can summon the smith to take those shackles off you and give them to him.

STALAGMUS (*ironically*). Since I have nothing to call my own, you are most generous.

(*The actors come to the front of the stage and address the audience.*)

Members of the audience, this play was composed on good moral principles and nothing improper was put into it. There is no illicit love affair, no substitution of children, and no young man secretly in love buys the freedom of a prostitute without his father's knowledge. Writers produce few comedies of this kind, in which the good become better. Now then, if the play pleases you, and if we have pleased you and not annoyed you, then show us your appreciation: those of you who wish that virtue should be rewarded, give your applause.

The Rope
(Rudens)

A COMEDY

by

PLAUTUS

⚜ ⚜ ⚜

translated by
Samuel Lieberman

DRAMATIS PERSONAE

ARCTURUS, a star, who speaks the prologue
SCEPARNIO, a slave of Daemones
PLESIDIPPUS, a young Athenian
THREE YOUNG MEN (who speak no lines), friends of Plesidippus
DAEMONES, an elderly farmer of Cyrene
PALAESTRA }
AMPELISCA } slave girls of Labrax
PTOLEMOCRATIA, elderly priestess of Venus
FISHERMEN OF CYRENE
TRACHALIO, a slave of Plesidippus
LABRAX, a procurer of Cyrene
CHARMIDES, his friend, a Sicilian Greek
TURBALIO and SPARAX, overseer-slaves of Daemones
GRIPUS, a fisherman, slave of Daemones

Scene: A rough rocky coast in North Africa, near the Greek city of Cyrene. To the left of the stage stands a temple of Venus, with an altar in front. To the right stands the cottage of Daemones.

Prologue

ARCTURUS. In the city of the celestials I am a fellow citizen of him who controls all peoples, seas, and lands. As you can see, I am a bright shining star, a light in the heavens, which always rises at its appointed times here and in the sky. My name is Arcturus.

At night I am in the sky among the gods, gleaming brightly; by day I walk among mortals. There are also other stars which drop from heaven to earth. Jupiter who is ruler of gods and men distributes us among the various nations so that we may learn the deeds and characters of men, the extent of their righteousness and honesty, so that he may aid each one with his bounty as need be.

Those who start false lawsuits with false evidence and those who win claims in court by perjured testimony, we write down their names and report them to Jupiter. Daily he learns who has been seeking to do wrong here on earth. If there is someone who is trying to win a case by perjured testimony about damages, or who wins a case before a judge by false evidence, Jupiter tries these cases all over again up in heaven, and he fines them with a heavier fine than what they won in court. The names of the good men he has written down on separate tablets.

Now the wicked have got it into their heads that they can placate Jupiter by gifts and sacrifices, but they are wasting their efforts and their expense. This is because no prayer by perjurers is acceptable to him. If a man is good and righteous, he will more easily have his prayer answered by the gods than one who is wicked. So that is why I am advising you who are good men and who lead your lives righteously and honestly—continue in this way, so that you may rejoice for having done so. And now, since this is the reason I came out here, I will explain the play to you.

First of all, Diphilus, whose Greek play this is based on, wants you to know that this city (*Pointing to stage behind him.*) is Cyrene. There lives Daemones on his farm and in his cottage, right by the sea. He is an elderly man who came here from

Athens as an exile. He's not a bad fellow and he didn't lose his country for doing wrong actually, but while he was helping others he got into trouble himself and lost his hard-earned possessions through kindness. He also lost his young daughter when she was a little girl. The man who stole her sold her to a very wicked man, a procurer, and he brought her, now a young woman, here to Cyrene.

A young man from Athens, her native city, saw her coming home from the music school and fell in love with her. He went to the procurer and arranged to buy the girl for thirty minas. So he paid a deposit and bound himself by an oath. The procurer, being the kind of man he is, didn't give a hang for his pledged word or what he had promised the young man on his oath. He happened to have a guest staying with him, a scoundrelly old Sicilian from Agrigentum, a traitor to his city. This man began to praise the girl's beauty as well as that of the other slave girls who belonged to his host. He began to urge the procurer to go with him to Sicily. The place, he said, was full of libertines, and there he could become rich. He convinced him that the biggest market for slave girls was in Sicily.

They secretly hired a ship, and at night the procurer took from his home everything he owned and loaded it on the ship. To the young man who had bought the girl he said he wanted to fulfill a vow to Venus—this here (*Pointing.*) is Venus' temple—and he invited the young man to meet him here for breakfast. Then right away he himself got on board and sailed away with the young women. Others told the young man what had happened, that the procurer had left. The young man came to the harbor, but their ship was already far out at sea.

Since I had seen the girl carried way, I brought help to him and ruin for the procurer at the same time. I stirred up a wintry storm and raised high waves in the sea. For I, Arcturus, am the stormiest of all stars. I am violent when I rise and more violent when I set. Now both of them, the procurer and his guest, are sitting on a stone, shipwrecked. Their ship is smashed. Meanwhile the girl and another slave girl, who had become frightened during the storm, leaped from the ship into a rowboat. Now the waves are bearing them from a rock to shore by the cottage where the old exile lives, and the wind has blown the roof tiles off his roof. That slave who is coming out is his. (SCEPARNIO *comes out of* DAEMONES' *cottage.*) Soon the young man who bought the girl from the procurer will come here— you'll see him.

Good-bye. May your enemies despair!   (*Exit.*)

Act I

(Sceparnio, who has come out of the cottage toward the end of the Prologue, is getting ready to dig for clay to repair the roof.)

SCEPARNIO. Oh immortal gods! What a storm Neptune sent us last night! The wind took the roof right off the house. How can I describe it? It wasn't just an ordinary wind, but more like the storm in Euripides' play *Alcmena*,[1] the way it tore all the roof tiles away! Well, anyway, there's more light in the house now, and windows where none were before.

(Enter left PLESIDIPPUS and three friends, all wearing cloaks and armed with swords.)

PLESIDIPPUS *(to friends)*. I've taken you away from your own occupations, but the reason for which I brought you has not come off, and I was not able to catch the procurer at the harbor. But I didn't want to fail in my hopes because of inactivity on my part. That's why, my friends, I've detained you so long. Now I've come here to Venus' temple where the procurer said he was going to hold services.

SCEPARNIO *(aside, looking down at the ground)*. If I were smart, I would prepare some of this damned clay.

PLESIDIPPUS *(alerted)*. Someone near me is speaking.

DAEMONES *(coming out of his cottage)*. Hey, Sceparnio!

SCEPARNIO *(turning)*. Who's calling me?

DAEMONES *(amiably)*. The man who paid out money for you.

SCEPARNIO *(ruefully)*. As if you had to tell me that I am your slave, Daemones!

DAEMONES. We need a lot of clay, so dig up a lot of earth. *(Looking up at the house.)* I see I have to cover up my whole roof, for it has light coming through more holes than a sieve.

PLESIDIPPUS *(approaching DAEMONES)*. Good morning, Father, and, indeed, good morning to both of you.

---

[1] The mother of Hercules. The specific reference here is unknown, since this play of Euripides is not extant.

SCEPARNIO (*impudently, to* PLESIDIPPUS). Tell me, are you male or female, that you call him father?

PLESIDIPPUS. I am a man, of course.

SCEPARNIO. Then look for your father somewhere else if you are a man.

DAEMONES (*sadly*). I once had a little daughter, an only child. I lost her. (*Sighs.*) I never had a male child.

PLESIDIPPUS. The gods will grant you one some day!

SCEPARNIO (*impatiently*). May they grant you, by Hercules, whoever you are, a lot of trouble for keeping busy men busy here with your talk.

PLESIDIPPUS (*pointing to the cottage*). Do you people live here?

SCEPARNIO (*impudently*). Why do you ask? Are you spying on the place so you can rob us later?

PLESIDIPPUS (*irritated and sarcastic*). It's certainly fine and proper for a slave to interrupt when his master is present and to speak discourteously to a free man!

SCEPARNIO (*equally sarcastic*). And it's certainly proper for a shameless impudent man to come barging up to somebody else's home to bother people where he has no business!

DAEMONES. Keep quiet, Sceparnio! (*To* PLESIDIPPUS.) What is it you want, young man?

PLESIDIPPUS. A thrashing for that fellow (*Indicating* SCEPARNIO.) for talking out of turn when his master is around. But if you don't mind, I would like to ask you a few questions.

DAEMONES. I'm at your service, even though I'm a bit busy.

SCEPARNIO (*to* PLESIDIPPUS). Why don't you go to the swamp and cut some reeds with which we can cover the roof while there's clear weather?

DAEMONES (*to* SCEPARNIO). Keep quiet! (*To* PLESIDIPPUS.) If there is something you want, speak up.

PLESIDIPPUS. Tell me, have you seen a man around here with curly gray hair—a rascal, a perjurer, a wheedler——

DAEMONES. Oh, many such—for it's because of men like that I live in poverty.

PLESIDIPPUS. Here, I mean—who brought two young women with him to the temple of Venus, and who was making preparations for religious services, today or yesterday?

DAEMONES. No, by Hercules, young man! Not for the last few days have I seen anyone sacrificing there, and it is not possible for anyone to sacrifice without my knowledge. They are always asking me for water, or fire, or dishes, or a knife, or a spit, or a pot for the entrails, or something. Need I say more? It looks as if I got my dishes and dug my well for Venus, not for myself! But there's been none of that for the past few days now.

PLESIDIPPUS. From what you say, it's all up with me!

DAEMONES. If it's up to me, may you live and be happy!

SCEPARNIO (*to* PLESIDIPPUS). Say, if you go visiting temples to fill up your belly, you'd better start out with a good breakfast at home.

DAEMONES (*to* PLESIDIPPUS). You mean you were invited here for breakfast and the man who invited you didn't turn up?

PLESIDIPPUS. Exactly.

SCEPARNIO (*to* PLESIDIPPUS). It's no concern of mine that you'll go home from here without breakfast. But take my advice: you'd better go after Ceres rather than Venus. Venus may provide love, but Ceres provides food.

PLESIDIPPUS (*indignantly to* DAEMONES). That fellow has been making fun of me and he's going too far!

DAEMONES (*suddenly looking out toward the sea*). Oh immortal gods! What is that, Sceparnio? People along the shore?

SCEPARNIO (*looking in the same direction*). If you ask me, they must have had quite a bon voyage party before setting sail.

DAEMONES. How so?

SCEPARNIO. Because it looks to me as though they had a bath after the party last night.

DAEMONES (*excitedly*). Their ship was wrecked in the sea!

SCEPARNIO. That's right. The way our house and roof tiles were wrecked on land.

DAEMONES. Bah! Human beings, how puny you are! (*Pointing.*) Look how the survivors are swimming!

PLESIDIPPUS (*trying to see, to* DAEMONES). Where are those people? Point them out to me.

DAEMONES (*pointing*). In this direction, on the right. Do you see? Along the shore.

PLESIDIPPUS. I see. (*To his friends.*) Come along. I only hope it is that damned rascal I am looking for. (*To* DAEMONES *and* SCEPARNIO, *by way of parting.*) Take care of yourselves. (*Hurries off left with his friends.*)

SCEPARNIO (*as a parting shot to* PLESIDIPPUS). You don't have to tell us. We'll remember to do it ourselves. (*Looking out again.*) Oh Palaemon, holy companion of Neptune, who is said to be a friend of Hercules! What a sight I see!

DAEMONES. What do you see?

SCEPARNIO. I see young women, sitting in a rowboat, all alone, two of them. How they are being tossed about, the poor girls!

Bravo! Bravo! Very good! The wave has turned the boat away
from the rock toward the shore! No helmsman could ever have
done as well. I don't think I ever saw bigger waves. They are
safe if they avoid those breakers. Now, now they're in danger!
A wave has thrown one of them out! But she is in shallow water,
she'll easily swim to shore. Bravo! Do you see that girl, how
the wave has thrown her out of the water? She has gotten up.
She's making her way in this direction. She's safe! Now the
other girl has leaped from the boat on to solid bottom. She
has fallen on her knees into the waves from fright! (*Looking
intently.*) She's safe, she's getting out of the water. Now she's
on the shore. But, damn it, she's turning to the right and is
going to destruction! Mm! She'll be going in the wrong direction
now!

DAEMONES. What do you care?

SCEPARNIO. If she falls down to the rock for which she's
heading, she'll pay dearly for going the wrong way.

DAEMONES (*ironically*). If you're going to eat at their expense,
Sceparnio, you ought to take care of them, I suppose. But if
you're going to eat with me, I want you to give me a hand.

SCEPARNIO. Right you are, and fair enough.

DAEMONES. Come along, then.

SCEPARNIO. I'm coming.

(DAEMONES *re-enters the cottage, followed by* SCEPARNIO.)
(*Enter* PALAESTRA *from the shore, to the right of the spectators.
Her clothes are dripping wet.*)

PALAESTRA. The things that happen to people are less wretched
in the telling than in the actuality. It's when you are really
experiencing them that you feel the bitterness.

Is this what pleases the gods—that I should be in this
plight, frightened and shipwrecked on an unknown shore? Shall
I say that this is what a miserable person like me was born for?
Is this my reward for being a good woman? I would have deserved to earn this amount of suffering if I had sinned against
my parents or the gods. But if I did my best to avoid this, then,
O gods, you have treated me indecently, unfairly, and worse
than I deserve. For how will we be able to tell the sinners from
the innocent if this is the way you honor the innocent?

If I knew that I or my parents had acted wickedly, I would
be less sorry for myself. But it is because of my master's sins
that I suffer. His wickedness brings me harm. Now he has lost
his ship and everything in the sea. This (*Pointing to herself.*) is
all that is left of his possessions. Even the girl who was with me
in the boat has fallen out. Now I am all alone. If at least I had

her safe with me, she would help make my sufferings less severe.

What is there to hope for now? What plan can I make to help myself? I am utterly alone in this lonely place. Here there are only rocks and the roaring sea, and there is no sign of a soul anywhere. What I'm wearing is all I possess, and I don't know where I'll get food or a place to find shelter. What hope is there to make me want to live? I don't know where I am or where I've been. If at least there were someone to show me a road or a path out of this place—because by now I just don't know whether to go this way or that way, and I don't even see a cultivated field anywhere nearby. (*Shudders.*) I'm cold, I'm lost, I'm scared! Everything is against me. (*Starts to cry.*)

Oh, my poor parents, you don't know that I am as miserable as I am. I was born absolutely free, but it was no use. Am I now less a slave than if I were born a slave? And there was no advantage even for the people who brought me up.

(AMPELISCA *comes into view, also dripping wet, miserable, and looking for* PALAESTRA.)

AMPELISCA (*unhappily*). What is better for me, what is more to my advantage than to put an end to my life? Life isn't worth living any more and my heart is filled with so many fearful worries. This is how things stand: I don't care to live any more, I've lost the hope that cheered me. I've gone back and forth everywhere and crept through every hole in the rocks looking for my fellow slave girl, searching for her with my voice, my eyes, and my ears. I can't find her anywhere, and I have no idea where to go or in which direction to look for her. And all this time I have not met anyone who could tell me. There are no lonely lands more lonely than this place and this region! But if she's alive, as long as I live, I will not stop looking for her.

PALAESTRA. Whose voice do I hear nearby?

AMPELISCA (*alerted*). Oh, who is this speaking nearby?

PALAESTRA. Good Hope, I beg you, come to my aid!

AMPELISCA. Will you free poor me from this fear?

PALAESTRA. Surely it's a woman's voice that reaches my ears.

AMPELISCA. It's a woman, a woman's voice reaches my ears!

PALAESTRA. Is it Ampelisca, I hope?

AMPELISCA. Is it you, Palaestra, that I hear?

PALAESTRA. Why don't I call her by name so that she will hear me. (*Calling.*) Ampelisca!

AMPELISCA. Oh, who is it?

PALAESTRA. It's me, Palaestra.

AMPELISCA. Tell me, where are you?

PALAESTRA. Right here, by Pollux, I'm in terrible trouble.

AMPELISCA. I'm your partner in that, and my share is no less than yours. I'm longing to see you.

PALAESTRA. So am I to see you.

AMPELISCA. Let's follow our voices with our steps. Where are you?

PALAESTRA. Here I am. Come right up to me and face me.

AMPELISCA. I certainly will. (*Comes closer.*)

PALAESTRA. Take my hand.

AMPELISCA (*stretches out her hand*). Here.

PALAESTRA (*taking her hand and looking at her*). Tell me, are you really alive?

AMPELISCA. You really make me want to live now, now that I can touch you. I can hardly believe that I am holding you. Please embrace be, my hope. (*They embrace with intensity.*) How you free me of all my troubles!

PALAESTRA. That's exactly what I was going to say. (*Releasing the embrace.*) But now we'd better get out of here.

AMPELISCA. Where shall we go?

PALAESTRA. Let's follow the shore here.

AMPELISCA. I'll follow wherever you like. Shall we keep going this way with our clothing all wet?

PALAESTRA. The situation being what it is, we must endure it. (*Notices the temple.*) But look, what is this?

AMPELISCA. What?

PALAESTRA. Look at this temple, will you?

AMPELISCA. Where is it?

PALAESTRA. On the right.

AMPELISCA. I see that the place seems fit for the gods.

PALAESTRA. There must be people not far away. It's such a charming place. Whoever the god is, I pray that he may free us from this trouble, and that he may help us poor, helpless, troubled girls, somehow or other.

(*Enter from the temple* PTOLEMOCRATIA, *elderly priestess of Venus.*)

PTOLEMOCRATIA. Who are they who offer prayers to my divine patroness? For the voices of people praying has made me come out here in a hurry. A good and kindly goddess and a not begrudging mistress is she whose favors they seek, and she is very gracious.

PALAESTRA. We give you greeting, Mother.

PTOLEMOCRATIA. Greetings to you, girls. But where do you come from with your clothes so wet and dressed so sadly?

PALAESTRA. The place we just walked from is not far from here, but the place we rode from is very far away.

PTOLEMOCRATIA. Then surely you rode on a wooden horse over sea-blue ways?

PALAESTRA. Exactly.

PTOLEMOCRATIA. Then it would have been more proper for you to come here clad in white, bringing sacrificial victims. It is not the custom to come to this shrine the way you are.

PALAESTRA (*somewhat annoyed*). But when we were both cast up from the sea, where did you expect us to get victims to bring here? (*Both girls in desperation kneel to the ground and clasp the priestess' legs in supplication.*) Now we embrace your knees, utterly destitute, we who are in an unknown place, not knowing where to turn, and we beg you to receive us under your roof and keep us safe and have pity on our afflictions. We have no place to go and no hope to look forward to and nothing to call our own except what you see on us.

PTOLEMOCRATIA. Give me your hands, both of you. Get up off your knees. (*They rise.*) There is no woman more compassionate than I. But I myself am poor and in need, girls. I can hardly keep body and soul together. I serve Venus at my own expense.

AMPELISCA. Then this is Venus' temple, is it?

PTOLEMOCRATIA. It is. I am known as the priestess of this temple. But I will make you as welcome as I can to whatever I have. Come with me, this way.

PALAESTRA. You are most friendly and kind to honor us in this way.

PTOLEMOCRATIA. And so I should.

(*All three enter the temple.*)

Act II

(*Enter Fishermen, left, coming from town to their work on shore.*)

FISHERMEN. A poor man's life is miserable in every way, especially when he can't earn a living and hasn't learned a decent trade. Then of necessity he has to be satisfied with whatever he has at home. From our appearance you can tell exactly how rich we are. These hooks and these fishing rods are the tools of our trade. Daily we come out here to forage for fish. This is our gymnastic and athletic exercise. We fish for sea-urchins, limpets, oysters, squid, mussels, sea nettles, clams, and fluted scallops. Then we try fishing with hooks and from rocks. We catch our food in the sea. If success doesn't come our way and no fish are caught, then we sneak home salted and washed clean and go to sleep without supper. And the way the sea is now violently heaving there is no hope for us. Unless we catch some shellfish, dinner's surely over for us. Now let us venerate good Venus here that she may graciously help us today.

(*Enter Trachalio from town, looking for his master.*)

TRACHALIO. I've always made it my business never to disregard my master's wishes. When he went out a while ago, he said he was going to the harbor and ordered me to meet him here at Venus' temple. (*Looks around, trying to find* PLESIDIPPUS.) Ah, very good. There I see some people standing around whom I can ask. I'll approach. (*Approaches the* FISHERMEN; *heartily.*) Good morning, pillagers of the sea, shellfishers and fishhookers, you nation of starvation. How are you doing? Starving as usual?

FISHERMEN (*with dour humor*). As a fisherman should—from hunger and thirst and false hope!

TRACHALIO. Tell me, while you've been standing here, did you happen to see a young man come along, of determined appearance, with a ruddy complexion and strong, who was leading with him three men dressed in cloaks carrying swords?

FISHERMEN. No one of that description came here today, that we know.

TRACHALIO. Well, then, did you see an old man, bald as Silenus, a man of good size, with a big belly, curly eyebrows and a frowning face—a cheat, a thing of hate to gods and men, a curse, full of vice and lewdness, who was escorting two rather pretty young girls?

FISHERMEN (*spitting*). Any man endowed with such virtues and accomplishments had better go to hell than to Venus!

TRACHALIO. But did you see him, tell me?

FISHERMEN. Absolutely nobody came here. Good day!

(*They go off.*)

TRACHALIO. Good day to you. Just as I thought. What I was suspecting has happened. My master has been cheated! The rascally procurer has left the country. He has boarded ship and taken the girls with him. (*Punches his fist into his hand.*) A prophet, that's what I am! He even invited my master here for breakfast, the seed of sin! Now I'd better stay right here and wait till my master comes. If I see the priestess of Venus, I'll ask her the same questions. Maybe she knows something more. She'll tell me.

(TRACHALIO *takes a few steps toward the temple, when* AMPELISCA *comes through the doorway carrying a pitcher.*)

AMPELISCA (*to* PTOLEMOCRATIA, *inside*). I understand. (*Pointing.*) You mean that cottage over there, next to the temple. I'm to knock on the door and ask for water.

TRACHALIO (*alerted*). Whose voice comes flying to my ears?

AMPELISCA (*similarly*). Oh! Who is this speaking?

TRACHALIO (*in surprise*). Whom do I see? Is that Ampelisca coming out of the temple?

AMPELISCA (*in surprise*). Is that Trachalio whom I see, Plesidippus' valet?

TRACHALIO (*delighted*). It's she!

AMPELISCA (*likewise*). It's he! Trachalio, hello!

TRACHALIO (*effusively*). Hello, Ampelisca! How are you doing?

AMPELISCA (*ruefully*). I'm spending the best years of my life miserably!

TRACHALIO. Don't say things like that! Things are bound to get better for you.

AMPELISCA. All sensible people should face the truth and speak it. But where is your master Plesidippus?

TRACHALIO. What a question! He's inside, I expect.

AMPELISCA. No, by Pollux, he isn't. And neither has any other man come here.

TRACHALIO. He hasn't come?

AMPELISCA. You speak the truth.

TRACHALIO. I don't usually, Ampelisca. But how soon will breakfast be ready?

AMPELISCA. What breakfast are you talking about?

TRACHALIO. Well, surely you people are holding religious services here, aren't you?

AMPELISCA. What in the world are you dreaming about?

TRACHALIO. I'm sure your master Labrax invited my master Plesidippus to breakfast here.

AMPELISCA. By Pollux, I shouldn't be surprised at what you tell me. If he has cheated gods and men, he has only acted like the procurer he is.

TRACHALIO. So you are not holding services here, you people and my master?

AMPELISCA. You're dreaming!

TRACHALIO. Then what are you doing here?

AMPELISCA. When we were in lots of trouble, and in greatest fear and in danger of losing our lives, destitute of help and resources, the priestess of Venus here welcomed us into her house, Palaestra and me.

TRACHALIO. You mean Palaestra is here too, my master's beloved?

AMPELISCA. Certainly!

TRACHALIO. That's good and pleasant news you give, Ampelisca. But about your danger, I'd like to know what happened to you.

AMPELISCA. Our ship was wrecked last night, my dear Trachalio.

TRACHALIO (*surprised and dubious*). What? Your ship? What kind of story is that?

AMPELISCA. You mean you didn't hear about the way the procurer wanted to carry us away secretly to Sicily and loaded on the ship everything he had at home? Now everything he ever had is gone.

TRACHALIO (*joyously*). Oh, you delightful Neptune, bless you! Nobody throws the dice more cleverly than you. You certainly threw him a smart one! You've ruined a perjuring scoundrel! (*To* AMPELISCA.) Where is Labrax the procurer now?

AMPELISCA (*with satisfaction*). He drowned in the sea, I suppose. Neptune treated him to some mighty big cups last night!

TRACHALIO (*similarly*). By Hercules, he certainly couldn't help but drink himself to death last night! (*Hugs her.*) Oh how I love you Ampelisca, how sweet you are, how honeyed the words you speak! (*Releases her.*) But you and Palaestra, how were *you* saved?

AMPELISCA. I'll tell you. Both of us got frightened and jumped out of the ship onto a rowboat, because we saw the ship was being swept toward the rocks. I hurriedly loosed the rope that held the boat while they stood there frightened. The storm carried us in the boat away from them toward the right. And so, tossed by the winds and the waves, we were in great danger and misery all night long. At last, today, the winds brought us to shore exhausted.

TRACHALIO (*joshing*). I know. That's the way Neptune is— like a finicky markets inspector. If any goods are not up to standard, he dumps the whole lot!

AMPELISCA (*pretending annoyance*). Oh, go to hell, you!

TRACHALIO. The same to you, my dear Ampelisca! (*With conviction.*) I knew the procurer was doing what he did! I often said so. I should let my hair grow and go into business as a fortuneteller.

AMPELISCA. Did you and your master take steps to prevent his getting away when you knew about it?

TRACHALIO. What was he to do?

AMPELISCA (*somewhat indignant*). He loved her, and you ask what he was to do? He could have guarded her day and night! He should have been always on the watch! (*Disparagingly.*) But then, by Castor, what can you expect? Plesidippus watched over her about as much as he cared for her.

TRACHALIO (*offended*). Why do you say that?

AMPELISCA. It's quite evident.

TRACHALIO. Is that so? Even when a man goes to the baths, though he guards his clothes there very carefully, they get stolen. Because the man who watches out for thieves can't tell whom to keep his eye on there. A thief easily sees the man he has *his* eye on, but the watcher doesn't know who is a thief. But lead me to her.

AMPELISCA. Go right into the temple here. You'll find her there sitting as a suppliant and crying.

TRACHALIO. I'm sorry to hear that. Why is she crying?

AMPELISCA. I'll tell you. This is what fills her heart with anguish. The procurer took away from her the little box in which she had the means of identifying her parents. She is afraid it's become lost.

TRACHALIO. Where was the little box?

AMPELISCA. Right there on the ship. The master had locked it into his trunk, so she wouldn't have the chance of identifying her parents.

TRACHALIO. Oh what a cruel trick! To force a girl who ought to be free to be a slave!

AMPELISCA. And now it has probably gone to the bottom of the sea together with the ship, and all the procurer's gold and silver with it.

TRACHALIO (*consolingly*). I have a feeling someone has dived down and retrieved it.

AMPELISCA. That's why she's unhappy, the poor girl, at having been deprived of those things.

TRACHALIO. Then it's all the more necessary for me to go in and console her so that she should not torment herself so. For I know that many good things happen to many people after they've given up all hope.

AMPELISCA. And I know that hope has deceived many people who had hopes.

TRACHALIO. Therefore taking things as they come is the best way to make trouble palatable. I'm going in if you don't mind.

(*Enters the temple.*)

AMPELISCA. Go ahead. (*Turns toward the cottage.*) I'll attend
to what the priestess told me to and ask for water from the
neighbor here. For she said if I ask in her name, they'll give it
to me right away.

I think I've never seen an old woman who is more deserving
of having gods and men treat her kindly. How charmingly,
how generously, how honorably and ungrudgingly she received
us when we were frightened, needy, wet, cast out, and exhausted
—just as if we were her own daughters! How she got busy and
heated water so we could wash! Now I won't delay any longer
and will ask for water as she told me. (*Knocks at* DAEMONES'
door.) Hello! Is anybody in the house? Is anybody opening the
door? Is anybody coming out?

(SCEPARNIO *opens the door and comes out.*)

SCEPARNIO. Who is it who is so impudently trying to damage
our door?

AMPELISCA. It's me.

SCEPARNIO (*comes closer; admiringly*). Hey! What do we have
here? Something nice! By Pollux, a pretty girl!

AMPELISCA (*formally*). Good morning, young man.

SCEPARNIO (*relishing the sight of her*). And to you too, young
lady!

AMPELISCA. I've come to see you.

SCEPARNIO. I'll receive you most hospitably if you'll come a
little later, in the evening, the way a pretty girl like you deserves.
For I have nothing with which to honor you properly so early
in the day. So what do you say, my pretty little beauty? (*Tries
to embrace her.*)

AMPELISCA (*freeing herself*). Hey! You're being a little too
forward!

SCEPARNIO. Oh immortal gods! She's the very image of Venus!
What a merry twinkle in her eyes! Oh what a complexion—
skinned like a peached—I mean skin like a peach! What breasts!
And her lips, made for kissing! (*Tries to embrace her again.*)

AMPELISCA (*eluding him again*). I'm not the hometown harvest
feast! Take your hands off me, will you!

SCEPARNIO. Can't I give a nice little pat to a pretty girl like
you?

AMPELISCA. When I have more time, then I'll give you a
chance to play and pet. But now, if you'll be so kind, I've been
sent here for a definite purpose. So tell me if you'll help me or
not.

SCEPARNIO. What is it you want?

AMPELISCA. Seeing what I have *on* me (*Indicating the pitcher*.) anyone with sense can easily tell what I want.

SCEPARNIO. Seeing what I have on *me* (*making an obscene gesture toward himself*), anyone with sense could easily tell what *I* want.

AMPELISCA. The priestess of Venus told me to ask for water for her here.

SCEPARNIO. Well, I'm the boss around here. If you don't ask me, you won't get a drop. We dug that well with our own tools and toil. Without a lot of sweet coaxing you can't get a drop from me.

AMPELISCA (*sweetly*). Why do you begrudge me water, which a stranger grants a stranger?

SCEPARNIO (*teasing*). Why do you begrudge me a favor which a fellow citizen grants a fellow citizen?

AMPELISCA (*sweetly*). Why, certainly, sweetheart, for you I'll do everything you want.

SCEPARNIO (*aside, delighted*). Oho! I'm doing well! She's already calling me sweetheart! (*To* AMPELISCA.) You'll get your water. You won't love me for nothing. (*Holding out his hand.*) Give me the pitcher.

AMPELISCA. Here, take it. Bring it back quickly, please.

SCEPARNIO. Just wait there. I'll be back soon, dear.

(*Goes into the cottage with the pitcher.*)

AMPELISCA (*impatiently*). How will I explain to the priestess my delaying here so long? (*Looks out toward the sea.*) Even now I get terribly frightened when I look out to sea. (*With a sudden tenseness.*) But, oh, what do I see far off on the shore? My master, the procurer, and his Sicilian guest! I thought both of them had perished in the sea. My luck! So now that misfortune of ours lives longer than we thought. But why am I standing here? I'd better hurry into the temple and tell Palaestra about it, so that we can take refuge at the altar before the rascally procurer comes and finds us. (*Hurries to the temple door.*) I'll take refuge here right away. That's what the situation demands.

(*Runs into the temple.*)

(SCEPARNIO *comes out, carrying the pitcher filled with water.*)

SCEPARNIO (*smiling; aside*). Oh, immortal gods! I never thought there was so much pleasure in water! How I enjoyed drawing it up! The well seemed much less deep than before. And I drew the water out without any effort at all! (*Pleased with himself.*) Knock wood! I'm quite a lady-killer the way I started this love affair today! (*Expecting* AMPELISCA *to be there.*) Here's your water, you beautiful creature. There, that's the way

—I want you to treat me the way I treat you, so that you will please me. (*Looking around.*) But where are you, sweetheart? Take the water, will you? Where *are* you? (*Aside.*) She certainly loves me, I'd say. (*Smiling.*) She's playing hide-and-seek, the naughty girl! (*To the absent* AMPELISCA.) Where are you? Aren't you going to take this pitcher? Where *are* you? Don't be a tease! Seriously now, aren't you going to take this pitcher? (*Looking all over.*) By Hercules, I don't see her anywhere! She's making fun of me. By heaven, then, I'll put the pitcher down here in the middle of the road. (*Starts to do so.*) But wait! What if someone takes it away from here, the sacred pitcher of Venus? I may get into trouble! By Hercules, I'm afraid that woman has set a trap for me so that I should be caught with the sacred pitcher of Venus. Of course, then the magistrate will have good reason to send me to jail if someone has seen me with it. For it's got lettering on it and sings its own song about whom it belongs to. (*Approaches the temple.*) Now, by Hercules, I'll call the priestess out here so she can take the pitcher. I'll go up to the door here. (*Does so.*) Hello! Ptolemocratia, come and take this pitcher of yours! Some young woman brought it over to me. It's got to be carried in. (*Aside.*) I've got enough work to do without having to carry water in to them too!   (*Enters the temple.*)

(*Enter* LABRAX *from the shore, right, followed after an interval by his guest* CHARMIDES, *both dripping wet.*)

LABRAX (*annoyed*). Any man who wants to be both pitiful and penniless should entrust himself and his life to Neptune. For if anyone has any dealings with him, he loses everything he has the way I did. Damn it, Lady Liberty, you were clever when you refused to set foot in Hercules' ship. (*Looking around.*) But where is that guest of mine who ruined me? (CHARMIDES *wearily appears.*) There he comes!

CHARMIDES (*trying to catch up with* LABRAX). Where in Hades are you hurrying, Labrax? I can't keep up with you at that vigorous pace!

LABRAX (*bitterly*). If only you had died on the gallows in Sicily before I ever set eyes on you! It's your fault that this terrible misfortune has happened to me!

CHARMIDES. If only I had spent the day in a prison cell instead of being taken to your house! I pray the immortal gods that as long as you live all your guests should be just like you.

LABRAX. I took bad luck into my house when I took you in! Why did I have to listen to a criminal like you?! Why did I have to go away?! Why did I ever get on a ship where I lost even more property than I had?

CHARMIDES. By God, I'm not surprised your ship was wrecked when it carried a crook like you and your crookedly acquired possessions!

LABRAX. You've reduced me to ruin with your smooth talk!

CHARMIDES. The dinner I had with you was more damnable than what was once served to Thyestes and Tereus! [2]

LABRAX (*suddenly retching*). God! I feel awful! Hold my head, will you please. (*Vomits.*)

CHARMIDES (*holding* LABRAX' *head; bitterly*). There now, by Pollux, vomit your lungs out!

LABRAX (*straightening up*). Alas, Palaestra and Ampelisca, where are you now?

CHARMIDES. Furnishing food for fishes in the sea, I suppose.

LABRAX (*angry again*). Beggary, that's what you've helped bring me to, while I listened to your big-talking, bluffing lies!

CHARMIDES (*mockingly*). You really ought to thank me the way I deserve for helping to add some salt to a tasteless fellow like you!

LABRAX. Why don't you leave me and go to hell!

CHARMIDES. You go! I already came close enough to it when I came along with you.

LABRAX. Oh! Is there anyone alive more miserable than I?

CHARMIDES. I am much more miserable than you, Labrax.

LABRAX. Why?

CHARMIDES. Because I don't deserve it, but you deserve what you got.

LABRAX (*turning to the reeds along the shore*). Oh reeds, reeds, how lucky you are! No matter how wet it is, you always stay gloriously dry!

CHARMIDES (*shivering*). I must be training for the army. I'm sh-shivering so, everything I s-s-say sh-shakes like a s-s-spear!

LABRAX (*shivering*). By g-god, Neptune, you're a c-cold bath-man. Ever since I l-left you, even with my c-clothes on, I'm f-f-freezing!

CHARMIDES (*trying to warm himself*). He hasn't even built a hot-drink stand. All he serves are salted and cold drinks! (*Shudders.*)

LABRAX (*trying to warm himself*). How blessed are the black-smiths who sit among their hot coals. They always keep warm!

CHARMIDES. I w-wish I was lucky enough to be a d-d-duck, so that even when I got out of the w-water I was always w-w-warm.

[2] Both these characters of myth and tragedy were served the cooked flesh of their children in vengeance, Thyestes by his feuding brother Atreus, and Tereus by his angry wife. (See note 3.)

LABRAX. What if I hired myself as a pair of castanets in the theater?

CHARMIDES. Why?

LABRAX. Because you can hear my teeth rattle so loud.

CHARMIDES. I think I quite deserved that bath I got.

LABRAX. How so?

CHARMIDES. Because I had the audacity to go with you on the ship in which you moved me from dry land to the sea.

LABRAX. I listened to *you.* You were promising me that Sicily was the biggest market for courtesans. There, you said, I could be rolling in wealth.

CHARMIDES. Were you expecting, you filthy beast, that you would swallow the whole island of Sicily?

LABRAX. I wonder what whale swallowed my trunk in which all my gold and silver was packed?

CHARMIDES. The same one, I suppose, that swallowed my satchel which was full of gold and silver in its pocket.

LABRAX. Alas! I am reduced to this one tunic and this miserable cloak. I'm utterly ruined!

CHARMIDES. You and I can go into partnership—we have equal shares.

LABRAX. At least if my young women were saved, there would be some hope. Now if young Plesidippus, from whom I took a deposit for Palaestra, sees me, he'll make plenty of trouble for me.

CHARMIDES. Why are you unhappy, you fool? By Pollux, as long as your tongue still wags in your head, you still have the means of settling your affairs with everybody.

(SCEPARNIO *comes out of the temple.*)

SCEPARNIO. What is it all about, I wonder? The two young women here in the temple are clasping the statue of Venus and weeping—scared of some man, the poor girls. They say that last night they were tossed about in the sea and that today they were cast ashore.

LABRAX (*approaching*). Excuse me, young man, where are the women you are talking about?

SCEPARNIO. Here in the temple of Venus.

LABRAX. How many are they?

SCEPARNIO. As many as you and I.

LABRAX (*half to himself*). Could they be mine?

SCEPARNIO. I'm sure I don't know.

LABRAX. What do they look like?

SCEPARNIO. Real pretty! I could make love to either of them. All I'd need is a few drinks.

LABRAX. You're sure they're girls?

SCEPARNIO. You are a pest! Go see for yourself if you like.

LABRAX (*his spirits rising*). They must be my girls in here, Charmides, old friend!

CHARMIDES (*brusquely*). May Jupiter damn you, whether they are or not!

LABRAX. I'll break in on them here in the temple. (*Hurries in.*)

CHARMIDES. Break into the pit for all I care! (*To* SCEPARNIO.) Please, stranger, get me a place to sleep.

SCEPARNIO (*pointing to the temple grounds*). Sleep there, wherever you wish. Nobody will stop you. It's public property.

CHARMIDES. But you see how I'm dressed, with my clothes all wet. Take me to your house, lend me some dry clothes to wear till mine dry out. I'll repay you, and with thanks, when I get a chance.

SCEPARNIO (*pointing*). There's a reed mat—it's the only dry thing I have. If you want, I'll give it to you. That's what I drape around myself, that's what I usually cover myself with if it rains. Give me your clothes. I'll get them dried. (*Reaches for* CHARMIDES' *cloak*.)

CHARMIDES (*resisting*). Hold on there! Now that I've got cleaned out in the sea, you won't be satisfied unless I get cleaned out here on land too?

SCEPARNIO (*offended*). I don't give a damn whether you get cleaned out or smeared up! I am not going to trust you with anything unless I get something as security. So you can sweat with the heat or die of cold, or get sick or stay healthy—I'm not wasting my time with an ill-mannered barbarian as a guest in my house! I've had enough arguments!

(*Goes into the cottage and slams the door.*)

CHARMIDES. You've gone already? He must be a slave dealer, whoever he is. He has no pity. (*With sudden decision.*) But why should I stand here all wet and miserable? I'd better go into Venus' temple to sleep off this—hangover which I got from drinking more than I should have if I had had any sense. Neptune poured sea water into us as if we were cheap Greek wines— full of salt—and hoped our stomachs would be cleared out with his salty cupfuls. In short, if he had continued to entertain us a little longer, we would have gone to sleep right then and there. As it is, he sent us home half-dead. Now I'll go and see what the procurer (*With a smirk.*), my drinking companion, is doing inside.   (*Enters temple.*)

Act III

(*Enter Daemones from his cottage.*)

DAEMONES (*pensive*). The gods mystify people in wondrous ways and send us strange kinds of dreams. Not even when we are sleeping do they let us rest. For example, I had a dream last night, a strange one, which I can't understand. A monkey seemed to be trying to climb up to a swallow's nest in order to get at the young birds, but it could not seize them. Then the monkey seemed to approach me and ask me to lend it a ladder. I answered that swallows were Athenians since they were descended from Philomela and Procne,³ and I pleaded with it not to harm my fellow citizens. Then the monkey seemed to become more ferocious and threatened to do me harm. It was going to take me to court. Then somehow or other, I became angry, seized the monkey by the middle, and locked the vicious beast in chains. Now all day I haven't been able to figure out what the dream refers to. (*A sound of shouting from the temple.*)

But what is the noise I hear in the temple of Venus, my neighbor? That's quite surprising! (*Turns toward the temple.*)

(TRACHALIO *runs out of the temple, shouting.*)

TRACHALIO (*loudly*). Ho! Citizens of Cyrene! Help, I beg you! Farmers, neighbors, bring help to the helpless and destruction to the despicable! Prevent the power of the impious from being greater than that of the innocent who do not wish to be notorious for crime! Teach a lesson to shamelessness, reward modesty! Make it possible to live here by law rather than be vanquished by violence! Hurry to the temple of Venus, I implore your help again! You who live nearby and hear my call, bring

---

³ These Athenian princesses were turned into birds by the gods when Tereus, a Thracian king married to Procne, tried to slay the two women with an ax for serving him the cooked flesh of his and Procne's child. This horrible meal was revenge for Tereus' raping of Philomela and cutting out her tongue so that she should not be able to tell her sister. The girl, however, wove her story on a piece of embroidery which she sent to Procne. The gods turned Procne into a nightingale, Philomela into a swallow, and Tereus into a hoopoe. Daemones makes both sisters swallows.

aid to those who in the ancient manner have entrusted their person to Venus and Venus' priestess. Wring the neck of wrong before it gets at you!

DAEMONES (*to* TRACHALIO). What's this all about?

TRACHALIO (*kneeling and clasping* DAEMONES' *knees*). By your knees, I beg you, sir, whoever you are——

DAEMONES. Just let go of my knees and explain to me why you are making such a racket.

TRACHALIO (*getting up; emotionally*). I beg and beseech you, if you hope that your silphium crop and asafoetida [4] extract will be plentiful this year, and that it will arrive safe when it is exported to Capua, and—that your eyes should be free of the bleary eye disease——

DAEMONES. Are you in your right mind?

TRACHALIO (*still emotional*). ——Or if you expect to have a large supply of silphium seed, I beg you, don't begrudge giving me the help I ask, sir.

DAEMONES (*showing annoyance*). And I swear to *you*, by your shins and your ankles and your back, that you can hope for a rich vintage of elm switchings and that you will get a rich harvest of whippings this year! Now tell me, what is all this to-do that you are shouting about?

TRACHALIO. Why do you enjoy cursing me? I was hoping for all good things from you.

DAEMONES. I'm only blessing you, praying you get what you deserve.

TRACHALIO. Then please attend to this.

DAEMONES. What's the trouble?

TRACHALIO. There are two innocent women in here, in dire need of your help, to whom against law and right a terrible wrong has been done and is still being done in the temple of Venus. Also, the priestess of Venus is being shamefully attacked.

DAEMONES (*angrily*). Who is the man who is so bold as to dare to dishonor the priestess? But those women, who are they? What wrong is being done them?

TRACHALIO. If you give me a chance, I'll tell you. They have been embracing the statue of Venus as suppliants. Now a most presumptuous man wishes to tear them away. They are both supposed to be free women.

DAEMONES. Who is this who thinks so little of the gods?

TRACHALIO. Do you want me to tell you? A man full of fraud,

---

[4] Silphium is a plant of the parsley family, from which both a condiment and the medicine, asafoetida, were prepared. The crop and its derivatives were the chief products of ancient Cyrene and its rural environs.

crime, parricide, perjury—a most shameless, filthy godless law-breaker—in a word, a procurer! Do I have to describe him further?

DAEMONES (*with moral indignation*). By God! You're describing a man who deserves to be flogged!

TRACHALIO. Yes! And the criminal tried to choke the priestess, too!

DAEMONES. By Hercules, he's in for a lot of trouble for that! (*Calling into his house for his overseer-slaves.*) Turbalio, Sparax, come out here! Where are you?

TRACHALIO (*to* DAEMONES). Go into the temple, I beg you! Help them!

DAEMONES (*to slaves, who have not yet come out*). I won't call you again! (*Two big burly slaves come running.*) Come with me.

TRACHALIO (*to* DAEMONES). Come on now, tell them to knock his eyes out, the way cooks do to cuttlefish!

DAEMONES (*to slaves*). Pitch him out here by the legs like a butchered hog! (DAEMONES *and his two slaves enter the temple. Loud noises ensue.*)

TRACHALIO. I hear a tumult. The procurer is getting a going over with fists, I suppose. I only wish they would knock that reprobate's teeth out! But there, the women are coming out of the temple. They look frightened.

(*Enter* PALAESTRA *and* AMPELISCA *from the temple.*)

PALAESTRA (*her back to* TRACHALIO; *unhappily*). Now we are caught, utterly destitute of resources, help, aid, and protection. There is no safety in sight and no way to get safety. And we don't know where to turn. We are in such great fear—and our master has treated us with such great brutality and abuse! Why, the pitiless man roughly threw the aged priestess down and pushed her shamefully away! And he tore us by force from the statue in the temple. The way our prospects look now, we might just as well die! There is nothing better than death when you are in terrible trouble and things are miserable.

TRACHALIO (*aside*). What's this? What kind of talk is that? I must console them. (*Approaches them.*) Hello, Palaestra!

PALAESTRA (*surprised*). Who is calling?

TRACHALIO. Ampelisca!

AMPELISCA (*surprised*). Oh, who is it who calls?

PALAESTRA. Who is it who calls our names?

TRACHALIO. If you'll both turn around, you'll know. (*Both girls turn and see him.*)

PALAESTRA (*happily*). Oh, hope of my safety!

TRACHALIO. Keep quiet and be brave. Trust in me.

PALAESTRA (*returning to her unhappy mood*). If I could get the chance—before violence crushes me—the violence directed against me would be the violence I use against myself.

TRACHALIO. Ah, stop it! You're being very silly!

PALAESTRA. Stop trying to console me in my misery with soothing words. Unless you are really bringing help, Trachalio, it's all finished with us.

AMPELISCA. I'm determined to die rather than endure the procurer's brutality against me. But I'm only a woman after all, and when the thought of death comes into my mind, every part of my body is filled with fear. Oh gods, what a bitter day!

TRACHALIO. Have courage, both of you.

PALAESTRA. Well, what can I get courage from, tell me?

TRACHALIO. Don't be afraid, I tell you. Sit here on the altar.

AMPELISCA. How can that altar do us more good than the statue of Venus inside the temple here, which we had been embracing and from which we poor women were torn by force?

TRACHALIO. Just sit on it. I'll guard you here. Consider this altar as your camp—I'll defend you from here as your ramparts. Under the protection of Venus I'll march against the malice of the procurer. (*The girls get on the altar.*)

PALAESTRA (*in tears, prayerfully*). Oh kindly Venus, we obey thee and we both beg thee, embracing thy altar, our eyes filled with tears, on our knees, receive us into thy custody and protect us. Take vengeance on those wicked men who make little of thy temple and permit us to occupy this altar with thy peace. We were both cleansed with Neptune's help last night, so do not consider it improper and don't hold it against us if we are not as well cleansed as thou thinkst proper.

TRACHALIO (*also in attitude of prayer*). Venus, I know they are asking for what is fair. It is only right for thee to grant their prayer. Thou shouldst forgive them; fear has driven them to do this. People say thou wert born from the sea in a shell; do not spurn them who also came out of the sea. (DAEMONES *starts coming out of the temple.*) Ah, very good! Here comes the old man, my patron and yours!

(*Enter* DAEMONES *from the temple, followed by his slaves who are threatening* LABRAX.)

DAEMONES (*to* LABRAX, *angrily*). Get out of the temple! You're the most sacrilegious man who was ever born! (*To girls, whom he does not see because he is in front of the altar with his back to it.*) You girls go and sit on the altar. (*Looking for them.*) But where are they?

TRACHALIO. Here! look behind you.

DAEMONES (*turns around*). Very good! That's what we wanted. Now tell him to come over. (*One of the slaves gives* LABRAX *a shove; he approaches* DAEMONES.) What are you trying to do, break our laws and the gods' laws too? (*To one of his slaves.*) Give him a punch in the mouth! (*Slave does so.*)

LABRAX (*rubbing his face*). Ow! that's unfair! You'll pay for this!

DAEMONES. He still has the nerve to threaten?!

LABRAX (*sullenly*). I've been deprived of my rights! You're taking away my slave girls against my will!

TRACHALIO. Get yourself an arbitrator—any one of the rich men of the senate of Cyrene—to decide whether the girls should be yours and not free, and whether you shouldn't be clapped into jail and stay there for the rest of your life until you wear out your cell completely.

LABRAX (*to* TRACHALIO, *sarcastically*). I had no idea this morning—and the auspices didn't warn me—that I would be talking to a jailbird like you! (*To* DAEMONES.) It's you I'm dealing with, not him.

DAEMONES (*curtly*). First you discuss matters with him. He knows the facts.

LABRAX (*stubbornly*). I'm talking with *you*.

TRACHALIO. Nevertheless you've got to talk with me. Are those slave girls yours?

LABRAX. They are.

TRACHALIO. Well then, just try and touch either of them with your little finger, the tiniest bit.

LABRAX (*defiantly*). What if I touch them?

TRACHALIO. Right away, by Hercules, I'll make you into a punching ball, and while you're up in the air, I'll go at you with my fists, you lying perjurer!

LABRAX. I'm not permitted to take my own slave girls from the altar of Venus?

DAEMONES (*determinedly*). You're not permitted. That's the law here among us.

LABRAX (*scornfully*). Your laws have nothing to do with me. I'm going to take them out now. You, old man, if you've taken a liking to them, you have to pay me hard cash. Or if it's Venus they please, she can have them if she pays for them.

DAEMONES. Gods pay you money! (*Shaking his fist.*) Now, so you should know how I feel, just try to use force against them the least little bit, even in fun, and I'll send you out of here so decorated you won't recognize yourself! (*To slaves.*) Now

you fellows, when I nod to you, if you don't knock his eyes out,
I'll trim you with switches like reeds on holiday myrtles!

LABRAX. So, you're using force.

TRACHALIO. *You're* talking about force, you scourge of shame!

LABRAX (*to* TRACHALIO). You triple jailbird, you dare speak
insultingly to me?

TRACHALIO. All right, granted—I'm a triple jailbird and you
are an absolutely upright man—is that any less reason why
they shouldn't be free?

LABRAX. What do you mean, free?

TRACHALIO. And they are ladies, far superior to you, by
Hercules, and from mainland Greece. One of them was born in
Athens of free-born parents.

DAEMONES (*surprised*). What are you saying?

TRACHALIO. This girl (*Pointing to* PALAESTRA.) was born free
in Athens.

DAEMONES. She's my fellow citizen, you mean?

TRACHALIO. Aren't you a Cyrenean?

DAEMONES. No. I was born, raised and brought up in Athens.

TRACHALIO. Then defend your fellow citizen, sir.

DAEMONES (*sadly*). Oh my daughter, when I look at this girl,
though you are gone, you remind me of my unhappiness! Three
years old she was when I lost her! If she's alive she would be
her age, I know. (*Wipes away tear.*)

LABRAX (*unmoved*). Whoever they are, I paid money to their
previous owner for both of them. What do I care whether they
were born in Athens or Thebes, as long as they serve properly
as slaves!

TRACHALIO. Is that so, you shameless rascal? You wolf, you
seducer of virgins, you steal children from their parents and
ruin them in your shameless business? Now as for this other girl
(*Indicating* AMPELISCA.), what her native land is I don't know,
but I do know that she is much finer than you are, you filth!

LABRAX (*sarcastically*). Do they belong to you?

TRACHALIO. Come on, let's have a contest and see whose back
shows the biggest liar. If you don't have more welts on your back
than a warship has nails, then I'll be the biggest liar. Then when
I've inspected your back, take a look at mine. If it doesn't turn
out so smooth that any leather flask maker will say that the skin
is the best and soundest for his kind of work, why shouldn't I
slash you up with whips till I'm satisfied? Why do you look at
the girls? If you touch them, I'll tear your eyes out for you!

LABRAX. Well, just because you forbid me I'm going to take
them both away with me, once and for all.

DAEMONES. How will you do that?

LABRAX. I'll bring Vulcan and his fire. He's against Venus.[5] (*Goes over to the cottage.*)

TRACHALIO. Where is he going?

LABRAX (*at the cottage*). Hey, is anyone here? Hey!

DAEMONES. If you touch that door, may the gods help me, you'll get a rich crop of punches in your face!

SLAVE (*from the door of the cottage*). We have no fire. We live on dried figs. (*Closes door.*)

DAEMONES. I'll give you fire! (*Shakes his fist.*) I'll give you a bunch of burns on your head!

LABRAX. I'm going to get fire somewhere.

DAEMONES. And what if you find it?

LABRAX. I'll make a big fire here.

DAEMONES. Why? To burn out the inhuman part of you?

LABRAX. Why, I'll burn them alive, those two on the altar. That's what I want.

DAEMONES. By Hercules, I'll grab you by your beard and throw you on the fire, and when you are half-roasted I'll throw you out as carrion for the vultures! (*Getting a sudden thought.*) Now that I come to think of it, *he* is the monkey I dreamed about last night, who wanted to seize the young swallows out of the nest against my wishes.

TRACHALIO (*to* DAEMONES). You know what I'd like to ask you, sir? That you protect them, defend them by force while I get my master.

DAEMONES. Yes, find your master and bring him here.

TRACHALIO. And watch out that *he* (*indicating* LABRAX) doesn't——

DAEMONES. He'll be badly off if he so much as touches them or tries to.

TRACHALIO. Take care of them.

DAEMONES. I'm taking care. Go ahead.

TRACHALIO. Guard him, too—that he doesn't get away. For we promised the hangman to deliver him today or pay a whole talent.

DAEMONES. Just go. I'll take care of everything properly.

TRACHALIO. I'll be back soon.   (*Goes off to town.*)

DAEMONES. Procurer, would you rather quiet down with a beating or without a beating if you have a chance?

---

[5] In the *Odyssey* (VIII, 266–366), Vulcan (Hephaestus) is the husband of Venus (Aphrodite), but the goddess of love is unfaithful to him, especially with Mars (Ares). The betrayed husband takes an amusing revenge by binding the two lovers in an invisible net while they are in the act and calling on all the gods to see their "shame."

LABRAX. I don't give a hoot for what you say, old man. They are mine and I'll drag them from the altar by the hair in spite of you and Venus and Jupiter supreme.

DAEMONES. Just try and touch them!

LABRAX. I certainly will touch them, by Hercules!

DAEMONES. Then go on, just move closer to them.

LABRAX. Just tell both of those slaves of yours to move back a bit.

DAEMONES. Instead they'll move closer to you.

LABRAX. Oh, no, they won't, I don't think so.

DAEMONES. What will you do if they move closer?

LABRAX. I'll move back. (*Threateningly.*) But, old man, if I ever bump into you in town, no one will ever say I'm a procurer if I don't finish you off good and proper.

DAEMONES. You just do what you threaten. But now, in the meantime, you'll get yourself a lot of punishment.

LABRAX. How much, really?

DAEMONES. As much as a procurer like you needs.

LABRAX. I don't give a damn for your threats. Whether you like it or not, I'll get both these girls.

DAEMONES. Just touch them!

LABRAX. I certainly will touch them!

DAEMONES. You touch them and you know what will happen to you. (*To one of his slaves.*) Turbalio, run out and bring two clubs from the house.

LABRAX. Clubs?

DAEMONES (*to* TURBALIO). But good stout ones. Hurry, quickly. (TURBALIO *hurries off. To* LABRAX.) I'll see to it today that you get the welcome that you deserve.

LABRAX. Too bad. I foolishly lost my helmet in the ship. It would have come in handy now if I had it with me. May I at least call out their names?

DAEMONES. You may not. (TURBALIO *is seen leaving the cottage.*) Ah! Good! Here he comes with the clubs now. (TURBALIO *approaches with two clubs.*)

LABRAX. By God! Those things could give you quite a ringing in the ears!

DAEMONES. There, Sparax, take one of the clubs from him. Now, one of you stand on one side of him, the other stand on the other. Both of you stand there. That's it! Now, listen. If he so much as touches them with his finger against their will, and if you don't entertain him so well with those things that he won't know the way to go home, that's the end of both of you. If he calls anyone by name, you answer instead of the girls there.

If he wants to go away from here, quick as you can, wrap those clubs around his legs.

LABRAX. They won't even let me get out of here?

DAEMONES. I've said enough. (*To slaves.*) And when that slave who went to get his master comes back with him, you two go right home. But keep your eyes on things here very carefully. (*The slaves take up positions on both sides of* LABRAX, *with their clubs ready.*)

LABRAX. Well, I'll be damned! Temples certainly go through quick changes! This used to be Venus' shrine, now it's Hercules' [6] the way the old man has set up these two statues here (*Pointing to the slaves.*) with their clubs! Now I just don't know where I can find refuge considering that both are rough on me—the land and the sea. (*Tries calling.*) Palaestra!

FIRST SLAVE (*answering for* PALAESTRA). What do you want?

LABRAX. Oh no! I beg to differ! The Palaestra who answers me is not mine. (*Calling.*) Hey, Ampelisca!

SECOND SLAVE (*to* LABRAX). You'd better watch yourself!

LABRAX. All right! For statues, these men give pretty good advice. But listen, hey fellows! Will it hurt you any if I go a little closer to them?

SLAVE. No, not us.

LABRAX. Will it hurt me?

SLAVE. No, not if you watch out.

LABRAX. What should I watch out for?

SLAVE (*brandishing his club*). Hm! A sound thrashing!

LABRAX. Please, I'd like to go away.

SLAVE (*threateningly*). Go away, if you want.

LABRAX. It's really very kind of you. Thank you very much. But I'd rather not leave.

SLAVE. You stand there.

LABRAX. By Pollux, I've had very bad luck in every way today. Now I'm determined to go ahead and win the girls by siege.

(*Enter* PLESIDIPPUS *energetically with* TRACHALIO.)

PLESIDIPPUS (*to* TRACHALIO). He used violence on my sweetheart? He wanted to drag her from the altar by force?

TRACHALIO. Exactly.

PLESIDIPPUS. Why didn't you kill him right then and there?

TRACHALIO. I had no sword.

PLESIDIPPUS. You could have taken a stick or a stone?

---

[6] One of the most common representations of Hercules in ancient art was of the hero in a lion's skin bearing a club. Hence Labrax' comment on the two slaves standing guard like statues in Venus' temple with clubs poised.

TRACHALIO. What? I should go after a man with stones, like after a dog, even though he is of the vilest?

LABRAX (*seeing* PLESIDIPPUS). Now I'm a goner for sure! Here is Plesidippus. He'll soon sweep the floor with me, dust and all!

PLESIDIPPUS. Were the women still sitting on the altar when you went off to meet me?

TRACHALIO. They are still sitting there now.

PLESIDIPPUS. Who is guarding them there?

TRACHALIO. Some old gentleman, a neighbor of Venus. He helped a great deal. He is guarding them now with his slaves. I entrusted the job to him.

PLESIDIPPUS. Take me to the procurer right away. Where is that fellow?

LABRAX. Good morning!

PLESIDIPPUS (*sternly*). I'm not wasting time with greetings. Choose quickly which you want—to go peacefully to court with a rope around your neck or be dragged? Choose while you can.

LABRAX (*blandly*). I want neither.

PLESIDIPPUS (*to* TRACHALIO). Go right down to the shore on the run, Trachalio. Tell those men I brought along to meet me in town by the harbor, so that they can hand him over to the hangman. Then come back here and take over the guarding. I'll drag this rascal to court as a runaway. (TRACHALIO *leaves. To* LABRAX, *trying to pull him.*) Come on! On to court with you!

LABRAX (*resisting*). What crime have I committed?

PLESIDIPPUS. You're asking me? Didn't you take a deposit from me for the girl and then sail away with her?

LABRAX. I didn't sail *away* with her.

PLESIDIPPUS. Why do you deny it?

LABRAX. Because, by Pollux, I sailed *here* with her. I couldn't sail away with her, unfortunately. (*Smirks.*) I told you I would be here at the temple of Venus. Do I prove false? Am I not here?

PLESIDIPPUS. You can tell your case in court later. Here you've talked enough. (*Starts putting a rope around* LABRAX' *neck.*)

LABRAX (*calling to* CHARMIDES). I beg you, Charmides, help me. I'm being taken to court with a rope around my neck. (*Struggling.*)

CHARMIDES (*coming out of the temple*). Who speaks my name?

LABRAX. Do you see how I'm being taken away?

CHARMIDES. I see and I am happy at the sight.

LABRAX. Won't you help me?

CHARMIDES. Who is the man who is taking you away?

LABRAX. The young man, Plesidippus.

CHARMIDES. Well, you've made your bed, now sleep in it. You'd better take yourself off to jail cheerfully. You've got what many people want.

LABRAX. What is that?

CHARMIDES. To find what they are looking for.

LABRAX. Come along with me, please.

CHARMIDES. That's just like you! You are being taken to jail and you ask me to come with you. You're still holding back, are you?

LABRAX (*hopelessly*). I'm as good as dead!

PLESIDIPPUS. I wish it were true. (*To the girls.*) You, dear Palaestra and Ampelisca, wait here till I return.

SLAVE. I advise that they come to our house till you return.

PLESIDIPPUS. Very good. That's very kind of you.

LABRAX. You're robbing me!

SLAVE. What do you mean, *robbing*. (*To other slave.*) Grab him!

LABRAX (*turning to* PALAESTRA). I beg you, please, Palaestra! (*She turns away.*)

PLESIDIPPUS. Come on, jailbird!

LABRAX (*to* CHARMIDES). My dear guest——

CHARMIDES. I'm not your guest. I repudiate the relationship.

LABRAX. So you spurn me?

CHARMIDES. That's what I'm doing. I had one drink with you. That was enough!

LABRAX. May the gods bring you misfortune!

CHARMIDES. On your head may it fall! (PLESIDIPPUS and LABRAX *move off toward town.* PALAESTRA, AMPELISCA *and* DAEMONES' *slaves enter the cottage.* CHARMIDES *remains alone.*) I have an idea that different people turn into different animals. That procurer, I think, is turning into a stockdove. For his neck will be in the stocks before long. He will make his nest in jail today. But I'll go there to be his lawyer, so that with my help he can be more quickly—condemned. (*Exit* CHARMIDES *toward town.*)

Act IV

(Daemones comes out of his cottage, pleased with himself.)

DAEMONES. That was a good thing I did today, helping the young women—and delightful! I've found myself two protégées —and both so pretty and young, too. But my nuisance of a wife watches my every move to see that I don't show a liking for the girls.

But I wonder how my slave Gripus is doing. He went off at night to the sea to fish. God! He would have been wiser if he had stayed at home in bed. For with the storm we had last night and the way it's blowing up now, he is wasting his efforts and his net. Seeing how rough the sea is, I'll probably be able to fry in my fingers whatever he has caught today. *(Sound of a voice from the house.)* But my wife is calling me to breakfast. I'm going back in. Soon she'll fill my ears with her idle chatter. *(Re-enters the house.)*

(Enter GRIPUS from the beach, dragging a trunk in a net by a long rope tied around it.)

GRIPUS *(joyfully)*. To Neptune, my patron, I now give thanks, to him who dwells in salty realms full of fish, for sending me from his realms richly laden and returning me from his confines laden with much loot, with my fishing boat safe and sound, a boat which in the midst of a turbulent sea put into my possession a new rich catch! It is just marvelous and unbelievable how delightfully successful my fishing has been today! And yet of fish I haven't caught a single ounce, only what I'm carrying in the net here.

Now I wasn't lazy and I got up while it was still dark, preferring gain to sleep and rest. Though a storm was raging, I tried to find something with which to make bearable my master's poverty and my slavery, and I spared no efforts. A lazy man is good for nothing and I hate that kind of person utterly. A man who wants to get his chores done in time should be wide awake. He should not wait till his master rouses him. For those who like to stay in bed, sleep away their chances of gain and get loss instead.

Now look at me—I who have not been idle have found a way to be idle in the future if I should wish to. I've found this in the sea (*Indicates the trunk.*), whatever there is in it. Whatever there *is* in it is heavy too! I think there is gold in here, and there is nobody around who knows of it but me! Now you have a chance, Gripus, of freeing yourself from the masses. Now this is what I'll do, here is my plan. I'll approach my master cleverly and shrewdly. I'll promise to pay him little by little to set me free. Then at last, when I'm free, I'll get myself land and a house and slaves. I'll get big ships and be a merchant—I'll be a king among kings. (*Relishing his future.*) Then I'll build myself a yacht, just to enjoy myself, and I'll imitate Stratonicus, the world traveler, and sail to all the cities in the world. When my name becomes famous, I will build a great city and name it Gripus as a monument to my fame and feats. And there I will establish a great kingdom. Ah, these are great things I'm planning in my mind!

Now I'll hide this trunk. (*Ruefully.*) But I, this king among kings, am meanwhile scheduled to have breakfast seasoned with some sour wine and salt and without any dainty relishes.

(*Enter* TRACHALIO, *who grabs the rope.*)

TRACHALIO. Hey there, wait!

GRIPUS. What should I wait for?

TRACHALIO. Till I tie up this rope for you which you are dragging.

GRIPUS (*annoyed*). Just let go!

TRACHALIO. But, by Pollux, I'm helping you. Do a good turn for a good man and it doesn't go to waste, you know.

GRIPUS. There was a terrible storm last night. I don't have any fish, young man, and don't expect me to have any. Don't you see that I'm bringing back a wet net without any of the scaly school in it?

TRACHALIO. Oh, I'm not asking for any fish. I just want a word with you.

GRIPUS. You bore me to death, whoever you are! (*Starts to go.*)

TRACHALIO. I will not let you get away from here. Wait. (*Tugs at the rope.*)

GRIPUS. You'd better watch it there! Why the hell do you pull me back?

TRACHALIO. Listen!

GRIPUS. I'm *not* listening!

TRACHALIO. Well, you certainly *will* listen!

GRIPUS. Why don't you say what you want?

TRACHALIO. Well, now, it's worth listening to, what I want to tell you.

GRIPUS. So tell me what it is.

TRACHALIO (*looking around*). Take a look. Is anyone following near us?

GRIPUS. Is it any of my concern?

TRACHALIO. Certainly. Can I depend on your discretion?

GRIPUS. Just say what it's all about.

TRACHALIO. Quiet and I'll tell you, if you give me your word that you will keep your word.

GRIPUS. I give you my word I'll keep my word, whoever you are.

TRACHALIO. Now listen. I saw somebody stealing something. I knew the owner from whom it was stolen. So I went to the thief and made this proposition to him: "I know the person who was robbed. Now if you are willing to give me half, I will not tell the owner." He didn't answer me. Now then, what do you think he ought to give me? I hope you say half.

GRIPUS. Why, even more. For if he doesn't give it to you, you ought to tell the owner, it seems to me.

TRACHALIO. I'll take your advice. Now give me your attention, for this whole thing applies to you.

GRIPUS. What have I done?

TRACHALIO. That trunk you have there—I've known the person it belongs to for some time.

GRIPUS. And what of it?

TRACHALIO. And how it was lost.

GRIPUS (*heatedly*). And *I* know how it was found, and *I* know the person who found it, and *I* know the one who owns it now! And this is not one bit more your concern than what you said concerns me. *I* know the one to whom it now belongs, *you* know the one to whom it once belonged. No one will get it away from me. Don't you expect to be able to!

TRACHALIO. The owner wouldn't get it if he should show up?

GRIPUS. Don't fool yourself! For this there is no owner alive except me, who caught it while fishing.

TRACHALIO. Is that so?

GRIPUS. Will you say that any fish in the sea are mine? Those I catch, if I do catch any, are mine. I consider them as mine. And they cannot be claimed by anyone, and no one can demand a part of them. I sell them in the market place publicly as my goods. The sea is certainly shared by everybody.

TRACHALIO. I agree. But why, then, does that give me less of a share in the trunk? It was found in the sea that is shared by all.

GRIPUS (*heatedly*). Of all the shameless nerve! If what you say were right, the fishermen would be ruined! For as soon as the fish were brought to the market, no one would buy, everyone would demand his share of the fish. They would say they were caught in the common sea.

TRACHALIO (*excitedly*). What do you mean, you impudent rascal? Do you compare a trunk with fish? Do they look like the same thing?

GRIPUS. It's not up to me. When I let down my net and my hook, whatever clings to them I pull out. Whatever the net and hook have caught is most certainly mine.

TRACHALIO. It certainly isn't if you have picked up some luggage.

GRIPUS. Philosopher!

TRACHALIO. You poisoner, did you ever see a fisherman catch a trunkfish or bring any to market? You simply can't take up all the trades you want and claim to be both a trunkmaker and a fisherman, you filth! Either you've got to show me a fish which is a trunk or you don't carry off something that didn't grow in the sea and doesn't have fish scales.

GRIPUS. You mean you never before heard of a trunkfish?

TRACHALIO. You crook, there isn't any.

GRIPUS. Why certainly there is. I'm a fisherman, I know. But it's rarely caught and even less often comes on land.

TRACHALIO. It won't work. You think you can fool me, you jailbird.

GRIPUS. Considering the color this is, very few of this color are caught. There are some with red skins—big ones too. And there are black ones——

TRACHALIO. I know. If you don't watch out, by Hercules, you'll turn into a trunk with two colors—black and blue, first one then the other!

GRIPUS. What a terrible mess this has turned out to be!

TRACHALIO. We're wasting time talking and the day is passing. Decide whom you want as judge to settle the matter for us.

GRIPUS. Judge Trunk.

TRACHALIO. Did I hear you right?

GRIPUS. Yes, you did.

TRACHALIO. You're a fool!

GRIPUS (*sarcastically*). And you're one of the Seven Wise Men!

TRACHALIO. You will not take that trunk away today unless

you get some mediator or arbitrator by whose decision this matter is settled.

GRIPUS (*sarcastic*). You're in your right mind, are you?

TRACHALIO (*sarcastic*). No, I'm batty!

GRIPUS. And I'm touched in the head, you think! I will not let this trunk go.

TRACHALIO. Say one more word and I'll bash my fists into your head! Then, if you don't let this go, I'll squeeze all your juice out, the way water is squeezed out of a new mop!

GRIPUS. If you touch me, I'll fling you to the ground the way I do with a sea squid! (*Showing a fist.*) You want to fight?

TRACHALIO. Why fight? Why don't you rather divide the loot in half?

GRIPUS. You won't share any of this except a good punch in the nose. Don't try to. (*Turns to go.*) I'm going.

TRACHALIO (*pulls at rope*). Then I'll turn the ship around, so you can't get away. Stay here!

GRIPUS. If you're the man at the prow of the ship, I'll be at the helm. (*Tugs from his end.*) Let go of the rope, you scoundrel!

TRACHALIO. I'll let go. You let go of the trunk.

GRIPUS. You won't get a scrap of profit out of this today, damn it!

TRACHALIO. You can't cow me by being contrary. Either I get my share or the matter is handed over to an arbitrator or you give security.

GRIPUS (*helpless*). But I fished it out of the water——

TRACHALIO. And I looked on from the shore.

GRIPUS. ——with my effort, my work, my net, my boat!

TRACHALIO. If the owner should come along, would I who saw from a distance that you had it be less of a thief than you?

GRIPUS. Not at all.

TRACHALIO. Hold on, you whipping block! By what reasoning am I not a partner and yet a thief? Explain it to me, will you?

GRIPUS. I don't know, and I don't know those city laws you people have. All I say is that this is mine.

TRACHALIO. And I say that it's also mine.

GRIPUS. Wait! I've just discovered a way by which you can be neither a partner nor a thief.

TRACHALIO. How?

GRIPUS. Let *me* go away from here, and you go quietly along *your* way. And you won't report me to anybody and I won't give you anything. You keep quiet and I'll keep mum. That's the best and the fairest thing.

TRACHALIO. You're willing to make me an offer?

GRIPUS. I've already made it: you go away, let go the rope, and don't bother me.

TRACHALIO. Wait while I make *you* an offer.

GRIPUS. Please, by Hercules, just get out of here.

TRACHALIO. Do you know anyone in these parts?

GRIPUS. Well, neighbors, obviously.

TRACHALIO. Where do you live around here?

GRIPUS (*cautiously*). Far down there, in the very last fields.

TRACHALIO. Are you willing that the man who lives in this cottage should be our arbitrator?

GRIPUS. Just let go the rope a little, while I go off a bit and think it over.

TRACHALIO. All right. (*Slackens the rope as* GRIPUS *moves away a few steps.*)

GRIPUS (*aside*). Hurray! I'm saved! The loot is mine forever! He is inviting me to my own master as arbitrator, here inside my own back-yard. Master won't give up a penny of his own. He (*Indicating* TRACHALIO.) doesn't even know what kind of an offer he has made. I'll accept the arbitrator. (*Turns toward* TRACHALIO.)

TRACHALIO. Well then?

GRIPUS. Although I know for certain that this is mine by right, I'll do what you suggest rather than fight with you now.

TRACHALIO. Now you're being agreeable!

GRIPUS. Though you are summoning me to an unknown arbitrator, if he is trustworthy even if he is unknown to me, I'll be happy to know him. If not, even if he is known to me, I won't have any more to do with him.

(DAEMONES *comes out of his house accompanied by* PALAESTRA *and* AMPELISCA, *followed by the slaves* TURBALIO *and* SPARAX.)

DAEMONES (*apologetic*). Honestly, girls, I really want to do everything you want me to, but I'm afraid that (*Uncomfortably.*) my wife may throw me out of the house because of you. She will say that I've gotten myself mistresses right under her nose. (*Making a gesture of helplessness.*) You two had better take refuge at the altar rather than I.

PALAESTRA } (*starting to cry*). Heaven pity us! What will be-
AMPELISCA }   come of us!

DAEMONES. I'll keep you safe. Don't fear. (*To slaves, more sternly than necessary to hide his embarrassment.*) Why do you follow us out? Since I am here, no one will do them any harm. Go on back home now. (*Assuming a military bearing.*) Guards dismissed! (*Slaves return to the house.*)

GRIPUS (*sees* DAEMONES; *cheerfully*). Good morning, Master!

DAEMONES. Good morning, Gripus! How did it go?

TRACHALIO (*to* DAEMONES.) Is this your slave?

GRIPUS. I'm not ashamed of it.

TRACHALIO. I'm not talking to you!

GRIPUS. Then get away from here.

TRACHALIO. Please answer me, sir. Is this your slave?

DAEMONES. He is mine.

TRACHALIO. Well, that's fine! And hello again!

DAEMONES. Hello to you too! Aren't you the one who went to fetch your master a short while ago?

TRACHALIO. I am the one.

DAEMONES (*generously*). What can I do for you now?

TRACHALIO. You're sure he's yours?

DAEMONES. He is.

TRACHALIO. It's very good that he is!

DAEMONES. What's it all about?

TRACHALIO (*angrily*). He's a crook, that's what he is!

DAEMONES. What did he do to you that's so bad?

TRACHALIO (*angrily*). I want his ankles broken!

DAEMONES. Why? What are you two quarreling about?

TRACHALIO. I'll explain.

GRIPUS. No, I'll explain.

TRACHALIO. I'm making the complaint, if I'm not mistaken.

GRIPUS. If you really have any sense of decency you'll make yourself scarce.

DAEMONES. Gripus, pay attention and keep still.

GRIPUS (*annoyed*). You'll give a stranger a chance to speak before one of your own?

TRACHALIO. Look how he can't shut up! As I began to say, that procurer whom you drove out of the temple—well, this fellow (*Indicating* GRIPUS.) has his trunk there.

GRIPUS (*indignantly*). I don't have it!

TRACHALIO. You deny what I see with my own eyes?

GRIPUS. Well I wish you couldn't see! I have it and I don't have it. What right do you have to interfere in what I'm doing?

TRACHALIO. By what right you have it, whether lawfully or unlawfully—that's what concerns me.

GRIPUS. Didn't I pull it out of the water? So there's no reason for you to send me to the hangman. If I caught it in my net in the sea, how is it yours rather than mine?

TRACHALIO (*to* DAEMONES). That's just a lot of talk! The thing happened the way I'm telling you.

GRIPUS (*indignantly*). What do you mean?

Trachalio. What I would say as plaintiff. (*To* Daemones.) Shut him up, will you, sir, if he is yours.

Gripus (*sarcastically*). So? You want the same thing done to *me* that *your* master does to you! Maybe your master shuts you up all the time, but ours doesn't do that!

Daemones (*to* Trachalio). He has you there! Now what do you mean? Tell me.

Trachalio (*to* Daemones). I'm not demanding a share of what is in that trunk for myself, and I never said it was mine. But in it is a little box belonging to this girl (*Indicates* Palaestra.) who I told you was free-born.

Daemones. You mean the one you said was my fellow citizen?

Trachalio. Exactly. And the toys which she played with as a little girl are in that little box which is there inside the trunk. The box is of no use to him (*Indicating* Gripus.) and will help the poor girl—if he gives it to her—to look for her parents.

Daemones. I'll make him give it to her. Rest assured.

Gripus (*indignantly*). I won't give her a thing, no sir!

Trachalio. I'm asking for nothing but the little box and the toys.

Gripus. What if they are of gold?

Trachalio. What is that to you? Gold will be repaid in gold, silver will be exchanged for silver.

Gripus. First let me see the gold; then I'll let you see the box.

Daemones (*to* Gripus). You'd better watch out for a thrashing and shut up! (*To* Trachalio.) You continue speaking as you began.

Trachalio. I beg only one thing of you—that you should have pity on this woman, if this trunk really belongs to the procurer, as I suspect. On this point I can tell you nothing certain, except that it is my opinion.

Gripus (*to* Daemones). You see? The rascal is setting a trap!

Trachalio (*to* Daemones). Let me go on speaking, as I began. If this trunk belongs to the villain whose I say it is, these women will be able to recognize it. Order him to show it to them.

Gripus (*sarcastically*). Is that so? Show it to them?!

Daemones (*reasonably*). It's not unfair what he says, Gripus —that they be shown the trunk.

Gripus. On the contrary, by Hercules, it's utterly unfair!

Daemones. Why so?

Gripus. Because if I show it to them, right away they will, of course, say they recognize it.

Trachalio (*blowing up*). You archcriminal! You think everyone is just like you, you archperjurer, you!

Gripus. I'm willing to allow all that, provided my master is on my side.

Trachalio. He may be standing on your side, but he will be taking evidence from my side.

Daemones. Gripus, pay attention! (*To* Trachalio.) Explain in a few words what you want.

Trachalio. I've already told you, but if you didn't understand me well, I'll say it again. These two girls, as I've already said, should be free. This one (*Indicating* Palaestra.) was kidnaped as a little girl from Athens.

Gripus. Tell me. What has this got to do with the trunk—whether they are slaves or free?

Trachalio (*to* Gripus). You want me to tell everything all over again, villain, so that there won't be enough time?

Daemones. Never mind the insults and explain to me what I have asked.

Trachalio. There should be a wicker box in that trunk in which are things by which she can identify her parents, things she had with her when she disappeared from Athens, as I said before.

Gripus. May Jupiter and the gods make you disappear from the earth! What do you mean, you poisoner? Are those girls dumb? Can't they speak up for themselves?

Trachalio. They are keeping silent because a silent woman is always better than a talkative one.

Gripus. Then in that case, you are neither a man nor a woman, because you're no good whether you're talking or silent! (*To* Daemones.) Tell me, will I ever have a chance to talk today?

Daemones (*annoyed*). If from now on you say one more word, I'll smash your head in for you!

Trachalio. As I began to say, sir, I am asking you to order him to return the little box to them. If he wants any money for it he will be given it. Whatever else there is in the trunk, let him keep for himself.

Gripus. Now, at last, you are saying that because you know I have a right to it. But all along you were asking for a half-share.

Trachalio. Why even now I still want that.

Gripus. I've seen hawks pounce the way you do without getting away with a thing!

Daemones (*to* Gripus). Can't I shut you up without a thrashing?

GRIPUS. If that fellow keeps quiet, I'll keep quiet. If he speaks, let me give my side of it!

DAEMONES. Just hand over that trunk you have there, Gripus.

GRIPUS. I'll entrust it to you provided that if none of those things are in it, you'll return it to me.

DAEMONES. You'll get it back.

GRIPUS (handing over the trunk). Take it.

DAEMONES. Now, Palaestra and also Ampelisca, listen to what I say. Is this the trunk in which you were saying the little box is?

PALAESTRA. It is.

GRIPUS (aside). Oh, too bad for me! I am a goner! Even before she took a good look she says it's in there.

PALAESTRA. I'll make it clear and simple for you. There should be a small wicker box in that trunk. I'll tell you what you will find in it item by item. Don't show me anything. If I am incorrect, I will have spoken to no purpose, and you people will keep for yourselves whatever is in there. If I turn out to be correct then I beg of you that my things be returned to me.

DAEMONES. Very good. To my mind your request is absolutely just.

GRIPUS. But to mine utterly unjust! What if she's a witch or a fortune-teller and identifies correctly everything that's in there? Will the fortune-teller keep it?

DAEMONES. She will not get it unless she identifies correctly. And she is certainly no fortune-teller! So untie the trunk so that I may see as soon as possible what the truth is.

GRIPUS (takes the rope off the trunk). Here it is. It's untied.

DAEMONES. Open it up. (GRIPUS does so.) I see the little box. (Takes it out and holds it up.)

PALAESTRA (excitedly). That's it! Oh my parents! I have you enclosed in here! In this I placed my chances and hopes of identifying you.

GRIPUS. Then the gods must really be angry at you, whoever you are, for shutting your parents up in such a small space!

DAEMONES. Gripus, come over here. It's your case that's before the court. You, girl, from over there, at a distance, tell what is inside and how it looks. Describe everything. I swear to you, if you make the least little error and later try to correct yourself, you will be making a big mistake.

GRIPUS. That's a just rule you're stating.

TRACHALIO (to GRIPUS). By Pollux, he's not asking you, for you're unjust.

DAEMONES. Speak up now girl. Gripus, pay attention and keep still. (*Holds the box, looking into it.*)

PALAESTRA. There are children's toys.

DAEMONES. Yes, I see them here.

GRIPUS. I'm beaten at the beginning of the battle. (*To* DAEMONES.) Wait! Don't show her.

DAEMONES (*to* PALAESTRA). What do they look like? Answer in detail.

PALAESTRA. First there's a little gold sword with lettering on it.

DAEMONES. Tell me—on this little sword—what letters are there?

PALAESTRA. My father's name. Then on the other side there is a little double-headed ax, also golden, with lettering on it. My mother's name is on the little ax.

DAEMONES. Now, wait! Tell me—on the little sword—what is your father's name?

PALAESTRA. Daemones.

DAEMONES (*excitedly*). Oh immortal gods! Where are my hopes?

GRIPUS. No, by Pollux, where are mine?

TRACHALIO (*to* DAEMONES). Continue, I beg you. Don't stop!

GRIPUS. Take it easy, or go to Hell, you two!

DAEMONES (*to* PALAESTRA). Tell me the name of your mother which is here on the little ax.

PALAESTRA. Daedalis.

DAEMONES (*emotionally*). Ah, the gods want me to be saved!

GRIPUS (*glumly*). And me ruined!

DAEMONES. She must be my daughter, Gripus!

GRIPUS (*glumly and bitterly*). Let her be, for all I care! (*To* TRACHALIO.) May all the gods destroy you who saw me with your eyes today! And me too, damned fool that I am, for not looking around a hundred times to make sure that no one was watching before I pulled the net out of the water!

PALAESTRA. Then there is a little silver sickle and two little clasped hands and a little windlass——

GRIPUS. Why don't you blow yourself to hell with your windlass or your wind, big or little!

PALAESTRA (*unperturbed*). And a gold locket which my father gave me on my birthday.

DAEMONES (*very excited*). It's she, certainly! I can't keep myself from embracing her! (*Embraces* PALAESTRA.) Oh, my daughter, welcome home! I am the father who reared you! I am Daemones and your mother, Daedalis, is there inside!

PALAESTRA (*emotionally*). Oh, dear, dear father! How good to see you again!

DAEMONES. It's so good to see you! How happy I am to embrace you!

TRACHALIO. It's wonderful that you folks got the happiness that your goodness deserves!

DAEMONES (*indicating the trunk*). Here, take the trunk and carry it inside if you can, will you, Trachalio. (TRACHALIO *picks up the trunk.*)

TRACHALIO (*gloating, to* GRIPUS). Well, Gripus, you rascal! Look at you now! I want to congratulate you on how badly things turned out for you.

DAEMONES (*gaily*). Come, my dear daughter, let's go in to your mother. She will be able to complete the identification with further proofs, for she took care of you more than I did and knows all your tokens better.

PALAESTRA. Let's all go in since we are all doing this together. Come with me, Ampelisca.

AMPELISCA (*giving* PALAESTRA *a hug*). I'm very glad that the gods love you. (*All go in except* GRIPUS.)

GRIPUS. Am I a stupid wretch for fishing out that trunk today? Or rather, when I fished it out, for not burying it somewhere in a lonely spot? Damn it, I had a feeling my catch would turn out to be a stormy one since it turned up in such stormy weather! Damn it, I believe there is a lot of gold and silver in that trunk! (*Shrugs in disappointment.*) Why don't I go in and just quietly hang myself—for a little while at least, until I get over my disappointment?

(DAEMONES *comes out, very happy.*)

DAEMONES. Oh immortal gods! Who is more fortunate than I who have unexpectedly found my daughter? Isn't it true though —if the gods want to help a man, somehow the prayers of the good get to be answered? This morning I neither hoped nor believed it would happen to me. Yet all unexpectedly I have found my daughter. (*Shakes his head, as if hardly able to believe it.*) I shall give her in marriage to a young man of excellent family, a free-born Athenian, a relative of mine. I want him brought here as soon as possible and have ordered his slave to leave at once for the market place to get him. But I'm surprised that he hasn't left yet. I'll go up to the door. (*Does so and looks in.*) What a sight! My wife is holding my daughter in close embrace. The way she is pouring out her love is almost excessive and distasteful. (*Calls inside through the open door.*)

You'd better give your kissing a rest a while, Wife, and fix up the house so that when I come in I can hold services to the household gods for bringing our family together again. We have sacrificial lambs and pigs at home. But why do you delay, Trachalio? (*Sees* TRACHALIO *coming out.*) Ah, very good! There he is coming out now. (TRACHALIO *comes out.*)

TRACHALIO. I'll find Plesidippus, wherever he is, and bring him back with me at once.

DAEMONES. Tell him how things turned out . . . about my daughter. Ask him to drop everything and come here.

TRACHALIO. All right.

DAEMONES. Tell him I shall give him my daughter in marriage.

TRACHALIO. All right.

DAEMONES. And that I know his father and that he is related to me.

TRACHALIO. All right.

DAEMONES. But hurry.

TRACHALIO. All right.

DAEMONES. Now get him here so that dinner may be prepared.

TRACHALIO. All right.

DAEMONES. Everything all right?

TRACHALIO. All right. But do you know what I want of you? That you remember what you promised me—that I be set free today.

DAEMONES. All right.

TRACHALIO. Talk Plesidippus into setting me free.

DAEMONES. All right.

TRACHALIO. And get your daughter to ask him. She will easily win him over.

DAEMONES. All right.

TRACHALIO. And that Ampelisca should get married to me when I am free.

DAEMONES. All right.

TRACHALIO. And that I may be repaid in deed for what I've done.

DAEMONES. All right.

TRACHALIO. Everything all right?

DAEMONES. All right. I'm repaying you in your own terms. But hurry. Get to town at once and bring him back here.

TRACHALIO. All right. I'll be here soon. Meanwhile get everything else ready that is necessary.

DAEMONES. All right. (TRACHALIO *hurries off to town.*) May Hercules damn him with his all rightness! No matter what I said to him he kept filling up my ears with "all right."

(*Enter* GRIPUS *from the house.*)

GRIPUS (*furtively*). How soon can I speak to you, Daemones?

DAEMONES. What about, Gripus?

GRIPUS. About the trunk. If you're smart, be smart. Keep a good thing which the gods grant you.

DAEMONES. Does it seem right to you that I should say that something which belongs to someone else is mine?

GRIPUS. Something which I found in the sea?

DAEMONES. That's all the luckier for the one who lost it, and all the less reason why the trunk should be yours.

GRIPUS. That's why you are a poor man, because you are too scrupulously honest!

DAEMONES (*in a moralizing tone*). Oh Gripus, Gripus, in a man's lifetime there are many traps into which he may fall if he is foolish. And, by Pollux, usually some bait is put into these traps. If some greedy fellow greedily goes for the bait, he is caught in the trap by his own greed. The man who uses his mind, and cleverly and prudently watches himself, may enjoy his honest gains a very long time. But that kind of loot, it seems to me, is going to be looted itself and leave with a higher pile than what it came with.

Should I hide something brought to me which I know to be someone else's? Never will Daemones do a thing like that! The justest course for the wise man is not to be an accomplice of his slaves in their wrongdoing. I want nothing to do with lucre gained by collusion.

GRIPUS. I recently watched comic actors uttering those kinds of wise saws and being applauded for it when they revealed those wise moral teachings to the audience. But when the people went off in different directions, each to his own home, no one acted the way those actors had bidden them.

DAEMONES (*annoyed*). Go inside! Don't be a nuisance and hold your tongue! I'm not going to give you anything, so don't waste your breath.

GRIPUS. And I pray to the gods that whatever is in that trunk, whether gold or silver, should all turn to ashes! (*Goes into the house in a huff.*)

DAEMONES. That's what we get for having good-for-nothing slaves! If he had gotten together with some other slave, he would have involved himself and the other in theft. While *he* would think that he had loot, he himself would be loot—and loot would be taking loot. (*Exit into his cottage.*)

(*Enter* PLESIDIPPUS *and* TRACHALIO *from town, gaily.*)

PLESIDIPPUS (*very happy*). Tell me everything again, my dear,

dear Trachalio, my freedman, or rather, my patron—my very father! Palaestra has found her father and mother?

TRACHALIO (*in the same mood*). Yes, she did!

PLESIDIPPUS. And she's from the same city as I?

TRACHALIO. So I gather.

PLESIDIPPUS. And she's going to marry me?

TRACHALIO. So I suspect.

PLESIDIPPUS. Do you think he'll betroth her to me today?

TRACHALIO. That's what I figure.

PLESIDIPPUS. Well, shall I congratulate her father on finding her?

TRACHALIO. That's what I figure.

PLESIDIPPUS. What about her mother?

TRACHALIO. I figure so.

PLESIDIPPUS. Why, then, do you figure so?

TRACHALIO. Because you ask me, I figure.

PLESIDIPPUS. So tell me, what do you figure it at?

TRACHALIO. I just figure.

PLESIDIPPUS. Add it up then. Don't keep always figuring.

TRACHALIO. So I figure.

PLESIDIPPUS. I'd better run, eh?

TRACHALIO. I figure so.

PLESIDIPPUS. Or should I rather take my time, the way I'm doing?

TRACHALIO. I figure so.

PLESIDIPPUS. When I arrive should I also greet her?

TRACHALIO. I figure so.

PLESIDIPPUS. Her father too?

TRACHALIO. I figure so.

PLESIDIPPUS. Then her mother?

TRACHALIO. I figure not.

PLESIDIPPUS. And then? When I arrive should I embrace her father?

TRACHALIO. I figure not.

PLESIDIPPUS. Her mother?

TRACHALIO. I figure not.

PLESIDIPPUS. What about Palaestra herself?

TRACHALIO. I figure not.

PLESIDIPPUS. Damn it! He's lost his reckoning! Now when I want him to, he doesn't figure any more.

TRACHALIO (*gaily*). You're crazy! Come on.

PLESIDIPPUS (*in high spirits*). Lead on, my patron, wherever you like! (*They enter* DAEMONES' *house.*)

Act V

(*Enter* Labrax *from town, sadly.*)

Labrax. Is there any mortal alive today who is more miserable than I? Plesidippus has just won his case against me in the special court, and Palaestra has been removed from my possession by the judges. I am ruined! (*Sighs.*) I believe procurers must really be sons of Joy, because everyone enjoys it when something bad happens to a procurer. (*With decision.*) Now I'll go into the temple of Venus to see the other girl who belongs to me, so that at least I can take *her* away. She's all that is left of my possessions.

(*Enter* Gripus *from* Daemones' *house carrying a spit which he proceeds to clean.*)

Gripus (*grumbling; half-addressing those inside the house*). I swear, by tonight you'll never see Gripus alive again unless I get the trunk back.

Labrax (*aside*). Oh! Whenever I hear the trunk mentioned my heart starts pounding as if a stick were beating my breast!

Gripus (*as before*). That rascal is a free man, and I who caught the trunk in my net and fished it out, you refuse to give me anything. (*Rubs viciously on the spit.*)

Labrax (*aside, excitedly*). Oh, immortal gods! My ears perked up at what he said.

Gripus. By Hercules, I'll put up signs everywhere with letters a yard long, saying if someone has lost a trunk with much gold and silver in it, to come to Gripus. You people won't make off with it as you are trying to.

Labrax (*aside, excitedly*). By God! My trunk! That fellow knows who has it, I think. I must go over to him. Gods, I pray you, come to my aid!

(*Someone is heard calling* Gripus *from inside the house.*)

Gripus (*to those inside*). Why do you call me back in? I want to clean this outside. For, by Pollux, it's made of rust, not of iron! The more I brush off the rust, the thinner it gets. This spit is surely bewitched. It's wasting away in my hands. (*Continues cleaning.*)

LABRAX (*approaching*). Young man, good day.

GRIPUS. May the gods love you, you without the haircut!

LABRAX. What are you doing?

GRIPUS (*rubbing vigorously*). I'm cleaning a spit.

LABRAX. Feeling well, I hope.

GRIPUS. What are you? A medico or something?

LABRAX. Not at all! Add one letter to that and you'll know what I am.

GRIPUS. Then you are a mendicant.

LABRAX. You've hit the nail on the head!

GRIPUS (*looking him over*). You look like one. What happened to you?

LABRAX. Last night the ship that I shared with another man was wrecked. I lost everything on it that I ever owned, unhappily.

GRIPUS (*interested*). What did you lose exactly?

LABRAX. A trunk with much gold and silver in it.

GRIPUS. Do you remember at all what exactly was in the trunk which you lost?

LABRAX. What difference does it make, when it's gone?

GRIPUS. Nevertheless . . .

LABRAX (*pretending indifference*). Never mind. Let's talk about something else.

GRIPUS. What if I know who found it? I want to know the identifying marks from you.

LABRAX. Eight hundred pure gold double drachmas were in it in a pouch, and, besides, a hundred philippics in a leather moneybag separately.

GRIPUS (*aside*). By the gods, that's a lot of loot! I should get a big reward. The gods watch over people. I'll leave here well enriched with loot. Surely it's his trunk. (*To* LABRAX.) Continue listing the rest.

LABRAX. And there will also be a large silver talent of full weight in a purse, and besides a bowl, a drinking cup, a pitcher, a jug and a ladling cup.

GRIPUS. By Pollux! You *really* had some splendid possessions!

LABRAX (*sadly*). That's an unhappy and very depressing word, "had," now that I have nothing.

GRIPUS. What would you be willing to give the man who traces it and tells you where it is? Speak up quickly.

LABRAX. Three hundred double drachmas.

GRIPUS (*scornful*). Trifles!

LABRAX. Four hundred.

GRIPUS. Stinking cobwebs!

LABRAX. Five hundred.

GRIPUS. An empty nutshell!

LABRAX. Six hundred.

GRIPUS. Tiny little maggots you're talking of!

LABRAX. I'll give you seven hundred.

GRIPUS. You're getting warm, but not warm enough.

LABRAX. I'll give you a thousand double drachmas.

GRIPUS. You're dreaming!

LABRAX. I'm not adding anything more!

GRIPUS. Then go away.

LABRAX. Listen to me! If I really go away, I won't be here. Do you want eleven hundred?

GRIPUS. You're asleep!

LABRAX. Tell me how much you want.

GRIPUS. A sum to which you need not add anything if you don't want to—a large talent. I can't go a penny lower. So just say yes or no.

LABRAX. What's the use? I can't help myself, I see. You'll get the talent.

GRIPUS (*moving over toward the altar in front of the temple*). Just come over here. I want Venus to bind you in this with an oath.

LABRAX (*follows him*). Whatever you like, command me.

GRIPUS. Touch the altar of Venus.

LABRAX (*does so*). I'm touching it.

GRIPUS. You must swear by Venus here.

LABRAX. What should I swear?

GRIPUS. What I tell you.

LABRAX. Dictate whatever you wish. (*Aside.*) Considering the oaths I already have stored up at home, I really will not need anyone's help in this.

GRIPUS. Hold this altar.

LABRAX. I'm holding it.

GRIPUS. Swear you will give me the money on the same day you get possession of your trunk.

LABRAX. Agreed.

GRIPUS (*dictating*). "Venus of Cyrene, I call you to witness: If I find the trunk which I lost in the ship with the gold and silver safe, and if it returns into my possession then I to Gripus here. . . ." (*To* LABRAX.) say it and touch me.

LABRAX. Then I to Gripus here—I'm speaking, Venus, so that you may hear—will give a large silver talent at once.

GRIPUS. Say that, if you go back on your word, Venus should

destroy you, body and soul and business. Moreover, let this be binding on you when you have sworn.

LABRAX. If I transgress in anyway counter to what I have sworn, Venus, I pray to you that all procurers will be miserable.

GRIPUS. And that will happen anyway even if you keep your word. (*They return from the altar to the front of the cottage.*) You wait here. Now I'll go get my old master to come out. Ask him for the trunk at once. (*Goes in.*)

LABRAX (*aside*). If he actually does give me back the trunk, I don't owe him a penny. It's still up to me, no matter what my tongue may swear. But I'll keep quiet. There! He's coming out, bringing the old man.

(DAEMONES *and* GRIPUS *come out.*)

GRIPUS (*to* DAEMONES). Come this way.

DAEMONES. Where is that procurer?

GRIPUS (*to* LABRAX). Hey, you! (*Indicating* DAEMONES.) Here you are. He has the trunk.

DAEMONES. I have it and I admit I have it, and if it's yours, you may have it. (*Signals to* GRIPUS, *who runs into the house and brings out the trunk.*) Everything that was in it you will find safe and sound. Take it if it's yours. (*Hands it to* LABRAX.)

LABRAX (*takes the trunk; examines it*). Oh, immortal gods! It *is* mine! Hello, trunk!

DAEMONES. Is it yours?

LABRAX. You ask? Even if it belonged to Jupiter himself, by Hercules, it is still mine!

DAEMONES. Everything is safe inside except that a single little box with children's toys was taken out—those through which I found my daughter today.

LABRAX. What daughter?

DAEMONES. Palaestra, the girl who belonged to you. She turned out to be my daughter.

LABRAX. That's very fine, by Hercules! Since you had the good fortune to get your heart's desire, I'm very happy for you.

DAEMONES. That's not so easy for me to believe.

LABRAX. Well then, by Hercules, just so you should know I'm happy about it (*Brazenly.*) you don't have to pay me a penny for her. I give her to you as a gift.

DAEMONES (*ironically*). That's very kind of you, by Pollux.

LABRAX. Why, it's very kind of you, really, by Hercules.

GRIPUS (*impatiently, to* LABRAX). Hey, you! Now that you have your trunk.

LABRAX (*disregarding* GRIPUS' *urging*). So I have.

GRIPUS (*as before*). Well? Hurry up!

LABRAX. What should I hurry up about?

GRIPUS. About paying me the money.

LABRAX. I'm not giving you anything, by Pollux, and I don't owe you anything.

GRIPUS. What do you think you're doing? You don't owe me?

LABRAX. No, I certainly don't.

GRIPUS. Didn't you swear to me?

LABRAX. I swore and I'll swear again if it gives me pleasure. (*Brazenly.*) Oaths were invented for keeping property not for losing it.

GRIPUS (*holding out his hand, angrily*). Hand over the large silver talent, will you, you lying perjurer!

DAEMONES. Gripus, what is that talent you are demanding?

GRIPUS. He swore to give it to me.

LABRAX (*smirking*). I enjoy swearing. Are you the high priest to condemn me for perjury?

DAEMONES (*to* GRIPUS). What did he promise you the money for?

GRIPUS. If I restored this trunk to his possession, he swore to give me a large silver talent.

LABRAX (*to* GRIPUS). Name someone as your representative with whom I can go before an arbitrator, and we'll see whether you didn't make a fraudulent contract and (*Smirking.*) whether I'm under twenty-five and therefore under age for contracts.

GRIPUS (*pointing to* DAEMONES). Have him as my representative.

LABRAX. We need someone else.

DAEMONES (*aside, considering future possibilities*). Now I couldn't get it away from him (*Eying* GRIPUS.) if I decide against him. (*Looking at* LABRAX. *To* LABRAX, *sternly.*) Did you promise him money?

LABRAX. I admit I did.

DAEMONES. What you promised my slave is supposed to be mine. Don't you, procurer, try any procurer's honesty here. You can't.

GRIPUS (*to* LABRAX). Did you think you found someone to cheat? You've got to give me a decent sum of money. Then I'll immediately give it to my master here so that he will set me free.

DAEMONES (*to* LABRAX). Therefore, since I was kind to you and through my efforts these things were saved——

GRIPUS. No, by Hercules, through my efforts. Don't say yours.

DAEMONES (*aside to* GRIPUS). If you're smart you'll keep

quiet! (*To* LABRAX.) Then it's also proper for you to thank your benefactor well.

LABRAX. Surely you're speaking with full recognition of my rights?

DAEMONES. It would be surprising if I should put myself out to look out for your rights alone.

GRIPUS (*aside*). I'm saved. The procurer is weakening. Freedom is in the offing.

DAEMONES (*to* LABRAX). He found your trunk and he is *my* slave. Furthermore, I saved the trunk containing a large sum of money.

LABRAX. I thank you, and as for the talent, there is no reason why *you* should not get what I swore to *him*.

GRIPUS. Hey, you! Then give it to me if you are smart.

DAEMONES (*to* GRIPUS). Are you keeping quiet or not?

GRIPUS. You pretend you are acting in my interest, but you are paving the way to your own! By Hercules, you won't swindle me of that even if I've lost the other loot.

DAEMONES. You'll get a walloping if you say another word!

GRIPUS. By Hercules, you make me sick! I won't keep quiet unless I'm shut up with a talent.

LABRAX (*to* GRIPUS). He's helping you. Keep quiet.

DAEMONES. Come aside here, procurer.

LABRAX. Very well. (*Approaches* DAEMONES.)

GRIPUS. Act openly. I don't want any murmuring and whispering.

DAEMONES (*aside to* LABRAX.) Tell me, how much did you pay for the second young woman, Ampelisca?

LABRAX. I paid a thousand for her—a talent.

DAEMONES. Do you want me to make you a splendid offer?

LABRAX. I certainly do.

DAEMONES. I'll go halves with you on the talent.

LABRAX. Very kind of you.

DAEMONES. For the second girl—so that she should go free— take half for yourself and give me the other half.

LABRAX. By all means!

DAEMONES. For that half I'll free Gripus through whom you found your trunk and I my daughter.

LABRAX. That's very kind of you. Thank you very much. (*They return to* GRIPUS.)

GRIPUS. So? How soon do I get the money?

DAEMONES. It's all settled, Gripus. *I* have it.

GRIPUS. But I'd rather have it, by Hercules.

DAEMONES (*joshingly*). There's nothing here for you. Don't expect it. I want you to release him from his oath.

GRIPUS. Damn it! I'm hanged if I don't hang myself! Never again will you cheat me after today.

DAEMONES (*to* LABRAX). Dine with us here today, procurer.

LABRAX. Good! Your offer is accepted with pleasure.

DAEMONES (*slapping* GRIPUS *on the back, as if to indicate everything will be all right*). Come inside, both of you. (*Turning to audience.*) Spectators, I would invite you also in to dinner if it weren't that I'm serving nothing and have no food at home, and if I didn't believe also that you have been invited out to dinner. But if you are willing to give this play your loud applause, all of you down to the age of sixteen will be invited to make a night of it at my house. (*To* LABRAX *and* GRIPUS.) But you two, you eat here today.

LABRAX. } Good.
GRIPUS. }

DAEMONES (*to audience*). Give us your applause.

The Brothers
(Adelphoe)

A COMEDY

by
TERENCE

❧ ❧ ❧

translated by
Samuel Lieberman

DRAMATIS PERSONAE

MICIO, uncle and adoptive father of Aeschinus.
DEMEA, his older brother and actual father of Aeschinus.
SANNIO, a procurer, dealer in slave-girls.
AESCHINUS, a sophisticated young man-about-town.
SYRUS, his faithful slave, a man in his forties.
CTESIPHO, younger brother of Aeschinus, rather countrified.
SOSTRATA, a widow, neighbor of Micio.
CANTHARA, an elderly nurse, slave of Sostrata.
PAMPHILA, young daughter of Sostrata.
GETA, slave of Sostrata, a man in his late forties or fifties.
HEGIO, an elderly man, relative of Sostrata.
DROMO, a young slave of Micio.
CANTOR (singer), who appears only at the end to ask for audience's applause. (See Introduction, p. 15.)

Appearing briefly in the action of the play but speaking no lines:
BACCHIS, a courtesan, slave girl of Sannio.
PARMENO, a slave of Aeschinus.

Place: A street in Athens. Two houses face on the street. Near the middle of the stage the audience can see the large main door and a smaller one belonging to Micio's house. The large door at the left belongs to Sostrata's house. A narrow lane on the audience's right leads from the street toward the country. There is a lane also on the left after Sostrata's house.

Time: The action starts in the morning and continues through the late afternoon.

Prologue

Since it has come to the author's attention that his writing is being subjected to unfair criticism and that his detractors are putting the play which we are about to present in the worst light, he is going to give evidence regarding himself, and you will be the judges as to whether what he has done ought to be praised or blamed.

There is a Greek comedy by Diphilus [1] called *The Suicide Pact*. Plautus made this into a Roman comedy by the same name. In the Greek play, in one of the early scenes, there is a young man who steals a courtesan away from a procurer. This scene was left intact by Plautus, who omitted it from his play. This scene has been taken over by our author in *The Brothers* and translated word for word. The play we are about to present is completely new. You may judge for yourselves whether you think plagiarism has been committed, or whether rather a scene which was passed over and not used has been retrieved for a Roman audience.

Now as to the statement by those ill-wishers to the effect that men of noble rank always help the author and collaborate with him in his writing. What they consider to be a serious accusation, the author considers to be the highest praise, namely that he pleases those who please all of you and the Roman people as a whole—those men whose efforts in war, in peace, in public activity everyone has availed himself of, according to his convenience, without reservations.

Finally, don't expect me to give you the plot of the play. The old men who come on first will disclose part of it as they play their parts.

May your good will encourage the author and give him renewed energy for writing.   (*Exit.*)

[1] A writer of New Comedy in the Hellenistic era. Only fragments of his work are extant. (See Introduction, p. 11.)

161

Act I

(*Enter Micio, calling to a slave.*)

MICIO. Storax! (*Gets no answer.*) So, Aeschinus didn't come home last night from dining out, nor have any of the slaves who had gone out to escort him home!

This is certainly a true saying: If you go out somewhere and don't get home when you are expected, it is better that what your enraged wife says or imagines has happened to you rather than that which your loving parents will fear has happened. For if you stay out late or don't come home, a wife thinks you are making love, or are being made love to, or you're drinking and indulging yourself, and that you are having a good time without her, while she is having a rotten time. But a parent? Because my son hasn't come home, what thoughts I think! How many worries assail me! Maybe he's become sick, or maybe he's had an accident, or maybe he's broken a leg or something! Bah! That any man should get or set his heart on something that is dearer to him than himself.

Actually, I am not his real father, but my brother is. And—from our early youth on—he has been of an entirely different temperament from me. I like this easygoing, sophisticated city life and leisure, and—something men such as he think fortunate—I've never been married. He is just the opposite in every respect. He lives in the country. He is always thrifty and stern. He got married and had two sons. I adopted the older one and brought him up from early childhood. I love him and consider him as my own son. He is my delight, he is the only thing that's dear to me. I do the best I can to make him feel the same toward me. I give him money, I overlook things, I don't consider it necessary for him to do everything by my orders. To sum up, the kind of things that others do in secret without their fathers' knowledge—the kind of things that come with youth—these things I've trained my son not to hide from me. For a boy who has learned to lie and deceive his father and will dare to, will also dare to do it to others.

I believe it is better to control children by developing in them a moral sense and a sense of honor than by fear. This point of view my brother opposes and dislikes. He often comes up to me shouting, "What are you doing, Micio? Why are you spoiling our young man? Why does he carry on love affairs? Why does he drink? Why do you supply him with funds for these things? Why do you indulge him in such an extensive wardrobe? You are awfully foolish!"

He is awfully stern, far beyond what is justified and good, and he is making a big mistake in my opinion if he believes that control is greater and more effective if it is imposed by force than if it is exercised by friendliness. This is my philsophy and this is my conviction: A person who does his duty through fear of punishment will be afraid only as long as he thinks he will be found out. If he expects that he will not be found out he will return to his natural instinct. The person whom you win over by kindness will act sincerely. He will be eager to return like for like. In your presence or away from you he will be the same. This is what it means to be a father, to train a son to do right of his own free will rather than through fear of another. This is the difference between a father and a master. A father who is unable to do this should admit that he cannot control his children.

But isn't that the very man I was talking about? It certainly is. He looks somewhat cross to me. I suppose, as usual, he will start quarreling. (DEMEA *approaches*.)

(*To* DEMEA.) I'm happy to see you, Demea. Hello!

DEMEA (*very upset*). Ah, opportunely met! You're just the man I was looking for!

MICIO. Why are you so upset?

DEMEA (*angry*). With Aeschinus in our family, you ask why I am upset? Didn't I tell you this would happen?

MICIO. There you go again. What did he do?

DEMEA (*angrily*). What did he *do*? He who has no shame and no fear and thinks the laws were not made for him!

MICIO. Why, what is it this time?

DEMEA. He smashed down a door and broke into somebody's house. He beat up the householder and his servants very severely. Then he eloped with a girl there that he is in love with. Everyone is loudly complaining at his outrageous actions. People come up to me on the street and talk to me about it. It's the only topic of conversation everywhere.

It's about time he followed the example of his brother. Doesn't he see that his brother doesn't get involved in anything like that, but stays on the farm sober, hardworking, and serious?

His brother hasn't done anything even remotely like this. When I talk of him, Micio, I'm also talking about you. You allow him to be ruined—you spoil him!

Micio (*blandly*). There is no one more unjust than a man of limited experience, who thinks that if he hasn't done something himself, it can't be right.

Demea (*indignantly*). What do you mean?

Micio. That you, Demea, have the wrong idea about this. It's no disgrace—take my word for it—for a young man to chase after women and to get drunk. It isn't! Nor is it so terrible to smash down a door. If you and I didn't do these things when we were young, it is because we were too poor to be able to. And now you take credit for not doing what you couldn't afford to do anyway. That's wrong! For if we had had the wherewithal we would have done it too.

Now that boy of *yours*—on the farm—if you are a man of intelligence, you'll allow him to do these things while they're still suitable to his age, rather than have him do them later, when he's finally carried you out in your coffin—which he's probably waiting for—when he'll really be too old to sow wild oats.

Demea (*angry*). Good god Jupiter! Insane, you're just insane! And you want to drive *me* crazy too! It is not a disgrace for a young man to do what he did?

Micio. Now listen. Don't keep hammering away at me about the same thing over and over. You gave your son over to me to be adopted, so now he's mine. If he has done something wrong, it's my responsibility, it's my problem. He gives expensive parties, he gets drunk, he reeks of perfume: it comes out of my pocket. He has an affair with a girl: he'll get money from me as long as it suits me. When he stops getting money from me, she'll probably throw him out of her house. He smashes down a door: it will be rebuilt. He gets his clothes torn: the tailor will repair them. I have, thank the gods, the means to pay for all this and it doesn't bother me financially. So finally, either stop nagging or get somebody to arbitrate and I'll show you that you're wrong in this matter.

Demea (*disgusted*). What's the use! You should learn to be a father from those who really know about fatherhood!

Micio. You may be his father by birth, but I'm his father by upbringing and guidance.

Demea. You? Guidance?

Micio. If you continue in this way I'm going!

Demea. Is that so?

MICIO. Do I have to keep hearing the same thing all the time?

DEMEA (*serious*). I'm concerned.

MICIO. I'm concerned too. But, Demea, let us each worry about his own—you about one son, I about the other. If we are both to worry about both, it amounts to your asking back for the boy you gave me.

DEMEA (*hurt*). Now, Micio!

MICIO. That's the way it seems to me.

DEMEA. All right! If that's the way you want it! (*Getting angry again.*) Let him squander, let him ruin, let him go to hell! It's no concern of mine! But if I hear any word from now on——

MICIO. Demea, you're getting angry again?

DEMEA. You don't believe me? Am I asking back for what I gave you? But I'm worried. I'm not a stranger. If I object—— All right, I'll stop. You want me to take care of one, I'll take care of one. And thank the gods, *he* is the way I want him to be. That fellow of yours, he'll realize some day—but I don't want to say anything harsher against him.   (*Exit.*)

MICIO. What he says is not wholly without foundation, and yet it is not the whole story. And I won't say that this doesn't bother me. But I don't want to show him I'm worried. For this is the kind of man he is. Though I try to calm him down and oppose him vigorously and restrain him, yet he hardly takes it the way a normal human being should. But if I were to encourage him in his anger I would surely go crazy with him.

And yet Aeschinus does carry on a little too much in this area of activity, it seems to me. What courtesan has he not made love to? To which has he not given presents? But lately— I suppose he began to get fed up with all of them—he said he wanted to get married. I was hoping his youthful ardor had cooled down. I was happy. And now he's at it again! Yet, whatever it is, I want to find out and I'll meet him if he is in the Forum.   (*Exit toward Forum.*)

Act II

(A scuffle is taking place in front of the house in which Aeschinus lives with Micio. Aeschinus is trying to take Bacchis into the house and Sannio is trying to prevent him. Aeschinus' slave PARMENO assists his master.)

SANNIO *(screaming)*. I beg you, fellow citizens, help a poor innocent man! Come to my aid, I'm helpless!

AESCHINUS *(to BACCHIS)*. Take it easy! *(Gesturing toward door.)* Now, stand right there. Why do you keep looking back? There's no danger. He won't touch you as long as I'm near you.

SANNIO. I certainly will, in spite of all of you.

AESCHINUS *(to BACCHIS)*. Though he is a scoundrel, he won't take a chance of getting another beating today.

SANNIO. Aeschinus, listen to me. So you won't say you were ignorant of my character—I am a procurer.

AESCHINUS. I know.

SANNIO. But a man whose integrity is as good as anyone's anywhere. And though you may later try to clear yourself by saying you didn't intend to do this harm to me, I don't give *this* for it. *(Snaps his fingers.)* Take my word for it, I'll sue you in court for this. I know my rights! And you will not be able to clear yourself with words for the wrong you've done me in fact. I know the kind of excuses you fellows give: *(Mimicking.)* "I'm sorry. I wish it hadn't happened. I'll give you my oath you didn't deserve this shameful and undeserving treatment." Meanwhile I've already been treated outrageously and undeservedly.

AESCHINUS *(to BACCHIS, disregarding SANNIO)*. Go right ahead and open the door.

SANNIO. You don't give a hang for what I just said?

AESCHINUS *(to BACCHIS, as before)*. Now you, go right in.

SANNIO. Well, I won't let her. *(Tries to block door.)*

AESCHINUS *(to PARMENO)*. Go over there, Parmeno. *(Pointing or gesturing to where Sannio is standing.)* You went too far on that side. Stand here, next to him. There, that's what I want. Now don't take your eyes off mine, so that if I nod there will be no delay in your giving him a punch in the jaw.

SANNIO. I'd like to see him try it!

AESCHINUS (*nods to* PARMENO, *who punches* SANNIO). There, take that! Let the woman go!

SANNIO (*rubbing his jaw*). Ow! What an outrage!

AESCHINUS. He'll give you another if you don't watch out. (PARMENO *hits* SANNIO *again.*)

SANNIO. Ow! My poor face!

AESCHINUS (*to* PARMENO). I didn't nod. But it's better to make a mistake in that direction. (*To* BACCHIS.) Now go in.
(*Exit* BACCHIS *into house.*)

SANNIO (*to* AESCHINUS). What's this all about? Do you think you're the king around here, Aeschinus?

AESCHINUS. If I were, you'd get decorated the way you really deserve.

SANNIO. What did I ever do to you?

AESCHINUS. Nothing.

SANNIO. So? Don't you know what I am?

AESCHINUS. I don't want to know.

SANNIO. Did I ever touch anything of yours?

AESCHINUS. If you had, you would really be out of luck.

SANNIO. Why should *you* have her? She's mine! I paid good money for her. Answer me.

AESCHINUS. It's better not to have an argument here in front of the house. But if you continue to bother me, you'll be dragged inside and get the life lashed out of you!

SANNIO. Lashes? For a free man?

AESCHINUS. That's what you'll get.

SANNIO. You filthy crook! And they say that in this town liberty is equal for all!

AESCHINUS. If you've finished raging, listen to me now, if you don't mind.

SANNIO. Have I been raging, or have you been raging at me?

AESCHINUS. Never mind that and let's get down to business.

SANNIO. What business? What should I get down to?

AESCHINUS. Are you willing now for me to tell you what concerns you?

SANNIO. I'm willing, as long as it's fair.

AESCHINUS (*sarcastically*). Well, a pimp, and he doesn't want me to speak unfairly!

SANNIO (*defiantly*). Pimp I am; the corrupter of all young men, I admit—a perjurer, a plague, but I've never done *you* any harm.

AESCHINUS. By Hercules, that's all that's lacking!

SANNIO. Please, get back to business, as you began, Aeschinus.

AESCHINUS. *You* bought her for twenty minas—may you live to regret it! I'll give you the same amount for her.

SANNIO (*shocked*). What? Suppose I don't want to sell her to you, will you force me?

AESCHINUS (*confidently*). Not at all!

SANNIO. I was afraid you would.

AESCHINUS. And I don't think she *should* be sold. She's a free woman. And I'm going to court with a formal claim that she is freeborn. Now you decide which you like better, to accept the money or prepare your case in court. Think it over till I come back, pimp. (*Exit into house.*)

SANNIO. Oh, Supreme Jupiter! I'm not at all surprised that people go crazy from the wrongs they suffer! He dragged me out of my house, he beat me up, and against my will he took away my slave girl. I'm still in pain from the five hundred blows in the face and more he gave me. (*Sarcastically.*) And in return for these injuries he demands that the girl I bought should be handed over to him at cost price! (*Still sarcastic.*) Surely, since he has well earned her, let him have her! He's only demanding his rights! (*Back to normal worried tone.*) Well, all right, I'm willing. If he only pays me the money I spent. But I can make this prediction: When I say I'm willing to give her to him at that price, there will be a witness on the spot to say I sold her. Then I can't sue for damages. About the money—I'll see it in my dreams. He'll say, "Soon. Come back tomorrow!" This also I can bear, provided he finally pays me, though it's unjust.

(*Resignedly.*) But I suppose that's the way things are. When you get into this business you have to accept and bear silently the wrongs young men do to you.

But nobody will pay me. I'm just wasting my time with these calculations.

(*Enter* SYRUS, *still talking to* AESCHINUS *as he leaves the house.*)

SYRUS. Well, no need to say more. I'll go over to him. I'll get him to accept eagerly, I assure you, and even to say he has been well treated. (*To* SANNIO.) What's this, Sannio? I hear you had a bit of a row with my master?

SANNIO. I never saw a more unevenly matched contest than the one between us. We both got quite worn out—he with beating and I with getting the beating!

SYRUS. Your fault!

SANNIO. What was I to do?

SYRUS. You ought to have given in to the young man.

SANNIO. How could I have given in better when I kept giving him my face to slap all day?

SYRUS. Come on, you know what I mean. There are times when it's better to forget about money. The profit is sometimes greater that way. Bah! You were afraid that if you gave up a little of your rights and gave in to the young man, you wouldn't make any profit, you utter fool, you!

SANNIO. I don't spend my money on hopes.

SYRUS. You'll never make your fortune. Go on! You don't know how to lead people on.

SANNIO. I suppose that way is better. But I have never reached such a pitch of cunning that I could keep from preferring to take what I could get at the moment.

SYRUS (*flatteringly*). Come on, I know your mind. As if twenty minas mean anything to you, as long as you gratify him! (*Slyly.*) Besides, there is a rumor that you are about to leave for Cyprus——

SANNIO. Hm.

SYRUS. ——and that you have bought many things here to take there—that a ship has been hired. So I can understand that you can't quite make up your mind now. When you get back from there, I expect, you will attend to this.

SANNIO (*firmly*). I won't stir a foot anywhere! (*Aside.*) They've got me, by Hercules! So this was the hope with which they started!

SYRUS (*aside*). He's scared. I've given him something to worry about.

SANNIO (*aside*). The enormity of it! Look at that! He has caught me just at the crucial moment! I've bought many slave girls, and there are other things that I am taking from here to Cyprus. If I don't get there for the market, I'll suffer enormous losses. But if I let this matter go now and then attend to it when I get back, I'll get nothing. The matter will have grown cold. They'll say, "Now you've finally come? Why did you let it go? Where were you?" So it's better to lose something now than to stay here so long or sue for it later.

SYRUS. Well, have you finally figured up what you think is coming to you?

SANNIO. Is this the right way for him to act? That Aeschinus should start a thing like this! To try to grab her from me by force!

SYRUS (*aside*). He's weakening. (*Aloud.*) I have this one

suggestion. See if you like it. Rather than run the risk, Sannio, of all or nothing, split the difference. He'll scrape together ten minas somewhere.

SANNIO (*indignantly*). Oh god! Now there is even doubt about whether I get my investment back! Doesn't he have any shame? He's loosened all my teeth. My head is all one swelling from his blows. And on top of that he cheats me. I'm not going anywhere!

SYRUS (*blandly*). As you please. Anything else you want before I go?

SANNIO. Yes, by Hercules, this at least I beg of you, Syrus. However this thing turns out, rather than to go to court, let me get back what is mine, at least the money I paid for her, Syrus. (*Ingratiatingly.*) I know you've not previously enjoyed my friendship, but you'll find I have a good memory and am grateful. (*Hands* SYRUS *a tip.*)

SYRUS. I'll do the best I can. (*Aside.*) But I see Ctesipho. He is happy about his girl friend. (*Turns from* SANNIO.)

SANNIO. What about what I asked you?

SYRUS. Just wait awhile.

(*Enter* CTESIPHO *from the Forum, looking happy.*)

CTESIPHO (*aside*). You are happy to receive a favor from anyone when you need it, but the real joy is when a person who is obligated to do so, does you a favor. Oh, Brother, Brother, what can I say in your praise? I know full well that I can never praise you so highly but that your goodness would surpass it! So let me just say that I think I have this one thing that no one else has, a brother second to none in his mastery of the finest qualities.

SYRUS (*catching sight of* CTESIPHO, *affectionately*). Ah, Ctesipho!

CTESIPHO (*cordially*). Ah, Syrus! Where's Aeschinus?

SYRUS (*pointing to house*). In there. He's waiting for you at home.

CTESIPHO (*giving a sound of joy*). Hm!

SYRUS. What is it?

CTESIPHO. What is it? Through his efforts I'm really living! What a wonderful fellow! My good comes first with him. Accusations, bad reputation, my troubles and my delinquencies he takes upon himself. Nothing can beat him! (*Sound of the door.*) Is that the door I hear?

SYRUS. Wait, wait! He is coming out.

(*Enter* AESCHINUS *from the house.*)

AESCHINUS. Where is that heathen?

SANNIO (*aside*). He's looking for me. Is he bringing anything out? Damn! I see nothing!

AESCHINUS (*to* CTESIPHO, *disregarding* SANNIO). Ah, just in time! You're the very one I was looking for. Well, Ctesipho? Everything is safe. You can really put an end to your sadness.

CTESIPHO (*warmly*). I really can when I have a brother like you. Oh my dear Aeschinus, my dear brother! (*Embracing him.*) Ah, I'm afraid to praise you any further to your face. You will think I'm doing it to flatter you rather than because I am grateful.

AESCHINUS (*affectionately*). Go on, don't be foolish! As if we don't know one another well enough now. The only thing that grieves me is that we got to know one another so late, and that matters almost reached the point where no one could have helped you, even if they had wanted to.

CTESIPHO. I was ashamed.

AESCHINUS (*affectionately and elder-brotherly*). Ah, that was foolishness, not shame! To think you almost left the country because of such a little thing! Shame on you! I pray the gods it never happens.

CTESIPHO (*abashed*). I was wrong.

AESCHINUS (*to* SYRUS). What does our friend Sannio finally say?

SYRUS. He's softened.

AESCHINUS. I'll go to the Forum to get money to pay him. (*To* CTESIPHO.) You go inside to her, Ctesipho.

SANNIO (*to* SYRUS). Syrus, keep at him.

SYRUS (*to* AESCHINUS). Let's go. For *he* (*Indicating* SANNIO.) is in a hurry to get to Cyprus.

SANNIO. Not quite as much in a hurry as you wish. I'm still here, I've got plenty of time.

SYRUS (*to* SANNIO). You'll get your money. Don't be afraid.

SANNIO. But all of it!

SYRUS. You'll get all of it. Just keep quiet and come along.

SANNIO. I'm coming. (*Exit* SANNIO *following* AESCHINUS; SYRUS *about to leave.*)

CTESIPHO. Hey, hey, Syrus!

SYRUS. What is it?

CTESIPHO. I beg you, by Hercules, pay off that filthy rascal as soon as possible, so he won't get more irritated, or then this thing will somehow leak out to my father and then I'll die of shame!

SYRUS. It won't. Don't worry. You go inside and enjoy yourself with her, and order the dining couches spread for us and everything else prepared. And when this business is transacted, I'll return home with provisions.

CTESIPHO. Yes, please do. And since this has turned out well, let's have a wonderful time today!

(*Exeunt,* CTESIPHO *indoors, and* SYRUS *after* AESCHINUS *toward Forum.*)

Act III

(*Enter from her house Sostrata, a matron of more than middle age, and her elderly nurse, Canthara, a slave. Inside, Sostrata's pregnant daughter, Pamphila, is beginning to have labor pains, and her moans are heard from time to time.*)

SOSTRATA (*worried*). Tell me, Nurse, what is going to happen now?

CANTHARA. What's going to happen, you ask? Everything will be all right, I expect, by Pollux.

SOSTRATA (*to* PAMPHILA, *inside, consolingly*). The pains are only beginning, dear.

CANTHARA (*to* SOSTRATA). You act as though you had never attended a pregnancy, as if you never gave birth yourself. There's nothing to be afraid of.

SOSTRATA (*worriedly*). Oh, god! I have no one. We are all alone! And Geta isn't here, and I have no one to send for the midwife or to summon Aeschinus.

CANTHARA. Oh, he will be here soon. Not one day goes by but he comes here.

SOSTRATA. He is the only one who can help me in my troubles.

CANTHARA. Under the circumstances, things could hardly have turned out better than they did, considering that when she was seduced *he* was the one involved—such a fine, good-natured young man of such an important family.

SOSTRATA. Yes, you're certainly right. I pray the gods keep him safe for us.

(*Enter* GETA *at a distance, coming from Forum. The women see him, but he does not notice them.*)

GETA (*agitated*). Now is the time when even if everybody should join together in planning a way out of this calamity that has fallen on me, my mistress, and her daughter, they wouldn't be able to do any good. So many obstacles have suddenly loomed up around us that it is impossible to get out from under: violence, poverty, injustice, helplessness, disgrace! What an age this is! What crimes are committed in it! People have no respct for religion and morality, and he—what an impious scoundrel!

SOSTRATA (*alarmed*). The gods help a poor woman! What's wrong? Why is Geta running in such alarm?

GETA. His promise, his oath, pity means nothing to him and doesn't stop him! And the fact that she is about to give birth—the poor girl whom he shamefully seduced by violence—that doesn't bother him at all!

SOSTRATA. I just can't make out what he is saying.

CANTHARA. Please, let us get closer, Sostrata.

GETA. God! I can hardly control myself—I'm so burnt up with anger! There is nothing I'd like better than to come face to face with that whole family while my grief and anger are still fresh. If I could only take vengeance the way I want to I'd consider that sufficient punishment. (*Fiercely.*) First I would snuff out the life of the old man himself—he begot that criminal. Then that instigator Syrus—what a wreck I would make of him! I'd grab him by the middle, lift him up in the air, and smash him on his head right to the ground, so that his brains would spatter over the street! And the young man himself—I would tear out his eyes and then I would send him flying head first! The others—I would hurl them, drive them, seize them, beat them and lay them flat! But I'd better hurry and tell my mistress this terrible news!

SOSTRATA. Let's call him. (*Calling.*) Geta!

GETA. Huh! Whoever you are, let me alone.

SOSTRATA. It's me, Sostrata!

GETA (*turning around*). Where is she? (*Noticing her.*) You're just the one I was looking for. I wanted to see you. You showed up just in time, Mistress.

SOSTRATA (*in alarm*). What is it? Why do you tremble so?

GETA (*sighing*). Ah, me! (*Keeps moaning.*)

SOSTRATA. Why do you hurry, dear Geta? Catch your breath.

GETA. Utterly!

SOSTRATA. What does this "utterly" mean?

GETA. We are ruined! We're finished!

SOSTRATA. So speak up, I beg you! What is it?

GETA (*with an expression of despair*). Ah!

SOSTRATA. What do you mean "Ah," Geta?

GETA. He has deserted our family!

SOSTRATA (*frantic*). Oh! I'm dying! Why?

GETA. He has fallen in love with someone else!

SOSTRATA. Oh, my god!

GETA. And he doesn't hide it either. He eloped with her from a procurer—openly!

SOSTRATA. Are you really certain of this?

GETA. Certain! I saw it with my own eyes, Sostrata.

SOSTRATA (*in despair and weeping*). Oh, the troubles I have! What can you believe now? Or whom can you believe? Our Aeschinus—who was our whole life? Who was our only hope of salvation? Who used to swear he could never live one day without her? Who said he would place the child in his father's arms and beg him to let him marry her?

GETA. Mistress, stop your crying and consider rather what has to be done next about this. Should we just accept it or should we tell someone?

CANTHARA (*disapproving, in shocked tones*). Oh no! My dear man, are you crazy? Do you think this should be made known to *anyone?*

GETA. I don't like the idea. In the first place the matter itself indicates that he has developed unfriendly feelings toward us. Now, if we announce it openly, he will deny it. I'm sure of it. (*To* SOSTRATA.) Your good name, your daughter's life will be in jeopardy! Then, even if he should confess completely it will not be worthwhile marrying her to him since he is in love with another girl. Therefore, no matter how, it must be kept quiet.

SOSTRATA (*determinedly*). Ah, not on your life! I won't do it!

GETA. What will you do?

SOSTRATA. I'll make it known.

CANTHARA. Uh! My dear Sostrata, consider what you're doing.

SOSTRATA. Things can't be worse than they are right now. First of all she has no dowry. Then, on top of that, what was almost as good as a dowry, she has lost. She can't be offered in marriage as a virgin. This is the only thing left for us to do: Face him with it. If he starts to make denials, I have some evidence—a ring that he lost here. Finally, Geta, since I know in my heart that I am not to blame—far from it—and no money transaction nor anything else unworthy of her or me has taken place, I'll go to court.

GETA. Well, if that's the way you want it. I give in, since your suggestion is better.

SOSTRATA (*to* GETA). Go as quickly as possible, and tell

Hegio, our next of kin, the whole story, from beginning to end. He was the best friend of my husband Simulus and he loved us very much.

GETA. Yes, by Hercules, there is no one else to look after us.

SOSTRATA. You, my dear Canthara, run, hurry, fetch the midwife so that when we need her there will be no delay.

(GETA *and* CANTHARA *go off on their errands.* SOSTRATA *re-enters the house.*)

(DEMEA *enters from Square toward* MICIO'S *house.*)

DEMEA (*angry*). Damn it! I've just heard that my son Ctesipho was involved with Aeschinus in the abduction. That's all I need to complete my misery, if he can lead the one who was still good for something into delinquency! But where should I look for him? I suppose he's taken him into some dive somewhere. That filthy lecher has corrupted him! I'm sure of it. (SYRUS *approaches.*) But there I see Syrus coming. Now I'll find out from him where he is. But, by Hercules, he's one of the gang. If he realizes that I'm looking for Ctesipho, he'll never tell me, the scoundrel. I won't let on that that's what I want.

SYRUS (*aside*). We've just told old Micio the whole thing, exactly as it happened. I never saw anyone more pleased!

DEMEA (*overhearing*). Oh Jupiter! The folly of the man!

SYRUS. He praised his son. To me who had advised him in this, he gave thanks.

DEMEA. I'll burst!

SYRUS. He counted out the money on the spot. Besides, he gave me half a mina to go marketing. That's the way I like to see money spent!

DEMEA (*aside, ironically*). Hm! Give him (*Pointing to* SYRUS.) the job if you want something properly taken care of.

SYRUS (*noticing* DEMEA). Ah Demea, I hadn't noticed you. What's doing?

DEMEA. What's doing? I just can't stop wondering at your conduct, yours and the others.

SYRUS (*lightly, purposely mistaking* DEMEA'S *meaning*). Damn foolish, isn't it? I'll tell you the truth, it's absurd! (*Calling into the house.*) Clean the rest of the fish, Dromo. Let that big eel play in the water a while. When I get back he'll be boned, not before.

DEMEA. Such disgraceful conduct!

SYRUS. I don't like it either, and I often scream at them. (*Shouting to slaves inside.*) These salted fish, get them well soaked!

DEMEA. Gods help me! Is he doing it on purpose or does he think he'll be praised for it if he ruins a son? Oh, woe, woe, woe! I think I can see the day coming when he'll run away from home, without a penny, to enlist in the army somewhere.

SYRUS. Ah, Demea, that's what it means to be wise—not only to see what is right in front of your nose, but to anticipate what is going to happen in the future.

DEMEA. Is that music girl with you, eh?

SYRUS. She's inside.

DEMEA. You don't say? And is he going to keep her in the house?

SYRUS. I suppose so. He's crazy enough to.

DEMEA. To permit such goings on!

SYRUS. His father is easygoing to the point of foolishness and excessively permissive.

DEMEA. I'm ashamed and disgusted with my brother!

SYRUS (*flatteringly*). There is a big difference between the two of you—and I'm not saying this just because you're present—a big difference. You, every inch of you, are wisdom personified. He—his head is up in the clouds. Would you permit yours to do this kind of thing?

DEMEA. Would I permit him? Wouldn't I have smelled it out six months before he even started on anything?

SYRUS. You're telling *me* how sharp and wide-awake you are?

DEMEA. May my son only be the way he is now, that's all I ask.

SYRUS. As each one *wants* his son to be, that's the way he'll be.

DEMEA. What about him? Have you seen him today?

SYRUS. Your son? (*Aside, with a gesture.*) I'll drive him off to the country. (*To* DEMEA.) He's been in the country for some time, busy with something, I think.

DEMEA. Are you sure he's there?

SYRUS. I'm sure, I was the one who escorted him.

DEMEA. Very good. I was afraid he was hanging around here.

SYRUS. And he was quite angry.

DEMEA. What about?

SYRUS. He got into a quarrel with his brother in the Forum about the music girl.

DEMEA. You don't say?

SYRUS. My, he didn't shut up! For just as the money was being paid out he happened to come along unexpectedly. He began to shout, "Oh Aeschinus, that you should do such disgraceful things! That you should commit such acts unworthy of our family!"

DEMEA. Oh, I could cry with joy!

SYRUS. "You're not just wasting money," he said, "you're wasting your life!"

DEMEA. Heaven spare him, that's my hope! He is just like his ancestors!

SYRUS (*making a gesture indicating that he not only agrees with DEMEA, but would even go further*). Hwee!

DEMEA. Syrus, he's just filled with those good old maxims.

SYRUS (*making a gesture as if to say: You don't have to tell me!*). Phee! He's got somebody at home to teach him!

DEMEA. I make every effort. I overlook nothing. I train him. Finally I tell him to examine everybody's lives as if in a mirror. And to take other people as examples for himself. "This you should do!" I say.

SYRUS. Absolutely right!

DEMEA. "This you should avoid!"

SYRUS. Clever!

DEMEA. "This is praiseworthy!"

SYRUS. That's the way!

DEMEA. "This is wrong!"

SYRUS. Excellent!

DEMEA. And further——

SYRUS. I really don't have any time to listen to you now. I've found some fish that I like. I've got to be careful they don't spoil. For for us slaves this is as much a disgrace, Demea, as not to do the things you just mentioned. And as well as I can I instruct my fellow slaves with maxims of the same good old kind: "This is too salty. This is a little burned. This needs more washing. That's just right; remember to do it the same way next time." I advise them as carefully as I can according to *my* wisdom. Finally, Demea, I bid them look into the pans as into a mirror and advise them what has to be done. I realize that these things we do are trifles, but what can you do? You've got to take people as they come. Anything else you wish to say before I go?

DEMEA. Yes, you people should have better sense.

SYRUS. Are you going to the country now?

DEMEA. Right away.

SYRUS. Sure, what would you do here where if you did have something good to teach, no one would listen!

DEMEA. Well, I'll be off, since the one for whose sake I had come here has gone to the country. I concern myself with him alone since he is my responsibility. If this is the way his brother wants to be, let Micio himself look after *him*. (HEGIO *appears at a distance*.) But who is it that I see in the distance? Isn't it

Hegio, my fellow tribesman? [2] (*Peering.*) If I'm seeing right, it *is* he, by Hercules. Ah, he has been a friend of mine from boyhood on! Ah, by the good gods! We certainly have a shortage of citizens of that kind nowadays, men of the good old-fashioned virtues and dependability. You'd have to wait a long time before *he* started any trouble for the community. How happy I am when I see people of this kind still around. I'll wait for him so that I can greet and speak to him.

(HEGIO, *accompanied by* GETA, *approaches* SOSTRATA'S *house.*)

HEGIO (*shocked*). Oh, immortal gods, what a disgraceful thing, Geta! What are you telling me!

GETA. That's what happened.

HEGIO. From such a family such ungentlemanly and irresponsible actions! Oh Aeschinus, acting like that is certainly not something you learned from your father!

DEMEA. Evidently he has heard about the music girl. Now it upsets an outsider. To his father it doesn't mean a thing. Ah me! How I wish he were around and could hear this!

HEGIO. If they don't do what they are obliged to, they won't get away with it!

GETA. Our hopes are all in your hands, Hegio. You are the only one we have. You are our patron; you are our father. The old master, when he died, entrusted us to you. If you desert us, we are lost.

HEGIO. Don't say that! I certainly won't do that, nor could I do such a thing and still do my duty as a kinsman.

DEMEA. I'll approach. Hello, Hegio, I hope you are well.

HEGIO. Oh, I was looking for *you* particularly. Hello, Demea.

DEMEA. Why, what's the matter?

HEGIO. Your eldest son Aeschinus, the one you gave your brother for adoption, has done something which is neither good nor honorable.

DEMEA. What did he do?

HEGIO. You know my friend Simulus—he was about our age.

DEMEA. Why, yes.

HEGIO. Aeschinus seduced his virgin daughter.

DEMEA (*horrified*). What!

HEGIO. Wait, you haven't heard the worst of it, Demea.

DEMEA. Is there anything more?

HEGIO. Yes, more. For what's done is done and has to be borne somehow. You know how these things happen—night, love, wine,

---

[2] For certain political, religious, and other community purposes, the Athenians were divided into groupings called tribes. Members of the same tribe felt a certain kinship.

youth—it happens to people. When he realized what he had done he went to the girl's mother of his own accord, weeping, begging, pleading, giving his promise, swearing he would marry her. It was forgiven, it was hushed up, it was believed. The girl became pregnant from those embraces. Now she is in the ninth month, and that fine fellow—*he,* if you please, has found himself a music girl to live with. He's deserted the girl who is pregnant.

DEMEA. Are you certain of what you are saying?

HEGIO. The girl's mother is available, the girl herself, the facts themselves, and also Geta, who is not a bad or incompetent man as slaves go. He keeps them going, he alone supports the whole family. Take him aside, tie him up, seek out the truth.

GETA. More than that—torture me,[3] by Hercules, if it isn't so, Demea. He won't deny it finally. Let me have him face to face.

DEMEA (*aside*). I'm ashamed! I don't know what to do or what to answer him.

PAMPHILA (*heard from inside the house in pain*). Oh, I can't stand it! The pains are killing me! Juno of childbirth, help me! Save me, I beg you!

HEGIO (*sympathetically and pityingly*). Hm! (*To* GETA.) She must be giving birth now, I suppose?

GETA. Certainly, Hegio.

HEGIO (*meditatively*). Hm! (*To* DEMEA.) She is begging you people to keep your word now, Demea—that you should do voluntarily what obligation compels you. I pray the gods that you will do what is proper. But if your family's intentions are otherwise, Demea, I'll defend her and her dead father with all the power at my command. He was my kinsman. We were brought up together from childhood. We were together in military service and at home. We both bore dire poverty together. Therefore I'll move heaven and earth, I'll get what they want. I'll go to court if I have to! I'll even give up my life rather than abandon them! What's your answer?

DEMEA (*uncomfortable*). I'll see my brother and talk to him, Hegio.

HEGIO. But, Demea, make sure you keep *this* clearly in your mind. You people are very well off, you people are very powerful, rich, fortunate and well known. Therefore you people especially ought to know what is fair and right and do it willingly. (*Turns to go.*)

---

[3] The reference is to a Roman rather than to a Greek practice. Since slaves were legally not persons but property, their testimony was not admissible in court. The Romans, however, sometimes resorted to torture in order to get information from them, since they assumed that slaves would never willingly inform on their masters.

DEMEA. Come back. (HEGIO *turns back*.) Everything that's fair and proper will be done.

HEGIO (*pleased, but dignified*). Very nice of you to do it. (*To* GETA.) Geta, lead me in to Sostrata.

(*Exit into house with* GETA.)

DEMEA (*aside*). I *told* him this would happen! If only this were the end of the matter! But—this kind of excess freedom *has* to end in great disaster! I'll look for my brother to spew all this out on him. (*Exit toward Forum*.)

(SHORT INTERVAL)

HEGIO (*coming out of* SOSTRATA'S *house*). So, you can rest easy, Sostrata, and you can relieve her mind as much as you can. I'm going to meet Micio if he is in the Forum and tell him what happened in detail. If he is going to do what his duty requires, let him act. But if his intentions on this matter are otherwise, let him give me an answer so that I will know as soon as possible what to do. (*Goes off toward Forum*.)

Act IV

(*Ctesipho comes out of Micio's house in conversation with Syrus*.)

CTESIPHO. You say my father has gone to the country?

SYRUS. Yes. Some time ago.

CTESIPHO. You really mean it?

SYRUS. He's at the farm. Right now, I suppose, he must be working away in the fields.

CTESIPHO. If only he were. If only he'd get so tired out—not that I wish him any harm—that he wouldn't be able to get out of bed for three days straight.

SYRUS. I hope so—maybe even longer than that, if possible!

CTESIPHO. Yes, for I so desperately wish to spend this day as I began it—in perpetual happiness! And that country—I hate it just because it is so near. If it were further away night would overtake him before he could return again. As it is, when he sees I'm not there he'll come running back here. I'm sure of it. He will ask where I've been, saying: "I haven't seen you all day." What will I say?

Syrus. Nothing comes to mind?

Ctesipho (*desperately*). Nothing *ever* does.

Syrus. So much the worse for you! Doesn't your family have a client, a friend, someone you owe a visit?

Ctesipho. We have. Then what?

Syrus. Then you might have been helping them out with something.

Ctesipho. When I actually did not? It can't be done.

Syrus. It can.

Ctesipho. By day, maybe. But if I spend the night here, what reason should I give, Syrus?

Syrus. Ah, how I wish it were the custom to help our friends at night. Well, you take it easy. I know very well the way his mind works. When his temper is at its worst, I make him as gentle as a lamb.

Ctesipho. How?

Syrus. He loves to hear himself praised on your account. I make you a god in his eyes. I speak about your good qualities.

Ctesipho. Mine?

Syrus. Yours. Right away tears spring to his eyes with joy. He's like a child. (*Suddenly notices* Demea.) Uh-oh! There you are!

Ctesipho. What is it?

Syrus. Speak of the devil!

Ctesipho. My father?

Syrus. It's him all right!

Ctesipho. Syrus, what do we do?

Syrus. You just hide inside. I'll handle it.

Ctesipho. If he asks you anything, you haven't seen me anywhere. You understand?

Syrus. Can't you stop it?

Ctesipho *runs into* Micio's *house and conceals himself within the doorway. Enter* Demea.)

Demea (*aside*). I am out of luck! First I can't find my brother anywhere at all. Then while I'm looking for him, I see a hired man from my farm. He says my son is not in the country. And I don't know what to do!

Ctesipho (*from doorway, whispering*). Syrus.

Syrus. What is it?

Ctesipho. Is he looking for me?

Syrus. Yes!

Ctesipho. Oh god!

Syrus. Now cheer up.

Demea. By Pollux, what bad luck! I just can't understand it.

Unless this is what I was born for, to bear troubles. I'm the first one to sense trouble for us, I'm the first to find anything out, and again I'm the first to report it. If anything happens, I'm the only one to feel bad about it.

SYRUS (*aside*). He makes me laugh. He says he is the first one to know. He's the only one who *doesn't* know everything!

DEMEA. Now that I'm back, I'll go see, maybe my brother has returned.

CTESIPHO (*from inside door, peeking out*). Syrus, make sure he doesn't come bursting right in here!

SYRUS. Will you keep quiet?! I'll watch out.

CTESIPHO. By Hercules, I won't leave this up to you today. I'll shut myself up with her in some inside room. That's the safest thing.

SYRUS. Go on! But I'll get rid of him.

DEMEA (*seeing* SYRUS). There's that scoundrel Syrus.

SYRUS (*pretending to be talking to himself*). No, by Hercules, I just can't take it any more, and there is nobody who can, even if he wants to, if things go on at this rate! I just want to know how many masters I have! What a miserable life this is!

DEMEA (*aside*). What is he growling about? What does he want? (*To* SYRUS.) Tell me, my good man, is my brother at home?

SYRUS. What's this damn "my good man" business? I'm as good as dead.

DEMEA. What's the matter with *you?*

SYRUS. You're asking? Ctesipho pretty nearly killed me and that music girl with his fists! (*Groans.*)

DEMEA. Hm? What are you talking about?

SYRUS (*whining, showing his lip*). Here, look how he split my lip!

DEMEA. What for?

SYRUS. He says it was at my instigation that she was bought.

DEMEA. Didn't you just tell me that you had escorted him to the country?

SYRUS. I did. But he came back later raging. He didn't pull any punches. He ought to be ashamed to beat up an old man! Why I carried him in my arms when he was a child only so big.

DEMEA. Good for him. (*Proudly.*) Ctesipho, you take after your father. Now that's what I call a man!

SYRUS. You praise him? He'd better keep his hands to himself in the future if he's wise.

DEMEA. Bravely done!

SYRUS (*sarcastically*). Very, because he was victorious over a wretched woman and me, a poor slave, who did not dare to hit back. Sure, very brave!

DEMEA. He couldn't have done better! Just as I do, he understands that you are at the head of this business. But is my brother inside?

SYRUS (*still acting aggrieved*). He isn't.

DEMEA. I'm trying to think where I can find him.

SYRUS (*pretending sullenness*). I know where he is, but I won't tell anybody today.

DEMEA (*sputtering angrily*). Hey, what's this you say?

SYRUS (*sullen*). Just so.

DEMEA (*raising his staff*). You'll get your head smashed in!

SYRUS (*pretending the answer has been forced out of him, reluctantly*). Well, I don't know the man's name but I know the place where he is.

DEMEA. So tell me the place.

SYRUS. Do you know the arcade by the butcher shop straight down this way?

DEMEA. Certainly, I know it.

SYRUS (*pointing and gesturing*). Pass down this way, straight up the street. When you get there, there is a hill before you. Head down it. Then on this side you'll see a little shrine. There is an alley next to it.

DEMEA. Which one do you mean?

SYRUS. The one that has a wild fig tree nearby.

DEMEA. Yes, I know.

SYRUS. Go straight through here.

DEMEA. But that's a blind alley!

SYRUS. That's right by Hercules! Hah! What do you think of me? I made a mistake! Go back again to the arcade. Actually it will be much nearer and you will have less chance of losing your way. Do you know the house of the rich man, Cratinus?

DEMEA. I do.

SYRUS. When you have passed by it, go straight down the street to the left. When you come to the temple of Diana, go to the right. Before you come to the city gate at the pool itself, there is a small mill and directly opposite it is a workshop. That's where he is.

DEMEA. What is he doing there?

SYRUS. He is having sun chairs made with oaken feet.

DEMEA. So you people can sit in the sun and get drunk! Very fine! But I'd better hurry and get to him.

(*Hurries off along lane on left.*)

SYRUS. Go on, go! I'll give you a work-out today the way you deserve, you old bag of bones.

What the hell is keeping Aeschinus? The dinner will be ruined! As for Ctesipho, he's completely engrossed in lovemaking. I'm going to look out for myself now. I'll go off and help myself to each and every one of the delicious dishes for dinner and I'll enjoy this day doing a little leisurely drinking.

(*Exit into house.*)

(*Enter* MICIO *and* HEGIO *together from Forum.*)

MICIO. I find no reason why I should be praised so highly, Hegio. I'm just doing my duty. I'm correcting a wrong for which we are responsible. Unless you imagined that I am one of those people who think that a wrong is being done *them* if you complain of a wrong which they themselves have done and they blame you in addition. Because I don't act that way, you thank me?

HEGIO (*smiling*). Ah, not at all. It didn't enter my mind that you are otherwise than you are. But I would appreciate it if you would come in with me to the girl's mother and tell her exactly what you told me—that this suspicion has arisen because of Aeschinus' brother, that the music girl is his brother's.

MICIO. If that's what you think is the right thing to do and if it is necessary, let's go.

HEGIO. You are very kind. That way you will relieve her mind. She's been just wasting away with grief and misery, and you will have done your duty. But if you think otherwise, I'll tell her myself what you've said to me.

MICIO. No, no, I'll go.

HEGIO. You are very kind. For some reason or other, people whose circumstances are not too favorable are more suspicious. They are the more likely to take everything as an insult. Because of their helplessness they always believe they are being made fools of. Therefore it will have a greater calming effect if you see her and clear yourself in person.

MICIO. What you say is right and true.

HEGIO. So, please follow me this way inside.

MICIO. Certainly.   (*They enter* SOSTRATA'S *house.*)

(*Enter* AESCHINUS *from Forum.*)

AESCHINUS (*looking very distraught*). I'm in a torment of emotions! That this terrible calamity should suddenly have fallen on me! It's so bad that I don't know what to do or how to act! My arms and legs are feeble with dread. My heart is frozen with fear. I can't settle on any plan in my mind. Ah, how shall I free myself from this anguish? This great suspicion has now fallen on me—not that I don't deserve it.

Sostrata believes that I bought this music girl for myself. The old nurse indicated this to me. For when she was on her way for the midwife, I happened to see her. At once I approached her and asked how Pamphila was getting along: Has her time come? Is that why you are going for the midwife? She screamed out, "Get away, get away, Aeschinus! Enough of your fine talk! You've fooled us enough! Our trust in you has deceived us enough!"

"Hm? What is this all about, please?" I asked her. "Good-bye and good luck!" she said. "Keep the girl that pleases you!"

I realized at once that they suspected me, but I controlled myself anyway, so as not to tell the old chatterbox anything about my brother and have it all come out in the open.

Now what should I do? Should I tell her she belongs to my brother—a matter which must not by any means get out. Well, never mind. It can be done in such a way that it won't get out. But I'm afraid they won't believe it. So many of the facts point to me. *I* was the one who seized her. *I* paid the money. She was taken to my house.

I admit that I was at fault too in this affair with Pamphila. What a fool I was not to have told my father the whole story exactly as it happened. I could have persuaded him to let me marry her if I had asked him. But I kept putting it off till now. Now at last rouse yourself, Aeschinus! But this comes first. I'll go over to them to clear myself. I'll approach the door. (*Approaches, raises his hand to knock.*) Oh, god! I shiver when I start to knock. (*Knocks.*) Hello! Hello! It's Aeschinus! Open the door, someone! (*Listens.*) Somebody is coming out. (*A sound of footsteps from the inside door.*) I'll slip in here. (*Goes to side.*)

(Micio, *coming out, finishes his conversation with* Sostrata.)

Micio. Do as I said, Sostrata. I'll get Aeschinus to tell him what we have arranged here. (*Aside.*) But who was knocking at the door?

Aeschinus (*aside*). By Hercules, it's my father! I'm sunk!

Micio (*sees him*). Aeschinus!

Aeschinus. What are you doing here?

Micio. Was it you knocking at the door. (Aeschinus *does not answer. Aside.*) He keeps quiet. Why don't I have a little fun with him for a while? It will serve him right, since he was not willing to tell me anything about this. (*To* Aeschinus.) You don't answer?

Aeschinus. *I* didn't knock on that door, as far as I know.

MICIO. So? I was wondering what business you had here. (*Aside.*) He is blushing. Everything will be all right.

AESCHINUS. Tell me, please, Father, what business did *you* have in there?

MICIO. *I* had none. But a friend of mine has just brought me in from the Forum to act as his counselor.

AESCHINUS. What about?

MICIO. I'll tell you. Some poor women live here—I don't think you know them. In fact, I'm sure of it. For they only moved in recently.

AESCHINUS. So what about them?

MICIO. There's a girl with her mother.

AESCHINUS. Go on.

MICIO. The girl's father is dead. This friend of mine is her next of kin. According to the law, he is supposed to marry her.

AESCHINUS. Good god!

MICIO. What's the matter?

AESCHINUS. Nothing. It's all right. Go on.

MICIO. He came to take her away with him. He lives in Miletus.

AESCHINUS. You mean to take the girl away with him?

MICIO. Yes.

AESCHINUS (*Aside*). I'm losing my mind! (*Aloud.*) What about the women? What do they say?

MICIO. What do you think they say? Nothing, of course. The mother *has* mentioned that she has just borne a child by some other man, but she didn't name the man. This other fellow has first claim, she said; the girl doesn't have to be given to my friend.

AESCHINUS. Well, doesn't this seem right to you?

MICIO. No!

AESCHINUS. Why not? Is he actually going to take her away, Father?

MICIO. Why shouldn't he?

AESCHINUS (*with emotion*). You and your friend are being very harsh, pitiless and, Father, even if I say it more openly, rather uncivilized.

MICIO. Why?

AESCHINUS. You're asking me? How do you think the poor fellow who was her lover is going to feel—who for all I know, poor fellow, still loves her desperately—when he sees her being torn from him and led away from his sight? That's an awful thing to do, Father!

MICIO. Why so? Who betrothed her? Who gave her away? To

whom was she married and when? Was the father of the groom there to give his consent? Why marry a girl whom his family doesn't know?

AESCHINUS. Was a girl of that age supposed to sit at home and wait until a relative came here all the way from Miletus? That's what you should have said, Father, and that's the position you should have defended.

MICIO. Ridiculous! Should I speak against the case which I have come to support? But why is it our concern, Aeschinus? What do we have to do with them? Let's go. (AESCHINUS *starts to cry.*) What's this? Why the tears?

AESCHINUS. Father, I beg you, listen!

MICIO (*kindly*). Aeschinus, I've heard everything and I know. I love you. That's why the things you do are so much my concern.

AESCHINUS. I only wish I deserved your love, as long as you live, Father. I am so sorry and ashamed to look you in the face for the wrong I've done.

MICIO. I honestly believe you. For I know your noble nature. But I'm afraid you have been too careless. In what kind of city do you think you are living, tell me? You seduced a young girl whom you had absolutely no right to touch. That was your first big mistake; it was big but human. Other good men have often done likewise. But after that happened, tell me, did you take any consideration or exercise any foresight as to what should be done or how it should be done? If you yourself were ashamed to speak up, how could I find out? While you were hesitating, nine months passed. You made her and yourself miserable and the child as well, so far as it depended on you. Why? Did you think the gods would make it come out right for you while you slept? I hope you aren't as dilatory about other matters. (AESCHINUS *looks crestfallen.*) Cheer up. You'll marry her!

AESCHINUS (*skeptical*). Hm!

MICIO. Cheer up, I say!

AESCHINUS. Father, I beg you, you aren't fooling me, are you?

MICIO. I fool you? Why?

AESCHINUS (*still close to tears*). I don't know. I so desperately want it to be true that I'm all the more fearful.

MICIO. Go home and pray to the gods in preparation for escorting your bride in the wedding procession. Go on.

AESCHINUS (*becoming more cheerful*). What? A wedding? Right now?

MICIO. Right now.

AESCHINUS. Now?

Micio. As soon as possible.

Aeschinus. May all the gods hate me, Father, if I don't love you at this moment more than anything or anyone!

Micio. Well, and what about *her!*

Aeschinus (*effusively*). Just as much!

Micio (*ironically*). Very kind of you!

Aeschinus. But wait, where is that Milesian?

Micio. He's finished! He is gone. He has boarded ship. (Aeschinus *suddenly gets a look of understanding.*) But what are you waiting for?

Aeschinus (*affectionately*). Go on, Father! *You'd* better pray to the gods. I'm quite certain they will listen to you, for you are a much better man than I.

Micio. I'm going in to see to what preparations have to be made. You, do as I said, if you're wise. (*Exit* Micio *into his house.*)

Aeschinus (*pleased*). What do you think of that! Did you ever see a father act this way with a son? If he were my brother or my best friend, how could he comply more with my wishes? Isn't he to be loved? Isn't he to be pressed to my heart? Honestly! And that's why he caused me such worry: he is so kind that he wanted to let me know indirectly that I shouldn't by chance do anything against his wishes. Now that I know, I'll be careful. But let me hurry inside so that I won't cause any delay for the wedding.   (*Enters house.*)

(*Enter* Demea, *tired, from area of Forum.*)

Demea. I'm tired out with walking. May great Jupiter blast you, Syrus, together with your directions! I've dragged myself all over the town—to the city gate, to the pool—where haven't I been! And there wasn't any shop there and there wasn't anybody who said he saw my brother. Now I'm going to sit down and stay at home until he returns.

(Micio *comes out of his house speaking to his house slaves or to* Aeschinus.)

Micio. I'll go now. I'll tell them we are ready.

Demea. Why, there he is! (*To* Micio.) I've been looking for you for some time, Micio!

Micio. What about?

Demea (*angry and sneeringly*). I have some more disgraceful acts to report, monstrous ones, of that good young man of yours.

Micio (*pretending astonishment*). You don't say!

Demea. Unheard of, atrocious!

Micio (*with amused deprecation*). Oh, now!

Demea. You don't know what kind of a man he is!

MICIO. I know.

DEMEA. Ah, you fool, you imagine I'm talking about the music girl? This latest is an assault against a respectable girl—a citizen!

MICIO. I know.

DEMEA (*outraged*). Oh ho! You know and you allow it?

MICIO. What shouldn't I allow?

DEMEA. Tell me, you don't shout, you don't rage?

MICIO. No. Of course, I'd prefer——

DEMEA (*interrupting angrily*). A child has been born!

MICIO. Gods bless him!

DEMEA (*vehemently*). The girl hasn't a penny!

MICIO. I've heard.

DEMEA. And she is to be married without a dowry.

MICIO. Evidently.

DEMEA. What is going to happen now?

MICIO (*calmly*). Of course, what the situation demands. The girl will move to our place.

DEMEA (*desperate*). Oh, Jupiter! Does it have to be that way?

MICIO. What more could I do?

DEMEA (*angry*). What could you do? If you are not actually upset at the matter, you could at least pretend to be, like a decent human being!

MICIO. Why, I've already given my consent to the marriage. The matter is settled. The wedding is taking place. I've removed all fear. This is more like a decent human being.

DEMEA (*puzzled*). But are you really pleased that this happened, Micio?

MICIO. Not if I could change it. But since I can't now, I'm making the best of it. Life is just like a game of dice. If the throw most needed doesn't turn up, then you try to correct by your skill the throw that did turn up.

DEMEA. You a corrector? By your skill twenty minas have been wasted on a music girl, who ought to be got rid of somewhere as soon as possible—if not at cost price, then for nothing.

MICIO. She doesn't have to be and I am not particularly eager to sell her.

DEMEA. Then what are you going to do?

MICIO. She'll be at my home.

DEMEA. God help us! A wench and a respectable wife in one house?

MICIO. Why not?

DEMEA. Are you in your right mind?

MICIO. I think I am.

DEMEA. May the gods help me! Knowing your foolishness, I suppose you're doing it to have someone to sing and dance with!

MICIO (*leading him on*). Why not?

DEMEA. And the new bride will learn how to do this too?

MICIO. Of course!

DEMEA. And you'll dance between them holding a daisy chain!

MICIO (*mockingly*). That's a good idea.

DEMEA. A good idea?

MICIO (*humorously*). And you'll join us if necessary.

DEMEA. Ah me! Aren't you ashamed of all this?

MICIO (*good-humoredly*). Now come, Demea, stop being so angry and make yourself jolly and happy, as you should be at the wedding of a son. I'll go to see the bride's family. Then I'll come back here.   (*Exit into* SOSTRATA'S *house.*)

DEMEA. Oh Jupiter, what a life! What morals! What madness! A wife without a dowry, a music girl in the house, a home full of extravagance, a young man debauched with luxury, and an old man in his dotage! The goddess of Health and Sanity herself, even if she wanted to, can't help this family any more.

Act V

(*Some time later. Syrus, rather drunk, comes out of Micio's house.*)

SYRUS. By Pollux, Syrus my boy, you've taken care of yourself—sweetly—and you did the job nicely. (*Smiles and gives a drunken gesture of satisfaction.*) Go on! But now that I'm brimming over with everything, I'd like to take a nice little walk here. (*Walks drunkenly.*)

DEMEA (*shocked, aside*). Look at that, will you! An example of discipline!

SYRUS (*seeing* DEMEA). Why here is our old Demea! What's up? Why are you so gloomy?

DEMEA. Oh you rascal!

SYRUS. Now, now! You're just wasting words here, Old Wisdom!

DEMEA (*angrily and threateningly*). If you belonged to me——

SYRUS (*interrupting*). You'd be rich as Pluto, Demea, and you would get your affairs in order.

DEMEA (*disregarding* SYRUS' *words*).——I would make you an example for all.

SYRUS. What for? What have I done?

DEMEA. In that turmoil and in the midst of the greatest wrong-doing, you get drunk, you rascal, as if you'd had a great success!

SYRUS (*aside*). I sincerely wish I had not come out here.

(DROMO, *another slave of* MICIO, *comes out.*)

DROMO. Hey, Syrus, Ctesipho is asking for you—he wants you to come back in.

SYRUS (*trying to hush him up*). Get away!

(DROMO *returns inside.*)

DEMEA. What is he saying about Ctesipho?

SYRUS. Nothing.

DEMEA. Oh ho, you gallowsbird, is Ctesipho inside?

SYRUS. He isn't.

DEMEA. Why did he mention his name?

SYRUS. There's another one by that name, a little bit of a parasite. Do you know him?

DEMEA (*taking a step toward* MICIO's *house*). I'll soon know.

SYRUS (*tries to block him*). What are you doing? Where are you going?

DEMEA. Let me go!

SYRUS. Don't, I tell you! (*Tries to hold him.*)

DEMEA. Take your hand off me, scoundrel! (*Holds up his staff.*) Or do you prefer to have me spatter your brains out here? (*Disengages himself from* SYRUS *and goes in.*)

SYRUS. Well, away he goes! By Pollux, a fine companion I am, especially to Ctesipho! What should I do now? Unless—(*Thinks for a moment.*) I'll go off to a corner somewhere while this uproar quiets down and sleep off this wine I have drunk. That's what I'll do.   (*Goes into house by a side door.*)

(MICIO *comes out of* SOSTRATA's *house.*)

MICIO. Everything is ready at our house, exactly as I said, Sostrata. So whenever you wish——(*Sound of a door slamming.*)——I wonder who slammed the door of my house so hard!

(DEMEA *comes out of* MICIO's *house in great agitation.*)

DEMEA. Oh god! What should I do? What should I *do*? What should I scream or what should I moan? O sky, O earth, O seas of Neptune!

MICIO. Well, there you are. He's found out everything. That's what he is screaming about. That does it! We're going to have a quarrel. I must help him.

DEMEA. There he is, the universal corrupter of our children!

MICIO. Please control your anger and come to your senses.

DEMEA (*controls himself with difficulty*). I am controlling myself, I'm stopping all accusations. All right. Let's consider the matter as it stands. Did we not give our word, both of us—and you were the one who suggested it—that you would not concern yourself with my son and I would not concern myself with yours? Answer me.

MICIO. It is true. I don't deny it.

DEMEA. Then why is he now drinking at your house? Why do you harbor my son? Why do you buy him a mistress, Micio? Is your interference in any way less unfair than mine? Since I don't concern myself with your boy, don't concern yourself with mine.

MICIO. What you say is not fair.

DEMEA. No?

MICIO. For there is an old saying: "Friends share things together."

DEMEA (*sarcastic*). Clever! It's a fine time to talk that way.

MICIO. Listen a moment if you don't mind, Demea. First of all, if the expenses that the boys incur is bothering you, I ask you to consider this: At first you were raising the two boys on your own income because you thought your property would be enough for two and you then believed I would probably get married. Keep to that old plan of former days. Save, acquire, be thrifty, make sure to leave them as much as possible in inheritance. Get your glory for that! Allow them to use my wealth, which has grown far beyond my expectations, for their extravagances. Nothing will be lost from the principal—that is, your estate. Whatever they get from my funds, consider all that as coming from profits. If you are willing to seriously consider this in your mind, you will save all of us a lot of trouble.

DEMEA. Never mind the money. Consider the character of the two.

MICIO. Wait. I know. I was coming to that. There are many signs in a person, Demea, from which an inference may easily be drawn, when two people are doing the same thing. So that you can often say, "This person may do this without harm; that person may not." Not because the thing done is different, but because the person doing it is. These signs I see in them, so that I am confident they will turn out the way we want them to. I see they are wise, have understanding, show fear at the proper time, and love one another. You can tell that their natures and hearts are noble. Any time you wish you can bring them back in line. But you may fear that they are a little too careless for their own good. Oh my dear Demea, in all other respects we become wiser and wiser with age, but old age brings only this one defect to people: we all become more tenacious about possessions than necessary. Age will make them sufficiently keen about that too.

DEMEA (*ironically*). Provided those very good arguments and that liberal attitude of yours doesn't corrupt them completely!

MICIO. Quiet. It won't happen. Now enough of this discussion. Give yourself over to me today. Brush away your frowns.

DEMEA. I suppose that is what the occasion demands. I must do it. But tomorrow, at dawn, I'm going back to the country with my son.

MICIO. Tonight, for all I care! But today just make yourself merry.

DEMEA. And that music girl—I'll take her along with me to the country.

MICIO. You will have won a victory. That way you will make your son even more attached to your farm. Only make sure you keep her.

DEMEA. I'll see to that! And I'll get her all covered with cinders, smoke and mill dust from cooking and grinding flour! Besides that, I'll have her gather straw at noon. I'll get her as dried up and black as coal!

MICIO (*mockingly*). Good. Now you seem smart to me. And then I would force your son to sleep with her even if he doesn't want to.

DEMEA. You're laughing at me. You're lucky to have the kind of attitude you do. (*Getting serious.*) I feel——

MICIO. Ah, you're continuing?

DEMEA. No, no. I'm stopping now.

MICIO. Well, then, go inside and let us devote this day merrily to the business for which it is intended. (*They go into the house together.*)

(*Some time later:* DEMEA *comes out feeling rather good.*)

DEMEA (*to audience*). Never has anyone taken a careful inventory of his life without realizing that circumstances, age, and experience always bring something new and teach some lesson. The result is that the things you thought you really knew you don't know and through experience you repudiate what you have considered of prime importance. That's what has happened to me. Now that my course is nearly run, I'm giving up the hard life which I have lived till now. Why is that? I have found out in fact that nothing is better for a man than affability and forbearance.

It's easy for anyone to see that from the examples of my brother and myself. *He* has always lived his life in leisure, attending parties. He is easy-going, doesn't get excited, offends nobody, smiles at everybody. He has lived for himself, he has spent money on himself: everybody speaks well of him and loves him. I, on the other hand, am looked upon as a rustic—stern, cross, thrifty, bad-tempered, and stingy. And I got married—what a miserable life I've had with that! Sons were born—another worry. And what do you think? While I have striven to make as much as I could for them, I have worn away my life and my best years. Now that my life is almost over, this is the fruit of my labors for them—hatred. He on the other hand enjoys all the advantages of fatherhood without the hardships. Him they love, me they hate. Him they trust with their plans. Him they adore. It's at his house that both of them are. I am deserted. That he should live long, that's what they hope. As for me, they are probably looking forward to my death.

That's how it is—I brought them up with great effort on my part and he has made them his at little expense. I have all the grief and he gets the joy! Well, now, let's try the opposite! Let's see whether I am able to speak pleasantly, and act kindly, since this is what he challenges me to. I also want to be loved by my family and be made much of. If that's what happens through giving and being indulgent, I won't play second fiddle. The money will give out, but that bothers me least of all since I'm the oldest in the family. Let those who survive me worry.

(*Enter* Syrus *from the house, at some distance from* Demea.)

Syrus. Ah, Demea, your brother says please don't go away too far.

Demea. Who is this? (*Effusive.*) Oh, our dear Syrus! Glad to see you! How are you? How are things?

Syrus (*a bit surprised*). Oh, pretty good.

Demea. Excellent! I've just used three expressions contrary to my nature: "Oh, my dear," "How are you?," "How are things?" Show yourself a not ignoble slave, and I'll be glad to do you a kindness.

Syrus (*suspiciously*). Thank you.

Demea. I mean it, Syrus. Actually try it some time in the near future.

(Geta *comes out of* Sostrata's *house.*)

GETA. Mistress, I'm going to see how soon they will call for the bride. (*Sees* DEMEA.) But there's Demea. (*To* DEMEA.) Best wishes to you!

DEMEA (*genially*). And what is your name, my dear man?

GETA. Geta.

DEMEA. Geta, you are a man of greatest value. I've come to that conclusion today. For to me particularly that slave is to be highly regarded who is as concerned about his master as you are for yours, Geta. And if the occasion should ever arise I'll be glad to do you a favor. (*Aside.*) I'm practicing affability and it's proceeding very well!

GETA. Very good of you to think of me this way.

DEMEA (*aside*). Little by little I'll have the masses in my pocket!

(AESCHINUS *comes out of the house, impatient.*)

AESCHINUS. They're killing me with their eagerness to make this a really fancy wedding! They are wasting the day with their preparations.

DEMEA (*genially*). How are things, Aeschinus?

AESCHINUS. Ah, my dear Father! Is this where you were?

DEMEA. By Hercules, really your father by affection and blood, who loves you more than anything! But why don't you get your bride and start the wedding procession?

AESCHINUS. I wish I could. But I am still waiting for the flute player and the people who are to sing the wedding hymn.

DEMEA. Hah! Do you want to listen to an old man like me?

AESCHINUS. What about?

DEMEA. Don't bother with these things—wedding songs, processions, lamps, flute players—and have them break down the garden wall between the two houses at once. Lead her through the breach in the wall. Make it all one home. Lead her mother and all her family over to us, here.

AESCHINUS. That's a good idea, most delightful Father.

DEMEA (*aside*). Hooray, now I'm called delightful! My brother's house will become a thoroughfare, he'll bring a crowd and confusion into his home, and he'll lose a lot of money through the expense. But what do I care? I, the delightful fellow, earn their gratitude. Let me see that big spender count out twenty minas now! (*To* SYRUS.) Syrus, hurry up and get it done.

SYRUS. I? What?

DEMEA. Break down the wall. (*To* GETA.) Go and lead them through.

GETA. May the gods be kind to you, Demea, since you are such a well-wisher to our family.

DEMEA. I think they deserve it. (*Exit* GETA. *To* AESCHINUS.) What do *you* say?

AESCHINUS. That's what I think.

DEMEA. It's much better than having the young mother led through the street in her condition.

AESCHINUS. Really, there couldn't be a better suggestion, as I see it, dear Father.

DEMEA. That's the way I am, all the time. But there is Micio, coming out.

(MICIO *comes out, a bit baffled.*)

MICIO. My brother ordered it? Where is he? (*Sees* DEMEA.) Are *you* ordering this, Demea?

DEMEA. I certainly am. I am ordering that in this way and every other way we should make every effort to make this family one with us, to cherish, to aid, to unite.

AESCHINUS. That's what I hope, Father!

MICIO. My intention is not otherwise.

DEMEA. More than that! It's the right thing for us to do! First of all there is his wife's mother.

MICIO. There is. What then?

DEMEA. She is a fine, respectable woman.

MICIO. So they say.

DEMEA. She's rather elderly.

MICIO. I know.

DEMEA. And long past the age of childbearing. And there is no one to look after her. She's alone.

MICIO (*in some alarm*). What is he driving at?

DEMEA. It is the right thing for you to marry her, so go ahead and do it.

MICIO. I—get married too?

DEMEA. Yes, *you.*

MICIO. *Me?* (*Shocked.*)

DEMEA. Yes, you, I say.

MICIO. You're joking!

DEMEA (*to* AESCHINUS). If you were a man, he would do it.

AESCHINUS (*to* MICIO, *pleadingly*). Father, dear!

MICIO (*annoyed*). Why do *you* listen to him, you ass?

DEMEA (*to* MICIO). No use. It can't be otherwise.

MICIO. You're mad!

AESCHINUS (*to* MICIO). Please do it for me, Father.

MICIO (*to* AESCHINUS). You're crazy! Go away!

DEMEA. Come on, grant your son's request. (*Pointedly.*) Be indulgent!

MICIO. Are you really sane? Should I become a newly-wed at

the age of sixty-five and marry a decrepit old woman? Is that the kind of match you are proposing for me?

AESCHINUS. Do it. I promised them.

MICIO (*sarcastically*). You *promised* them! Be generous with yourself, my boy!

DEMEA. Come, come! What if he asked you for something greater?

MICIO. As if this isn't the greatest he could ask!

DEMEA (*wheedling*). Be a good fellow!

AESCHINUS. Don't refuse.

DEMEA. Do it, promise.

MICIO. Won't you let me alone?

AESCHINUS. Not unless I make you agree.

MICIO. So, you're trying to force me!

DEMEA. Come on, Micio, be obliging.

MICIO. Even though this seems to me wrong, stupid, absurd and utterly alien to my way of life, if you two want it so strongly, all right, I'll do it.

AESCHINUS. Thank you.

DEMEA. Thanks, I really appreciate it. (*Gets a new idea.*) But——

MICIO. What?

DEMEA. I'll tell you, now that my wish is accomplished.

MICIO. What more is there now?

DEMEA. There is this Hegio, their closest relative, our relative by marriage now—a poor man. It would be fitting for us to do something nice for him.

MICIO. Do what?

DEMEA. There is this bit of farmland, just out of town, which you usually rent out to strangers. We could let *him* use it so he could farm it and get some benefit from it.

MICIO. You call that a *little* bit of land?

DEMEA. Even if it's a lot, you ought to do it. He is her guardian, he is a good man, he is one of us now. It's right to give it to him. I have finally accepted the truth of that saying you spoke so well and wisely a short time ago: "It is a common fault of all of us that we become too tenacious about possessions in our old age." This defect we should avoid. It's a true saying and ought to be carried out in practice.

AESCHINUS (*pleadingly to* MICIO). Father!

MICIO (*wearily*). That's what you want? All right. The farm will be given to Hegio whenever he wishes.

AESCHINUS. I'm happy.

DEMEA. Now you are really my brother—in spirit as well as

in flesh. (*Aside, with a chuckle*.) I'm attacking him with his own weapons!

(*Enter* SYRUS *from the house.*)

SYRUS. What you ordered has been done, Demea.

DEMEA (*affably*). You're a worthy fellow. Therefore, by Pollux, it is my considered opinion that you deserve to be free.

MICIO. He should be free? For doing what, tell me?

DEMEA. Many things.

SYRUS. Oh, my dear Demea, you're a good man, by Pollux. I conscientiously took care of both of them from childhood on. I taught them, I advised them, I have always given them all the good precepts I could.

DEMEA (*ironically*). That's obvious. And even beyond that, your achievements extend to such things as buying provisions without cheating your master, picking up prostitutes, arranging lavish all-day parties. These are the accomplishments of no ordinary man!

SYRUS. What a charming fellow you are, sir!

DEMEA (*ironically*). Finally, today in the matter of buying the music girl he was the chief accomplice, and it was he who supervised it. He ought to be rewarded. The others will be the better for it. Finally, Aeschinus here wants it to be done.

MICIO (*to* AESCHINUS). Do you want this to be done?

AESCHINUS (*earnestly*). I do wish it.

MICIO. Well, then, if you wish it—Syrus, ho! Come over here to me. (MICIO *performs the informal ceremony of manumission. He strikes or taps the slave with his hand, turns him around and lets him go, saying the words which follow.*) Be free, henceforth!

SYRUS. Thank you very much! I thank you all, but you especially, Demea.

DEMEA. I'm very happy.

AESCHINUS. I too.

SYRUS. I believe you. If only my happiness could be made complete by having my wife Phrygia freed with me!

DEMEA. A very fine woman!

SYRUS. You know? She was the first to give the breast to your grandson, Aeschinus' son, today.

DEMEA (*pretending to take an absurdity seriously*). Well then, by Hercules, seriously, now, if she was the first to do it, there is no doubt but that she deserves to be freed.

MICIO. For a thing like that!

DEMEA. For a thing like that. (*To* MICIO.) As a final inducement, you can have from me as much money as she's worth.

SYRUS (*gratefully*). May the gods bring you everything you wish, Demea!

MICIO. You've done very well today, Syrus.

DEMEA. He will if you do your duty and lend him a little spending money to start out with. He will return it to you.

MICIO (*who has had enough*). I'll give him less than that! (*Snaps his fingers to signify "nothing."*)

AESCHINUS (*referring to* SYRUS). He is a worthy man.

SYRUS (*to* MICIO). I'll give it back to you, by Hercules. Just lend it to me!

MICIO. I'll think it over later.

DEMEA (*to* SYRUS). He'll do it.

SYRUS (*to* DEMEA). O most excellent man!

AESCHINUS (*to* DEMEA). O my dearest Father! (SYRUS *leaves.*)

MICIO (*to* DEMEA). What's this? What has so suddenly changed your character? What whim? What is this sudden generosity?

DEMEA. I'll tell you: I've done it to show you that the fact that the boys think you good natured and a good sport comes not from a proper way of life nor from your fairness or goodness, but from consenting, indulging, and spending, Micio. (*Turning to* AESCHINUS.) Now if my way of life is objectionable to you and your brother, Aeschinus, for the very reason that I did not give in to all your requests on every occasion, whether just or unjust, I'll stay out of your way. Squander, buy, do whatever your hearts desire. But if you would rather have this—that those things which because of your youth you don't see in their proper light, and desire the more passionately and consider the consequences too little—if in these situations you want me to check you, correct you, and yield where it is proper, here I am, at your service to do it for you.

AESCHINUS. We put ourselves in your hands, Father. You know better what must be done. But about my brother—what is to be done?

DEMEA. I give my permission. Let him have her. But let that be his last fling!

MICIO (*to* DEMEA). You are right there.

CANTOR. Your applause, please.

Phormio

A COMEDY

by
TERENCE

❦ ❦ ❦

translated by
Samuel Lieberman

DRAMATIS PERSONAE

DAVUS, a slave, friend of Geta

GETA, slave of Demipho

ANTIPHO, son of Demipho

PHAEDRIA, his cousin, son of Chremes

DEMIPHO, an elderly Athenian

PHORMIO, a parasite, friend of Antipho and Phaedria

HEGIO, CRATINUS, and CRITO, elderly Athenians, friends and advisors of Demipho

DORIO, a procurer

CHREMES, an elderly Athenian, brother of Demipho

SOPHRONA, elderly nurse of Antipho's wife, Phanium (Phanium does not appear on stage)

NAUSISTRATA, wife of Chremes

(CANTOR [singer], a member of the cast who calls for applause at the end)

Scene: A street in Athens, leading on the spectator's right to the center of town, or market place, on the left to the harbor. At the back of the stage, from left to right, stand the houses of Chremes, Demipho, and Dorio.

Prologue

There is an old playwright who, being unable to drive our playwright from his profession and reduce him to idleness, is trying to scare him away from writing by malicious accusations. He keeps saying that the plays which the author wrote previously are feeble in thought and poorly expressed because he never writes about a young man mad with love who sees a doe running away from dogs who are chasing her while she cries and begs for help.[1] But if the older playwright knew that this play, which was successful at its first performance, was more successful than his because of the efforts of its star actor, he would have been less bold to attack than he was.

Now if there is anyone who says or thinks: "If the old playwright had not attacked him, the younger one would not have found anything to say in his prologue unless he had someone to criticize," let such a person have this for an answer: That the prize is offered to all those who practice playwriting. The other is doing everything he can to drive the author from his profession into starvation. The author has wished only to respond, not to provoke. If the other had carried on the rivalry with kind words, he would have heard kind words in return. Let him understand that he is simply getting back in kind what he himself has introduced. I shall now make an end of speaking of him, though he is not finished with offensive conduct on his part.

Now give your attention to what I would like to say. I bring you a new comedy which in Greek is called *The Claimant,* and which the playwright calls *Phormio* in Latin, because the one who plays the main role is Phormio, a parasite through whom particularly the action will be carried on, if you grant the author your favor. Give us your help, show us your good will by being quiet, so that we don't have the same bad luck we had before, when because of a disturbance our company was driven from the stage. Our place upon the stage has now been restored to us by the assistance of your kindness and good will.   (*Exit.*)

---

[1] This is evidently a reference to some sentimental incident in a play by the hostile "old playwright," Luscius Lanuvinus. The work is not extant.

Act I

(*Enter Davus, a slave, from the right side of the stage as seen by the audience, carrying a small bag of money.*)

DAVUS. My very good friend and fellow townsman Geta came to see me yesterday. For some time he's been depositing his small bit of savings with me. He came to have me close out his account. And that's what I've done. (*Holds up the money bag.*) I'm bringing it to him. For I hear his master's son has married. I suppose (*Gesturing with the bag.*) this is a gift he has scraped together for the bride.

What an unfair arrangement it is—that those who have little should always add something to the possessions of the rich. What the poor fellow has saved bit by bit from his monthly allowance, denying his own needs, every bit of it she will grab away, little thinking with what labor it was acquired.

Later Geta will be hit with another gift—when the young mistress gives birth. Then by another—when the child has a birthday; and then when they initiate it into the religious cult. Each of these gifts the mother will take for herself, but the child will be the pretext for the donation. (*Shakes his head.*)

But isn't that Geta I see there?

(*As* DAVUS *speaks this last line,* GETA *is coming out of the house of his master,* DEMIPHO.)

GETA (*turning to speak to someone inside*). If a red-headed fellow comes looking for me——

DAVUS (*to* GETA, *interrupting*). Here he is! Don't bother.

GETA (*turning toward* DAVUS). Oh! I was just on the point of going to meet you, Davus. (*Approaches.*)

DAVUS (*holding up money bag*). Here, take it! It's all here! You'll find the amount is exactly what I owe you, and good coins too.

GETA (*takes the bag*). Thank you! I really appreciate your taking the trouble.

DAVUS (*sardonically*). Considering the way people are these days, things have come to such a pass that if someone returns to you what is yours, you're supposed to be most thankful! (*Looks at* GETA.) But why .re you looking so unhappy?

GETA. I? (*Worriedly.*) You can't possibly know in what dread, in what danger we are here!

DAVUS (*sympathetic*). What is it all about?

GETA. You'll find out if only you'll keep quiet about it.

DAVUS. Go on, will you! Don't be silly! A person you trust with your money you're afraid to trust with your words? What have I got to gain by betraying you?

GETA. Well, then, listen.

DAVUS. I certainly will.

GETA. Our old man's brother, Chremes—do you know him, Davus?

DAVUS. As well as I know you.

GETA. It happened that both of them had to go on a trip—the brother to Lemnos and the old man, my master, to Cilicia to visit an old friend of his. This friend offered him all kinds of inducements by letter, promising him everything short of mountains of gold.

DAVUS. When he already had so much wealth, and was rolling in it?

GETA. You don't have to tell me! That's the kind of man he is.

DAVUS. Oh, if I were only a rich man! (*Implying he would know how to use money properly.*)

GETA. So when the two of them went away, they left me as a sort of guardian for their sons.

DAVUS. Oh, Geta! That was a tough assignment you got!

GETA. *That* I learned by experience. I know this much: my guardian spirit must have been angry when I was left here in that job! At first I started out trying to restrain the boys and opposing them. (*Making a gesture of impossibility.*) What's the use of talking? As long as I was faithful to the old gentlemen, I kept getting my shoulders ruined from the beatings.

DAVUS. That thought occurred to me. For it's utter folly to swim against the tide.

GETA. So, I began to do everything their way, to give in to whatever they wanted.

DAVUS. You sure knew how to take advantage of the market.

GETA. *Our* young man—nothing wrong at first. But this fellow Phaedria, his cousin, at once found himself a girl, a lute player, and he fell desperately in love with her. She was the slave of a procurer, and Phaedria had no money with which to buy her from him. So there was nothing he could do but feast his eyes on her, follow her around, walk with her to the music school and back. Having little else to do, the other two of us helped Phaedria along.

Exactly opposite the place where the music school was where the girl was taking lessons there was a barbershop. Here we generally used to wait for her until she was ready to go home. One day, while we're sitting there, a young man comes in with tears in his eyes. We look at him in surprise and ask him what's the matter. "I've never realized until just now," he says, "what a heavy burden poverty is. I've just seen a young girl, here in the neighborhood, mourning her dead mother. The girl was pitiful. The body was laid out in the hallway, and she had nobody with her to offer condolences—and no one was there, no friend or relative except an old woman to help with the funeral. It was just pitiful! The girl herself was of remarkable beauty."

Why say more? He moved us all. Right then and there Antipho, my young master, says to the two of us, "Would you like to go take a look?" And Phaedria says, "Certainly! Let's go! You lead the way, if you don't mind."

We go, we come over, we see. A beautiful girl! And even more remarkable—she had no aids to beauty. Her hair was disheveled, her feet bare, she was unkempt, in tears, her clothing messy. So that if her beauty had not been of great power in itself, these things would have extinguished it.

The one who was in love with the music girl only said, "Quite a girl!" But ours——

DAVUS (*interrupting*). I know already. He fell in love.

GETA. And how! Wait till I tell you how it turned out! The next day he went straight to the old woman. He pleaded with her to arrange a rendezvous with the girl. But the old woman refused and said he was not doing the proper thing. The girl was an Athenian citizen, she said, well brought up, of respectable parents. If he wanted to marry her, he could do it legally, but otherwise she refused.

Our young man didn't know *what* to do. He wanted to marry her and at the same time was afraid of his absent father.

DAVUS. Wouldn't his father have given his consent on his return?

GETA. Give his consent to a girl without a dowry—a nobody? Never!

DAVUS. So what happened finally?

GETA. What *happened?* There is a parasite, Phormio, a shrewd operator—may all the gods destroy him!

DAVUS. What did *he* do?

GETA. He gave us this plan that I'll tell you about. He said, "There's a law that girls who are orphans should be married to those who are their nearest kin, and the same law orders the kinsmen to marry them. I'll say you are a relative and I'll bring suit against you. I'll pretend to be a friend of the girl's father and we'll go to court. Who her father was, who her mother, how she is related to you—all these I'll make up. Since you will not refute any of these statements—a situation which will be good and advantageous to me in the suit—I'll obviously win. When your father comes back, he'll start a quarrel with me. What do I care? She'll be ours by then."

DAVUS. The nerve of the man! It's almost funny!

GETA. Antipho let himself be persuaded and they did it. He came to court. He lost the case. He married her.

DAVUS (*surprised*). What are you saying!

GETA. Exactly what you hear.

DAVUS (*in sympathetic alarm*). Oh, Geta! What's going to happen to you?!

GETA (*unhappily*). I don't know, by Hercules! But one thing I do know: whatever Fortune brings, we'll just bear it and make the best of it.

DAVUS. Quite right! Spoken like a man!

GETA. I have every hope in myself.

DAVUS. Splendid!

GETA (*ruefully*). I suppose I'd better get myself a special pleader to intercede for me and to say, "Please let him go this time. But if he does anything again in the future, I won't intervene." As long as he doesn't add, "When I leave here you can kill him."

DAVUS. What about the cousin who was tagging along after the lute player? How are things going with him?

GETA. As of now, badly.

DAVUS. He hasn't much money to pay, I suppose?

GETA. Absolutely nothing but sheer hope.

DAVUS. Has his father returned yet?

GETA. Not yet.

DAVUS. And your old master—when do you expect him?

GETA. I don't know for certain, but I've just heard that a letter from him was just delivered to the customs officers. I'll go and get it.

DAVUS (*getting ready to leave*). Well, Geta, is there anything more you want of me?

GETA (*cordially*). Only that everything should be well with you! (*They embrace or shake hands, and* DAVUS *leaves in the direction of the market place.*)

GETA (*calls inside*). Hey, boy!——Is no one coming out here? (*A slave boy hurries out.* GETA *gives him the bag with the money.*) Here, take this. Give it to my wife, Dorcium.

(GETA *goes off left toward the harbor.*)

(*Enter* ANTIPHO *and* PHAEDRIA *from* CHREMES' *house, both looking unhappy.*)

ANTIPHO (*unhappily*). To think that it has come to the point, Phaedria, that whenever I think of the arrival of my father, who always wanted only the best for me, I get scared! (*Shakes his head.*) But if I had not been thoughtless, I would be looking forward to his arrival the way I should.

PHAEDRIA. What do you mean?

ANTIPHO. You ask me, you who were my accomplice in this bold misdeed? If only Phormio had not had the idea of persuading me to do it! If only I had not been so eager to let him push me into it! That was what started my wrongdoing. I wouldn't have gained possession of her— (*As if indifferent and philosophical about the whole thing.*) so I would have been miserable for a few days! But at least these worries would not be torturing my mind every day——

PHAEDRIA (*unsympathetic and ironical*). Uh huh!

ANTIPHO. ——while I wait to see how soon my father will come and break up my marriage.

PHAEDRIA. Other people are unhappy because they don't have *any* love, you're miserable because you have an overabundance! You're just abounding with love, Antipho. Why, by Hercules, your life is certainly enviable and most desirable. So help me Heaven, if I might enjoy the girl I love as long as you, I'd be willing to pay for it with my life! Just compare the two of us! What do I have? (*Bitterly.*) Nothing! What do you have? Plenty! Not to mention the fact that you have got, at no expense, a freeborn, respectable girl—that you have, as you would have wished, a wife whom you don't have to be ashamed to introduce anywhere.

You're well off—if only you had one thing more, the ability to put up with the situation as it is. But if you had dealings with that procurer the way I have, then you'd realize! That's the way most of us are—it's human nature—we're always dissatisfied with what we have.

ANTIPHO. Why, on the contrary, *you* seem the fortunate one to me, Phaedria, you who have the freedom of choice, the power to decide whether to hold on to your love or give it up. *I* find myself in the unhappy position that I haven't the choice of either giving it up or of keeping it. (*Looks in the direction of the harbor.*) But what's that? Is that Geta coming running here? It *is* he! Oh, I'm terribly afraid about the kind of news he is bringing me!

(*Enter* GETA *from the left, hurrying and troubled. He doesn't see the young men.*)

GETA (*to himself*). You're done for, Geta, unless you get yourself some kind of plan in a hurry! Big troubles are suddenly threatening you and you are utterly unprepared! I know neither how to avoid them nor how to extricate myself from them. Our audacious moves can no longer be kept hidden.

ANTIPHO (*to* PHAEDRIA). What is he so excited about?

GETA (*as before*). And I don't have a moment to lose! My master is here!

ANTIPHO (*to* PHAEDRIA). What is this trouble he's talking about?

GETA (*as before*). When he hears what we've done, how can I keep him from anger? Should I speak? I'll make him flare up. Should I keep quiet? I'll stir him up. Should I try to clear myself? I'll be wasting my breath. Oh, I feel miserable! At the same time I fear for myself, I'm also torn with worry for Antipho. *He's* the one I'm sorry for, *he's* the one I'm really fearful for, it is *he* who now makes me hesitate. For if it were not for him I would have looked out for myself properly, and I would have gotten even with the old man for his anger. I would have packed some things together and would be taking to my heels out of here at once.

ANTIPHO. What is this flight and theft he is planning?

GETA (*desperately*). I've got to find Antipho! But where? On what street should I start looking for him?

PHAEDRIA (*to* ANTIPHO). He's just spoken your name.

ANTIPHO. I'm afraid he's bringing me some really bad news.

PHAEDRIA. Ah! Are you crazy?

GETA. I'll go on home. That's where he usually is.

PHAEDRIA. Let's call him over.

ANTIPHO (*to* GETA). Stay right there!

GETA (*turning around*). You sound bossy enough, whoever you are.

ANTIPHO. Geta!

GETA. It's he! The very one I wanted to see.

ANTIPHO (*excited*). Tell me! What news do you bring? And be brief about it, if you can.

GETA. I will.

ANTIPHO. So speak up!

GETA (*excitedly*). Just now—at the harbor——

ANTIPHO (*alarmed*). My . . . ?

GETA (*helplessly*). You've understood!

ANTIPHO (*desperately*). I'll die!

PHAEDRIA (*concerned, but not quite understanding*). Hm.

ANTIPHO (*as before*). What should I do?

PHAEDRIA (*to* GETA). What do you mean?

GETA. I saw his father!

ANTIPHO. What do I do now against this sudden disaster? *I'm in trouble!* But if I am reduced to the misfortune of being torn from you, Phanium, my life is not worth living!

GETA. Since that's the case, Antipho, we've got to be all the more on the alert. Fortune helps the brave.

ANTIPHO. I'm not in control of myself.

GETA. But, Antipho, now especially you've got to take hold of yourself. For if your father notices that you're scared, he'll think you've done something wrong.

PHAEDRIA. That's true.

ANTIPHO (*helplessly*). I can't change myself!

GETA. What would you do if you now had to do something even more difficult?

ANTIPHO. Since I can't do this, I'd be even less able to do that.

GETA (*throwing up his hands*). It's no use, Phaedria. Obviously! Why do we waste our efforts here in vain? I'd better go.

PHAEDRIA. And I too.

ANTIPHO (*screwing up his courage*). Please, what if I make believe? Is that all right?

GETA. You're just talking!

ANTIPHO (*to both, trying to appear calm*). Look at my face. Here! (*Puts on a weak expression of calm and determination.*) Is this good enough?

GETA (*looks at him, dissatisfied*). No!

ANTIPHO (*tries another expression*). How about this?

GETA (*warming*). Almost.

ANTIPHO (*tries again, with success*). What about this?

GETA (*approving*). That's good! There! Hold it! And when he questions you, keep your answers to a minimum—just answer what he asks and no more, so that he won't get angry and beat you down with his harsh words.

ANTIPHO. I understand.

GETA. Say you were unwilling, but you were forced——

PHAEDRIA. ——by law, by the court.

GETA (*to* ANTIPHO). You understand? (*Catches sight of* DEMIPHO *on his way home from the harbor*.) But wait! Who is that old man way down the street there? (*Alarmed*.) It's the master!

ANTIPHO (*losing his nerve*). I can't stay! (*Starts to leave*.)

GETA (*to* ANTIPHO). Hey! What are you doing? Where are you going, Antipho? Stay, I tell you!

ANTIPHO (*stopping for a moment*). I know myself and my weak points. (*Leaves*.)

PHAEDRIA (*looks at* GETA, *who looks at him*). Well, Geta, what's going to happen now?

GETA. *You'll* be upbraided soon. *I'll* be strung up and whipped unless I'm badly mistaken. (*Suddenly gets an idea*.) But listen! What we were just trying to get Antipho to do—that's what we ourselves ought to do, Phaedria.

PHAEDRIA. Never mind the "ought to." Just tell me what to do.

GETA. Do you remember the way you fellows once talked when you first started the affair? About how to ward off blame—that the case was just, easy, sure to win, fair as could be?

PHAEDRIA. I remember.

GETA. Well, that's the kind of talk we need now, or, if possible, something even better and cleverer.

PHAEDRIA. I'll do my best.

GETA. Now you go up to him first. (*Indicating* DEMIPHO.) I'll stay in hiding here—in reserve—to be ready if you don't do too well.

PHAEDRIA. All right, let's go!

Act II

(*Enter Demipho angry. Phaedria and Geta stand on one side, in an alley between the houses out of the old man's sight, but hearing what he says*.)

DEMIPHO (*shouting*). So! Antipho has got married without my permission! And my authority means nothing to him! Never mind my authority! Has he no respect for my feelings, my indignation? And has he no shame either? What insolence—to do a thing like that! (*Bitterly.*) Oh, Geta, Geta! I left *you* as his advisor! Where were *you?*

GETA (*to* PHAEDRIA, *ironically*). Here it comes! He's finally remembered me.

DEMIPHO (*as before*). What will they say to me? What excuse will they make up, I wonder?

GETA (*aside, ironically*). I'll think of something. Don't worry about that.

DEMIPHO (*as before*). Will he say to me, "I did it unwillingly. The law forced me"? That's a good excuse, I admit.

GETA (*aside, ironically*). Good!

DEMIPHO (*continuing his monologue*). But with your eyes wide open, without opening your mouth, you threw up your case and handed it over to your adversaries—did the law force you to do that, too?

PHAEDRIA (*aside, to* GETA). That's a hard one to answer.

GETA (*aside to* PHAEDRIA). I'll find an answer. Just leave it to me.

DEMIPHO (*irritatedly*). I don't know what to do! It's happened so unexpectedly it's hard to believe! I'm so wrought up I can't think straight! (*A bit more calmly.*) That's why at the very time when things are going particularly well everyone must prepare his mind for the worst, so as to know how to bear the troubles that may face him—dangers, losses. When returning from abroad a person should always think of the possibility of bad news when he arrives: a son's transgression, a wife's death, a daughter's illness. He must realize that these are common occurrences in life and that they can happen—so that nothing that does happen will come as a shock. Whatever turns out counter to his forebodings he must consider a gain.

GETA (*aside, to* PHAEDRIA, *wryly*). You know, Phaedria, it's hard to believe how far I surpass the Master in wisdom. I've already prepared my mind for all the possible misfortunes I may face when my master returns—grinding away in the mill, getting a beating, shackles on my feet, hard labor in the fields. None of these will come as a shock to me. Whatever turns out counter to my forebodings, all that I will count as a gain.

But why don't you go up to him and start a conversation as though nothing had happened?

(PHAEDRIA *comes out of his hiding place toward* DEMIPHO.)

DEMIPHO (*catching sight of him*). I see Phaedria, my brother's son, coming up to me.

PHAEDRIA (*with pretended warmth*). Greetings, Uncle!

DEMIPHO (*dourly*). Greetings! But where is Antipho?

PHAEDRIA (*as before*). I'm happy to see you well on your arrival.

DEMIPHO (*ironically*). I dare say. But answer my question.

PHAEDRIA. He's well. He's around. Well, do you find everything to your liking?

DEMIPHO (*sadly*). I wish it really were!

PHAEDRIA (*innocently*). Why do you say that?

DEMIPHO (*sarcastically*). You ask, Phaedria? A fine marriage you fellows arranged here in my absence!

PHAEDRIA. Oho! Is that why you're angry at him?

GETA (*aside*). What a clever actor!

DEMIPHO (*angrily*). Why *shouldn't* I be angry at him? I'm just itching to catch sight of him, so that he'll realize right now that *he* is to blame for my changing from a good-natured father to a (*Emphatically.*) very stern one.

PHAEDRIA. And yet, Uncle, he has done nothing for you to get angry at.

DEMIPHO. They're all the same! They're all alike! If you know one you know them all.

PHAEDRIA. It's not so at all!

DEMIPHO. One does something wrong, the other one is at hand to defend his case! When this one is the offender, the other one is ready to defend. They must exchange roles with one another.

GETA (*aside*). Unsuspectingly the old man has painted a perfect picture of their actions.

DEMIPHO. For if this were not so, Phaedria, you would not be standing here as his defense counsel.

PHAEDRIA (*with pretended sincerity*). If Antipho is to blame, Uncle, for having too little concern for fortune and reputation, I don't plead his case to prevent him from getting what he deserves. But if somebody out of spite happened to set a trap for our youth and got the better of us, is it our fault or that of the judges, who often because of ill-will take away from the rich or because of pity give to the poor?

GETA (*aside*). If I didn't know the case, I would believe he is speaking the truth.

DEMIPHO. But is there any judge who could know the justice on your side when you don't say a word in rebuttal, the way he did?

PHAEDRIA. Antipho just did his duty as a young freeborn gentleman. When he came before the judges he couldn't express his thoughts—his shyness made him so timid and tongue-tied.

GETA (*aside*). He's doing very well! But I'd better go over to the old man as soon as possible. (*Comes out of hiding and approaches* DEMIPHO.) Master! Greetings! I'm happy to see you back!

DEMIPHO (*sarcastically*). Oh, hello, you fine guardian, you pillar of the family, to whom I entrusted my son on leaving here!

GETA. For some time I've been listening to you accuse all of us undeservedly and me most undeservedly of all! What did you want me to do in this matter? The laws do not permit a man who is a slave to plead a case. And his testimony is inadmissible.

DEMIPHO. All these points I grant you. I grant your statement: "Being a young man and inexperienced he was frightened." I concede that you are a slave. But if she really is a relative, it wasn't necessary to keep her as a wife! You fellows could have done what the law allows—you could have given her a dowry and he could have found her another husband. For what reason did he prefer to marry her, a penniless girl?

GETA. It wasn't a reason but money that was lacking.

DEMIPHO. He should have gotten it somewhere.

GETA. Where? There's nothing easier to say.

DEMIPHO. Well, if there was no other way, he should have borrowed it.

GETA. Well! Fine words you speak! As if anyone would have trusted him while you are alive!

DEMIPHO (*angrily*). No! It's not going to be this way! It can't! Do you think I'm going to let her stay married to him for one day? He doesn't deserve such gentle treatment. I want that *man* pointed out to me and to be shown where he lives.

GETA. You mean Phormio?

DEMIPHO (*distastefully*). That patron of the woman.

GETA. I'll get him here soon.

DEMIPHO. Where is Antipho now?

GETA. Out.

DEMIPHO (*to* PHAEDRIA). Get going, Phaedria! Find him and bring him here!

PHAEDRIA. I'm going—right down the street there.

GETA (*aside*). Sure! To his girl Pamphila's!

DEMIPHO. I'm going home now to pay my respects to the household gods. Then I'll go to the market place and call several of my friends to help me in this matter, so that I won't be unprepared if Phormio comes.

(DEMIPHO *enters his house.* PHAEDRIA *and* GETA *go off on their errands.*)

(*After a short interval of time* PHORMIO *and* GETA *enter from the direction of the market place.*)

PHORMIO (*to* GETA). You say he was so afraid to face his father that he went away?

GETA. Absolutely!

PHORMIO. And Phanium has been left all alone?

GETA. Yes!

PHORMIO. And the old man is angry?

GETA. Very much so!

PHORMIO. So the whole thing is dumped in *your* lap, Geta! You cooked up this mess and you've got to eat it all. Gird up your loins!

GETA. I beg you——

PHORMIO (*not listening, but thinking out his plan*). If he asks . . .

GETA. Our hopes are with you.

PHORMIO (*as before*). By Ceres! What if he tries to give her back?

GETA (*continuing his appeal to* PHORMIO). You drove him to it!

PHORMIO (*still planning*). I've got it!

GETA (*unhappily*). *I* helped him!

PHORMIO (*to* GETA, *confidently*). Get the old man! All my plans are already drawn up in my mind.

GETA. What are you going to do?

PHORMIO (*confidently*). What do you want? Isn't it that Phanium should stay, and I free Antipho from the charge of wrongdoing and divert all of the old man's anger onto me?

GETA (*joyously*). Oh, you are a brave man and a friend! But I'm often afraid that your bravery will finally land you in jail.

PHORMIO. Ah, that's not likely. I've had experience with danger, and my feet know the way out by now. (*Boastfully.*) How many men do you think I've beaten half to death? Foreigners as well as citizens? The better I know the way the more often I try it. Now tell me, have you ever heard of a suit for damages being brought against me?

GETA. Why is that?

PHORMIO. Because nets are not set against hawks and kites who do us harm. They are set for those who do us no harm, because there's profit in the latter, but with the former it's a waste of time and effort. Those who face dangers from all directions are the ones who can be robbed of something. They know I have nothing.

You'll say, "They'll fine him and condemn him to slavery when he can't pay." But they don't want to keep feeding a man who likes to eat. And they are wise in my opinion, if they don't wish to repay wrongdoing with the greatest benefits!

GETA (*with feeling*). It's impossible for Antipho to thank you the way you really deserve!

PHORMIO. On the contrary, no one can really thank a *patron* the way he really deserves. You come to a party perfumed and just out of a bath, your mind at ease, while your patron is consumed with worry and expense. While everything is being done to please you, *he* is grumbling with annoyance. You are free to laugh, you can take a drink before he does, you can take your place at the table before him. Then a puzzling meal is served.

GETA (*surprised*). What do you mean by "puzzling"?

PHORMIO (*smiling*). It's a meal that's so good and so full that you're puzzled about which dish you'd like to eat best. So when you consider how many delightful and dear things a patron supplies, wouldn't you think he is a manifest god?

GETA (*sees* DEMIPHO *approaching and nudges* PHORMIO). The old man is here! Decide what you're going to do. The first clash is the fiercest. If you stand up to *it,* then you can play him as you please.

(*Enter* DEMIPHO *with three respectable citizens of his own age,* HEGIO, CRATINUS, *and* CRITO, *all very serious and dignified. The three are to advise* DEMIPHO *and act as a sort of informal court of arbitration between him and* PHORMIO. GETA *and* PHORMIO *stay out of their sight at first but can hear what is being said.*)

DEMIPHO (*to his friends*). Have you ever heard of anyone more outrageously treated than I? Please act as my advisors in this matter. (*They nod solemnly.*)

GETA (*to* PHORMIO). He is angry!

PHORMIO (*to* GETA). Now watch this. I'll shake him up. (*Aloud so the others can hear, with pretended indignation.*) Oh immortal gods! Demipho denies that this girl Phanium is a relative of his? *She's* not a relative says Demipho!

GETA (*also audible to the others, the rest of the ensuing conversation being really for the others' ears*). He denies it.

PHORMIO. And he says he doesn't know who her father was?

GETA. He says he doesn't.

DEMIPHO (*to his friends*). I think that's the very man I was talking about. Come with me. (*They come closer to* GETA *and* PHORMIO.)

PHORMIO. And he says he doesn't know who Stilpo was?

GETA. He says he doesn't.

PHORMIO (*at the height of pretended indignation*). Just because the poor girl was left in poverty, her father becomes an unknown and she is neglected. Look at what greed does!

GETA (*pretending loyalty*). If you accuse my master of malice, you'll hear from him!

DEMIPHO. The nerve of him! He comes accusing me just like that!

PHORMIO. Now I have no reason to be angry with the young man if *he* doesn't know him well. After all, her father was already elderly, a poor man, whose whole life was spent in hard work—he usually stayed in the country. There he had some land to work which he rented from my father. The old man used to tell me that Demipho, his relative, was neglecting him. But what a man! The best man I ever saw in all my life!

GETA (*ironically*). May you turn out to be the way you say he was!

PHORMIO (*pretending anger*). Go to hell! If I didn't have this opinion of him, I wouldn't now be undertaking these hostilities against your family for the sake of the girl whom he spurns so meanly.

GETA (*with pretended loyalty*). Do you persist in speaking badly of my master in his absence, you piece of filth?!

PHORMIO. Well, he deserves it!

GETA (*indignantly*). You don't say, you jailbird!

DEMIPHO (*trying to get GETA's attention and calm his apparent anger*). Geta!

GETA (*to PHORMIO, as before*). You blackmailer, you law-twister!

DEMIPHO (*louder*). Geta!

PHORMIO (*aside to GETA*). Answer him.

GETA. Who is this man? (*As if seeing DEMIPHO for the first time.*) Ah!

DEMIPHO (*sympathetically*). Keep quiet.

GETA (*to DEMIPHO*). All day, in your absence, he hasn't stopped uttering insults, which you don't deserve, but which *he* deserves.

DEMIPHO (*to GETA, as before*). Stop it now. (*To PHORMIO, coldly polite.*) First of all, I ask you, if you don't mind, to be so kind as to answer me. Who do you say that friend of yours was? Explain it to me. And how did he say he was related to me?

PHORMIO. You're fishing for information, as if you didn't know.

DEMIPHO. I know him?

PHORMIO. Yes!

DEMIPHO. I say I don't. You say I do, so recall him to my memory.

PHORMIO. What, man, you don't know your own cousin?

DEMIPHO (*sneeringly*). You amaze me! Tell me his name.

PHORMIO (*stalling*). Name?

DEMIPHO (*beginning to feel triumphant*). Certainly! (*Waits for an answer which is not forthcoming.*) Why are you silent now?

PHORMIO (*flustered, mumbling half-aside*). Damn me! By Hercules, I've forgotten the name!

DEMIPHO. Well, what do you say?

PHORMIO (*aside to* GETA). Geta, if you remember what we once said the name was, prompt me. (*Aloud to* DEMIPHO, *stalling.*) Hm, I won't tell you! As if you don't know—you've come here to test me!

DEMIPHO. I test you?

GETA (*whispering to* PHORMIO). Stilpo.

PHORMIO. And yet, what do I care? It's Stilpo.

DEMIPHO. Who did you say?

PHORMIO. Stilpo is the man I say you knew.

DEMIPHO. I neither knew him nor was anyone by that name ever a relative of mine.

PHORMIO. Is that so? Aren't you ashamed before these gentlemen? (*Indicates* DEMIPHO's *three friends.*) But if he had left her ten talents of money——

DEMIPHO (*angry*). May the gods damn you!

PHORMIO. ——you would be the first to remember how far back you two are related, going back to your grandfather and your great-great grandfather.

DEMIPHO (*sarcastically*). Exactly as you say. If I had ever gone to court to put in my claim I would have stated how she is related to me. *You* do the same! Tell me, how is she related?

GETA (*pretending loyalty*). Bravo, master! Well done! (*To* PHORMIO.) Now you, you'd better watch out!

PHORMIO. I explained it very clearly to the judges when I had to. If it was false why didn't your son refute it at that time?

DEMIPHO (*bursting out*). You're telling me about my son? His stupidity just can't be described the way it deserves!

PHORMIO (*sarcastically*). Then you who are so wise, go before the magistrates so they can give you a decision again about the same case, since you are the king around here, and you alone are entitled to get a second decision on the same case!

DEMIPHO. Even though a wrong has been done me, still,

rather than go to court or listen to you tell me (*Sarcastically*.) how she's related, if she is—since the law orders me to give her a dowry, here are five minas and take her away. (*Holds out money*.)

PHORMIO. Ha! Ha! Ha! (*Sarcastically*.) You're a nice fellow!

DEMIPHO. What's the matter? Am I asking for something unfair? Or shouldn't I obtain what the law of the land allows?

PHORMIO (*with a show of indignation*). So that's the way it is, is it? Just like with a prostitute? When you're finished with her, the law bids you pay her fee and send her away? (*Pauses for effect*.) But in the case of a woman who is a citizen, in order that she should not suffer shame because of poverty, the law orders that she be wed to her nearest kin to spend her life with one man. And *you* forbid that?

DEMIPHO. Exactly! To her nearest kin. But how are we her nearest kin, by what relationship?

PHORMIO. Come now! As the saying goes, "Don't try a case already decided."

DEMIPHO. Don't try? Why, I won't stop till I get what I want!

PHORMIO. You're talking nonsense!

DEMIPHO. Just wait and see!

PHORMIO. Anyway, we have nothing to do with you, Demipho. It was your son who was ordered to marry her, not you. You were too old for that.

DEMIPHO. Well, just consider that he is saying what I am now saying. And anyway I will not let him stay in the house with her for a wife.

GETA (*aside to* PHORMIO). He is *angry*.

PHORMIO (*to* DEMIPHO). You'll think better of it!

DEMIPHO. Are you prepared to use every means against me, you wretch?

PHORMIO (*aside to* GETA). He's afraid of us even though he is doing his best to hide it.

GETA (*aside to* PHORMIO). You've made a good beginning.

PHORMIO (*to* DEMIPHO). Why don't you accept what you have to? You will be doing what is proper for you to do, and we can be friends.

DEMIPHO (*angrily*). Am I asking you for your friendship? Do I want to see or hear you?

PHORMIO. If you accept her you will have someone to delight your old age. Consider your time of life.

DEMIPHO (*sarcastic*). Let her delight you! Keep her for yourself!

PHORMIO. Don't be so angry.

DEMIPHO. Look here! There's been enough talk. If you don't hurry up and take the woman away, I will throw her out. (*Dismissing the matter.*) I've said my say, Phormio!

PHORMIO. If you touch her in any way other than it is proper to touch a free woman, I'll bring suit against you for heavy damages. *I've* had *my* say, Demipho! (*To* GETA, *aside.*) If there is any need for me, hey, I'll be home.

GETA (*to* PHORMIO, *aside*). I understand.

(PHORMIO *stalks off right.*)

DEMIPHO. What great trouble and worry has he brought me, that son of mine who has tied me and himself up in this marriage! And he doesn't give me a chance to see him, so that I may at least know what *he* says about this matter or what *he* thinks. (*To* GETA.) Go, see whether he hasn't come home by now.

GETA. I'm going. (*Goes off into* DEMIPHO'S *house.*)

DEMIPHO (*to his friends*). You see what the situation is. What do I do? Tell me, Hegio.

HEGIO. I? I defer to Cratinus, if you don't mind.

DEMIPHO (*turns to* CRATINUS). What do you say, Cratinus?

CRATINUS. You want my opinion?

DEMIPHO. Yes, yours.

CRATINUS (*with great deliberation*). I would like you to do what is to your advantage. This is what I think: it is right and proper that what your son did in your absence should be cancelled and things restored to their original condition. And you will achieve it. That's my opinion.

DEMIPHO. Now you speak, Hegio.

HEGIO (*choosing his words carefully*). I believe Cratinus has spoken with due deliberation. But, it's true as they say, "As many men so many minds." Everyone to his own way, I don't think that what has been done by law can be rescinded. And it is not good for one's reputation to undertake it.

DEMIPHO. Crito, you speak!

CRITO. I think it needs further deliberation.

HEGIO (*preparing to leave with the other two, politely*). Is there anything further you want of us?

DEMIPHO (*annoyed*). You've done very well—I'm more undecided now than I was before!

(*The three counselors walk toward the market place with great dignity.*)

GETA (*coming out of the house*). They say he has not yet returned.

DEMIPHO. My brother is the one I should wait for. Whatever

advice he gives me on this matter I'll follow. I'll go ask at the harbor when he's coming back. (*Goes off left.*)

GETA (*aside*). And I'll look for Antipho to tell him what has happened here. But there he is! I see he is returning just in time.

Act III

(*Antipho enters, very remorseful.*)

ANTIPHO (*to himself*). Really now, Antipho, you and your faint heart are much to be blamed. The idea of running away and giving others the job of protecting the girl who is your whole life! Did you think that others would handle your affairs better than you? For no matter what else happened, you should certainly take thought now for the girl you have at home so that she won't be deceived in her faith in you and suffer harm. Poor girl, all her hopes and resources now depend on you and you alone.

GETA (*coming over*). To tell you the truth, Master, all the time you were away, we have been criticizing you for leaving.

ANTIPHO. I was looking for you!

GETA. But in spite of that we did not fail you.

ANTIPHO. Tell me, please, how do things stand? What are the prospects? Does my father suspect anything at all?

GETA. Not a thing.

ANTIPHO (*somewhat hopeful*). Is there any hope for the future?

GETA. I don't know.

ANTIPHO (*disappointed*). I see.

GETA. Except that Phaedria has not stopped making every effort for you.

ANTIPHO (*ruefully appreciative*). As usual!

GETA. Also Phormio is proving exactly as energetic in this matter as in others.

ANTIPHO (*eagerly*). What has he done?

GETA. He put a damper on your very angry father.

ANTIPHO. Bravo, Phormio!

GETA. And I have gone on doing whatever I could.

ANTIPHO (*effusively*). My dear Geta, I love you all!

GETA. That's how things are now, as I've told you. It's only the beginning. So far things are calm. Your father is waiting till your uncle comes back.

ANTIPHO (*worried*). Why is he waiting for him?

GETA. Well, he says he wants his advice to guide him on what has to be done in this matter.

ANTIPHO (*depressed again*). How frightened I've suddenly become at the thought of seeing my uncle return safe and sound! For by his decision alone, from what you say, I either live or die.

GETA (*peering in the distance*). Here's Phaedria!

ANTIPHO. Where?

GETA. There he is—coming out of his playground. (*Snickers.*) (PHAEDRIA *and* DORIO, *the slave dealer, come out of the latter's house at the right of the stage;* PHAEDRIA *is very distressed.* ANTIPHO *and* GETA *stand at a side watching.*)

PHAEDRIA (*pleading*). Dorio, listen—please!

DORIO (*indifferent*). I'm not listening.

PHAEDRIA. Just a little while?

DORIO. Why don't you leave me alone?

PHAEDRIA. Listen to what I'm saying!

DORIO. I'm getting sick and tired of hearing the same thing a thousand times!

PHAEDRIA. But now I'll tell you something you'll be glad to hear.

DORIO. Speak up! I'm listening.

PHAEDRIA (*earnestly*). Can't I convince you to wait for just three more days? (DORIO *turns his back and starts to return to his house.*) Wait! Where are you going?

DORIO (*sneeringly*). I was *wondering* whether you had anything new to offer me.

ANTIPHO (*aside to* GETA). Ai! I'm afraid that that procurer might——

GETA (*aside to* ANTIPHO). ——get his head handed to him? I was afraid of the same thing myself.

PHAEDRIA. Don't you trust me?

DORIO (*sarcastically*). You're a veritable fortune-teller!

PHAEDRIA. But if I give you my *word?*

DORIO. Fairy tales!

PHAEDRIA. Just do me this favor and you'll say it was an excellent investment!

DORIO. Words!

PHAEDRIA. Trust me—you'll be happy you did! It's the truth, by Hercules!

Dorio. Idle dreams!

Phaedria. Take a chance. It's not a long time!

Dorio. You're singing the same old song.

Phaedria (*desperately*). You're my relative, you're my—parent, you're my friend, you're——

Dorio. Just babble on!

Phaedria. Are you so hard and heartless that you can't be moved by pity and prayers?

Dorio. Are you so thoughtless and impudent beyond measure that you think you can take me in with your fine speeches and take my slave girl away without paying?

(Phaedria *is at a loss.*)

Antipho (*aside to* Geta). It's pitiful!

Phaedria (*sadly*). Ah, the truth is too much for me!

Geta (*aside*). How alike the two boys are!

Phaedria (*aside*). Why couldn't this blow have hit me when Antipho was not occupied with other troubles of his own!?

Antipho (*approaching with* Geta). What's this all about, Phaedria?

Phaedria. Oh, Antipho! You lucky, lucky fellow!

Antipho (*bewildered*). I?

Phaedria. You have somebody safe at home to love, and you've never had the experience of being beset by this kind of misfortune.

Antipho. I have somebody *safe* at home? On the contrary, as the saying goes—I have a tiger by the tail, and I don't know how either to let go or hold on.

Dorio. That's just what I have with this fellow.

Antipho (*to* Dorio, *ironically*). Hey, you'd better be careful you don't get too kindhearted for a procurer! (*To* Phaedria.) Has he done anything?

Phaedria. He? Like the brute he is, he has gone and sold my Pamphila!

Antipho. What? Sold her? (*Horrified.*)

Phaedria (*sadly and definitely*). He sold her.

Dorio (*exploding sarcastically*). What a terrible thing to do! I sold a slave girl bought with my own money!

Phaedria. I've been pleading with him to wait for me and cancel his agreement with the other fellow—just three more days until I get the money that has been promised me by friends of mine. (*To* Dorio *again, pleading.*) If I don't give it to you then, you don't have to wait a single hour more!

Dorio. Again, the same thing, dinning into my ears?

Antipho (*to* Dorio). It's not a long time he is asking for. Let him have it! And he will pay you back double for the favor you do him.

DORIO (*impatient*). Those are just words!

ANTIPHO (*to* DORIO). You'll allow Pamphila to be sent out of this city? Then in addition you have the heart to tear apart these two people who are in love?

DORIO (*ironically*). Neither I nor you have the heart to!

GETA (*disgusted, to* DORIO). May all the gods give you what you deserve!

DORIO (*to* PHAEDRIA). Counter to my usual practice, I was patient with you for many months while you promised and brought no money, but kept crying. Now instead of all that I have found a customer who pays and doesn't weep. So step aside for your betters!

ANTIPHO (*to* PHAEDRIA). But certainly, by Hercules, if I remember correctly, you *did* have a definite date agreed on by which you were to pay him?

PHAEDRIA. I did.

DORIO. Do I deny that?

ANTIPHO (*to* DORIO). Well, has it already passed?

DORIO. No, but the other fellow's date had been set ahead of his.

ANTIPHO. Aren't you ashamed of the deception?

DORIO (*bluntly*). Not at all, as long as it's to my advantage.

GETA (*angrily*). You heap of filth!

PHAEDRIA. Dorio, is that the way to behave?

DORIO (*smugly*). That's the way I am. If you like me that way, do business with me.

ANTIPHO. To cheat like that!

DORIO (*blandly, with a "no hard feelings" air*). Why, on the contrary, he cheats me! For he knew that I was this kind of person, but I thought he was different. *I'm* disappointed in *him!* I'm not the least bit different to him from what I've always been. But no matter how things are, here's what I'll do. The soldier said he was giving me the money tomorrow. If you bring it first, Phaedria, I'll follow my rule—first come first served. Good-bye.
(*Returns to his house.*)

PHAEDRIA (*looking at* ANTIPHO *and* GETA *with dismay*). What can I do? Where will I suddenly find the money for him, when a poor wretch like me has less than nothing? If only he had listened to my pleas to wait just three more days—it was promised!

ANTIPHO (*to* GETA). Shall we allow him to be so unhappy, when, as you've said, he has been helping me like a good friend? Why don't we try to do him a kindness in return. He needs it!

GETA. I agree, that's only fair.

ANTIPHO. Well, then, you're the only one who can save him.

GETA. What should I do?

ANTIPHO. Find the money.

GETA. I wish I could. But tell me where.

ANTIPHO. His father is back.

GETA. I know. But what then?

ANTIPHO. Ah! A word to the wise is sufficient.

GETA. *That's* what you mean?

ANTIPHO. Yes.

GETA (*indignantly*). By Hercules, that certainly is a nice thing you're suggesting! Go on! It's enough of a triumph for me that I didn't get into trouble because of your marriage without your telling me now to stick my neck in a noose for his sake too!

ANTIPHO (*to* PHAEDRIA). He's right.

PHAEDRIA. What, Geta? Am I a stranger to you, too?

GETA. That's not the point! But isn't it enough that the old man is already angry at all of us without stirring him up further, so that there will be no room left for entreaties?

PHAEDRIA (*hopelessly*). Shall another man take her out of my sight to some unknown place? (*Sighs.*) Well then, while you still have the chance and while I'm still here, speak to me, Antipho—look at me!

ANTIPHO. What for? What are you going to do? Tell me.

PHAEDRIA (*desperately*). Wherever in the world she is carried off to, I am determined to follow her or die!

GETA. May the gods help you in what you are going to do! But be careful!

ANTIPHO (*To* GETA). Look, can't you give him some help?

GETA. "Some help." But what?

ANTIPHO. Think of something, I beg you, so he won't do something desperate that we'll all be sorry about later, Geta.

GETA. I'm thinking. He's safe as far as I can see. But I'm still afraid of trouble.

ANTIPHO. Don't be afraid. We'll bear the good and bad together with you.

GETA (*to* PHAEDRIA). How much money do you say you need?

PHAEDRIA. Only thirty minas.

GETA (*surprised*). Thirty? My, she's very expensive, Phaedria!

PHAEDRIA. She's really cheap at that price.

GETA. All right, all right, I'll manage to get the money.

PHAEDRIA (*effusively*). Oh, you're wonderful!

GETA (*to* PHAEDRIA). Now get yourself away from here.

PHAEDRIA. I need it soon!

GETA. You'll get it soon. But I need to have Phormio as an assistant in this job.

ANTIPHO. He's ready and waiting. You can most confidently give him any difficult assignment. He'll carry it out.

GETA. Then let's go to him quickly.

ANTIPHO. Is there anything you need my help for?

GETA. No. But go home and cheer up that poor girl of yours who I know is sitting in there (*Indicating* DEMIPHO's *house.*) pale with fear. What are you waiting for?

ANTIPHO. There's nothing I'd like better to do.

(*Goes into the house.*)

PHAEDRIA (*to* GETA). How are you going to do it?

GETA. I'll tell you on the way. But let's get away from here.

(*They leave toward the market place.*)

Act IV

(*Chremes and Demipho are on their way home from the harbor, where Chremes has just disembarked.*)

DEMIPHO. Well? Did you accomplish what you went to Lemnos for? Did you bring your daughter back with you?

CHREMES (*sadly*). No.

DEMIPHO. Why not?

CHREMES (*ruefully*). When her mother saw that I was staying away and neglecting them too long while the girl was growing up, she set sail with the whole family for my place.

DEMIPHO. Why, then, did you stay there so long, when you had heard that?

CHREMES. Well, I got ill, and that delayed me.

DEMIPHO. How did you get ill? What illness?

CHREMES. You ask? (*Sadly.*) Old age itself is an illness! But I heard from the skipper who brought them here that they'd arrived safe and sound.

DEMIPHO. Have you heard what happened to my son while I was away, Chremes?

CHREMES. Yes, and it has certainly upset my plans. For now if I offer my daughter in marriage to someone outside the family,

I shall have to explain exactly how she is my daughter. I knew I could trust *you* as well as myself. The outsider, if he wants to marry into my family will keep quiet as long as there are good relations between us. But if we should have a falling out, he will know more than he should know. And I'm afraid too that somehow my wife will find out all about it. If that happens, all that's left for me is to clear out and leave home. For of everything I have I am the only thing that really belongs to me.

DEMIPHO. I know that this is so, and your troubles are my worry too—and I'll never stop trying and never grow weary until I have accomplished what I promised you.

(*Enter* GETA, *who has just seen* PHORMIO.)

GETA (*aside*). I've never seen anyone cleverer than Phormio! I came over to tell him that money is needed and to ask how it can be raised. I was hardly half through speaking when he understood the whole situation! He was happy, he praised me, he asked about the old man. He thanked the gods that he had been given an opportunity to show that he was a friend to Phaedria no less than to Antipho. I told him to wait in the market place, saying I would bring the old man over. (*Seeing* DEMIPHO.) But there he is! (*Peering.*) But who is that behind him? Uh-oh! Phaedria's father has arrived! But why get scared, idiot that I am? Because I'm offered two people to cheat instead of one? I think it's more convenient to have two strings to my bow. (*Warming to the possibilities.*) I'll start by working on the one I had intended to originally. If he gives me the money, that's good enough. But if there's nothing doing with him, I'll go after the new arrival. (*Gesturing toward* CHREMES.)

(ANTIPHO *comes out of the house, but does not see* GETA *at first.*)

ANTIPHO (*aside*). I wonder how soon Geta will get back. (*Suddenly sees* CHREMES *and* DEMIPHO.) But I see my uncle standing there with my father! Oh, how I fear what my uncle's arrival may lead my father to! (*Gets out of their sight.*)

GETA (*aside*). I'll approach them. (*Does so.*) Ah, greetings, my dear Chremes!

CHREMES. Greetings to you, Geta.

GETA. It's a pleasure to see you back safe and sound.

CHREMES. Thank you.

GETA. How do you find things? Many changes around here since you left, aren't there?

CHREMES. Many.

GETA. Yes, did you hear about Antipho—what happened?

CHREMES. Everything.

GETA (*to* DEMIPHO). Did you tell him? (*To* CHREMES.) An intolerable outrage to be so deceived!

CHREMES. That's what I was just talking about with Demipho.

GETA. Well, now! I also have been thinking the matter over carefully in my mind, and I have found a solution, I think.

CHREMES (*eagerly*). What is it, Geta?

DEMIPHO (*hopefully, but guardedly*). What solution?

GETA (*to* DEMIPHO). When I left you, I happened to meet Phormio.

CHREMES. Who's Phormio?

DEMIPHO. He's the one who . . . her . . . (*His answer trails off in gestures.*)

CHREMES. I understand.

GETA. I decided I'd better sound him out first. So I got him alone and said, "Phormio, why don't you see to it that we settle these matters between us with good grace rather than with bad grace? My master is a gentleman and is shy of lawsuits. Now, everyone else, indeed all his friends, with one voice, have advised him to kick her out." (DEMIPHO *and* CHREMES *look interested.*)

ANTIPHO (*aside, alarmed*). What is he starting now and what will he end up with?

GETA. And I went on, "You'll say that he will pay the penalty of the law if he throws her out? That point has already been gone into." "Oh ho!" I said to Phormio, "you'll certainly be sweating if you start up with that man! That's how eloquent he is. (DEMIPHO *looks pleased.*) But even supposing he loses his case, still, for him it's not a case in which his rights as a citizen are at stake, but only money. But for you?" (DEMIPHO *nods.*) After I felt the fellow was being softened up with these words, I said, "We're alone here now. Come on, tell me what you want to be given in cash so that my master should be free of lawsuits, that she should take herself off, and that you shouldn't bother us?" (DEMIPHO *looks as if he is not sure he likes this.*)

ANTIPHO (*aside, worried*). Ye gods! Is he out of his mind?

GETA. "For I know very well," I told him, "that if you mention a figure that will have the least particle of justice in it, you and my master will not have any more words about it."

DEMIPHO (*a bit put out*). Who told you to say that?

GETA. Why, we couldn't get where we want to in any better way.

ANTIPHO (*aside*). I'm dead!

DEMIPHO (*interested*). Go on talking.

GETA. At first the fellow raged like a madman!

CHREMES. Tell me, how much did he ask for?

GETA. How much? Much too much.

CHREMES. *How* much? Tell me.

GETA. Someone should give him a whole talent—sixty minas!

DEMIPHO (*sputtering*). Damn him! By Hercules, has he no shame?!

GETA. That's exactly what I told him. "Why," I said, "what if he were marrying off an only daughter? It was of no benefit to him that he didn't raise a daughter; a girl has been found to claim a dowry from him!" To make a long story short, leaving out all his impertinences, here are his final words. "At first," he said, "I wanted to marry the daughter of a friend of mine, as was right. For I began to think of the disadvantages to my friend's daughter, a rather poor girl, if she were married to a rich man. It would really be slavery for her. But to tell you the truth, I needed the bit of money she would bring, to pay off my debts. And even now, if Demipho is willing to give me the amount I am getting from the girl who is betrothed to me, I would like nothing better than to marry Antipho's girl."

ANTIPHO (*aside, alarmed and annoyed*). I don't know what to think! Is he doing it out of stupidity or malice? Does he know what he is doing, or is he just blundering?

DEMIPHO. What if he is up to his ears in debt?

GETA. He says he has a field mortgaged for ten minas.

DEMIPHO. All right, all right! Let him marry her. I'll give it to him.

GETA (*quickly*). He says he also has a small house on which he owes ten more.

DEMIPHO (*raising his voice*). Stop! That's too much!

CHREMES. Don't shout. You can get the second ten from me.

GETA. He says he has to buy a slave girl as a maid for his wife. Then he needs a bit of furniture—and then there are the expenses for the wedding. For these things add ten minas more, he says.

DEMIPHO (*firmly and angrily*). Then let him bring a thousand suits against me! I'm giving nothing! What does that dirty crook think he is doing? Trying to make a fool of me?

CHREMES (*appeasingly, to* DEMIPHO). Come now, I'll pay it. Calm down. Just see to it that your son marries (*With emphasis.*) the girl we want.

ANTIPHO (*aside, desperately*). Oh! Geta! You've destroyed me with your deceptions!

CHREMES. The other girl is being thrown out for my sake. It's only right that I should lose the money.

GETA. "Make certain you let me know as soon as possible," he said, "if they are giving her to me, so I can give up my friend's daughter. I must be sure. For her family has already decided to give me a dowry."

CHREMES. Let him have her at once. Let him give notice that the other engagement is off. Let him marry this girl.

DEMIPHO (*with feeling*). May this affair turn out badly for him!

CHREMES. Very opportunely I happen to have money with me right now. It's the profits from my wife's estates in Lemnos. I'll draw on that. I'll tell my wife you needed it, Demipho.

(CHREMES *and* DEMIPHO *go into the latter's house.*)
(ANTIPHO *comes out of his hiding place near his father's house.*)

ANTIPHO. Geta!

GETA. Hm?

ANTIPHO (*excitedly*). What did you do?

GETA (*pleased with himself*). I've cleaned the old men out of money!

ANTIPHO (*indignantly*). Is that all?

GETA. I don't know, by Hercules. That's all I was told to do.

ANTIPHO (*angrily*). Oh ho! You whipping block! You're not answering my question!

GETA (*surprised*). What are you talking about?

ANTIPHO (*heatedly*). What am I talking about? You've fixed it so that I might just as well hang myself! May all the gods and goddesses, above and below, damn you with the worst torments! (*Pointing scornfully at* GETA.) There he is! If you want someone to bring your ship from a calm sea onto the rocks, give *him* the job! What was the purpose of touching on this painful subject and mentioning my wife? It was the worst thing to do! My father was given the hope that she could be pushed out! And also, tell me: if Phormio accepts the dowry and marries her, what happens then?

GETA (*confidently*). He won't marry her.

ANTIPHO (*sarcastically*). Sure! But when they ask for their money back, I suppose he would rather go to prison for our sake!

GETA. There is nothing that cannot be distorted by telling it the wrong way. *You* disregard what is good and emphasize what is bad. Now listen to a different version.

As soon as he gets the money, he has to get married, as you say. I grant you that. (*Slyly.*) But surely he'll be given a *little* time to arrange the wedding ceremony, to send out invitations, to perform sacrifices. Meanwhile Phaedria's friends will give him what they promised. With that Phormio will pay the money back.

ANTIPHO. On what pretext? What will he say?

GETA. You ask? He'll say, "How many bad omens have appeared to me! A strange black dog wandered into my house. A snake fell from the rooftiles into the courtyard. A hen crowed. The soothsayer warns against it, the auspices forbid it. Imagine starting new business before the winter solstice!" (*Throws up hands and looks up to heavens in mock gesture of impossibility.*) Whatever is the best excuse, that's what he'll use.

ANTIPHO (*dubious*). If only it's done!

GETA. It will be done. Depend on me. (*Sees* DEMIPHO *coming out.*) Your father is coming out. Go, tell Phaedria the money is available.   (*Exit* ANTIPHO.)

(DEMIPHO, *holding a small bag of money, comes out with* CHREMES.)

DEMIPHO (*to* CHREMES). Rest easy, I tell you. I'll see to it that he doesn't cheat us. I won't let this (*Gesturing with the money bag.*) get out of my hands without having witnesses. In their presence I'll state to whom I'm giving it and for what reason.

GETA (*aside*). How cautious he is where there's no reason for it!

CHREMES. Yes. That's what we have to do. And hurry while he is still willing. For if the other girl insists too much, he may perhaps turn us down.

GETA (*aside*). You've hit the nail on the head!

DEMIPHO (*to* GETA). Well, lead me to him.

GETA. Without delay!

CHREMES (*to* DEMIPHO). When you've finished with this, go straight to my wife so she can meet with the girl before she leaves here. Let my wife say that we are giving her to Phormio in marriage so that she won't get angry. And let her say that he's much more suitable for the girl since he is much more closely related to her—also that we haven't shirked our duty. A dowry has been given to him, as much as he wanted.

DEMIPHO. What damned concern is that of yours?

CHREMES. It's very much my concern, Demipho. It's not enough to have done your duty if public opinion doesn't approve. I want this to be done with the girl's consent, so she won't say she was thrown out.

DEMIPHO. I could do that for you.

CHREMES. A woman gets on better with a woman.

DEMIPHO. All right, I'll ask your wife to do it.

CHREMES. Now I wonder where I can find my Lemnian family!

(DEMIPHO *goes toward the market place to find* PHORMIO. CHREMES *remains where he is on stage.*)

Act V

(*While Chremes is standing on the stage, Sophrona, Phanium's nurse, comes out of Demipho's house, very upset.*)

SOPHRONA. What am I to do? Where can a poor woman like me find a friend? To whom should I turn with these latest developments? Where can I seek aid? For I'm afraid that because of my urging my mistress may suffer terrible harm. I hear young Antipho's father is violently opposed to what his son did. (*Wrings her hands.*)

CHREMES (*looking up, aside*). Now who is that old woman who has just come out of my brother's house all upset?

SOPHRONA. It was our poverty that drove me to it, although I knew the marriage was shaky. So I recommended it in order that, until her father was found, her life would be secure.

CHREMES (*aside, getting excited*). By Pollux, unless my mind is playing tricks on me, or my eyesight is failing, I certainly see my daughter's nurse!

SOPHRONA. And he hasn't been traced yet . . .

CHREMES (*aside*). What do I do?

SOPHRONA. . . . the man who is her father.

CHREMES (*aside*). Shall I approach her or wait until I make out better what she is saying?

SOPHRONA. But if I can't find him, there is nothing for me to fear.

CHREMES (*looking carefully, aside*). It's she all right! I'll speak to her.

SOPHRONA (*noticing him*). Who is this speaking?

CHREMES (*calling*). Sophrona!

SOPHRONA. And he calls me by name!

CHREMES. Look at me!

SOPHRONA (*unbelieving*). Gods, I pray you, is this Stilpo?

CHREMES. No, it isn't.

SOPHRONA. You're not, you say?

CHREMES. Come away from here, away from the doors a little, on that side if you please, Sophrona. (*She moves toward him.*) Don't call me by that name hereafter.

SOPHRONA. Why? Tell me, please, aren't you the one you always said you were?

CHREMES. Sh!

SOPHRONA. Why are you afraid of those doors? (*Indicates* CHREMES' *house.*)

CHREMES. I have a wild beast of a wife shut up behind those doors. But that name, Stilpo—that's what I falsely called myself once, so that you people might not imprudently blurt out my real name by chance and have my wife find out about it later somehow.

SOPHRONA. So that's why we, poor women, could never find you here!

CHREMES (*cheerfully*). Well, tell me. What have you to do with the family whose house you just came out of? Where are my wife and daughter?

SOPHRONA (*with grief*). It's very sad.

CHREMES (*alarmed*). Why, what's the matter? Are they alive?

SOPHRONA. Your daughter is alive. Her mother, because of all her trouble and sorrow, died, poor woman.

CHREMES (*sadly*). That's too bad!

SOPHRONA. I, however, since I am an old woman, deserted, in need, unknown—I arranged, as well as I could, for the marriage of the girl to the young man who is the master of this house here. (*Indicates* DEMIPHO's *house.*)

CHREMES. To Antipho?

SOPHRONA. That's the very one I mean.

CHREMES (*alarmed*). What? Does he have two wives?

SOPHRONA (*smiling*). Oh, no! Please! He has only one—her alone.

CHREMES (*puzzled*). What about the other girl who is said to be a relative?

SOPHRONA. She's the one!

CHREMES. What do you mean?

SOPHRONA. It was done by collusion—so that the young man who loved her could have her without a dowry.

CHREMES (*relieved*). May the gods bless us! How often what you would not dare to wish for happens by chance! Now that I've arrived home, I inadvertently find my daughter married to the man I wanted and quietly, the way I wanted. What the two of us exerted every effort to accomplish, Antipho, all by himself, has accomplished with no supervision by us!

SOPHRONA (*worried*). Now consider what has to be done. The young man's father has arrived, and they say he is very much opposed to what has happened.

CHREMES. There's no danger. But by the gods and men, be very careful no one finds out she is my daughter!

SOPHRONA. No one will find out from me.

CHREMES. Come with me. We will hear the rest of the story inside.

(*The two enter* DEMIPHO'*s house.*)

(*Enter* DEMIPHO *and* GETA *from the market place.*)

DEMIPHO. It's our own fault that we make it worthwhile for people to be bad while trying our hardest to be considered good and kind. Out of the frying pan into the fire, as they say. Wasn't it enough to be wronged by him? Did we have to throw money his way too, so he should have enough to live on until he brings off some other outrage?

GETA (*playing along*). You're absolutely right!

DEMIPHO. Now this is the reward for those who act rightly and properly——

GETA. Very true!

DEMIPHO. ——so that we have handled this matter very foolishly.

GETA (*as if really concerned*). If only this procedure gets us out of our difficulty and he marries the girl!

DEMIPHO (*with alarm*). Is there still some doubt about it?

GETA. You never can tell, by Hercules—considering the kind of man he is—whether he may not change his mind.

DEMIPHO (*starting to boil*). What! Change his mind?

GETA. I don't know. But I mention it just in case.

DEMIPHO (*calming down*). Well, as my brother advised, I'll get his wife to come out here so she can talk with her. You, Geta, go on ahead and tell the girl that Nausistrata is coming.

(DEMIPHO *enters* CHREMES' *house.*)

GETA. Money has been found for Phaedria. About a severe scolding, there's not a word. Arrangements have been made that the girl should not leave here for the present. (*Looks satisfied.*) Now, what's next? What will happen? You're not out of the woods yet, Geta! You solve one problem to acquire another. There will be a reckoning yet, Geta! The threat of punishment which loomed over you all day has gone, but the number of lashes due you increases if you don't watch out.

Now I'll go home and tell Phanium not to be alarmed about Phormio or whatever Nausistrata says to her.

(*Enters* DEMIPHO'*s house.*)

(DEMIPHO *and* NAUSISTRATA *come out of her house, still in conversation.*)

DEMIPHO. Well, then, Nausistrata, with your customary tact get her to be pleased with what we are doing so that she will do what she has to willingly.

NAUSISTRATA. I'll do so.

DEMIPHO. Help me now with your assistance and resources just as you've always done.

NAUSISTRATA. I'm glad to do it. And, by Pollux, it's my husband's fault that I can do less than I should.

DEMIPHO. Why, what do you mean?

NAUSISTRATA. Because, by Pollux, he manages my father's carefully acquired properties too inefficiently. Why, from those estates we own my father used to make two silver talents a year! What a difference there is between two men!

DEMIPHO. Two talents, you say?

NAUSISTRATA (*bitterly*). And even in those days, when prices were much lower than now—two talents a year!

DEMIPHO. Remarkable!

NAUSISTRATA. What do you think of that!

DEMIPHO. Obviously!

NAUSISTRATA. I wish I had been born a man—I'd show him!

DEMIPHO. I'm sure you would.

NAUSISTRATA. How . . .

DEMIPHO (*solicitously*). Spare yourself, please, so you will be able to deal with her—so that the young woman does not tire you out.

NAUSISTRATA. I'll do as you say. But I see my husband coming out of your house.

(*Enter* CHREMES *from* DEMIPHO's *house.* DEMIPHO *approaches him, while* NAUSISTRATA *remains in front of her house.*)

CHREMES (*a bit worried*). Uh-hm, Demipho, have you given him the money yet?

DEMIPHO. I attended to it right away.

CHREMES. I wish you hadn't given it to him. (*Suddenly sees* NAUSISTRATA.) Oh, I see my wife. I almost said too much!

DEMIPHO. Why do you wish I hadn't, Chremes?

CHREMES (*trying to close the subject*). It's all right.

DEMIPHO. What are you up to? Have you spoken at all to Phanium as to why we are bringing Nausistrata to see her?

CHREMES. I dropped in there.

DEMIPHO. What does she say?

CHREMES (*not answering the question, but firmly*). She can't be sent away!

DEMIPHO (*puzzled*). Why can't she?

CHREMES. Because they both love one another very much.

DEMIPHO. What's that got to do with it?

CHREMES. Very much. Besides I found out she is related to us.

DEMIPHO. What? You're mad!

CHREMES. No. It's true. I'm not talking idly. I've recalled the circumstances.

DEMIPHO. Are you in your right mind?

NAUSISTRATA (*interrupting*). Now, I beg you, don't do wrong to a relative.

DEMIPHO (*brusquely*). She isn't!

CHREMES. Don't be so ready to deny it. Her father had a different name from the one she gave. That's why you went wrong.

DEMIPHO. Didn't she know her father?

CHREMES. She knew him. (*Gestures or winks to* DEMIPHO *to give him a hint so that* NAUSISTRATA *will not notice.*)

DEMIPHO (*not understanding the hint*). Why didn't she give his right name?

CHREMES (*annoyed*). Won't you ever give in and understand?

DEMIPHO (*puzzled*). But if you don't tell me anything?

CHREMES. You're killing me!

NAUSISTRATA (*to* DEMIPHO). I wonder what it's all about?

DEMIPHO. I assure you I don't know.

CHREMES. Do you want to know? So help me Jupiter, there is no one more closely related to her than you and I!

DEMIPHO. Gods help us! Let's go to her! We've got to clear this thing up one way or another together.

CHREMES. Ah! (*As if to say, "It's not so easy."*)

DEMIPHO. What's the matter?

CHREMES. Do you have so little faith in me?

DEMIPHO (*beginning to understand*). Do you want me to trust you? Do you want me to stop asking questions about the matter? Very well. I stop. Now what is to happen to our friend's daughter?

CHREMES. It's all right.

DEMIPHO. So we don't need her? (*Indicating* NAUSISTRATA.)

CHREMES. What for?

DEMIPHO. And the girl stays?

CHREMES. Yes.

DEMIPHO. Well then, you may go home now, Nausistrata.

NAUSISTRATA. Yes, it's certainly better for all concerned if she stays here rather than what you had planned. For she seemed a very nice and well-brought-up young lady when I saw her.

(*Exit into her house.*)

DEMIPHO (*very curious*). Now, what's this all about?

CHREMES (*cautiously*). Has she shut the door?

DEMIPHO (*looking up*). She has.

CHREMES (*excitedly*). Oh Jupiter! The gods certainly look out for us! I've found my daughter! She's married to your son!

DEMIPHO (*surprised*). What! How could it have happened?

CHREMES (*looking toward his door*). This place isn't safe enough to tell the story.

DEMIPHO. Then come inside to my house.

CHREMES. Now listen, I don't want our sons to find out about this.

(*The two go into* DEMIPHO'S *house*.)

(*Enter* ANTIPHO *from the market place*.)

ANTIPHO (*looking worried*). No matter what is the state of my own affairs, I'm happy that my cousin has what he wants. How sensible it is to set your heart on the kinds of desires for which, when things stand in the way of your attaining them, you can find a remedy with little effort! As soon as Phaedria found the money he was free of worry. But I have no way of extricating myself from my troubles. If my marriage is kept secret I'm in fear; if it is revealed I'm in disgrace. And I would not be going home now if I didn't have some hope held out to me of keeping her.

But where can I now find Geta? (*Looks up the street*.)

(*Enter* PHORMIO *from the same direction*.)

PHORMIO (*aside*). I received the money, handed it over to the procurer, and took the girl away. I've seen to it that Phaedria will have her for his very own. And she's no longer a slave; he has freed her. Now just one thing remains for me to accomplish —to get the leisure from the old men to do some drinking. I plan to spend the next few days on that. (*Smacks his lips*.)

ANTIPHO (*seeing him*). But it's Phormio! (*Approaching*.) Well?

PHORMIO. What do you mean?

ANTIPHO. What's Phaedria going to do now? How does he plan to enjoy his love to the fullest?

PHORMIO. He is going to take turns with you now. *He* is going to take over *your* role.

ANTIPHO. What role?

PHORMIO. Avoiding his father. And he asks that you take over his role—pleading his case for him. For he is going to be drinking at my house. I will tell the old men I am going to Sunium on business to buy the lady's maid whom Geta spoke about, so that when they don't see me here they won't think I am just squandering their money. (*Sound of a door.*) But the door is opening in your house.

ANTIPHO (*trying to hide*). Take a look! Who is coming out?

PHORMIO. It's Geta.

(ANTIPHO *returns to normal.*)

(GETA *emerges from* DEMIPHO's *house, not seeing anyone at first.*)

GETA (*exultantly*). Ah Fortune, Oh Lucky Fortune! With what benefits have you suddenly loaded this day for my master, Antipho, by your aid!

ANTIPHO (*to* PHORMIO). What does he mean?

GETA. And from his friends you have removed the burden of fear! But I must not delay now. I'll put the ends of my cloak on my shoulders (*Does so.*) and hurry to find him, so that he will know what has happened.

ANTIPHO (*to* PHORMIO). Do *you* understand what he is talking about?

PHORMIO (*with a gesture of ignorance*). Do you?

ANTIPHO (*similarly*). No.

PHORMIO. Neither do I.

GETA (*eagerly*). I'll go on to the procurer. That's where they are now.

ANTIPHO. Hey, Geta!

GETA (*not seeing* ANTIPHO; *very annoyed*). There you are! I'm not surprised! As usual, there's always somebody to call you back and delay you when you've started to run!

ANTIPHO (*louder*). Geta!

GETA (*as before*). By Hercules, he keeps it up! (*Contemptuously.*) You won't get the better of me by your insolence. (*Continues going.*)

ANTIPHO. Won't you wait?

GETA (*still not recognizing him and still annoyed*). Go and get yourself flogged!

ANTIPHO. That's what will happen to you if you don't stop, you whipping block!

GETA (*stopping*). That must be a member of my family—he threatens me with punishment. But isn't that whom I'm looking for? (*Looking carefully.*) It is! Up to him at once! (*Runs up to* ANTIPHO *in extreme elation.*) Oh most well-endowed of all men that exist! There are no two ways about it, Antipho—you are the only one who is loved by the gods!

ANTIPHO (*doubtfully*). If that were only so! But I'd like to be told how I am to believe that.

GETA (*eagerly*). Is it enough if I get you drenched in joy?

ANTIPHO (*sarcastic*). You devastate me!

PHORMIO (*coming up to* GETA). Cut out the promises! Just tell us what news you bring.

GETA. Oh, you were here also, Phormio?

PHORMIO. I was. But what are you waiting for?

GETA (*joyfully*). Listen to this! (*To* PHORMIO.) As soon as we gave you the money in the market place, we went right home. (*To* ANTIPHO.) Meanwhile the master sends me to your wife.

ANTIPHO. What for?

GETA. I won't bother to explain that, for it has nothing to do with the matter at hand, Antipho. (*Warming up to his story.*) When I started to go into the women's apartments, the slave-boy Mida comes running up to me. He grabs me by my cloak from behind, he jerks me back. I turn around and ask him why he is holding me back. He says it's forbidden to go in to the young mistress. "Sophrona has just brought in old Master's brother, Chremes," he says, and tells me that he is now in there with them. (*Looks at the other two for effect.*) When I've heard this, I continue on my way (*Imitating with his voice secrecy of action.*) up to the door of the room, but quietly, on tiptoe. (*Pauses.*) I get there, I stand close, I hold my breath, I apply my ear (*Imitative gesture.*) In that way I start to listen and that's how I overhear their conversation!

PHORMIO. Bravo, Geta!

GETA (*his eyes shining*). And at that moment I heard the most beautiful piece of news—so beautiful, by Hercules, that I almost shouted with joy!

ANTIPHO (*all ears*). What?

GETA (*smiling*). What do you think?

ANTIPHO (*doubtfully*). I don't know.

GETA (*almost beside himself*). And it's marvelous! Your uncle turns out to be the father of your wife Phanium!

ANTIPHO (*unbelieving*). What are you talking about?

GETA. A long time ago he had a secret affair with her mother in Lemnos.

PHORMIO. Nonsense! How would she not know her own father?

GETA. Believe me, Phormio, there must be some reason. But do you think, being outside the door, I could understand everything they were saying to one another inside?

ANTIPHO. Come to think of it, by Hercules, I also heard a story like that.

GETA. Here's something else, which will give you even more reason to believe. (*Pauses.*) Your uncle goes outside. Not much later he comes back with your father, and then both say you are

being given permission to keep her. Finally I am sent off to find
you and bring you home.

ANTIPHO (*joyously*). So take me! What are you waiting for?

GETA (*eagerly*). I'll do so at once!

ANTIPHO (*happily and gratefully*). Oh, my dear Phormio
good-bye and good wishes!

PHORMIO (*clapping him on the back*). My best wishes to you
Antipho! Well done, so help me gods! I'm very glad.

(ANTIPHO *and* GETA *go into* DEMIPHO's *house.* PHORMIO *remains outside alone, thinking aloud.*)

PHORMIO. Suddenly so much good fortune for them! And now
I've been given the supreme opportunity of outwitting the old
men and freeing Phaedria from his money worries, so that he
doesn't have to go begging from any of his friends. For this same
money, just as it's been given, will remain in his possession
whether they want it to or not! The course of events has shown
me how I can force this to happen.

Now I have to change my gestures and facial expression. I'll
go into this alleyway here nearby. Then I'll show myself to them
when they come outside. I don't intend to go to Sunium on business as I had pretended I was. (*Hides in alleyway.*)

(CHREMES *and* DEMIPHO *come out of the latter's house, both
smiling.*)

DEMIPHO. I give great thanks to the gods—and they deserve
it—that things have turned out so favorable for us! Now, as
quickly as possible, we must get hold of Phormio, before he
makes a mess of our thirty minas, so we can get them back.

PHORMIO (*leaves his hiding place, speaking aside, but so as to
be overheard*). I'll go and see Demipho, if he is at home, so
that . . .

DEMIPHO. Why, we were just going to see you, Phormio.

PHORMIO. For the same reason, perhaps?

DEMIPHO. Yes, by Hercules!

PHORMIO. I thought so. Why were you going to see me?

DEMIPHO (*deprecatingly*). A trifling matter.

PHORMIO. Were you afraid that I might not accomplish what
I had once taken upon myself to do? (*Proudly.*) Look here! No
matter how poor I am, there is still one thing I've been most
careful about—keeping my word!

CHREMES (*his mind on his daughter, to* DEMIPHO). Isn't she
a real lady, as I told you?

DEMIPHO. Very much so!

PHORMIO (*pressing his advantage*). So accordingly, this is what

I'm coming to announce, Demipho—I'm ready. Give me my bride whenever you wish. I've put all my other affairs aside, as is right, since I've noticed that this is what you so very much wanted.

DEMIPHO (*uneasily*). But this gentleman (*Indicating* CHREMES.) has urged me not to give her to you. "What will people say," he told me, "if you do it? Before, when it could have been done honorably, she wasn't given to him. Now, to be divorced and driven out is shameful!" Almost the same objections you made to me in person.

PHORMIO (*pretending indignation*). You two are certainly playing around with me in a high and mighty way!

DEMIPHO. How?

PHORMIO. You're asking me? Now I won't even be able to marry the other girl. How will I look if I go back to the girl I jilted?

CHREMES. Just say to her, "It seems that Antipho is unwilling to give the girl up."

DEMIPHO. And besides, my son *is* unwilling to give the girl up. So if you don't mind, go over to the market place and have the banker retransfer the money to my account, Phormio.

PHORMIO (*sarcastically*). You mean the money I then transferred to the accounts of those to whom I owed it?

DEMIPHO (*at a loss, to* CHREMES). What then shall we do?

(CHREMES *shrugs his shoulders slightly.*)

PHORMIO (*insistently*). If you want me to marry the girl you promised me, I'll marry her. But if the fact is that you want her to stay in your family, then the *dowry* stays with me, Demipho. For it is not fair for me to be cheated to help you people when out of consideration for you I have broken my engagement with the other girl who was to bring me as much dowry.

DEMIPHO (*angry*). To Hades with your high-toned airs, you vagabond! Do you think we don't know about you and your tricks?

PHORMIO (*pretending anger*). I'm getting angry!

DEMIPHO (*sarcastically*). Would you really marry the girl if she were given to you?

PHORMIO (*blandly*). Just give it a try!

DEMIPHO (*heatedly*). That my son should live with her at your house—that was the plan you fellows had!

PHORMIO (*innocently*). What *are* you talking about?

DEMIPHO (*roughly*). Come on! Hand over the money!

PHORMIO. Well then, hand over the girl!

DEMIPHO (*roaring*). You march straight to court!

PHORMIO. I'm telling *you!* If you persist in being unpleasant . . .

DEMIPHO (*challenging*). What will you do?

PHORMIO. I? (*Mildly threatening.*) Maybe you think I act a patron only for those without dowries. I also help those *with* dowries.

CHREMES. What's that to us?

PHORMIO. Nothing. (*Pointedly.*) I know a lady here (*Indicating* CHREMES' *house.*) whose husband has . . .

CHREMES (*flustered*). Er—uh—hm! (*Gesturing helplessly toward* PHORMIO.)

DEMIPHO (*puzzled, to* CHREMES). What is it?

PHORMIO (*relentlessly*). . . . . another wife in Lemnos . . .

CHREMES (*in despair*). I'm done for!

PHORMIO (*enjoying himself*). . . . . by whom he had a daughter and brought her up.

CHREMES (*as before*). I'm buried!

PHORMIO. And that is what I'm soon going to tell *her*. (*Indicating* CHREMES' house.)

CHREMES (*holding out his hands to* PHORMIO). I beg you don't do it!

PHORMIO (*pretending surprise*). Oh, were you the man?

DEMIPHO (*bitterly*). What sport he is making of us!

CHREMES (*defeated*). All right. We let you go.

PHORMIO. Nonsense!

CHREMES. What do you want? The money that you have you can keep.

PHORMIO (*ironically*). Thank you! (*Pretending anger.*) Then why, by Pollux, did you play around with me so foolishly, with your childish inability to make up your minds: "I won't." "I will." "I will." then "I won't." again. "Take it." "Give it back." "What was said is unsaid." "What was just settled is unsettled."

CHREMES (*distraught*). How or from whom did he find out?

DEMIPHO (*worried*). I don't know! And yet I'm sure I told nobody.

CHREMES (*as before*). It's like magic! May the gods help me!

PHORMIO (*aside, smiling*). I've fixed *their* wagon!

DEMIPHO (*disgruntled, to* CHREMES). Huh! That he should get such a large sum of money out of us while he laughs at us so openly! I'd rather die! (*Firmly.*) Stand up to it! Show your manly courage! You see that your misconduct has been given full publicity, and that you can no longer hide it from your wife. She'll take it better, Chremes, if we ourselves tell her what she is soon going to hear from others anyway. Then we will be able to take revenge on this filthy rascal in our own way.

PHORMIO (*aside.*) Oho! If I don't watch out, I'm stuck! They are preparing to go at me like gladiators—with no holds barred!

CHREMES (*to* DEMIPHO). But I'm afraid there is no way of pacifying her.

DEMIPHO. Keep your courage up! I'll restore good relations between you. We have this on our side, Chremes, that the girl's mother is no longer with us.

PHORMIO (*coming forward defiantly*). So that's how you're dealing with me? You're attacking very cleverly! (*Indicating* CHREMES.) He's going to be very sorry you goaded me, Demipho! (*To* CHREMES.) And what have *you* to say for yourself? After you did whatever you liked abroad and had no respect for this excellent lady (*Pointing to* CHREMES' *house.*) to keep you from insulting her in a most unheard of manner, you *now* come to wash away your sinful misconduct with tears? This is what I'll tell her and I'll make her so enraged with you that you won't be able to extinguish her anger even if you drip with tears.

DEMIPHO. Damnation! That's what the gods and goddesses should send you to! Did you ever see anybody so full of such damned effrontery! How is it that such a villain is not sent into exile into some god-forsaken wilderness for the good of society?!

CHREMES (*utterly helpless*). I've reached the point where I don't know what to say to him further!

DEMIPHO. I know! (*To* PHORMIO.) We're taking you to court. (*Lays a hand on him.*)

PHORMIO. To court? (*Smiles.*) Into here (*Points to* CHREMES' *house.*) if you like. (*Starts toward* CHREMES' *house.*)

CHREMES (*frantic*). Follow him! Hold him back while I call out the slaves!

DEMIPHO (*goes for* PHORMIO). I can't do it alone! Run up to him. (*Makes a grab for him.*)

PHORMIO (*turns to* DEMIPHO). That's one case of assault against you!

DEMIPHO. So take me to court! (CHREMES *grabs at* PHORMIO.)

PHORMIO. And a second case against you, Chremes! (*Frees himself.*)

CHREMES. Seize him! (*Tries it himself.*)

PHORMIO. So that's what you're doing! Well then, I must use my voice. (*Loudly.*) Nausistrata, come out!

CHREMES. Shut your dirty mouth! (*Vainly tries to grab hold of* PHORMIO *again.*) Look how strong he is!

PHORMIO (*calling.*) Nausistrata, I say!

DEMIPHO (*threateningly*). You won't keep quiet?

PHORMIO (*scornfully*). Keep quiet?

DEMIPHO (*to* CHREMES). If he doesn't come away with you, give him a few punches in the stomach!

PHORMIO. You can even gouge my eye out! I've got ways of getting even with you two properly! (*They tussle.*)

(NAUSISTRATA *comes out.*)

NAUSISTRATA (*looking around*). Who called my name? (*Sees the men still tussling.*) Hey! What's the commotion about, Husband? (*The fighting suddenly stops: there is silence.*)

PHORMIO (*to* CHREMES). Well, why are you now suddenly struck dumb?

NAUSISTRATA (*to* CHREMES). Who's this man? (*Indicates* PHORMIO.) Won't you answer me?

PHORMIO (*sarcastically*). You expect him to answer? He doesn't even know where he's at!

CHREMES (*frantically, to* NAUSISTRATA). Don't believe a word he says!

PHORMIO (*to* NAUSISTRATA). Go on, feel him! If he's not absolutely cold with fright, you can kill me.

CHREMES. It's nothing!

NAUSISTRATA. What is it then? What is he talking about?

PHORMIO (*to* NAUSISTRATA). You'll know soon enough. Just listen.

CHREMES (*scared*). Are you really going to believe him?

NAUSISTRATA. What is there not to believe, I ask you, when he hasn't spoken a word?

PHORMIO (*mockingly*). Poor fellow! He's delirious with fright!

NAUSISTRATA (*suspiciously*). By Pollux! It's not for nothing that you are so scared!

CHREMES. *I'm* scared?

PHORMIO. You certainly are! (*Challengingly.*) Since you're not scared, and what I tell her is nothing, then *you* tell her!

DEMIPHO. You villain! Should he tell it to help you out?

PHORMIO (*sarcastically*). Hey! You're certainly siding with your brother, aren't you?

NAUSISTRATA. Husband, won't you tell me?

CHREMES (*stammering with fear*). But . . .

NAUSISTRATA. What do you mean, "but"?

CHREMES. It's not necessary to speak!

PHORMIO. For you maybe, but she has to know. (*Spitefully, to* NAUSISTRATA.) In Lemnos——

NAUSISTRATA. What? What do you mean?

CHREMES (*to* PHORMIO, *desperately*). Won't you keep quiet?

PHORMIO. ——without your knowledge——

CHREMES (*hopelessly*). Good God!

PHORMIO (*triumphantly*). ——he got married!

NAUSISTRATA (*to* PHORMIO, *contemptuously, disbelieving*). My dear fellow, may the gods help you!

PHORMIO. But that's what he did!

NAUSISTRATA (*unhappily, accepting the truth*). Oh! may the gods help me!

PHORMIO (*pressing his advantage, maliciously*). And he had one child by her, a daughter, whom he acknowledged while your eyes were elsewhere!

CHREMES (*to* DEMIPHO, *groaning*). What do we do?

NAUSISTRATA. Oh immortal gods! What a deplorable and damnable thing to do!

PHORMIO (*to* CHREMES). What do you *do*? You've already done it!

NAUSISTRATA (*angry and disgusted*). Oh immortal gods! Did you ever hear of anything more shameful? That's men for you! But when it comes to their own wives, then they become old men! Demipho—I'm talking to you, for it just fills me with disgust to speak to *him*—so this is the meaning of those frequent visits and long stop-overs in Lemnos? So this was (*Sneeringly.*) the low prices which cut into our profits?

DEMIPHO (*trying to calm her*). I'm not denying, Nausistrata, that he deserves blame in this matter. But why not forgive and forget?

PHORMIO (*mockingly*). And now a few words for the dead.

DEMIPHO (*as before*). He didn't do it out of disrespect or dislike for you. (*Pleading.*) Overcome with wine, almost fifteen years ago, he made love to the young woman, and then the girl was born. He never touched her after that. The woman in question is dead—she's no longer with us. Therefore, I beg of you with your usual good nature, be forbearing now.

NAUSISTRATA. Why should I be forbearing? (*Half-tearful.*) I feel so miserable I don't want to have any more to do with this kind of thing! But how can I hope not to? Am I to expect that as he gets older he will sin less? He was already an old man then, if old age makes people respectable! Or do my looks and my age make me more attractive now, Demipho? What guarantee do you give me that I should expect or hope that it will not happen again in the future?

PHORMIO (*mockingly imitating an undertaker's announcement*). The funeral of Chremes is about to take place. All who find it convenient are invited to attend. That's the way I handle them! Well now, does anyone else want to attack Phormio? (*Vindictively*.) Just try it! I'll get him the same kind of beating by misfortune that *he* got. (*Indicating* CHREMES.)

DEMIPHO. Enough of these hard feelings, Nausistrata! You've been angry enough at your husband.

PHORMIO (*aside*). Well, let him come back into her good graces now. I've got my revenge. Now she has something she can nag him about for the rest of his life.

NAUSISTRATA (*to* DEMIPHO, *ironically*). I deserved this kind of treatment, I suppose! What do you want me to do now, Demipho? Recite item by item the kind of wife I was to him?

DEMIPHO (*sympathetically*). I know all about that as well as you.

NAUSISTRATA. Do you think I deserved what he did?

DEMIPHO. Not in the world! But since what's done can't be undone by recriminations, forgive and forget. He implores, he confesses, he makes a clean breast of it. What more do you want?

PHORMIO (*aside*). Well then, before she pardons him, I will look out for myself and Phaedria. (*To* NAUSISTRATA.). Oh, Nausistrata, before you answer him heedlessly, listen to me.

NAUSISTRATA. What is it?

PHORMIO. I got thirty minas out of him by a deception. I gave them to your son. He gave them to a procurer in payment for his mistress.

CHREMES (*shocked*). Eh? What do you say?

NAUSISTRATA (*to* CHREMES). Does it seem so unseemly to you that your son, a young man, has a mistress when you have two wives? Aren't you ashamed of yourself? How will you have the face to scold him? Answer me!

(CHREMES *looks down*.)

DEMIPHO (*to* NAUSISTRATA). He will do as you wish.

NAUSISTRATA. Better still, if you want to know my decision— I don't forgive him, or promise anything, or give an answer before I've seen my son. I entrust everything to *his* judgement. I'll do what *he* tells me. (*Nods decisively*.)

PHORMIO. You're a wise woman, Nausistrata.

NAUSISTRATA (*to* DEMIPHO, *ignoring* CHREMES). Is that good enough for you?

DEMIPHO. Good enough!

CHREMES (*aside, relieved*). Why, I'm getting off easy and better than I expected! Wonderful!

NAUSISTRATA (*to* PHORMIO). You sir, tell me what your name is.

PHORMIO. Phormio—a friend of your family and the best friend of your son Phaedria.

NAUSISTRATA (*cordially*). Phormio, from now on, by Castor, I'll do anything you say or wish!

PHORMIO. That's very kind of you!

NAUSISTRATA. Well, you deserve it!

PHORMIO (*mischievously*). Would you like to begin by doing something that will make me very happy, Nausistrata, and that will annoy your husband?

NAUSISTRATA. I do.

PHORMIO. Invite me to dinner!

NAUSISTRATA. By Pollux, you're certainly invited!

DEMIPHO. Let's go in.

NAUSISTRATA. Very well. But where is Phaedria?

PHORMIO. I'll have him here soon.

CANTOR (to *audience*). Our best wishes to you. Give us your applause.

The Woman of Andros (Andria)

A COMEDY

by

TERENCE

❖ ❖ ❖

translated by
Samuel Lieberman

DRAMATIS PERSONAE

SIMO, an elderly Athenian
SOSIA, his freedman and steward
DAVUS, slave of Simo
MYSIS, female servant of Glycerium
PAMPHILUS, a young man, son of Simo
CHARINUS, a young man, friend of Pamphilus
BYRRIA, slave of Charinus
LESBIA, a midwife
CHREMES, an elderly Athenian, friend of Simo
CRITO, an elderly citizen of Andros visiting Athens
DROMO, overseer of slaves to Simo
GLYCERIUM, the young Woman of Andros (does not appear on-
stage, but speaks one line offstage)
CANTOR (singer), a member of the cast who calls for applause at
the end.

Scene: A street in Athens, showing on one side the house of
Simo and on the other the house of Glycerium. An altar of
Apollo with cut branches on it stands near Simo's house. On the
right is a street leading to the center of town, and on the left a
street leading to the harbor.

Prologue

When the author first turned his attention to writing, he thought that the only responsibility he had was that whatever plays he wrote should please the public. But he knows that things have turned out quite differently. For he uses up his energies in writing prologues not to explain the plot, but to answer the malicious accusations of a hostile older writer. Now please listen to the kind of thing they find fault with. Menander wrote *The Woman of Andros* and *The Woman of Perinthos*. Anyone who knows one of these plays knows them both, for as they were written they differ not so much in plot as in theme and style. Our author admits that he transferred whatever was suitable from *The Woman of Perinthos* to his own *Woman of Andros* and used it for his own. This is what his detractors find fault with, and in doing so they argue that it is not proper to run two plays together into one. Are they trying to show by their knowledge that they know nothing? When they accuse him, they are accusing Naevius, Plautus, and Ennius [1] whom our author takes as his models and whose freedom in this matter he very much wants to emulate rather than the plodding accuracy of his detractors. So I warn them to keep quiet in the future and to stop their malicious attacks lest people come to know of their wrongdoings. Now give us your complete attention, be fair-minded, and learn the facts, so that you may be able to tell whether the author has any future to hope for, whether the plays which he will hereafter write, basing himself on Greek plays, should be seen by you or be driven from the stage before they appear.   (*Exit.*)

[1] The Roman poet Naevius, third century B.C., wrote tragedies, comedies, and an epic on the Punic Wars. Ennius, 239–169 B.C., highly revered by the Romans, was a great innovator in that he was the first to write an epic on a Roman subject in dactylic hexameter in Latin, *Annales.* He also wrote tragedies and a few comedies based on Greek works.

Act I

(*Enter Simo and Sosia from the right. Behind them are two slaves carrying provisions just purchased.*)

SIMO (*to slaves*). You two, carry those things inside. And hurry! (*Exeunt slaves into* SIMO's *house.*) Sosia, stay a while. There's something I want to say to you.

SOSIA. Consider it said—you want these things attended to properly. Right?

SIMO. No. Something else.

SOSIA. What is there that my culinary skills can accomplish for you more than this?

SIMO. It isn't your well-known skills in cooking that I need for the matter I have in mind, but those abilities that I always knew you had in you—trustworthiness and the ability to keep a secret.

SOSIA (*bowing slightly in acknowledgement*). I await your wishes.

SIMO. You know how just and mild your servitude to me was for you from the day I bought you, from childhood on. From a slave I made you my freedman, because you served in a manner worthy of a free man. The highest award I had I gave to you.

SOSIA. I am well aware of it.

SIMO. Not that I would change what I have done.

SOSIA. I'm happy that whatever I have done pleases you, Simo, and I am thankful that it has been appreciated by you. But all this disturbs me—for your mentioning it is like reproaching a man for not remembering a benefit conferred on him. (*With less humility.*) Why don't you say directly what it is you want of me?

SIMO. So I will. Let me start by telling you this first: the plans for marriage, which you believed to be real, are not real.

SOSIA. Then why did you pretend?

SIMO. I will tell you everything from the beginning. In this way you will understand my son's conduct, my plan, and what I want you to do in this matter. (*Pauses.*) Now, when my son had reached his majority, Sosia, and had attained the right to lead his life more independently—for before that how could you know or even begin to know his true nature as long as being under age, fear, and tutor restrained him?—

SOSIA. Very true.

SIMO. The kinds of activities that young men generally get interested in, such as raising horses or hunting dogs, or taking up with philosophers, in none of these was he particularly interested to the exclusion of the others, but he engaged in all of them in moderation. This pleased me.

SOSIA. And with good reason. For this I consider to be a particularly useful principle in life—not to go to extremes.

SIMO. That is the way he led his life: he got along well with others; he devoted himself to those he was with when he was with them; he adjusted himself to their interests, opposing no one and never putting himself at their head—in such a way as to most easily find popularity without ill-will and congenial friends.

SOSIA. He led his life wisely. For nowadays conformity breeds friends and sincerity breeds unpopularity.

SIMO. Meanwhile, about three years ago a woman moved into this neighborhood from Andros, driven by poverty and her relatives' neglect, a woman of outstanding beauty and in the bloom of youth.

SOSIA. Ai! I'm afraid the woman from Andros brings trouble of some kind.

SIMO. At first she lived respectably, though frugally and in difficult circumstances, trying to make a living with wool and loom. But then (*In the tone of a "man of the world."*) one lover approached her offering payment, and then a second likewise— and since all human nature is more inclined to pleasure than to hard work, she accepted their terms and was in business.

As it turned out, the young men who then happened to be her lovers introduced my son to her house so that he might dine with them. At once I thought to myself, "He's surely caught. He's smitten." I used to watch their slave-boys coming and going in the morning and would ask them, "Well, boys, tell me, will you, who had Chrysis last night?" That was the Andrian woman's name, you see.

SOSIA. I understand.

SIMO. They would say Phaedrus, or Clinias, or Niceratus. These three were then her lovers at the same time. "Eh, and what about Pamphilus?" I would say. "Him? Oh, he contributes his share and dines with them." That made me happy. I would ask the same way on another day. I found out that there was nothing whatever involving Pamphilus. In fact, I thought him a well tested example of continence. For when anyone is in the company of people of such character and yet doesn't get his passions aroused by it, you can be sure that he himself is able to maintain control over his behavior.

Not only was *I* pleased with this, but with one accord everyone said complimentary things about him and praised my good fortune in having a son endowed with such character. But why go on? Attracted by his reputation, Chremes approached me to offer his only daughter in marriage to my son, with a very large dowry. I was delighted. I agreed to their betrothal, and today was set for the wedding.

SOSIA. Then what is in the way of its taking place?

SIMO. You'll hear. About a few days after these things happened our neighbor Chrysis died.

SOSIA. Oh good! I'm glad. I was afraid for him because of Chrysis.

SIMO. Then my son began to spend lots of time with those who had been her lovers. He helped them with the funeral arrangements; he would be sad at times, occasionally bursting into tears. At the time I was pleased by it. I thought to myself, "After only a slight acquaintance he feels so strongly about her death. What if he had been her lover? How will he feel for *me,* his father?" These I thought were the acts of a kindly nature and a gentle heart. But why delay? I even went to the funeral for his sake, suspecting nothing wrong.

SOSIA. Hm! What do you mean?

SIMO. You'll find out. (*Pauses*). Her body is carried out of the house, we follow in the funeral procession. Meanwhile among the women who happen to be there I saw one young woman who looked—— (*His voice indicates admiration.*)

SOSIA. Beautiful, I suppose.

SIMO (*nods*). ——and with a face so gentle, so beautiful, that nothing could surpass it. Since she seemed to me to be grieving more than the other women and since her beauty was beyond the others', so fair and noble, I approached the maids in attendance and asked who she was. She was Chrysis' sister, they said. Right then it struck me. Aha! So that's it! That's the meaning of those tears, that's the reason for that compassion!

SOSIA. How I fear what you are leading up to!

SIMO. Meanwhile the funeral goes on. We follow. We come to the tomb, she is placed on the pyre, there is weeping. In the meantime the sister whom I mentioned has approached rather dangerously close to the flames, quite heedlessly. At that moment Pamphilus, pale with fright, reveals his well hidden and secret love. He runs over, clasps the girl around the waist, and says, "Glycerium dear, what are you doing? Why are you trying to destroy yourself?" Then she—in such a way that you could easily tell their deep love for one another—throws herself weeping into his arms, so tenderly.

Sosia. You don't say?

Simo. I returned from there angry and much put out. And yet, I had no sufficient cause for scolding him. He would say, "What have I done? What am I guilty of, or what sin have I committed, Father? She wanted to throw herself into the fire—I stopped her. I saved her." A proper way of putting it.

Sosia. You're right. For if you scolded him for helping save a life, what would you do if he committed damage or assault?

Simo. Next day Chremes came to me shouting that it was a shameless outrage, that he had found out that Pamphilus was practically married to this foreign woman. I did my best to deny that this was so. He insisted that it was a fact. Finally when I left him, it was clear that he refused to give his daughter in marriage.

Sosia. And your son, didn't you then . . . ?

Simo. Not even then was there a strong enough reason for scolding him.

Sosia. Why? Tell me.

Simo. He would say, "You yourself have set limits to this affair. The time is near when I must live according to someone else's wishes. Let me now live in my own way."

Sosia. Then what grounds for scolding do you have left?

Simo. If because of his love affair he is unwilling to get married, that finally is a punishable offense on his part. Now this is what I am working on—to find a real cause for scolding him if he should refuse, and also if that rascal Davus has any plan in mind, he may use it up now when his schemes are no hindrance. He, I believe, with every means at his disposal will do his utmost to obstruct the marriage more to annoy me than to oblige my son.

Sosia. What for?

Simo. You ask? Evil mind, evil intentions. Indeed, if I notice that he—but why go on? Yet if what I wish happens, that is if Pamphilus does not make any objections, there is still Chremes to be won over. And I am hoping he will be. Now it's your responsibility to do a good job of pretending the wedding is on, of frightening Davus, and of watching to see what my son is up to.

Sosia. Good enough. I'll take care of it.

Simo. Let's go in now. You go first, I'll come later.

(Sosia *enters the house.* Simo *remains outside.*)

Simo. I have no doubt that my son is unwilling to get married, judging how scared Davus got when he heard that the marriage would take place. (Davus *appears at* Simo's *door.*) But there he's coming out.

(Davus *comes out, not seeing* Simo *at first.*)

Davus. I was wondering whether we would get away with it so easily, and I was worrying what the outcome of my master's leniency would be. When he heard that his son was not going to be accepted in marriage, he didn't say a word to either of us and he didn't get upset about it either.

Simo (*aside*). But he *will* say a word about it now and it won't be, I assure you, without severe punishment for you.

Davus (*half-aside*). What he wanted was to lead us on while we were off our guard through our mistaken happiness and hopeful that our fear was now removed. In this way he wanted to catch us by surprise so that there would be no time to think up a plan for disrupting the marriage. Clever!

Simo (*half-aside*). What is the scoundrel saying?

Davus (*catching sight of him, aside*). It's my master, and I didn't see him in time!

Simo (*peremptorily*). Davus!

Davus. Yes, what is it?

Simo. Uh, come over here a moment.

Davus (*aside*). What does he want? (*Approaches* Simo.)

Simo. Well?

Davus. What about?

Simo. You're asking *me?* There is a rumor that my son has a mistress.

Davus. People are always spreading rumors, you know.

Simo. Are you paying attention to me or not?

Davus. Of course I am.

Simo. But I would be an unreasonable father to inquire now into what he did before. For what he did previously doesn't concern me at all. As long as his youth prompted this kind of thing, I allowed it, so that he might satisfy his desires. Now, this day starts him on another way of life, it demands a change in conduct. From now on I demand, or if I must, I ask you, Davus, that he return to the right path. What is this, you ask? All those who have love affairs are reluctant to get married.

Davus. So people say.

Simo. Then, too, if someone has (*Pointedly.*) a bad adviser in this matter, (*Pauses for effect.*) this adviser guides the young man's already love-sick heart toward the worse course of action.

DAVUS (*innocently*). I don't know what you're talking about.

SIMO. You don't, eh?

DAVUS. No. I'm Davus, not Oedipus the riddle-solver.

SIMO. Do you want me to speak plainly about the rest of what I have to say?

DAVUS. I certainly do.

SIMO (*bluntly*). If I notice you trying any tricks today to hamper the marriage or trying to show how crafty you are in this matter, I'll have you cut to ribbons with whips and sent to the mill to stay there till you die. (*Shaking a finger at* DAVUS.) And I give you my word and I warn you that I will never release you from there. Well, have you understood that? Or don't you understand even now?

DAVUS. Oh, thoroughly. You've explained yourself very clearly. You haven't beaten around the bush at all.

SIMO (*raising his voice*). I would rather let myself be fooled in anything else than in this matter.

DAVUS (*with slight mockery*). Please, sir, don't say such things.

SIMO (*angrily*). Are you making fun of me? You don't fool me one bit. But I'm telling you, don't do anything rash. And don't say you weren't warned. Watch out! (*Strides off into his house.*)

DAVUS (*aside*). Well, Davus my boy, there is no time for indolence and inactivity if I've correctly understand the old man's intentions on the marriage. If it isn't cunningly prevented, I and my young master are lost. And I'm not sure what to do, whether to help Pamphilus or listen to the old man. If I abandon Pamphilus I fear for his life, but if I help him out I'm afraid of the old man's threats—and it's hard to fool him. He has just found out about the love affair, so he's angry and watching to see that I am not devising some scheme about the marriage. If he feels I am, I'm finished. Or if he wants to, he will find some excuse, and rightly or wrongly will send me head first to the mill. (*Shudders.*) In addition to these troubles of mine something else has been added. This girl from Andros, whether she's his wife or mistress, is pregnant by Pamphilus. (*Throws up his hands.*) That's the reward for helping them—hearing of their reckless-ness, for it's an undertaking of lunatics not lovers. When she has given birth, whether it's a boy or a girl, they have decided to acknowledge it and bring it up. And they've made up a story between them that she is an Athenian citizen. (*Tries to express the preposterousness of it in his face.*) It goes like this: "Once upon a time there was an elderly merchant from this city. His ship was wrecked off the island of Andros and he died." At that time, they say, she was cast ashore and Chrysis' father took the little orphan girl into his home. Fairy tales! To me at least it doesn't sound believable. And yet they like the fiction. (*Shrugs his shoulders.*)

(MYSIS *appears at* GLYCERIUM'S *door on her way out.*)

MYSIS (*in a tone of annoyance, to another servant inside*). I've heard you, I've heard you, Archylis. You're telling me to get Lesbia the midwife. But honestly, by Pollux, she is a drunken reckless woman and not really the kind of person to whom to entrust a woman in her first pregnancy. I should get her anyway? (*The door slams shut.*) Look at how the old hag insists on her own way! Just because she's her crony and they get drunk together. Oh, gods, I pray you, give her an easy pregnancy—and that midwife, please let her make her mistakes on somebody else! (PAMPHILUS *appears at a distance.*) But why does Pamphilus look so pale and shaken? I'm afraid of what it may be. I'll wait and find out what sorrow his disturbed appearance reflects.

(*Enter* PAMPHILUS *in great distress.*)

PAMPHILUS. Is this the way for a human being to act? Is this the kind of thing a father should do?

MYSIS (*aside, alarmed*). What is that all about?

PAMPHILUS. Oh gods! What is this if not an affront? He had decided to get me married today. Shouldn't he have let me know in advance? Shouldn't he have consulted me beforehand?

MYSIS (*unhappily*). Oh my god! What is he saying?

PAMPHILUS. What is this? Has Chremes who had refused to give me his daughter in marriage changed his mind because he sees me unchanged? Is he so obstinate in his efforts to tear me away from Glycerium and make me miserable? If that happens I die completely. (*Clasps his hands together in despair.*) Oh gods and men, help me! Is there no way for me to escape marrying into Chremes' family? In how many different ways has he been scorned and spurned! It was all finished and done with. Hm! Rejected, I am recalled again. But for what reason? Unless it is what I suspect. The girl must be a horrible monstrosity, and since she can't be disposed of on anybody, they come to me.

MYSIS (*aside*). His words have made me miserable with fear.

PAMPHILUS. And what should I say of my father? Ah, to handle such an important matter with such indifference! Passing by me a while ago in the market place he says, "Pamphilus, you're to get married today. Go home and get ready." What he seemed to be saying to me was, "Get going and hang yourself." I was dumfounded. Do you think I could have uttered a word?

Or given any excuse, foolish though it might be and groundless and unreasonable? I was speechless! But if someone should now ask me what I would do if I had known in advance—I would do something to avoid doing this. (*With a gesture of despair.*) But now what should I try first? So many contradictory emotions have me in their grip pulling me in different directions—my love, pity for Glycerium, worry about the marriage, and then respect for my father who until now has treated me so leniently and allowed me to do whatever my heart desired. Can I turn against him? Oh, I am uncertain what to do.

MYSIS (*half-aside*). Oh, I'm afraid of what that "uncertain" will end up in. But now it's absolutely necessary either that he talk with her or that I say something to him about her. While his mind is in doubt it can be turned in one direction or another with a little push.

PAMPHILUS. Who is this talking? (*Sees* MYSIS.) Mysis, hello!

MYSIS. Oh, hello, Pamphilus.

PAMPHILUS (*anxiously*). How is she?

MYSIS. You ask? She is having labor pains, and she is also miserable with worry because your wedding has been set for today. Then too she is afraid you may desert her.

PAMPHILUS. What? Would I be able to do a thing like that? Would I allow myself to deceive the poor girl when she has entrusted her heart and her whole life to me, she whom I love so very dearly as my wife? *I* allow a girl of her character, taught and brought up in virtue and modesty, to be corrupted by force of poverty? I wouldn't do that.

MYSIS. I wouldn't have any fear if it depended on you alone. But I'm afraid that you may not be able to stand up to pressure.

PAMPHILUS. Do you think me so base, so unfeeling or so inhuman or barbarous, that neither intimacy nor love nor honor affect me and that they don't remind me to keep my word?

MYSIS. I know only this one thing, that she deserves that you should be mindful of her.

PAMPHILUS. "Mindful of her"? Oh Mysis, Mysis, even now those words of Chrysis concerning Glycerium are enscribed in my mind. When she was already dying she called for me. I came over. The rest of you were out of the room; we were alone. She began, "My dear Pamphilus, you see her beauty and her youth, and you are not unaware of (*Ironically.*) what good that will be to protect her modesty and her property. Therefore I beg of you by your right hand in mine and by your better self, by your promised word and by her helplessness, don't leave her and don't desert her. If I have loved you as my own brother, if she has always held you alone in the highest regard and has been considerate of you in everything, I give her to you as a husband, friend, guardian and father. Our property here I entrust to you and assign it to your protection." Thus she betrothed Glycerium to me. Death took her at once. (*Pauses.*) I accepted Glycerium and having accepted her I will keep her.

Mysis. That's my earnest hope.

Pamphilus. But why are you leaving the house?

Mysis. I'm going to fetch the midwife.

Pamphilus. Then hurry. And listen, not a word about the marriage, so that in her condition this won't be something else to——

Mysis. I understand.

(*She hurries off while* Pamphilus *remains, looking anxiously toward* Glycerium's *house.*)

Act II

(*Enter Charinus, looking unhappy, in conversation with Byrria.*)

Charinus (*in alarm*). What are you saying, Byrria? She is being married to Pamphilus today?

Byrria. That's true.

Charinus. How do you know?

Byrria. I've just heard it from Davus in the market place.

Charinus (*miserably*). Oh, god! Up to now my heart has been hovering between hope and fear, but now that hope has been taken away from me, my heart is worn out with worry and numb with exhaustion.

Byrria. Now, look here, Charinus. By Pollux, since what you want isn't possible, want what *is* possible.

Charinus. I want nothing but Philumena.

Byrria. Ah, how much better it is for you to make an effort to remove her from your mind than to say things that inflame your passions all the more to no purpose.

Charinus (*sharply*). All of us give good advice to the sick when we are well. If you were in my place you would feel differently.

Byrria. All right. Have it your way.

CHARINUS (*noticing* PAMPHILUS). But look, there's Pamphilus. I'm determined to try everything before I die.

BYRRIA (*aside*). What does he mean?

CHARINUS. I'll beg him, I'll implore him, I'll tell him of my love. I believe I'll convince him at least to postpone the wedding a few days. Meanwhile something will happen.

BYRRIA (*aside, dourly*). That "something" is nothing.

CHARINUS. Byrria, what do you think? Should I go over to him?

BYRRIA. Why not? If you accomplish nothing else, at least let him think that if he marries her, he will also be getting himself a lover for his wife.

CHARINUS. To Hades with those suspicions of yours, you scoundrel!

PAMPHILUS (*noticing* CHARINUS). I see Charinus. (*Approaching.*) Hello!

CHARINUS. Oh hello, Pamphilus. (*Earnestly.*) I come to you seeking hope, salvation, help and advice.

PAMPHILUS. By Pollux, I am in no position to give you advice and I certainly have no resources for helping you. But what is it all about?

CHARINUS. Are you getting married today?

PAMPHILUS. That's what they say.

CHARINUS (*emotionally*). Pamphilus, if you do this, today is the last time you see me.

PAMPHILUS. Why so?

CHARINUS. I'm afraid to speak. Tell him, please, Byrria.

BYRRIA. I'll tell him.

PAMPHILUS. What is it?

BYRRIA. He's in love with the girl you are to marry.

PAMPHILUS. He certainly doesn't feel the way I do. Now tell me, is there anything more between you and her, Charinus?

CHARINUS (*unhappily*). Ah, Pamphilus, nothing.

PAMPHILUS. How I wish there were!

CHARINUS. Now I beg you, by our friendship, by my love— don't get married to her. That's the main thing.

PAMPHILUS. *I'll* do my best.

CHARINUS. But if that is not possible, or if your heart is set on the marriage——

PAMPHILUS (*finding this absurd*). My heart set on it?

CHARINUS. ——at least put it off a few days while I go off somewhere (*Chokes up.*) so that I shouldn't see it.

PAMPHILUS. Now listen here, Charinus. I do not by any means think it the act of a gentleman to claim credit for a favor done by him when he doesn't deserve it. *I* am more eager to avoid the marriage than *you* are to obtain it.

CHARINUS (*relieved*). You have given me back my life.

PAMPHILUS. Now in any way you can, either you or Byrria here, make up, invent, find, work out a way by which she may be given to you. I'll work out a way by which she may not be given to me.

CHARINUS. Good enough.

PAMPHILUS (*sees* DAVUS *approaching*). Just in time, there's Davus, the man on whose advice I depend.

CHARINUS (*to* BYRRIA, *annoyed*). And you, by Hercules, you tell me nothing but what I don't need to know. Why don't you get away from me, and quickly?

BYRRIA. I certainly will, and gladly. (*Exit.*)

(*Enter* DAVUS *cheerfully from the direction of the market place.*)

DAVUS (*aside*). Good gods! What good news I bring! (*Looking around.*) But where shall I find Pamphilus, so that I may remove the fear he is now in and fill his heart with joy?

CHARINUS. He is happy about something.

PAMPHILUS (*to* CHARINUS). It's nothing. He just hasn't learned of my troubles yet.

DAVUS (*half-aside*). If he has heard that arrangements are being made for his wedding, I suppose he is now pale and shaken——

CHARINUS. Do you hear him?

DAVUS (*as before*). ——looking for me all over town. But where should I look for him? (*Musing.*) Now where should I go first?

CHARINUS (*to* PAMPHILUS). Why don't you speak to him?

DAVUS (*with decision*). I have it! (*Starts to go.*)

PAMPHILUS. Davus, stay where you are! Stop!

DAVUS (*turning around*). Who is it who—— (*Sees* PAMPHILUS.) Oh, Pamphilus, you're the very one I was looking for. (*Seeing* CHARINUS.) Good! Charinus too! Most opportunely. I want both of you.

PAMPHILUS (*sadly*). Davus, I'm done for!

DAVUS. Why don't you hear what I have to say?

PAMPHILUS. I'm doomed.

DAVUS (*reassuringly*). I know what you're afraid of.

CHARINUS (*to* DAVUS, *sadly*). My life, indeed, is definitely in doubt, by Hercules.

DAVUS (*cheerfully, to* CHARINUS). And what you're afraid of I also know.

PAMPHILUS. My wedding——

DAVUS. But I know, I tell you.

PAMPHILUS. ——today——

DAVUS. You keep hammering at me even though I know? (*Brightly.*) *You* are quaking with fear that you'll marry her, (*To* CHARINUS.) and *you* that you won't.

CHARINUS (*surprised*). You've got it right!

PAMPHILUS. That's it exactly.

DAVUS (*confidently*). And that's the very thing there's no danger of, trust me.

PAMPHILUS. I beg you, free me from this miserable fear as soon as possible.

DAVUS. Here, I'm freeing you. Chremes is no longer giving you his daughter in marriage.

PAMPHILUS. How do you know?

DAVUS. I know. Your father told me a while ago that he's marrying you off today—and also many other things which this is neither the time nor place to relate. At once I run hurrying to you in the market place, to tell you about it. When I don't find you I climb up a hill. I look around. Nowhere. By chance I see (*With a nod to* CHARINUS.) his slave Byrria. I ask *him*. He says he hasn't seen you. I'm annoyed. I think of what to do. Just as I'm returning, the whole thing begins to look suspicious to me on the face of it. "Hm," I say to myself, "very little marketing done. The Master is cross. A wedding all-of-a-sudden. It doesn't hang together."

PAMPHILUS. What are you getting at?

DAVUS. I go straight to Chremes'. When I get there, not a soul in front of the door. This makes me really happy.

CHARINUS. You're right.

PAMPHILUS (*to* DAVUS). Go on.

DAVUS. I wait. All that time I see no one going out, no matron-of-honor in front of the house, no decorations, no to-do. I come close to the door, I look in.

PAMPHILUS. I understand. It's a good sign.

DAVUS. Do these things seem to fit in with a wedding?

PAMPHILUS. I don't think so, Davus.

DAVUS. "Don't think so," you say! You don't rightly understand. It's a sure thing! When I left there, I even met Chremes' slave-boy. He was carrying a few vegetables and a few obols' worth of tiny fish for his master's supper.

CHARINUS. I've been freed today, Davus, thanks to you.

DAVUS. No, not at all.

CHARINUS. Why so? Surely he isn't still going to give her to Pamphilus?

DAVUS. Ridiculous fellow! As if he has to marry her to you if he doesn't give her to him—unless you see to it yourself, unless you ask the old man's friends to intercede for you, unless you seek her hand.

CHARINUS. That's good advice. I'll go, even though, by Hercules, I've often been disappointed in my hopes. Good-bye.

(Exit.)

PAMPHILUS. What does my father mean then? Why does he pretend?

DAVUS. I'll tell you. If he should get angry at you now, just because Chremes doesn't accept you as a husband for his daughter before he has seen how you feel about the marriage, he himself will feel he is unjust, and not unjustly. But if you refuse to get married, then he will put the blame on you. And then there will be trouble.

PAMPHILUS. I'll go through anything.

DAVUS. He's your father, Pamphilus. It's difficult. Then too, she is a woman alone and helpless. No sooner said than done, he'll find some pretext to expel her from the city.

PAMPHILUS *(taken aback)*. Expel her?

DAVUS *(nodding)*. Quickly.

PAMPHILUS. Then tell me what to do, Davus.

DAVUS. Say you'll get married.

PAMPHILUS *(shakily)*. Hm.

DAVUS. What's the matter?

PAMPHILUS. *(horrified)*. I should tell him that?

DAVUS. Why not?

PAMPHILUS. I'll never do it.

DAVUS. Don't refuse.

PAMPHILUS. Don't urge me.

DAVUS. Consider what happens if you do.

PAMPHILUS. I'll be shut out from her and be shut up in there. *(Indicating CHREMES' house.)*

DAVUS. That's not so. Here's the way I think it will be. Your father will say, "I want you to get married today." You will say, "I'll get married." Tell me, what will he have to quarrel with you about on this? You will upset all his plans which are now set, without any danger. For of this there is no doubt, that Chremes will not give you his daughter. And you won't on this account be letting up on what you are doing—keeping him from changing his mind. Tell your father you are willing so that even though he wants to, he can't justifiably get angry at you.

Now, as to your hope of something like, "I'll easily discourage any kind of marriage by the kind of life I lead. Nobody will accept me"—forget it. Your father will find a poor girl for you rather than allow you to be (*Ironically.*) corrupted. But if he will believe you are accepting the idea of marriage, you will have made him careless. He'll take his time about looking for another bride for you. Meanwhile something good will have happened.

PAMPHILUS. You think so?

DAVUS. There's absolutely no doubt about it.

PAMPHILUS (*worriedly*). Look at what you're asking me to do.

DAVUS. Quiet down, won't you?

PAMPHILUS. No, I'll speak out. We've got to be careful he doesn't find out that I'm the father of her child, for I've promised to acknowledge it.

DAVUS. Oh, what a foolhardy thing to do!

PAMPHILUS. I promised—she begged me to, so that she would know she isn't going to be deserted.

DAVUS (*resignedly*). It will be attended to. (SIMO *approaches at a distance.*) But here's your father. Be careful that he doesn't notice that you are unhappy.

(*Enter* SIMO *from the market place.*)

SIMO (*aside*). I'm coming back to see what they are up to, or what plans they are making.

DAVUS. (*aside to* PAMPHILUS). He has no doubt that you will refuse to get married. He comes with a speech well rehearsed in private somewhere, and he hopes he has found the words to tear you apart. So see to it that you keep your wits about you.

PAMPHILUS (*similarly to* DAVUS). If only I can, Davus.

DAVUS (*as before*). Believe me, I tell you, Pamphilus, your father won't say one word to you if you say you'll get married.

(*Enter* BYRRIA, *watchful, but keeping out of sight of the others.*)

BYRRIA (*aside*). My master told me to drop everything and watch Pamphilus today, so that I might see what he is doing about the marriage. That's why I am now following Simo here. And Pamphilus himself is right here with Davus, I see. Good. I'll get on the job.

SIMO (*aside*). I see they're both here.

DAVUS (*aside to* PAMPHILUS). Now, be on your guard.

SIMO (*commandingly*). Pamphilus.

DAVUS (*as before*). Look at him as if you suddenly notice him.

PAMPHILUS (*following instructions*). Ah, Father!

DAVUS (*aside to* PAMPHILUS). Very good.

SIMO (*to* PAMPHILUS). Today, as I told you, I want you to get married.

BYRRIA (*aside*). Now I'm afraid for our side about what he is going to say.

PAMPHILUS (*to* SIMO). Neither in this matter nor in any other will I ever oppose you in any way. (SIMO *has difficulty in hiding his surprise.*)

BYRRIA (*aside, surprised*). Hm?

DAVUS (*aside, to* PAMPHILUS). He's been struck dumb.

BYRRIA (*as before*). What did he say?

SIMO (*gravely, to* PAMPHILUS). You are behaving as a son should in agreeing with good grace to what I ask.

DAVUS (*aside to* PAMPHILUS, *triumphantly*). Was I right?

BYRRIA (*aside*). From what I hear, my master has lost a wife.

SIMO (*to* PAMPHILUS, *with some affection*). Go inside now, so you won't cause any delay when I need you.

PAMPHILUS. I'm going.   (*Exit into* SIMO's *house.*)

BYRRIA (*aside*). To think that you can't trust any man in anything! (*Shakes his head.*) It's true what people say—everyone prefers things to go better for themselves than for someone else. I've seen her. I remember she seemed a very good-looking young girl. So I can't blame Pamphilus if he has decided that *he* would rather embrace her in bed than that Charinus should. I'll make my report—so that my master can give me a blow for this blow.

(*Exit.*)

DAVUS (*aside*). Now he believes I am playing some trick against him, and that this is why I am staying out here.

SIMO (*ironically, to* DAVUS). Well, what does Davus have to say? Anything like before? Nothing? Hm?

DAVUS. Nothing further.

SIMO. And yet I was really expecting something.

DAVUS (*aside*). It turned out differently from what he expected, I see. That disturbs him.

SIMO. (*man-to-man*). Can you tell me the truth?

DAVUS (*cheerfully*). Nothing easier.

SIMO. Doesn't he feel *any* annoyance at the marriage because of his relationship to this foreign woman?

DAVUS. None at all. Or if he does, it's a feeling that will last a day or two, that's all—you know. Then it will stop. Why, he himself has thought this over and has come to a proper realization of things.

SIMO (*pleased*). Good for him.

DAVUS. As long as he was permitted and as long as it suited his age, he engaged in a love affair. But then he did it on the quiet. He was careful to avoid any scandal—as befitted an honorable man. Now he has to get married, so he has turned his thoughts to marriage.

SIMO. He seemed just a little put out to me.

DAVUS. Not because of this. But there *is* something about which he is annoyed with you.

SIMO. What can it be?

DAVUS. It's really unimportant.

SIMO (*curious*). What is it?

DAVUS (*making light of it*). Nothing.

SIMO (*impatiently*). Well, tell me. What is it?

DAVUS. He says—you've been too—stingy with your money.

SIMO. Me? !

DAVUS. Yes, you. "Hardly ten drachmas have been spent on provisions," he says. "He doesn't seem to be marrying a son. Which of my friends can I possibly invite to the wedding dinner under these circumstances?" says he. And if I have to say so myself, between you and me, you *have* been too stingy. That's not good.

SIMO (*irritated*). Shut up!

DAVUS (*aside*). I've got him worried.

SIMO. I'll see to it that these things are corrected. (*Aside.*) What does the old schemer mean? For if there's any mischief here, he's surely at the bottom of it.

(SIMO *and* DAVUS *remain onstage as the next act begins.*)

Act III

(*Enter Mysis from the direction of the market place, in conversation with Lesbia. They do not notice Simo and Davus.*)

MYSIS (*to* LESBIA). By Pollux, it's certainly the truth, as you say, Lesbia: hardly ever would you find a man faithful to a woman.

SIMO (*to* DAVUS). Is that the Andrian woman's maid?

DAVUS. What are you talking about?

SIMO. She is!

MYSIS (*to* LESBIA). But this Pamphilus now——

SIMO (*alerted*). What's *this*?

MYSIS. ——he kept his promise.

SIMO (*suspiciously*). Hm.

DAVUS (*aside, desperately*). If only he would become deaf and she dumb!

MYSIS (*as before*). For he ordered that any child she bore should be acknowledged and reared.

SIMO (*aside*). Oh Jupiter! What do I hear? It's all over, if she's really telling the truth.

LESBIA (*to* MYSIS). He's a young man with a fine character, from what you say.

MYSIS (*to* LESBIA). The very best. But come inside with me, so you'll be ready when she needs you.

(*They enter* GLYCERIUM'S *house.*)

SIMO (*angry*). What's this? Is he that mad? By a foreigner? Now I understand. Ah, now I've finally seen through it! How stupid of me!

DAVUS (*aside.*) What does he say he's seen through?

SIMO (*aside, craftily.*) The trick he is playing on me is just now beginning. They are pretending that she is giving birth to scare Chremes away.

GLYCERIUM (*inside the house, screaming*). Juno of Childbirth, help me, save me, I pray you!

SIMO (*scornfully*). Hah! So quickly? Ridiculous! As soon as she heard I was standing outside, she hurried it up. (*To* DAVUS.) You haven't timed the division of your acts properly, Davus.

DAVUS (*innocently*). Me?

SIMO (*mockingly*). Your actors haven't forgotten their lines, have they?

DAVUS. I don't know what you're talking about.

SIMO (*aside, eying* DAVUS). If this fellow had caught me unprepared in the midst of a real wedding, what a laughing-stock he would have made of me! Now he's in danger and it's smooth sailing for me.

(*After a brief interval* LESBIA *appears at* GLYCERIUM'S *door on her way out. She is in conversation with one of the maids inside.*)

LESBIA. So far, Archylis, I see in her all the signs that usually indicate a safe recovery. Now then, first get her bathed, and then give her to drink what I've ordered, and as much as I've prescribed. I'm coming back soon. By Castor, a fine boy has been born to Pamphilus. I pray the gods that he will live and be healthy, since Pamphilus is a good man and has avoided doing wrong to this fine young woman. (*Exit toward the market place.*)

SIMO (*to* DAVUS). Now who would not believe, knowing you, that you are at the root of all this.

DAVUS. At the root of what?

SIMO (*scornfully*). She couldn't tell the new mother what she had to do when she was with her, but yells it from the street to those inside after she has come out. Oh, Davus, do you have such a low opinion of me? Or do I really seem to you such a dupe that you would try to fool me with your tricks so obviously. At least do it artfully so that it really looks as if you're afraid I might find out.

DAVUS (*aside*). By Hercules, now *he's* certainly fooling himself, not I.

SIMO. I told you, I threatened you not to do it. Weren't you afraid? What good did it do you? Do you actually expect me to believe that she gave birth to Pamphilus' child?

DAVUS (*aside*). I understand what his mistake is and I know what to do.

SIMO. Why do you keep quiet?

DAVUS. What do you mean, "believe"? As if you didn't get a report that this would happen.

SIMO. Report? To me?

DAVUS (*flatteringly*). Oh now, then did you figure it out on your own that this was all make-believe?

SIMO (*aside*). He's making fun of me.

DAVUS. It *must* have been reported to you. For otherwise how could you have such a suspicion?

SIMO. How? (*Bluntly.*) Because I know you.

DAVUS. In other words, you're saying that this was done on my advice?

SIMO. I'm sure of it.

DAVUS. You don't really know the kind of man I am, Simo.

SIMO (*smiling knowingly*). I don't know you?

DAVUS. If I ever start to tell you anything, you immediately think you are being fooled.

SIMO (*scornfully*). Wrongly so, I suppose!

DAVUS. So, by Hercules, I haven't dared to say a word.

SIMO. This one thing I know for certain—no one has given birth here.

DAVUS. You're right. That's so. But nonetheless they will soon be bringing a child here in front of the door. I'm telling you now that this will happen, Master, so that you will be aware of it and not tell me later it was done by the scheming and planning of Davus. I want this opinion you have of me utterly removed.

SIMO. How do you know this?

DAVUS. I heard it and I believe it. Many things coincide to

lead me to make this guess. To begin with, she said she was pregnant by Pamphilus. This has proven false. Now, since she sees that wedding preparations are being made at your house, she quickly sends a maid to get the midwife to her and bring a child along. If she doesn't manage to have you see the child, there is no hindrance to the marriage.

SIMO. But tell me, when you had understood that they were planning this, why didn't you at once tell Pamphilus?

DAVUS. Well, who do you think dragged him away from her but me? For we all know how desperately he was in love with her—and now he is looking forward to marriage. So, in conclusion, give this job to me. You continue with the wedding preparations just as you are doing, and I am hopeful the gods will help us.

SIMO. No. You go in. Wait for me there and prepare what is necessary. (DAVUS *nods and enters* SIMO's *house.*) He hasn't convinced me completely into believing what he says. And yet, for all I know, what he says may all be true. But I don't put much stock in it. The important thing to me is what my son himself has promised me. Now I'll go and meet Chremes and ask him to accept my son in marriage. If I accomplish that, what else would I like better than to have the wedding take place today? For I have no doubt that if my son is unwilling to do what he promised, I can very properly compel him. (CHREMES *appears at a distance.*) And indeed just when I want him, here comes Chremes himself.

(*Enter* CHREMES.)

SIMO (*affably*). Greetings, Chremes.

CHREMES (*somewhat cross*). Oh, you're just the man I was looking for.

SIMO. And I was looking for you. I'm glad you're here.

CHREMES. Several people came up to me who said they had heard from you that my daughter was being married to your son today. I came to see whether you're crazy or they are.

SIMO. Just listen a moment and you'll know what I want of you as well as the answer to your question.

CHREMES. I'm listening. Tell me what you want of me.

SIMO (*earnestly*). By the gods, I beg of you, and by our friendship, Chremes—a friendship which began in our childhood and has increased with the years—and by your only daughter and my son whose salvation is entirely in your hands, I beg you to aid me in this matter that the wedding should take place as originally planned.

CHREMES (*taken aback*). Ah, don't implore me, as if just

because you ask this of me I must grant it to you. Do you think
he is different now from what he was before when I offered
him my daughter? If it's to the advantage of both of them for
the marriage to take place, get the wedding procession started.
But if more bad than good will come out of it for both, then
I beg you to consider our *common* good, as if she were your
daughter and I were Pamphilus' father.

SIMO. Well, that's the way I want it and that's what is behind
my request. And I wouldn't be asking you if the circumstances
themselves didn't prompt me.

CHREMES. What circumstances?

SIMO. Glycerium and my son are quarreling.

CHREMES (*ironically*). Really!

SIMO. It's so serious that I'm hoping for the possibility of a
complete separation.

CHREMES. Nonsense!

SIMO. I'm sure of it.

CHREMES. So much so that I can tell you this: lovers' quarrels
are love's renewal.

SIMO (*with a gesture of disagreement*). Hm. (*Insistently.*)
That's just what I'm asking you to help me prevent while
there is still time and while his ardor is held in check by angry
words. Before the machinations of these women and their
contrived tears move his love-sick heart to pity, let us get him
married. It is my hope that bound by intimacy with your
daughter and an honorable marriage, he will easily extricate
himself from his entanglements, Chremes.

CHREMES. That's the way it seems to you. But I don't think
that he can either remain faithful to my daughter, or that I could
endure it if he didn't.

SIMO. Well, how do you know unless you've tried it out?

CHREMES. But to try such an experiment on my daughter is a
serious matter.

SIMO. Surely. But the disadvantage finally comes down to this,
that it may end up in divorce—which the gods forbid! But if he
is straightened out, look at all the advantages. Most important
of all, you've restored a son to your friend, acquired a steadfast
son-in-law for yourself, and a husband for your daughter.

CHREMES. Well, then, all right. If you're so convinced that it's
a good thing, I don't want any advantage to you to be blocked
through me.

SIMO (*pleased*). It was with good reason I always thought
highly of you, Chremes.

CHREMES. But tell me something.

Simo. What?

Chremes. How do you know they are quarreling with one another?

Simo. Davus himself told me, and he is most deeply involved in their plans. And he urges me to hold the wedding as soon as possible. Do you think he would do that if he didn't know that my son wanted it too? You will soon hear it yourself from his own lips. (*Calling inside.*) Hey, call Davus out here! (*Davus appears at the door.*) There he is, coming out.

(*Enter* Davus.)

Davus (*to* Simo). I was on my way out to see you.

Simo. What for?

Davus. Why hasn't the bride been summoned? It will be evening soon.

Simo (*to* Chremes). Do you hear him? (*To* Davus.) I have for some time been not a little afraid, Davus, that you would do to me what the common run of slaves do, that is, deceive me with schemes because my son is having a love affair.

Davus. I do that?

Simo. I believed so, and fearing it I hid from the two of you what I am now going to tell you.

Davus. What?

Simo. I'll tell you, for I almost trust you now.

Davus. So you've finally learned what kind of man I am.

Simo. I had not intended to go through with the marriage.

Davus (*in mock surprise*). What? Not intended?

Simo. But I pretended for the purpose of testing the two of you out.

Davus. You don't say?

Simo. That's the truth.

Davus. Look at that! I never knew it. My! What a clever plan!

Simo. Now listen to this. When I sent you in, opportunely this gentleman came along.

Davus (*aside, fearfully*). Hm, are we going to be ruined after all?

Simo. I beg him to give us his daughter in marriage, and with difficulty I finally convince him.

Davus (*half-aside*). I'm done for!

Simo. Eh, what did you say?

Davus (*pretending cheerfulness*). Good, very good, I say.

Simo. Now there's no delay on *his* account.

Chremes. I'll go home now and tell them to get ready, and I'll report back here to you. (*Exit.*)

Simo. Now I ask you, Davus, since you alone have made this marriage possible for me——

Davus (*unenthusiastically*). I alone—that's true.

Simo. ——to continue doing your best to get my son straightened out.

Davus. I'll certainly do my best.

Simo. You can do it now while he's annoyed with her.

Davus. Rest assured.

Simo. Well then, where is he now?

Davus. I wouldn't be surprised if he's at home.

Simo. I'll go to him and tell him also what I've told you.

(*Exit into house.*)

Davus. That's the end of me. What reason is there why I shouldn't go straight from here to the mill? I have no grounds left for pleading for mercy. I've made a mess of everything. I've deceived my master; I've thrown my master's son into an unwanted marriage; I've made the wedding take place today against the expectations of Simo and the will of Pamphilus. Hm! That's cleverness for you! But if I had kept quiet, nothing bad would have happened. (Pamphilus *appears at the door of the house.*) But there, I see Pamphilus. I'm done for. If I only had some place from which I could jump off and kill myself!

(*Enter* Pamphilus.)

Pamphilus (*angry*). Where is that rascal who has ruined me?

Davus (*aside*). That's the end of me!

Pamphilus. Yes! I admit I deserved to have this happen to me because I am so incompetent, so lacking in judgment. To think that I entrusted my fortunes to a good-for-nothing slave! That's the reward for my stupidity. But he won't get away with it unpunished.

Davus (*aside*). I'll consider myself safe enough in the future if I can only get out of the troubles I'm in now.

Pamphilus. What can I say to my father? Shall I say I don't want to get married when I've just promised I would? How can I have the nerve to dare to do it? And I don't know what to do with myself now.

Davus (*aside*). Neither do I, but I'm considering this carefully. I'll say I'll find something so that I can postpone my punishment a bit.

Pamphilus (*suddenly seeing* Davus). Oh!

Davus (*aside*). He's seen me.

Pamphilus (*to* Davus). Well, my fine fellow, what do you have to say for yourself? Do you see that you've made me miserably entrapped by your plans?

DAVUS. But I'll get you out soon.

PAMPHILUS (*skeptically*). You'll get me out?

DAVUS. Certainly, Pamphilus.

PAMPHILUS. Just see that you do.

DAVUS. Why, I expect even better than that.

PAMPHILUS. Oh, you scoundrel! You expect me to believe you? *You* restore to normal my entangled and ruined affairs? (*Scornfully.*) Look at the man I relied on! The man who, when everything was going smoothly and calmly, today threw me onto the rocks of marriage! Didn't I *say* this would happen?

DAVUS (*contritely*). You did.

PAMPHILUS. What do you deserve?

DAVUS. Hanging. But give me a moment to get control of myself. I'll soon figure something out.

PAMPHILUS. Too bad I don't have the time to punish you as I want to. For this emergency permits me only to look out for myself, not to deal with you.

Act IV

(*While Pamphilus and Davus remain onstage, Charinus enters looking unhappy and angry.*)

CHARINUS. Is it credible or conceivable that anyone can be so heartless as to rejoice in misfortunes and get his own happiness at the cost of others' unhappiness? Ah, is it right? These are the very worst kinds of people. They are a bit ashamed to refuse you at the moment, but later when the time comes to carry out their promises, they are forced by necessity to reveal themselves in their true light. Then they make the most brazen statements: "Who are *you?* What are you to *me?* Why should I give my girl to *you?* Look here, to myself I come first." But if you should ask, "What about your promise?", then when they ought to, they are not ashamed. At the time when there is no need to, then they are afraid. But what should I do? Should I go up to him and complain about the wrong he is doing me? Should I heap insults upon him? Yet someone would say, "You won't accomplish anything." I'll accomplish much. I'll certainly make him uncomfortable and relieve my feelings.

PAMPHILUS (*seeing* CHARINUS, *apologetically*). Charinus, without intending to, I've spoiled things for both of us, unless the gods intervene somehow.

CHARINUS (*scornfully*). So, "without intending to" is it? You've finally found an excuse. (*Raising his voice.*) You've broken your promise!

PAMPHILUS (*annoyed*). "Finally"? What do you mean?

CHARINUS (*as before*). Are you still trying to lead me on with your words?

PAMPHILUS. What are you talking about?

CHARINUS. After I said I was in love with her she suddenly became desirable to you. To my misfortune I judged your nature by mine.

PAMPHILUS. You're making a mistake.

CHARINUS (*excitedly*). Did your happiness not seem complete enough for you unless you deluded me who loved her and unless you led me on with false hope? You can keep her! (*Turns away.*)

PAMPHILUS. Keep her? Ah, you don't know what great trouble I'm in, poor me, and what worries this scoundrel of mine has caused me by his plans.

(CHARINUS *turns to* PAMPHILUS *again.*)

CHARINUS. Why is it so surprising if he takes you as his example?

PAMPHILUS. You wouldn't say that if you knew me or the love I feel.

CHARINUS (*ironically*). I know. You've had an argument with your father, and so now he's angry at you and he can't force you to marry her today.

PAMPHILUS. On the contrary, just to show you how little you know of my problems—no preparations were being made for me to get married today, and no one was asking me to get married.

CHARINUS (*ironically*). I see. You were forced by your own free will.

PAMPHILUS. Now wait—you still don't understand.

CHARINUS. All *I* understand is that you are going to marry her today.

PAMPHILUS. Why do you make it so difficult? Listen to what I say. He never stopped pressing me to tell my father I would get married. He kept persuading and pleading until he finally made me do it.

CHARINUS. Who is the person who did that?

PAMPHILUS. Davus.

CHARINUS (*surprised*). Davus?

PAMPHILUS. He has made a mess of everything.

CHARINUS. For what reason?

PAMPHILUS. I don't know. Unless, I suppose, the gods were angry at me for listening to him.

CHARINUS (*to* DAVUS). Is this true, Davus?

DAVUS (*ashamedly*). It's true.

CHARINUS. Hm! What do you have to say for yourself? Oh, you villain! May the gods grant you a death worthy of your deeds! So tell me, if all his enemies wanted to throw him into marriage, what advice would they have given him other than this?

DAVUS. I was mistaken, but I'm not finished yet.

CHARINUS (*skeptically*). I know.

DAVUS. We've not succeeded this way, we'll try another. Unless you think that because there's been no success at first, this failure can't be turned into a means of saving the situation.

PAMPHILUS (*bitterly*). Why, no! I'm willing to believe that if you're really wide awake you can make me two marriages out of one.

DAVUS (*indignant*). I, Pamphilus, owe you this in my capacity as your slave, to try with every means at my disposal, night and day, to risk my life to help you. It's your duty to forgive me if anything happens counter to our expectations. What I've been trying to do hasn't succeeded, but I've done my best. Now, if you prefer, find something better yourself and dismiss me.

PAMPHILUS. All right. Just restore me to the position I was in when you started.

DAVUS. I'll do so.

PAMPHILUS. But you must do it now.

DAVUS. Hm.—But wait, I hear Glycerium's door opening.

PAMPHILUS. It doesn't concern you.

DAVUS (*meditatively*). I'm looking for a plan.

PAMPHILUS. Well, do you have one?

DAVUS. I'll have one for you soon.

(*Enter* MYSIS *from* GLYCERIUM'*s house*.)

MYSIS (*to* GLYCERIUM *inside*.) Wherever he is, I'll find your Pamphilus for you and bring him back with me. Don't fret yourself, my dear.

PAMPHILUS. Mysis.

MYSIS (*turning around*). Who is it? Ah, Pamphilus, it's very good that you're here.

PAMPHILUS. What's the matter?

MYSIS. My mistress told me to ask you to come to her now if you love her.

PAMPHILUS. Ah, damn! My troubles are beginning again. (*To* DAVUS.) Look at the way you've made us miserable with worry! That's why she wants to see me, because she's found out that wedding preparations are being made for me.

CHARINUS. How easily they could have been prevented if this fellow had kept quiet!

DAVUS (*annoyed, to* CHARINUS). Go ahead! Stir him up—as if he is not angry enough on his own account.

MYSIS. Yes, by Pollux, that's what it is and that's why she is unhappy and dejected.

PAMPHILUS. Mysis, by all the gods, I swear to you I will not desert her, not even if I know I will have everybody as my enemy. I wanted her, fortune gave her to me, we are good for one another. Away with those who want to part us! Nothing but death will take her away from me.

MYSIS. I am relieved.

PAMPHILUS. Not even Apollo's oracular responses are truer than the answer I've given you. If it will be possible to keep my father from believing that I am to blame for blocking the marriage, well and good. But if it will not be possible, I will take the direct way out and let him believe that I am the one that is standing in the way. What do you think of me now?

CHARINUS. That you are as badly off as I am.

DAVUS (*still meditatively*). I'm searching for a plan.

PAMPHILUS. Good boy! I know that whatever you attempt——

DAVUS. I'll surely get one worked out for you.

PAMPHILUS. I need one now.

DAVUS (*brightly*). I *have* one now.

CHARINUS. What is it?

DAVUS (*to* CHARINUS). I have one for him, not you—don't make any mistake about it.

CHARINUS. That's good enough for me.

PAMPHILUS. What will you do? Tell me.

DAVUS. I'm afraid this day may not be enough for me to carry it out, so don't think I have enough time to tell you about it now. Therefore you two get yourselves out of here. You're in the way.

PAMPHILUS. I'll go to see Glycerium. (*Exit into* GLYCERIUM'S *house.*)

DAVUS (*to* CHARINUS). What about you? Where are you going?

CHARINUS. You want me to tell you the truth?

Davus (*impatiently and ironically*). Yes, of course. Here comes the beginning of a long story.

Charinus. What will become of me?

Davus. Oho! You have a lot of gall! Aren't you satisfied that in postponing the marriage I am giving you an extra day?

Charinus. But, Davus——

Davus. What now?

Charinus. ——see to it that I marry her.

Davus. Ridiculous!

Charinus. Make sure you come to me if you are able to do anything.

Davus. Why should I come? I have nothing for you.

Charinus. But anyway—if you do.

Davus. Very well, I will if I have anything.

Charinus. I'll be home.   (*Exit.*)

Davus (*to* Mysis). You, Mysis, while I'm gone, wait for me here a while.

Mysis. What for?

Davus. You must.

Mysis. Don't be long.

Davus. I'll be back in a moment, I tell you.

(*Goes into* Glycerium's *house, leaving* Mysis *alone onstage.*)

Mysis. You can't be sure of anything! Gods help us! I used to think this Pamphilus was the greatest good for my mistress—a friend, lover, and husband, ready in any emergency. But look at the trouble the poor girl has been having from him. The bad she's had out of him is easily worse than the good. (Davus *comes out carrying a baby.*) But Davus is coming out. My dear fellow, what is *that,* for God's sake? Where are you taking the child?

Davus. Mysis, now I need your ready shrewdness and cleverness for this job.

Mysis. What *are* you up to?

Davus. Take him from me quickly and place him in front of our door.

Mysis. My goodness! On the ground?

Davus. Get yourself some branches from the altar here and spread them down.

Mysis. Why don't *you* do it?

Davus. Because if I happen to have to swear to my master that I didn't put him there, I can do it with a clear conscience.

Mysis (*spreads the branches*). I see. You've suddenly developed scruples, something new for you. (*Holding out her hands.*) Give him to me. (*She takes the child from* Davus.)

DAVUS. Move quickly so that you may learn what I am doing next. (MYSIS *places the child on the branches.*) Oh Jupiter!

(CHREMES *appears in the distance.*)

MYSIS. What's the matter?

DAVUS. The bride's father is coming. I'm discarding the plan I originally intended.

MYSIS. I don't know what you're talking about.

DAVUS. I'll pretend I'm just coming in here, from the right. You see to it that you support my story whenever necessary.

MYSIS. I don't understand at all what you're up to. But if you and Pamphilus have any need of my help—seeing that you are cleverer than I—I'll stand by so as not to hinder any advantage to you and your master.

(DAVUS *slips out of sight as* CHREMES *enters.*)

CHREMES. Now that I've made the necessary arrangements for my daughter's wedding, I've come back to tell them to start the wedding procession. (*Sees the child.*) But what's this? It's a child, by Hercules! (*To* MYSIS) Woman, did you place it here?

MYSIS (*looking uneasily for* DAVUS). Where is he?

CHREMES (*a bit offended*). Why don't you answer me?

MYSIS (*still worried about* DAVUS). He's nowhere around. Oh, what will I do now? The fellow has gone and left me.

DAVUS (*appearing suddenly from the right*). May the gods help me! What excitement in the market place! How many people are arguing there! Well, grain is dear this year. I don't know how else to explain it.

MYSIS (*to* DAVUS). Why in the world did you leave me here all alone?

DAVUS. Hm, what nonsense are you talking? (*Pretending surprise at the sight of the child.*) Tell me, Mysis, where is this child from? Who brought it here?

MYSIS. Are you in your right mind to ask me this?

DAVUS. Whom should I ask, then, when I see no one else here?

CHREMES (*aside*). I wonder where it's from.

DAVUS (*to* MYSIS). Are you going to tell me what I ask? (*Moves her away from* CHREMES a bit roughly.*)

MYSIS. Ow!

DAVUS (*quietly to Mysis*). Come over to the right.

MYSIS (*to Davus*). You're mad! Didn't you yourself——?

DAVUS (*quietly, so* CHREMES *should not hear*). If you say one word beyond what I ask you, watch out! (*Aloud.*) You're getting abusive, eh? Where is it from? Speak up!

MYSIS. From our house.

DAVUS. Ha! Ha! Ha! (*Ironically.*) Small wonder if the woman —a courtesan—has the nerve to do it!

CHREMES (*aside*). She's the maid from the Andrian woman's house as far as I can tell.

DAVUS (*in mock anger*). Do we seem to you the kind of people you can fool this way?

CHREMES (*aside*). I've come just in time.

DAVUS (*to* MYSIS). Now hurry up and pick the child up from the door here. (*Aside to* MYSIS.) Wait! Don't move from where you are!

MYSIS. May the gods destroy you! You're scaring me to death.

DAVUS. Am I speaking to you or not?

MYSIS. What do you want?

DAVUS. You're still asking? Tell me whose child you put down there.

MYSIS You don't know?

DAVUS. Never mind what I know. Tell me what I ask.

MYSIS. Your master's.

DAVUS. Which master's?

MYSIS. Pamphilus'.

CHREMES. (*aside*). Hm.

DAVUS. What? Pamphilus'?

MYSIS. Well, isn't it?

CHREMES (*aside*). I was right in always avoiding this marriage.

DAVUS. Oh, what a monstrous outrage!

MYSIS. Why are you shouting?

DAVUS. A child which I saw being brought to your mistress' house last night?

MYSIS (*indignantly*). Oh, you've got a lot of nerve!

DAVUS (*as if confirmed in his suspicions*). Sure! I saw Canthara all puffed out under her clothes.

MYSIS. I'm certainly grateful to the gods that there were some free women present when she was giving birth.

DAVUS. She surely doesn't know the kind of man he is whom she is trying to impress with this kind of thing. She thinks: "If Chremes sees the child placed in front of the house, he won't give his daughter in marriage." Why, he'll be all the more willing to do so.

CHREMES (*aside, with determination*). He certainly will not.

DAVUS. Now, just so you should understand me—if you don't pick up this child this instant, I'll fling it into the middle of the street and I'll roll you after it in the mud.

MYSIS. Fellow, you're definitely not sober.

DAVUS. One deception presses hard on another. (*Scornfully.*) I've heard it whispered that she is an Athenian citizen.

CHREMES (*aside*). Hm.

DAVUS. They are saying, "Forced by the laws, he'll marry her."

MYSIS (*indignantly*). Oho, tell me, *isn't* she a citizen?

CHREMES (*half-aside*). Unknowingly I almost fell into a ridiculous mess.

DAVUS. Who is speaking? (*Turns around.*) Oh, Chremes, you've come just in time. Listen.

CHREMES. I've already heard everything.

DAVUS. You don't say? Everything?

CHREMES. I've heard it, I tell you, from the beginning.

DAVUS. You've heard, then? Well, isn't that villainy for you? She should be taken away and hanged. (*To* MYSIS.) This is the gentleman. Don't think you're just tricking Davus.

MYSIS (*to* CHREMES). Oh my, oh my! Absolutely nothing I said is false, sir.

CHREMES. I know all about it. (*To* DAVUS.) Is Simo inside?

DAVUS. He is.

(*Exit* CHREMES *into* SIMO's *house.*)

(MYSIS *gets ready to pick up the baby and leave in a huff, but* DAVUS *holds her back.*)

MYSIS (*indignantly*). Don't touch me, you rascal! If I don't tell Glycerium all about this——

DAVUS (*smiling*). Oho, silly, don't you know what was going on here?

MYSIS. How should I know?

DAVUS. That's the father-in-law. There was no other way I could manage for him to find out what we want him to.

MYSIS. Hm. You should have told me beforehand.

DAVUS. Do you think it makes little difference whether you do everything spontaneously and naturally or with premeditation?

(MYSIS *takes the baby into the house and comes out again. Enter Crito, left.*)

CRITO (*looking around*). On this street I was told Chrysis lived. She preferred gaining wealth dishonorably to living in honorable poverty in her native land. By her death her property became mine by law. (*Sees* MYSIS *and* DAVUS.) But I see somebody to ask. (*Approaches.*) How do you do?

MYSIS. My! Isn't that Crito I see, Chrysis' cousin? It is!

CRITO. Oh, Mysis! How are you!

MYSIS. How do you do, Crito!

CRITO (*sadly*). So it's true about Chrysis? Hm.

MYSIS (*sadly*). Yes, she's left us poor souls, she's gone.

CRITO. And what about you people? How are things with you here? Well enough?

MYSIS. Us? With us it's like this—as the saying goes, since we can't do what we want, we do what we can.

CRITO. What about Glycerium? Has she found her parents yet?

MYSIS. If only she had!

CRITO. You mean she still hasn't? Then I haven't come here auspiciously. For, by Pollux, if I had known that, I would never have set foot here. Glycerium was always spoken of as her sister and so considered. She is in possession of whatever belonged to Chrysis. Now if I, a stranger, start litigations, I have enough warning from the example of others how easy and advantageous that will be for me. At the same time I think that by now she has some friend and defender, for she was already quite a young woman when she left Andros. People would cry out that I am an impostor, a beggar, chasing after an inheritance. Then too, it's not my wish to leave her impoverished.

MYSIS. Oh, most excellent guest! By Pollux, Crito, you're a gentleman of the old school.

CRITO. Now that I'm here, take me in to the house so that I may see her.

MYSIS. Certainly.

(*They enter* GLYCERIUM's *house*.)

DAVUS. I'll go with them. I don't want the old master to see me at this time.   (*Follows them in*.)

Act V

(*Enter Chremes and Simo from the latter's house*.)

CHREMES. My friendship to you has been sufficiently proven, Simo. I've taken enough risks, enough, so make an end of your pleading. In my willingness to oblige you I almost gambled away my daughter's life.

SIMO. On the contrary, now more than ever I ask and beg of you to fulfill in action the kindness you began in words.

CHREMES. Look how unfair you are in your eagerness. As long as you accomplish what you wish you give no thought to how far I should go in my kindness nor to what you are asking of me.

For if you should think for a moment, you would stop imposing unjust demands on me.

SIMO. Such as?

CHREMES. You have to ask me? Here's a young man all involved in a love affair with another girl, abhorring the very thought of marriage and you've been pressing me to subject my daughter to domestic discord and an insecure marriage so that by *her* suffering and *her* pain I should cure *your* son. You got what you wanted. I took the first steps as long as circumstances warranted. Now they do not. So accept the situation. They say she is a citizen, a child has been born—release us.

SIMO. By the gods I beg you not to allow yourself to believe them. It's to their greatest advantage that he should appear at his worst. All this was done and begun because of the impending marriage. When they have been deprived of the reason for doing these things, they will stop.

CHREMES. You're mistaken. I myself saw her maid arguing with Davus.

SIMO. I know.

CHREMES. They weren't pretending, since neither of them knew in advance that I would be there.

SIMO. I believe you, and Davus told me beforehand that they would do this, but somehow or other I forgot to tell you about it today as I intended.

(*Enter* DAVUS *from* GLYCERIUM's *house.* SIMO *and* CHREMES *withdraw to a side.*)

DAVUS (*to* GLYCERIUM *inside*). I'm telling you, you can rest easy now——

CHREMES (*to* SIMO). Well, there's Davus for you!

SIMO. Where is he coming out of?

DAVUS (*as before*). ——under my protection and that of your guest.

SIMO. What mischief is he up to now?

DAVUS. I never saw anything more convenient—the man, his arrival, or the time.

SIMO. The villain! Whom is he praising?

DAVUS (*continuing*). It's smooth sailing now.

SIMO. I must speak to him. (*Approaches* DAVUS.)

DAVUS (*aside*). It's my master! What should I do?

SIMO. Well, hello, my fine fellow.

DAVUS. Ahem, Simo. Oh, my dear Chremes. Everything is ready inside.

SIMO (*sarcastically*). You've taken care of things properly.

DAVUS. Summon the bride whenever you wish.

SIMO. Very nice. There is just this one thing more now. You've still got to answer this question: What business did you have in there?

DAVUS. Me?

SIMO. Yes.

DAVUS (*pretending innocence*). Me?

SIMO. Yes, you!

DAVUS (*stalling and stammering*). I just went in there——

SIMO. I've asked you a question.

DAVUS. ——together with your son.

SIMO. Pamphilus is inside? Oh, my head is splitting! Didn't you say they were angry at one another, you gallowsbird?

DAVUS (*brazenly*). They are.

SIMO. Then why is he there?

CHREMES (*sarcastically*). Why do you think? He's quarreling with her.

DAVUS. No, really, Chremes, by my honor now, let me tell you about a shocking thing that is happening. Some old man has just arrived—he's in there—bold and shrewd. To look at him he seems to be a man of the highest worth. There's an austere sincerity in his face and a sober truthfulness in his words.

SIMO. What are you trying to tell me?

DAVUS. Nothing, except what I've heard him say.

SIMO. And what does he say?

DAVUS. That Glycerium is an Athenian citizen.

SIMO (*scornfully*). Hm! (*Calling into his house.*) Dromo, Dromo!

DAVUS. What's the matter?

SIMO. Dromo!

DAVUS. Listen.

SIMO. If you say one more word—Dromo!

(*Enter* DROMO.)

DROMO. What do you wish, sir?

SIMO. Seize him and carry him inside, quickly!

DROMO. Whom?

SIMO. Davus.

DAVUS. What for?

SIMO. Because that's what I want. (*To* DROMO.) Seize him, I say.

DAVUS. What did I do?

SIMO (*implacably*). Seize him!

DAVUS. If you find that I have lied, you can kill me.

SIMO. I'm not listening. Now I'll give *you* a shaking-up.

DAVUS. Even though what I say is true?

SIMO. Even so. (*To* DROMO.) See that you tie him up and guard him. And listen—tie up his hands and feet. (*To* DAVUS.) Well now, by Pollux, as sure as I'm alive I'll show *you* today how dangerous it is to fool your master, and *him* how dangerous to fool a father.

(DROMO *takes* DAVUS *into the house*.)

CHREMES. Ah, don't be in such a rage.

SIMO. Oh Chremes—filial piety! (*Shakes his head.*) Don't you pity me? To have taken such great pains for such a son! (*Calls angrily.*) Come on, Pamphilus! Out here, Pamphilus! Don't you have any shame at all?

(*Enter* PAMPHILUS *from* GLYCERIUM'*s house.*)

PAMPHILUS. Who wants me? (*Sees his father.*) Uh—oh! It's my father!

SIMO (*bitterly*). What have you got to say for yourself, you——

CHREMES (*to* SIMO). Ah, better get to the point and never mind the insults.

SIMO. As if anything too harsh could be said against him. (*To* PAMPHILUS.) Well, tell me. Is Glycerium a citizen?

PAMPHILUS. So they say.

SIMO. "So they say"? What monstrous impudence is this? Doesn't he realize what he is saying? Isn't he sorry for what he has done? Look, does his face show any blush of shame? Can he be so headstrong that against the law and custom of his fellow-citizens, against the wishes of his father, he should insist on keeping her to his great disgrace!?

PAMPHILUS (*unhappily*). I feel miserable!

SIMO. Hm, just *now* you finally begin to feel this way, Pamphilus? You should have felt this way before, much before, when you resolved that somehow or other you must accomplish what you wanted. That was the day when it would have been truly fitting for you to say those words. But what do I care? Why do I torture myself? Why do I torment myself? Why do I trouble my old age with his senselessness? Should I pay the penalty for his sins? Why, no! Let him keep her! Good-by and good luck to him! Let him live with her! (*Makes a gesture of dismissal.*)

PAMPHILUS (*pleadingly, almost tearful*). Father, Father!

SIMO. What's this "Father, Father"? As if you need a father. You've got yourself a home, a wife, children without your father and his wishes. You've brought in witnesses to say she is a citizen of this town. You win!

PAMPHILUS. Father, may I say a few words?

SIMO. What will you say to me?

CHREMES. Nevertheless, Simo, listen to him.

Simo. Listen to him? Why *should* I listen, Chremes?

Chremes. At least let him speak.

Simo. All right, let him speak.

Pamphilus. I admit I'm in love with her. If that's a sin, I admit that too. I put myself in your hands, Father. Place any burden you wish upon me, command me. You want me to get married? To get rid of her? I'll do it and bear it as well as I can. This alone I ask of you: don't believe that this old man was suborned by me. Give me a chance to clear myself by bringing him here to you face to face.

Simo. Bringing him to me?

Pamphilus. Allow me, Father.

Chremes (*to Simo*). What he asks is fair. Give your consent.

Pamphilus. Please grant me this request.

Simo. All right, I grant it. (Pamphilus *hurries into* Glycerium's *house.*) I'm willing to do anything, as long as I don't find myself fooled by him, Chremes.

Chremes. For a great offense a small punishment should satisfy a father.

(Pamphilus *returns with* Crito.)

Crito (*to* Pamphilus). You don't have to keep begging me. Any one of these reasons is good enough to induce me to do what you ask—you, the truth, or my wishes for Glycerium.

Chremes (*surprised*). Is that Crito of Andros that I see? It certainly is!

Crito (*equally surprised*). Hello, Chremes! Good to see you!

Chremes. What brings you to Athens so unexpectedly?

Crito. It just so happened. Is this Simo?

Chremes. This is Simo.

Simo (*uncivilly*). So, you're the one who says Glycerium is a citizen of this town?

Crito. And you say she isn't?

Simo. And that's what you came here all prepared to say?

Crito. Why do you say that?

Simo (*angrily*). You're asking me? You think you'll get away with it? You think you're going to take young men, inexperienced in the world, well brought up, and lead them astray? Is that what you do, take advantage of them by enticements and promises?

Crito. Are you in your right mind?

Simo (*as before*). And cement love affairs with prostitutes by marriage?

Pamphilus (*aside*). I'm lost! I'm afraid the stranger will not stand up to this.

CHREMES. Simo, if you knew this man well enough, you wouldn't think so. This is a good man.

SIMO (*to* CHREMES). This man is good, you say? Then how did he just *happen* to arrive opportunely today, just in time for the wedding and never before? Is he really to be believed, Chremes?

PAMPHILUS (*aside*). If only I weren't afraid of my father, there is a good suggestion I have to make on this point.

SIMO (*to* CRITO, *with vehemence*). Adventurer!

CRITO (*annoyed*). Hm.

CHREMES. That's how he is, Crito. Don't mind him.

CRITO (*to* CHREMES). Let him be careful how he behaves. If he goes on saying whatever he wishes to me, he'll hear things he doesn't wish to hear. (*To* SIMO.) Am I the cause of your troubles? Are they any of my business? It's your problem. Can't you face up to it without getting so excited? You can tell soon enough whether the information which I am giving you is true or false. (*Pauses.*) Some time ago, a certain Athenian was shipwrecked and was washed ashore at Andros. With him was this one little girl. Then, being in need, the first one he happened to apply to for help was Chrysis' father.

SIMO. He is making up a story.

CHREMES. Let him continue.

CRITO. Does he persist in interrupting this way?

CHREMES (*soothingly*). Continue, Crito.

CRITO. He was my relative, the man who took him in. It's from him I heard that the shipwrecked merchant was an Athenian. Then the Athenian died.

CHREMES (*eagerly*). His name?

CRITO. His name so soon?

PAMPHILUS (*unable to hold in*). Phania.

CHREMES (*aside*). Oh, heaven help me!

CRITO. True, by Hercules. I think it *was* Phania. But this I know for certain—he said he was from the deme of Rhamnus.[2]

CHREMES (*aside*). Oh, Jupiter!

CRITO. This same information, Chremes, many other people in Andros heard at that time.

CHREMES (*aside*). Oh, if it's only what I hope! (*To* CRITO.) Uh, tell me. What about the little girl? Did he say she was his?

CRITO. No.

---

[2] Besides being organized by tribes, the Athenians were also divided up into *demes*, or wards, which were geographical subdivisions of the city and countryside for voting and other political purposes. Identification of a citizen included his name, his father's name, and his deme.

CHREMES. Whose then?

CRITO. His brother's daughter.

CHREMES (*excitedly*). She's certainly mine!

CRITO. What's this?

SIMO (*to* CHREMES). What are you saying?

PAMPHILUS (*aside*). Be all ears, Pamphilus!

SIMO (*to* CHREMES). What makes you think so?

CHREMES. This Phania was my brother.

SIMO. I know him and am aware of the fact.

CHREMES. He fled from the war here many years ago, and set out to join me in Asia Minor where I then was. He was afraid to leave the girl here at such a time. This is the first I've heard of what became of him since.

PAMPHILUS (*aside*). I'm almost beside myself! My feelings are such a turmoil of fear and hope and joy at such wonderful great and sudden good!

SIMO (*to* CHREMES). I am really ever so grateful that she turns out to be your daughter.

PAMPHILUS. I'm glad you are, Father.

CHREMES. But there is still a doubt remaining that bothers me.

PAMPHILUS (*half-joshingly*). With your scruples, you make a mountain out of a molehill.

CRITO (*to* CHREMES). What is it that bothers you?

CHREMES. Her name doesn't fit.

CRITO. Well, by Hercules, she did have another name as a child.

CHREMES. What name, Crito? Don't you remember it at all?

CRITO. That's what I'm trying to recall.

PAMPHILUS (*aside*). Should I let his bad memory stand in the way of my happiness when I can help myself in this matter? (*To* CHREMES.) Listen, Chremes, the name you are looking for is Pasibula.

CHREMES. Pasibula? (*Happily.*) That's *it!*

CRITO. *That's* it.

PAMPHILUS (*excitedly*). I've heard it from her a thousand times!

SIMO (*warmly*). I'm sure you believe me, Chremes, when I say that we all share in your happiness.

CHREMES. So help me the gods, I believe it.

PAMPHILUS (*hinting*). And now, Father, there is still something else . . .

SIMO. The way things have turned out has reconciled me to the situation.

PAMPHILUS. Oh delightful Father! And about my wife—since

she *is* my wife—(*Turning to* CHREMES.) Chremes doesn't plan to change things?

CHREMES. Your case is of the best (*Turning to* SIMO.) unless your father has some objection.

PAMPHILUS (*to* SIMO). You don't have any, do you?

SIMO (*affably*). Of course, I agree.

CHREMES. The dowry, Pamphilus, is ten talents.

PAMPHILUS. I accept.

CHREMES. I must hurry to my daughter. Do come with me, Crito, for I suppose she hardly knows me.

(*Exeunt* CHREMES *and* CRITO *into* GLYCERIUM's *house*.)

SIMO (*affably, to* PAMPHILUS). Why don't you have her moved to our house?

PAMPHILUS. That's a good idea. I'll give Davus the job.

SIMO. He can't.

PAMPHILUS. Why?

SIMO. Because he is busy with something else more in his line and bigger.

PAMPHILUS. What may that be?

SIMO. He's in chains.

PAMPHILUS. He's not rightly tied up.

SIMO (*laughing*). He certainly was when I ordered it.

PAMPHILUS. Please have him released.

SIMO. I'll do it at once.

PAMPHILUS. But hurry.

SIMO. I'm going in.   (*Exit into his house.*)

PAMPHILUS. Oh lucky, lovely day!

(*Enter* CHARINUS.)

CHARINUS. I've come back to see what Pamphilus is up to. And there he is.

PAMPHILUS (*musing*). Someone may perhaps think that I don't think this is real, but it is real, and right now I am delighted that it is. (*Smiles.*) What really makes the life of the gods eternal, I imagine, is that their happiness is everlasting. In that case I've attained immortality if no sorrow spoils my present happiness. But whom would I now most want to see to tell him about all this?

CHARINUS (*aside*). What's he so happy about?

(DAVUS *appears at the door, rubbing his sore arms.*)

PAMPHILUS. I see Davus. There's nobody else in all the world that I'd rather have with me now. I know that he alone will really and sincerely be happy at my happiness.

DAVUS (*looking around*). Where's Pamphilus, I wonder?

PAMPHILUS. Davus.

Davus. Who's that?

Pamphilus. It's me.

Davus (*coming forward*). Oh, Pamphilus.

Pamphilus (*excitedly*). You don't know what has happened to me.

Davus. You're right. (*Wryly.*) But what has happened to *me* I do know.

Pamphilus (*sympathetically*). And I do too.

Davus. That's the way it is in this world. *You* found out the bad I endured before I found out the good that happened to you.

Pamphilus (*eagerly*). My Glycerium has found her parents!

Davus. Wonderful!

Charinus (*aside, surprised*). Hm!

Pamphilus. Her father is a great friend of our family.

Davus. Who?

Pamphilus. Chremes.

Davus. That's very good news.

Pamphilus. And there's no obstacle to my marrying her.

Charinus (*aside*). Is he dreaming of what he wanted while awake?

Pamphilus. Then about the child, Davus——

Davus. Ah, enough! You're the only one whom the gods love.

Charinus (*aside*). I'm saved if this is true. I'll speak to him.

Pamphilus (*seeing him*). Who is this? Oh, Charinus, you come at just the right time.

Charinus. Congratulations!

Pamphilus. You heard?

Charinus. Everything. Come on, have some consideration for me in your good fortune. Chremes is now your father-in-law. I'm sure he will do everything you will want.

Pamphilus. I have it in mind. But it will be too long to wait until he comes out. Come in with me. He is in there with Glycerium now. You, Davus, go on home, hurry, and send over some people to bring her to my house. Why do you stand there? Get going.

Davus. I'm going. (*Exeunt* Pamphilus *and* Charinus *into* Glycerium's *house. To audience.*) Don't you wait until they come out here. The betrothal will take place inside. Whatever remains to be done will take place there.

Cantor. Your applause please.

Hippolytus,
OR
Phaedra

A TRAGEDY

by
SENECA

❧ ❧ ❧

translated by
Frank Justus Miller

DRAMATIS PERSONAE

HIPPOLYTUS, son of Theseus and Antiope, an Amazon
PHAEDRA, wife of Theseus and stepmother of Hippolytus
THESEUS, king of Athens
NURSE of Phaedra
MESSENGER
SLAVES AND ATTENDANTS
CHORUS of Athenian citizens

The Scene is laid throughout in the court in front of the royal palace at Athens, and the action is confined to the space of one day.

ARGUMENT

Theseus *had wed Antiope, the Amazon, and of their union had been born Hippolytus. This youth grew up to love the chase, austere and beautiful, shunning the haunts of men and scorning the love of women. Theseus had meanwhile slain Antiope, and married Phaedra, Cretan Minos' child.*

And now, for four years past, the king has not been seen upon the earth, for, following the mad adventure of his bosom friend, Pirithoüs, he has descended into Tartarus to help him steal away its queen, and thence, men think, he never will return.

Deserted by her lord, the hapless Phaedra has conceived a hopeless passion for Hippolytus; for Venus, mindful of her old amour with Mars, which Phaedra's ancestor, Apollo, had exposed, has sent this madness on her, even as Pasiphaë, her mother, had been cursed with a most mad and fatal malady.

(In the early morning, in the palace court at Athens. Enter Hippolytus with a large company of huntsmen armed with the various weapons of the hunt, and leading numerous dogs in leash. Hippolytus proceeds to assign the various tasks of the day to his followers.)

Hippolytus. Go, girdle the shadowy woods and the topmost ridges of the mount, you sons of Cecrops! With nimble feet wide wandering, scour the coverts that lie beneath rocky Parnes and in the vale of Thria, whose swift-flowing stream lashes its banks; climb the hills ever white with Rhipean snow. Here, here let others go, where the tall alder-thickets fringe the grove where meadows lie which Zephyr soothes with his dew-laden breath and calls forth the herbage of the spring, where scant Ilissos flows sluggishly along through meager fields, and with ungenerous stream creeps over unfruitful sands.

Go you by the left path where Marathon opens out her forest glades, where with their small following the suckling mothers seek nightly forage; and you, where rugged Acharneus tempers his frosts beneath the warm southwind.

Let one tread sweet Hymettus' cliff, another, small Aphidnae; too long unharried is that spot where Sunium thrusts out the shores of the curving sea. If any feels the lure of the forest, Phlye calls for him; there is the haunt of the boar, terror of husbandmen, famed by now for many a wound.

But do you cast off the leashes from the dogs that hunt in silence; still let thongs hold the keen Molossians fast, and let the savage Cretans tug on the stout bonds with well-worn necks. But the Spartans (for their breed is bold and eager for the prey) hold in carefully with a tighter knot. The time will come when the hollow rocks will re-echo with their bayings; now, with heads low-hung, let them snuff the air with keen nostrils, and with muzzles to earth quest through the forest haunts, while the light is still dim, while the dewy ground still retains the well-marked trail.

Let some of you make speed to load your necks with the heavy, wide-meshed nets, and others with the smooth-wrought snares. Let a line decked out with crimson feathers hedge the deer with empty terror. Thou shalt brandish the dart, thou with right and left hand together hurl the heavy oak-shaft with broad iron head; do thou lie in hiding and with shouts drive the game on in headlong rush; and thou, when victory is won, shalt free flesh from hide with thy curved hunting-knife.

And do thou be with thy follower, O manlike goddess,[1] for whose sovereignty earth's secret places are reserved, whose darts with unerring aim seek out the prey which drinks of the cool Araxes or sports on Ister's frozen streams. Thy hand aims at Gaetulian lions, thine at Cretan deer; and now with lighter stroke dost thou pierce swift-fleeing does. The striped tigers face thee, but the shaggy-backed bisons flee, and the wild ox with wide-spreading horns. All things that feed in the lonely fields, whether the Arabian knows them in his rich forests, or the needy Garamantian and the wandering Sarmatian on his desert plains, whatever the heights of the rough Pyrenees or the Hyrcanian glades conceal, all fear thy bow, Diana. If, his offerings paid, thy worshipper takes thy favor with him to the glades, his nets hold the tangled prey, no feet break through his snares; his game is brought in on groaning wagons, his hounds have their muzzles red with blood and all the rustic throng come home in long triumphant line.

---

[1] Diana.

Lo, goddess, thou dost hear me: the shrill-tongued hounds have given the sign. I am summoned to the woods. Here, here I'll hasten by the shortest way.   (*Exeunt.*)

(*Enter* PHAEDRA *from the palace.*)

PHAEDRA. O mighty Crete, the vast sea's mistress, whose countless vessels along every coast have held the deep, yea, whatever lands, even to Assyria, making a path for the prows of ships, old Nereus cleaves—why doest thou force me here, given over to an enemy's house as hostage, wife to my foe, to spend my days in wretchedness and weeping? Behold, fled is my lord afar and keeps his bridal oath as is the wont of Theseus. Through the deep shades of the pool which none recrosses is he faring, this brave recruit of a madcap suitor,[2] that from the very throne of the king of the dead he may rob and bear away his wife. He hurries on, a partner in mad folly; him nor fear nor shame held back. And there in the depths of Acheron he seeks adultery and an unlawful bed, this father of Hippolytus.[3]

But another, greater smart burdens my woeful breast. No rest by night, no deep slumber frees me from care. A malady feeds and grows within my heart, and it burns there hot as the steam that wells from Aetna's caverns. Pallas' loom stands idle and my task slips from my listless hands; no longer it pleases me to deck the temples with votive offerings, nor at the altars, midst bands of Athenian women, to wave torches in witness of the silent rites, nor with pure prayers and pious worship to approach the goddess[4] who guards the land once granted to her! My joy is to follow in pursuit of the startled beasts and with soft hand to hurl stiff javelins.

Whither, my soul, art tending? Why this mad love of forest glades? I recognize my wretched mother's fatal curse;[5] her love and mine know how to sin in forest depths. Mother, my heart aches for thee; swept away by ill unspeakable, thou didst boldly love the wild leader of the savage herd. Fierce was he and impatient of the yoke, lawless in love, leader of an untamed herd; yet he did love something. But as for me, what god, what Daedalus could ease my wretched passion? Though he himself[6] should return, mighty in Attic cunning, who shut our monster in the dark labyrinth, he could afford no help to my calamity. Venus, detesting the offspring of the hated Sun, is avenging through us

---

[2] Pirithoüs.

[3] From being merely the assistant of another in an unlawful deed, Theseus is here conceived as the principal in it.

[4] Pallas, patroness of Athens by the assignment of the gods.

[5] Her mother, Pasiphaë, mated with a bull.

[6] Daedalus.

the chains [7] that bound her to her loved Mars, and loads the
whole race of Phoebus with shame unspeakable. No daughter of
Minos' house hath found love's bondage light; it is ever linked
with guilt.

NURSE. O wife of Theseus, illustrious child of Jove, quickly
drive guilty thoughts from thy pure breast, put out these fires,
nor show thyself obedient to this dread hope of love. Whoever
at the outset has resisted and routed love, has been safe and con-
queror; but whoso by dalliance has fed the sweet torment, too
late refuses to bear the accepted yoke.

I know how the stubborn pride of princes, ill brooking truth,
refuses to be bent to righteousness; but whatever outcome fate
shall give I am ready to endure; freedom near at hand makes
the aged brave.

Best is the upright purpose and the unswerving path; next is
the shame, that knows some measure in transgressing. To what
end art thou hasting, wretched woman? Why heap fresh infamy
upon thy house and outsin thy mother? Impious sin is worse
than monstrous passion; for monstrous love thou mayst impute
to fate, but crime, to character. If because thy husband sees not
the realms of earth, thou dost believe thy guilt safe and devoid
of fear, thou errest. Suppose that Theseus is indeed held fast,
hidden away in Lethean depths, and must suffer the Styx eter-
nally; what of him, thy father, who holds the seas under his wide
dominion and gives laws to a hundred [8] peoples? Will he permit
so great a crime to lie concealed? Shrewd is the care of fathers.
Yet suppose that by craft and guile we do hide this great wickedness from him; what of him who sheds his light on all things, thy
mother's sire? [9] What of him who makes the heavens rock, brandishing Aetnean bolts in his glittering hand, the father of the
gods? Dost believe thou canst so sin as to escape the all-seeing
eyes of both thy grandsires?

But grant that heaven's kindly grace conceals this impious intercourse; grant that to incest be shown the loyalty which great
crimes never find; what of the ever-present penalty, the soul's
conscious dread, and the heart filled with crime and fearful of
itself? Some women have sinned with safety, but none with peace
of soul. Then quench the fires of impious love, I pray, and shun
a deed which no barbaric land has ever done, neither the Getae,
wandering on their plains, nor the inhospitable Taurians, nor
scattered Scythians. Drive this hideous purpose from thy chaste

[7] See Odyssey Bk. VIII, 266–366.
[8] The "hundred cities" of Crete.
[9] The Sun.

mind, and, remembering thy mother, shun strange matings. Dost purpose to share thy bed with father and with son, and receive in an incestuous womb a blended progeny? Then go thou on and overturn all nature with thy unhallowed fires. Why do monsters cease? [10] Why does thy brother's [11] labyrinth stand empty? Shall the world hear of strange prodigies, shall nature's laws give way, whenever a Cretan woman loves?

PHAEDRA. I know, nurse, that what thou sayest is true; but passion forces me to take the worser path. With full knowledge my soul moves on to the abyss and vainly seeks the backward way in quest of counsels sane. Even so, when the mariner urges his laden vessel against opposing seas, his toil goes for naught and the ship, vanquished, is swept away by the swift-moving tide. What can reason do? Passion has conquered and now rules supreme, and, a mighty god, lords it over all my soul. This winged god rules ruthlessly throughout the earth and inflames Jove himself, wounded with unquenched fires. Gradivus, the warrior god, has felt those flames; that god [12] has felt them who fashions the three-forked thunderbolts, yea, he who tends to the hot furnaces ever raging beneath Aetna's peaks is inflamed by so small a fire as this. Phoebus himself, who guides with sure aim his arrows from the bowstring, a boy of more sure aim pierces with his flying shaft, and flits about, baneful alike to heaven and to earth.

NURSE. It is base and sin-mad lust that has made love into a god and to enjoy more liberty, has given to passion the title of an unreal divinity. The goddess of Eryx [13] sends her son, indeed, wandering through all lands, and he, flying through heaven's void, wields wanton weapons in his boyish hands, and, though least of gods, still holds such mighty empire! It is love-mad souls that have adopted these vain conceits and have feigned Venus' divinity and a god's archery. Whoever rejoices in overmuch prosperity and abounds in luxury is ever seeking unaccustomed joys. Then that dire comrade of high estate, inordinate desire, steals in; wonted feasts no longer please, nor houses of simple fashion or modest cups. Why steals this deadly pest more rarely into humble homes, choosing rather the homes of luxury? Why does hallowed love dwell beneath lowly roofs and the general throng have wholesome impulses? Why has modest fortune self-control? Why, on the other hand, do rich men, propped on empire, ever grasp at more than heaven allows? He who is too

10 *i.e.* Why are no more monsters like the Minotaur produced?
11 The Minotaur.
12 Vulcan.
13 Venus.

powerful seeks power beyond his power. What becomes one endowed with high estate, thou knowest well; then fear and respect the sceptre of thy returning lord.

PHAEDRA. Love's is, I think, the mightiest sovereignty over me, and I fear no lord's return. Nevermore has he reached sight of the vaulted skies who, once plunged in perpetual night, has gone to the silent home.

NURSE. Trust not in Dis. Though he bar his realm, and though the Stygian dog keep guard o'er the grim doors, Theseus alone finds out forbidden ways.

PHAEDRA. He will give indulgence to my love, perchance.

NURSE. Harsh was he even to a virtuous wife; foreign Antiope found his hand severe. But suppose thou canst bend thy angry husband; who can bend this youth's stubborn soul? Hating the very name of woman, he flees them all, sternly devotes his years to single life and shuns the marriage tie. Thou wouldst know him of Amazonian breed.

PHAEDRA. Though he keep him to the peaks of snowy hills, though he course swiftly amongst the ragged rocks, still through the deep forests, over the mountains, it is my resolve to follow him.

NURSE. Will he stop for thee and yield himself to thy caresses? Will he lay aside his pure practices for impure love? Will he give up his hate for thee, when it is for hate of thee, perchance, he repels all women? By no prayers can he be overcome.

PHAEDRA. Wild is he; but wild things, we have learned, can be overcome by love.

NURSE. He will flee away.

PHAEDRA. Though he flee through the very seas, still will I follow.

NURSE. Remember thy father.

PHAEDRA. My mother I remember too.

NURSE. He shuns the whole race of women.

PHAEDRA. Then need I fear no rival.

NURSE. Thy husband will be here.

PHAEDRA. Yes, comrade of Pirithoüs!

NURSE. And thy father will be here.

PHAEDRA. He will be kind, Ariadne's father.

NURSE. By these gleaming locks of age, by this heart worn with care, by these dear breasts, I beg thee check this mad love and come to thy own relief. The wish for healing has ever been the half of health.

PHAEDRA. Not wholly has shame fled from my noble soul. I yield, dear nurse. Let the love which will not be controlled be overcome. Fair fame, I will not suffer thee to be defiled. This is the only way, the one sole escape from evil: let me follow my husband; by death will I forestall my sin.

NURSE. Check, O my child, the rush of thine unbridled spirit; control thy passion. For this cause do I deem thee worthy life, since thou declarest thyself worthy death.

PHAEDRA. I am resolved on death; I seek but the manner of my fate. With the noose shall I end my life, or fall upon the sword? or shall I leap headlong from Pallas' citadel?

NURSE. Can my old age permit thee thus to go headlong to thy death? Resist this mad impulse. No one can easily be recalled to life.

PHAEDRA. No argument can stay from perishing one who has resolved to die and ought to die. Therefore in protection of my honor let me arm my hand.

NURSE. O mistress, sole comfort of my weary years, if so unruly a passion weighs on thy soul, scorn thou this fame; scarcely does fame favor truth, being better to the worse deserving, worse to the good. Let us test that grim and stubborn soul. Mine is the task to approach the savage youth and bend the cruel man's relentless will.

(*Exeunt into the palace.*)

CHORUS. Thou goddess born of the cruel sea, who art called the mother of both Loves,[14] that wanton, smiling boy of thine, reckless alike with torches and with arrows, with how sure bow does he aim his shafts! His madness steals to the inmost marrow, while with creeping fire he ravages the veins. The wound he deals has no broad front, but it eats its way deep into the hidden marrow. There is no peace with that boy of thine; throughout the world nimbly he scatters his flying shafts. The shore that beholds the new-born sun and the shore that lies at his far western goal, the land lying beneath the burning Crab and the cold region of the Arcadian Bear, which sustains its ever-wandering husbandmen, all know these fires of his. He kindles the fierce flames of youth and in worn-out age he wakes again the extinguished fires; he smites maids' breasts with unknown heat, and bids the very gods leave heaven and dwell on earth in borrowed forms.

Phoebus as keeper of the Thessalian herd[15] drove his cattle along and, laying quill aside, called together his bulls on the unequal pipes. How often did he put on lower forms, even he[16] who made heaven and the clouds: now as a bird he fluttered his

---

14 Eros and Anteros (i.e., Love and Unrequited Love).
15 Phoebus kept the herds of King Admetus for a year.
16 Jupiter, who came to Leda in the form of a swan.

white wings with note sweeter than the dying swan; now with savage front as a wanton bull he lowered his back for the sport of maidens and through the strange kingdom of his brother's waves, using his hoofs in place of pliant oars, he breasted the deep sea and overcame it, a ferryman trembling for the prize [17] he bore. The radiant goddess [18] of the darksome sky burned with love and, forsaking the night, gave her gleaming chariot to her brother to guide in fashion other than his own. He learned to drive the team of night and to wheel in narrower circuit, while the axle groaned beneath the car's heavier weight; nor did the nights keep their accustomed length, and with belated dawning came the day. The son of Alcmena [19] laid by his quiver and the threatening skin of the huge lion, letting emeralds be fitted to his fingers and law be enforced on his rough locks; he bound his legs with cross-garterings of gold and within yellow sandals confined his feet; and in that hand, with which he but now bore the club, he spun out threads with flying spindle.

Persia and the rich, fertile realm of Lydia saw the fierce lion's skin laid aside, and on those shoulders, on which the royal structure of the lofty sky had rested, a gauzy cloak of Tyrian web. It is an accursed fire (believe those who have suffered) and all too powerful. Where the land is encircled by the briny deep, where the bright stars course through heaven itself, over these realms the pitiless boy holds sovereignty, whose shafts are felt in the lowest depths by the sea-blue throng of Nereids, nor can they ease their heat by ocean's waters. These fires the race of winged creatures feel. Goaded on by love, the bold bull undertakes battle for the whole herd; if they feel that their mates are in danger, timid stags challenge to war. At such a time swart India holds striped tigers in especial fear; at such a time the boar whets his death-dealing tusks and his jaws are covered all with foam; African lions toss their manes and by their roarings give token of their engendered passion. When Love has roused them, then the forest groans with their grim uproar. Love sways the monsters of the raging sea, sways elephants, claims as his own all nature; nothing is exempt, and hate perishes at the command of Love. Old grudges yield unto his fires. Why tell of more? Love's cares overwhelm harsh stepmothers. (*Enter* NURSE *from the inner palace*.) Nurse, tell the news thou bearest. How stands it with the queen? Has her fierce flame any bound?

[17] Europa, whom the god, in bull-form, carried over the sea to Crete.
[18] Diana, or Luna, the moon-goddess, who was in love with the shepherd, Endymion.
[19] Hercules, smitten with love for Omphale, the Lydian queen.

NURSE. No hope is there that such suffering can be relieved, and no end will there be to her mad fires. She is parched by a silent fever, and even though it is hidden away, shut in her heart, her passion is betrayed in her face; fire darts from her eyes; again, her weary gaze shrinks from the light; nothing long pleases her unbalanced soul, and her limbs by ever-shifting pangs are tossed in changeful wise. Now with failing steps she sinks down as if dying, and can hardly hold up her head on her fainting neck; now she lies down to rest and, heedless of slumber, spends the night in lamentations; she bids them to lift her up and again to lay her down, to loose her hair and again to bind it up; her raiment, with itself dissatisfied, is ever changed. She has now no care for food or health. She walks with aimless feet, wasted now in strength. Her old-time sprightliness is gone, and the ruddy glow of health no longer shines on her bright face; care feeds upon her limbs, her steps totter and the tender grace of her once beautiful form is fallen away; her eyes, which once shone like Phoebus' torch, no longer gleam with their ancestral fire. Tears fall down her face and her cheeks are wet with constant drops, as when on the top of Taurus the snows melt away, pierced by a warm shower.

But see, the palace doors are opening, and she herself, lying on golden couch, all sick of soul, rejects her wonted garments.

PHAEDRA. Away, ye slaves, with robes bedecked with purple and with gold; away, scarlet of the Tyrian shell, the webs which the far-off Chinese gather from the trees. Let a narrow girdle hold in my garments' unencumbering folds, let there be no necklace at my throat, let no snowy pearls, the gift of India's ocean, weigh down my ears, and let my hair hang loose, unscented by Assyrian nard. So, tossed at random, let my locks fall down upon my neck and shoulders and, moved by swift running, stream upon the wind. My left hand shall be busied with the quiver and my right wield a Thessalian spear. In such guise as the dweller by Tanaïs or Maeotis,[20] leaving cold Pontus' tract behind, led her hordes, treading Athenian soil, and, binding her locks in a knot, let them flow free, her side protected by a crescent shield; so will I betake me to the woods.

CHORUS. Cease thy complainings; grieving helps not the wretched. Appease the rustic divinity of our virgin goddess.

NURSE. O queen of groves, thou who in solitude lovest thy mountain-haunts, and who upon the solitary mountains art alone held holy, change for the better these dark, ill-omened threats. O great goddess of the woods and groves, bright orb of heaven,

20 *i.e.*, any woman of the race of Amazons.

glory of the night, by whose changing beams the universe shines clear, O three-formed Hecate, lo, thou art at hand, favoring our undertaking. Conquer the unbending soul of stern Hippolytus; may he, compliant, give ear unto our prayer. Soften his fierce heart; may he learn to love, may he feel answering flames. Ensnare his mind; grim, hostile, fierce, may he turn him back unto the fealty of love. To this end direct thy powers; so mayst thou wear a shining face and, the clouds all scattered, fare on with undimmed horns; so, when thou drivest thy car through the nightly skies, may no witcheries of Thessaly prevail to drag thee down and may no shepherd [21] make boast over thee. Be near, goddess, in answer to our call; hear now our prayers. (HIPPOLYTUS *is seen approaching.*) The man himself I see, coming to perform thy sacred rites, no comrade at his side. (*To herself.*) Why dost thou hesitate? Chance has given thee both time and place. Thou must employ thy arts. Why do I tremble? It is no easy task to dare a crime bidden by another, but whoso fears a sovereign's behests must lay aside and banish from his heart all thought of honor; shame is but an ill servant of a sovereign's commands.

HIPPOLYTUS. Why dost hither wend wearily thy aged steps, O faithful nurse, with troubled brow and face dejected? Surely my sire is safe, Phaedra is safe, and their two sons?

NURSE. Banish thy fear. The realm is in prosperous state, thy house is strong, flourishing under the smile of Heaven. But in this happy lot do thou show thyself less harsh; for distress for thee harasses my anxious heart, seeing that thou in thine own despite dost break thyself with heavy penances. If fate compels, it is pardonable to be wretched; but whoso of his own accord surrenders himself to misery and causes his own torment, he deserves to lose the happiness he knows not how to use. Nay, remember thy youth and relax thy spirit; go out at night, raising the festal torch; let Bacchus unburden thy weighty cares.

Enjoy thy life; it is speeding swift away. Now hearts are light, now love to youth is pleasing. Let thy heart rejoice. Why dost lie on a lonely couch? Free thy youth from gloom; lay hold on pleasures; loosen the reins; let not life's best days escape thee. God has portioned out its proper duties to each time of life and led this span of ours through its own stages; joy befits the young, a serious face the old. Why dost hold thyself in check and strangle thy true nature? That crop will give to the farmer the best return which in the tender blade runs riot with joyous growth, and that tree with lofty head will overtop the grove which no

[21] An allusion to Endymion.

grudging hand cuts down or prunes away. So will right minds be
reared unto a richer fruit of praise, if sprightly freedom nourish
the high-born soul.

Wilt thou, as a harsh woods-dweller, ignorant of life, spend thy
youth in gloom and let Venus be forgot? Is it man's allotted task,
thinkst thou, to endure hardship, curb horses in their swift course,
and wage savage wars in bloody battles? How various are the
forms of death that seize and feed on mortal throngs! the sea,
the steel and treachery! But suppose these lacking: by thy path
we make wantonly for murky death. The unwedded life let
barren youth applaud; then will all that thou beholdest be the
throng of one generation only and will fall in ruins on itself. In
his providence did the almighty father of the universe, when he
saw how greedy were the hands of Fate, give heed ever by fresh
progeny to make losses good. Come now, let love but be banished
from human life, love, which supplies and renews the impoverished race: the whole globe will lie foul in vile neglect; the
sea will stand empty of its fish; birds will be lacking to the
heavens, wild beasts to the woods, and the paths of air will be
traversed only by the winds. Follow, then, nature as life's guide;
frequent the city; seek out the haunts of men.

HIPPOLYTUS. There is no life so free and innocent, none which
better cherishes the ancient ways, than that which, forsaking
cities, loves the woods. His heart is inflamed by no mad greed of
gain who has devoted himself to harmless ranging on the moun-
tain-tops; here is no shouting populace, no mob, faithless to good
men, no poisonous hate, no brittle favor. No slave is he of kings,
nor in quest of kingship does he chase empty honors or elusive
wealth, free alike from hope and fear; him venomous spite assails
not with the bite of base-born tooth; those crimes that spawn
midst the city's teeming throngs he does not know, nor in guilty
consciousness does he quake at every sound, or frame lying words.
He seeks not in pride of wealth to be sheltered by a roof reared
on a thousand pillars, nor in insolence plates he with much gold
his rafter-beams. No streams of blood drench his pious altars, no
hecatombs of snow-white bullocks, sprinkled with the sacred meal,
bend low their necks; but his lordship is over the empty fields,
and beneath the open sky he wanders blameless.

His only craft is to set cunning snares for the wild beasts, and,
when weary with hard toil, he refreshes his body in Ilissos'
stream, chilled by the snows. Now he fares along the bank of
swift-flowing Alpheus, now traverses the lofty grove's deep places,
where cool Lerna is transparent with its crystal shoals, and the
silent forest-depths, wherein the complaining birds make music,

and the ash-trees and ancient beeches quiver, moving gently in the breeze. Sweet it is to lie on the bank of some vagrant stream, or on the bare sward to enjoy light slumbers, be it where some copious spring pours down its hurrying waters, or through budding flowers some brook murmurs sweetly as it glides along.

Fruit shaken from the forest trees stays his hunger, and berries plucked from the low bushes afford an easy meal. It is his passion to flee far from royal luxury. It is from anxious cups of gold that the proud drink! How sweet to catch up with the bare hand the water of the spring! Here slumber more surely soothes as he lays him down, carefree, on his hard bed. He guiltily plots no stealthy deeds in secret chamber and on a hidden couch, nor hides fearfully away in his labyrinthine palace; it is the air and light he seeks, and his life has heaven for its witness.

It was in such wise, methinks, they lived whom the primal age produced, in friendly intercourse with gods. They had no blind love of gold; no sacred boundary-stone, judging betwixt peoples, separated fields on the spreading plain; not yet did rash vessels plough the sea; each man knew only his native waters. Then cities were not surrounded with massive walls, set with many towers; no soldier applied his fierce hand to arms, nor did hurling engines burst through closed gates with heavy stones. Not yet did earth, suffering a master's rule, endure the hard toil of the yoked ox; but the fields, fruitful of themselves, fed nations who asked nothing more; the woods gave men their natural wealth, and shady caves afforded natural homes.

Unholy passion for gain broke up this peaceful life, headlong wrath, and lust which sets men's hearts aflame. Next came cruel thirst for power; the weaker was made the stronger's prey, and might took the place of right. At first men fought with naked fists, next they began to lay hand to deadly weapons and turned stones and rough clubs to the use of arms. As yet there was no light cornel-shaft, tipped with tapering iron; no long, sharp-pointed sword hung at the side; no helmets crested with plumes gleamed from afar; rage furnished arms. Warlike Mars invented new modes of strife and a thousand forms of death. From this source streams of blood stained all lands and the sea grew red. Then crime stalked unchecked through every home and no impious deed lacked precedent. Brother was slain by brother, father by the hand of son, husband lay dead by the sword of wife, and unnatural mothers destroyed their own offspring. I say naught of stepmothers; they are no whit more merciful than the beasts. But the leader of all wickedness is woman; it is she, cunning mistress of crime, besets our minds; it is by her foul adulteries so many cities smoke, so many nations war, so many people lie crushed beneath the ruins of their kingdoms, utterly overthrown. Let others be unnamed; Aegeus' wife alone, Medea, will prove that women are an accursed race.

NURSE. Why make the crime of few the blame of all?

HIPPOLYTUS. I abominate them all, I dread, shun, curse them all. Be it reason, be it instinct, be it wild rage: it is my joy to hate them. Sooner shall you mate fire and water, sooner shall the dangerous Syrtes offer to ships a friendly passage, sooner shall Tethys from her far western shore bring in bright dawn, and wolves gaze on does with eyes caressing, than I, my hate overcome, have kindly thought for woman.

NURSE. Oft-times does Love put curb on stubborn hearts and change their hate. Look at thy mother's kingdom; those warlike women feel the yoke of Venus. Thou bearest witness to this, of her race the only son.[22]

HIPPOLYTUS. I count it the one solace for my lost mother, that now I may hate all womankind.

NURSE (aside). As some hard crag, on all sides unassailable, resists the waves, and flings far back the flood importunate, so does he spurn my words.

But Phaedra is hurrying towards us, impatient of delay. Whither will fortune go? Whither will madness tend? (PHAEDRA enters and falls as in a swoon.) Her fainting body has fallen suddenly to earth and death-like pallor has overspread her face. (HIPPOLYTUS hastens to raise her in his arms.) Lift thy face, break silence. See, my daughter, thine own Hippolytus embraces thee.

PHAEDRA (recovering). Who gives me back to grief and again sets in my soul this fever dire? How blest was my unconsciousness of self!

HIPPOLYTUS. Why dost thou shun the sweet boon of life restored?

PHAEDRA (aside). Courage! my soul, essay, fulfil thine own behest. Fearless be thy words, and firm; who makes timid request, invites denial. The chief part of my guilt is long since accomplished; too late for me is modesty—I *have* loved basely. If I follow up what I have begun, perchance I may hide my sin behind the marriage torch. Success makes some sins honest. Come now, my soul, begin! (*To* HIPPOLYTUS.) Lend ear to me privately a little while, I pray. If any comrade of thine is here, let him withdraw.

HIPPOLYTUS. Behold, the place is free from all witnesses.

22 It is said that the Amazons were accustomed to kill all boys born to them. Hippolytus, being the son of Theseus, had been spared.

PHAEDRA. But my lips refuse passage to the words I seek to frame; some strong power urges me to speak, and a stronger holds me back. I call you all to witness, you heavenly powers, that what I wish—

HIPPOLYTUS. Thy heart desires something and cannot tell it out?

PHAEDRA. Light troubles speak; the weighty are struck dumb.

HIPPOLYTUS. Entrust thy troubles to my ears, mother.

PHAEDRA. Mother—that name is too proud and high; a humbler name better suits my feelings. Call me sister, Hippolytus, or slave—yes, slave is better; I will endure all servitude. Shouldst thou bid me walk through deep-drifted snows, I would not shrink from faring along the cold peaks of Pindus; shouldst thou send me through fire and midst deadly battle ranks, I would not hesitate to offer my breast to naked swords. Take thou in my stead the sceptre committed to my care, accept me for thy slave; it becomes thee to bear sway, me, to obey thine orders. It is no woman's task to watch o'er royal cities. Do thou, in the vigor of thy youth's first bloom, rule over the citizens, strong in thy father's power; take to thine arms thy suppliant, and protect thy slave. Pity my widowhood—

HIPPOLYTUS. The most high God avert that omen! In safety will my father soon return.

PHAEDRA. The overlord of the fast-holding realm and of the silent Styx has made no way to the upper world once quitted; and will he let the robber of his couch go back? Unless, perchance, even Pluto sits smiling upon love!

HIPPOLYTUS. Him surely the kindly deities will bring again. But while God still holds our prayers in doubt, with due affection will I care for my dear brothers, and so deserve of thee that thou shalt not deem thee widowed, and myself will fill for thee my father's place.

PHAEDRA (aside). O credulous hope of lovers, O deceitful love! Has he not said enough? I'll bring my prayers to bear upon him and attack. (To HIPPOLYTUS.) Have pity! hearken to the prayers my heart may not express. I long—and am ashamed—to speak.

HIPPOLYTUS. What, pray, is this thy trouble?

PHAEDRA. A trouble thou wouldst scarce believe could befall a stepmother.

HIPPOLYTUS. Words of doubtful meaning thou utterest with riddling lips. Speak out and plainly.

PHAEDRA. It is burning love that scorches my maddened heart. A hot fire glows deep in my inmost vitals and hides darkly in my veins, as when nimble flames dart through deep-set timbers.

HIPPOLYTUS. It is with pure love for Theseus thou dost burn?

PHAEDRA. Hippolytus, it is thus with me: Theseus' features I love, those former looks of his which once as a youth he had, when his first beard marked his smooth cheeks, when he looked on the dark home of the Cretan monster, and gathered in the long thread over the winding way. How glorious was he then! Fillets bound his locks, and his young face glowed with the blush of modesty; strong muscles lay beneath the softness of his arms; and his features were as of thy Phoebe or of my Phoebus—or, rather, were thy own. Such, yes, such was he when he won his foeman's [23] favor; just so he bore his head erect. In thee more brightly shines a beauty unadorned; all of thy sire is in thee, and yet some portion of thy mother's sternness blends with an equal charm; on Grecian face shows Scythian austerity. If with thy father thou hadst come to the shores of Crete, for thee and not for him would my sister have spun the thread. Thee, thee, O sister, wherever amidst the starry heavens thou shinest, I call to aid for a cause like to thine own. One house has ruined two sisters: thee, the father, but me, the son. (*She kneels to* HIPPOLYTUS.) See, a king's daughter lies fallen at thy knees, a suppliant. Without spot or stain, pure, innocent, I am changed for thee alone. With fixed purpose have I humbled myself to prayer; this day shall bring an end either to my misery or my life. Have pity on her who loves—

HIPPOLYTUS. Great ruler of the gods, dost thou so calmly hear crimes, so calmly look upon them? And when wilt thou send forth thy thunderbolt with angry hand, if now it is cloudless? Let all the sky fall in shattered ruin, and in murky clouds hide the day; let the stars be turned backward and, wrenched aside, go athwart their courses. And thou, star of stars, O radiant Sun, dost thou behold this shame of thy race? Hide thy light and take refuge in darkness. Why is thy right hand empty, O ruler of gods and men? Why is not the world in flames by thy forked lightning? Me let thy thunder smite, pierce me, me let thy swift-darting fire consume. I am guilty, I have deserved to die; I have stirred my stepmother to love. (*To* PHAEDRA.) Look thou! Am I fitted for adulteries? For such crime did I alone seem to thee an easy instrument? Has my austerity earned this? O thou, who hast out-sinned the whole race of women, who hast dared a greater evil than thy monster-bearing mother, thou worse than she who bore thee! She did but pollute herself with her shameful lust, and yet her offspring by its two-shaped infamy displayed her crime,

[23] *i.e.* Ariadne, daughter of the foe of Athens.

though long concealed, and by his fierce visage the hybrid child made clear his mother's guilt. That was the womb that bore thee. Oh, thrice and again blest of fate are they whom hatred and treachery have destroyed, consumed, and given unto death! O father, I envy thee; than thy Colchian stepdame [24] this is a curse, greater, greater far!

PHAEDRA. I, too, recognize the fortune of my house: we seek what we should shun; but I am not mistress of myself. Thee even through fire, through the mad sea will I pursue, yes, over crags and rivers, swollen by torrent streams; wherever thou shalt direct thy steps, there will I madly rush. Once more, proud man, I grovel at thy feet.

HIPPOLYTUS. Away with thy impure touch from my chaste body! What? Even rush into my arms! Out, sword, and mete her just punishment. See, with left hand in her twisted hair have I bent back her shameless head. Never has blood been more justly spilled upon thy altar, O goddess of the bow.

PHAEDRA. Hippolytus, now dost thou grant me fulfilment of my prayer; thou healest me of my madness. This is beyond my prayer, that, with my honor saved, it is by thy hands I die. (She grasps the sword and points it at her breast.)

HIPPOLYTUS. Begone, live, lest thou have thy wish; and let this sword, polluted by thy touch, quit my chaste side. (He throws his sword from him.) What Tanaïs will cleanse me, what Maeotis, with its barbaric waves rushing into the Pontic sea? Not great Father Neptune's self, with his whole ocean, could wash away so much of guilt. O woods! O beasts! (He rushes off into the depths of the forest.)

NURSE. Her sin has been found out. O soul, why dost stand inactive and aghast? We must throw the crime back on him himself, and ourselves charge him with incestuous love. Crime must be concealed by crime. It is safest, when in fear, to force the attack. Whether we first dared the sin or suffered it, since it was done in secret, who of his own knowledge is to testify? (She raises her voice in loud outcry.) Help, Athens, help! Faithful band of slaves, come to our aid! The ravisher, Hippolytus, with vile, lustful intent, is after us; he is upon us and threatens us with death; with the sword he is terrifying our chaste queen—ah! he has rushed headlong forth and, dazed, in panic flight, has left his sword. We hold the proof of guilt. But the stricken queen, revive her first. Let her dishevelled hair, her torn locks, stay even as they are, the marks of that great guilt. Bear her to the city. Now come back to consciousness, my mistress. Why dost tear

24 Medea, who had tried to murder Theseus.

thyself and shun the glances of us all? It is thinking makes impure, not circumstance.   (*Exeunt.*)

CHORUS. He fled like a raging tempest, swifter than cloud-collecting Corus,[25] swifter than flame which speeds on its way when a meteor, driven by the winds, extends its long-trailing fire.

Let fame compare with thee [26] all ancient beauty, fame, admirer of the olden time; as much fairer does thy beauty shine as gleams more brightly the full-orbed moon when with meeting horns she has joined her fires, when at the full with speeding chariot blushing Phoebe shows her face and the lesser stars fade out of sight. Such as he is the messenger of night, who brings the first shadows back, the Evening Star fresh bathed in ocean; and when the shadows have been driven away again, the Morning Star also.

And thou, Bacchus, from thyrsus-bearing India, with unshorn locks, perpetually young, thou who frightenest tigers with thy vine-clad spear, and with a turban bindest thy horned head—thou wilt not surpass Hippolytus' crisp locks. Admire not thou thy beauty overmuch; story has spread through every nation whom [27] the sister of Phaedra preferred to Bromius.

O beauty, doubtful boon to mortals, brief gift for but a little time, how swiftly on quick foot thou dost slip away!

Not so swiftly are the meadows, beauteous with early spring, despoiled by the hot summer's glow, when with solstitial fire midday rages, and the nights sweep headlong in their brief course. As lilies wither and their leaves grow pale, so do our pleasing locks fall from the head, and the bright glow which shines on youthful cheeks is ravished in a moment and no day takes not spoil of our body's beauty. Beauty is a fleeting thing. Who that is wise would trust so frail a blessing? Enjoy it while thou mayest. Time is silently undermining thee, and an hour, worse than the last, is ever creeping on.

Why seek desert places? Beauty is no safer in pathless regions. Hide thee in the woods when Titan has brought midday, and the saucy Naïds, a wanton throng, will encompass thee, wont in their waters to imprison shapely boys,[28] and for thy slumbers the frolicsome goddesses of the groves will lay their snares, the Dryads, who pursue Pans wandering on the mountains. Or else, looking down on thee from the starry heavens, the orb [29] that was born

25 The north-west wind.
26 Hippolytus.
27 *i.e.* Theseus, whom Ariadne would have preferred to Bacchus (Bromius) had not Theseus deserted her.
28 The poet has in mind the case of Hylas.
29 Luna. The reference is to Luna and Endymion.

after the old Arcadians [30] will lose control of her white-shining car. And lately she blushed fiery red, though no staining cloud obscured her bright face; but we, anxious for our troubled goddess, thinking her harried by Thessalian charms, made loud jingling sounds: yet it was thou [31] hadst been her trouble, thou the cause of her delaying; while gazing on thee the goddess of the night checked her swift course.

This face of thine let frosts more rarely ravage, let this face more seldom woo the sun; it will shine more bright than Parian marble. How pleasing is the manly sternness of thy face and the severe dignity of thine old-seeming brow! With Phoebus mayst thou match that gleaming neck. Him locks that will not be confined, streaming over his shoulders, adorn and robe; but thee a shaggy brow, thee shorter locks, lying in disarray, become. It is thine with manly strength to dare meet the rough and warlike gods and by the spread of thy huge body to overcome them; for even in youth thou dost match the muscles of a Hercules, art broader of chest than war-waging Mars. Shouldst thou be pleased to ride a horn-footed horse, with hand more agile on the rein than Castor's thou couldst guide the Spartan Cyllarus. Stretch thong with thumb and forefinger and shoot the dart straight with all thy might; still not so far, though skilled to hurl the dart, will Cretans send the slender shaft. Or should it please thee to shoot thy arrows into the sky, in Parthian fashion, none will come down without its bird, but, deep fixed in the warm breast, will bring prey from the very clouds.

To few men has beauty (scan the ages past) not brought its penalty. May God, more merciful, pass thee by unharmed, and may thy illustrious beauty pass over the threshold of shapeless age.

What would the woman's headlong madness leave undared? She is preparing outrageous charges against this guileless youth. Behold her guilty wiles! By her torn hair she seeks to be believed; she disorders all the glory of her locks, bedews her cheeks with tears. She is marshalling her plot by every art that woman knows. (*A man is seen approaching who proves to be* Theseus.) But who is this, wearing a regal dignity on his face and with head borne high? How like the young Pirithoüs he is in countenance, were his cheeks not so deathly pale and did not unkempt squalor stiffen in his bristling hair. See, it is Theseus himself, restored to the upper world.

[30] The Arcadians were said to be older than the moon.
[31] The chorus concludes that it was Hippolytus, and not Endymion, who of late had caused the moon's perturbations.

THESEUS. At last have I escaped the realm of eternal night, the dark world which in vast prison-house overshades the dead, and scarcely do my eyes endure the longed-for light. Now for the fourth time is Eleusis harvesting the bounty of Triptolemus,[32] as many times has Libra made day equal unto night, since dubious battling with an unknown fate has kept me between the ills of death and life. Though dead to all things else, one part of life remained to me—my sense of ills. Hercules was the end, who, when he dragged the dog by violence out of Tartarus, brought me, too, along with him to the upper world. But my strength is spent, has lost its old-time vigor, and my steps do falter. Alas, how hard a struggle it was from lowest Phlegethon to attain the far realms of air, at once to flee from death and follow Hercules!

But what is this tearful outcry that strikes my ears? Let someone tell me. Grieving and tears and woe, and on my very threshold sad lamentation?—auspices that well befit a guest from hell.

NURSE. Phaedra holds unbending purpose of self-murder; she scorns our tears and is on the very edge of death.

THESEUS. What cause for death? Why die, now that her husband is come back?

NURSE. That very cause has brought with it speedy death.

THESEUS. Thy riddling words some weighty matter hide. Tell me plainly what grief weighs on her mind.

NURSE. She discloses it to none; though sorrowing, she hides her secret grief and is resolved to take with her the woe whereof she dies. But come now, I pray thee, come; there is need of haste.

THESEUS. Unbar the closed portals of the royal house. (*The doors are thrown open and* THESEUS *encounters his wife just within.*) O partner of my couch, is it thus thou welcomest thy lord's return and the face of thy long-sought husband? Come, put away the sword from thy right hand, give me heart again, and whatever is driving thee out of life, declare it.

PHAEDRA. Alas, O Theseus, great of soul, by the sceptre of thy kingdom, by thy children's lives, by thy return, and by my body already doomed to dust, allow my death.

THESEUS. What cause forces thee to die?

PHAEDRA. If the cause of my death is told, its fruit is lost.

THESEUS. No one else shall hear it, save myself.

PHAEDRA. A chaste woman dreads her husband's ears alone.

THESEUS. Speak out; in my true heart will I hide thy secret.

PHAEDRA. Where thou wouldst have another silence keep, keep silence first thyself.

32 Wheat: Triptolemus taught man to sow and harvest wheat.

THESEUS. No means of death shall be granted unto thee.

PHAEDRA. If one wills to die, death can never fail.

THESEUS. Tell me what sin is to be purged by death.

PHAEDRA. That I still live.

THESEUS. Do not my tears move thee?

PHAEDRA. It is best to die a death to be wept by friends.

THESEUS. She persists in silence. Then by scourge and bonds shall her old nurse reveal whatever she will not tell. (*To attendants.*) Bind her with chains. Let the power of the scourge drag forth the secrets of her soul.

PHAEDRA. Hold! I will myself confess.

THESEUS. Why dost turn away thy sorrowing face and hide with veiling robe the tears that suddenly overflow thy cheeks?

PHAEDRA. Thee, thee, O sire of the heavenly gods, I call to witness, and thee,[33] bright radiance of celestial light, on whom as founder this house of ours depends—though sorely tempted, I withstood his prayers; to sword and threats my soul yielded not; yet did my body bear his violence. This stain of shame shall my blood wash away.

THESEUS. Who, tell me, was the destroyer of my honor?

PHAEDRA. Whom thou least thinkest.

THESEUS. Who is he? I demand to hear.

PHAEDRA. This sword will tell, which, in his panic terror, the ravisher left behind, fearing the gathering of the citizens.

THESEUS. Ah me! What villainy do I behold? What monstrous thing do I see? The royal hilt of ivory, embossed with tiny figures, gleams before me, the glory of the Athenian race. But he, whither has he escaped?

PHAEDRA. The slaves, here, saw him speeding swift away in headlong flight.

THESEUS. O holy Piety, O ruler of the heavens, and thou [34] who with thy billows dost sway the second realm, whence came this infection of infamy in our stock? Was that man nurtured by the land of Greece or by the Scythian Taurus and Colchian Phasis? The breed reverts to its progenitors and debased blood reproduces the primal stock. This, truly, is the madness of that warlike race,[35] to contemn Venus' laws and to prostitute the long-chaste body to the crowd. O abominable race, yielding to no laws of a better land! Even the very beasts do shun incestuous love, and instinctive chastity guards Nature's laws. Where are those features, that feigned austerity of the man, that rough garb,

---

[33] Phoebus, the father of Phaedra's mother, Pasiphaë.
[34] Neptune.
[35] The Amazons.

aping old-fashioned and archaic ways? Where thy stern manners and the sour severity of age? O two-faced life, thou keepest thy true thoughts hidden and dost clothe foul purpose with an aspect fair—chaste bearing hides unchastity; meekness, effrontery; piety, sin unspeakable; false men approve truth and the soft affect hardihood.

O thou lover of the woods, the boasted wild man, continent, rough, unstained, is it for me thou keepst thyself in check? With my couch, by such crime as this, was it thy pleasure to make first test of manhood? Now, now I give thanks to the heavenly powers that Antiope fell stricken by my hand, and that, descending to the Stygian pit, I did not leave to thee thy mother. Fugitive, traverse nations remote, unknown; though a land on the remotest confines of the world hold thee separated by Ocean's tracts, though thou take up thy dwelling in the world opposite our feet, though thou escape to the shuddering realms of the high north and hide deep in its farthest corner, and though, placed beyond the reach of winter [36] and his hoar snows, thou leave behind thee the threatening rage of cold Boreas, still shalt thou pay penalty for thy crime. Fugitive, through all thy hiding-places untiringly will I pursue thee; regions remote, blocked, hidden away, far separate, trackless, will I traverse, and no place shall stop me— thou knowest whence I am returned. Whither weapons cannot be hurled, thither will I hurl my prayers. My father of the sea granted me thrice to fashion prayers whereto the god would bow, and, calling upon Styx, confirmed the boon. (*To* NEPTUNE.) Now fulfil the sad [37] boon, O ruler of the sea! Let Hippolytus see the bright day no more, and in youth pass to the ghosts that are wrathful with his sire. Now bring aid, which my soul abhors, O father, to thy son; never should I squander this last boon [38] of thine, did not great ills overwhelm; in depths of Tartarus, in presence of dread Dis, and imminent menace of hell's lord, I was sparing of this prayer. Keep now thy promised faith. Father, dost thou delay? Why are thy waves yet silent? Now veil the night with dark clouds driven by the winds; snatch stars and sky from sight; pour forth the deep; and, rising high, summon the floods from Ocean's self.

CHORUS. O Nature, mighty mother of the gods, and thou, fire-bearing Olympus' lord, who through the swift firmament whirlest the scattered stars, and the wandering courses of the planets, who makest the heavens on swift axis turn, why dost thou take

36 *i.e.*, in the Hyperborean regions.
37 Because a father is asking the death of his son.
38 Theseus has already used two of his wishes, the first when he set out from Troezen to Athens, and the second when he was in the labyrinth.

such care to keep perpetual the pathways of the lofty sky, that now the hoar frosts of winter may strip the woods, now to the plantations their foliage come again, that now in summer the Lion's fervent heat may ripen the grain and the year regulate its powers? But why, again, dost thou, who holdest so wide sway, and by whose hands the ponderous masses of the vast universe are poised and wheel their appointed courses—why dost thou dwell afar, all too indifferent to men, not anxious to bring blessing to the good, and to the evil, bane?

Fate without order rules the affairs of men, scatters her gifts with unseeing hand, fostering the worse; dire lust prevails against pure men, and crime sits regnant in the lofty palace. The rabble rejoice to give government to the vile, paying high honors even where they hate. Warped are the rewards of uprightness sad virtue gains; wretched poverty dogs the pure, and the adulterer, strong in wickedness, reigns supreme. O decency, honor, how empty and how false!

But why does yon messenger haste hither with rapid pace, his sad countenance wet with grieving tears?

(*Enter* MESSENGER.)

MESSENGER. O lot bitter and hard, O cruel servitude, why calls fate upon me to bear unutterable tidings?

THESEUS. Fear not to speak out boldly the disaster, cruel though it be; I bear a heart not unprepared for suffering.

MESSENGER. My tongue refuses utterance to the grief-bringing woe.

THESEUS. Tell what mischance weighs down this shattered house.

MESSENGER. Hippolytus, woe is me, lies in lamentable death.

THESEUS. That his son was dead the sire has long since known; now is the ravisher dead. But tell the manner of his end.

MESSENGER. When with troubled steps he left the city, a fugitive, unfolding his swift way with flying feet, he quickly brought his prancing steeds beneath the high yoke and curbed their mouths with tight-drawn reins. Then much did he utter, communing with himself, and, cursing his native land, called oft upon his sire, and with loose reins fiercely shook the lash; when suddenly from out the deep the vast sea thundered and starward heaved itself. No wind was blowing on the briny sea, from no quarter of the calm sky came the noise, but a self-born [39] tempest stirred the peaceful deep. Not so violently does the south wind distress Sicilia's straits, nor so madly does the Ionian sea swell

[39] *i.e.* the commotion came from within the sea.

beneath the north-west's tyranny, when the cliffs tremble under the shock of waves and the white spray smites Leucate's summit. The mighty deep heaves up into a huge mound, and the sea, swollen with a monstrous birth, rushes to land.

Nor is that vast destruction piled up for ships; it is the land it threatens. With no light sweep the flood rolls forward; some strange thing in its burdened womb the heavy wave is carrying. What new land shows its head to the stars? Is a new Cyclad rising? The rocks, the sacred seat of the Epidaurian god,[40] were hid, and the cliffs famous for the crime of Sciron, and the land [41] which is hemmed in by two seas.

While we in dumb amaze are wondering what this means, behold, the whole sea bellows, and the cliffs on every hand echo back the sound; the highest peak is wet with dashed-up spray; it foams, and then in turn spews back the flood, as when a cavernous whale swims through the deep ways of ocean, spouting back streams of water from his mouth. Then the great globe of waters shivered, shook and broke, and brought to the shore a thing more terrible than our fear; the sea rushed landward, following its monster. My lips tremble in the telling. How the thing looked! how huge! A bull it was, towering high with a dark blue neck, and he reared a high mane upon his verdant crest; his shaggy ears stood up; his eyes flashed with changing color, now such as the lord of a wild herd might have, now such as one born beneath the sea—now his eyes dart flame, now they flash wondrous with cerulean gleam. His brawny neck with great muscles bulges and his wide nostrils roar with his gaping draughts of air. His breast and dewlap are green with clinging moss, and his long flanks with red seaweed are spotted. His hinder parts are joined into monstrous shape, and, all scaly, the huge beast drags his measureless length along. Such is that sea-monster of the outer ocean which swallows or crushes swift-flying ships. The lands quaked with fear; herds fled in frenzy in all directions through the fields, and the herdsman forgot to follow his cattle. All beasts fled from their wooded haunts; all hunters stood trembling, pale with chilling fear. Hippolytus alone, quite unafraid, with tight reins holds fast his horses and, terror-stricken though they are, urges them on with the encouragement of his familiar voice.

There is a deep passage towards the fields through the broken hills, hard by the neighboring stretches of the sea below. Here that huge creature sharpens his anger and prepares his wrath.

---

40 These altar-like rocks were sacred to Aesculapius.
41 Isthmus.

When he has gained his spirit, and with full trial rehearsed his wrath, he darts forth, running swiftly, scarce touching the surface of the ground with flying feet, and stands, in grim menace, before the trembling steeds. Thy son, rising up, confronts him with fierce, threatening look, nor does he change countenance, but loudly thunders: "This empty terror cannot break my spirit, for it was my father's task to conquer bulls." But straightway his horses, disobedient to the reins, seized the chariot and, roaming from the road, wherever frenzied terror carried them in their mad flight, there they plunged along and dashed amid the rocks.

But he, as a helmsman holds his ship steady on the boisterous sea, lest it give its side to the waves, and skilfully cheats the floods, in like manner guides his swift-moving steeds. Now he drags on their mouths checked by the tight-drawn reins, and now, oft plying the twisted lash, he forces them to his will. His companion [42] holds doggedly in pursuit, now racing alongside the horses, now making detour to face them, from every side filling them with fear.

But now they could flee no further; for he charged full front upon them, that bristling, horned monster of the deep. Then, truly, the plunging horses, driven by mad fear, broke from control, struggled to wrench their necks from the yoke, and, rearing up, hurled their burden to the ground. Headlong on his face he plunged and, as he fell, entangled his body in the clinging reins; and the more he struggled, the tighter he drew those firm-holding coils. The horses felt their deed, and now, with the light chariot, since none controlled, wherever fear bade on they dashed. Just so, not recognizing their wonted burden, and indignant that the day had been entrusted to a pretended Sun, the horses [43] flung Phaëthon far from his heavenly track. Far and wide the fields are stained with blood, and his head, dashed on the rocks, bounds back from them. The brambles pluck away his hair; the hard stones ravage that lovely face, and his ill-fated beauty is ruined by many a wound. The swift wheels drag his dying limbs; and at last, as he is whirled along, a tree, its trunk charred into a stake, stays him with its stock driven right through the groin and holds him fast, and for a little while the car stands still, held by its impaled master. Awhile that wound stays the team—then equally delay and their master, too, they break. Thereafter the thickets slash his half-dead body, the rough brambles with their sharp thorns tear him, and every tree-trunk has taken its toll of him. Now bands of his mourning servants are scouring the fields

[42] The monster.
[43] *i.e.* of the Sun.

through the places where Hippolytus was dragged, marked in a long trail by bloody traces, and his whimpering dogs are tracking their master's limbs. But not yet has the painstaking toil of his grieving friends availed to fill out his body. Has his glorious beauty come to this? He who but now was the illustrious partner of his father's throne, who but now, his acknowledged heir, shone like the stars, he is being gathered from every hand for his last burning, and collected for his funeral pyre.

THESEUS (*weeping*). O nature, all too potent, with how strong ties of blood dost thou hold parents! how we cherish thee, even against our wills! Guilty, I wished him dead; lost, I lament him.

MESSENGER. Not rightfully may any weep what he has willed.

THESEUS. Truly I deem this the crowning woe of woes, if fortune makes what we must loathe that we must long for.

MESSENGER. If thou still keepst thy hate, why are thy cheeks wet with tears?

THESEUS. Not that I lost, but that I slew, I weep.

CHORUS. How chance whirls round the affairs of men! Less does fortune rage midst humble folk, and more lightly God smites the more lightly blessed. Unnoticed ease keeps men in peace and a cottage bestows age untroubled.

The mountain-peaks, lifted to airy heights, catch east, catch south winds, mad Boreas' threats, and the rain-fraught north-west gale. Seldom does the moist valley suffer the lightning's blast; but Caucasus the huge, and the Phrygian grove of mother Cybele, quake beneath the bolt of high-thundering Jove. For in jealous fear Jove aims at that which neighbors on high heaven; but the low-roofed, common home never feels his mighty blasts. Around thrones he thunders.

On doubtful wings flies the inconstant hour, nor does swift Fortune pledge loyalty to any. He [44] who with joy beheld the clear, starry skies and bright day, the night [45] now left behind, in grief is lamenting his sorrowful return, and finds his welcome to his father's dwelling more doleful than Avernus' self.

O Pallas, ever to be revered by the Athenian race, for that thy Theseus looks on sky and upper world and has escaped from the pools of Styx, chaste one, thou owest naught to thine uncle, the all-devouring; unchanged the toll [46] remains for the infernal king.

What voice of wailing sounds from the high palace? And what would maddened Phaedra with the naked sword?

(*Enter* PHAEDRA *with a drawn sword in her hand.*)

---

[44] Theseus, who has but now returned from Hades.
[45] The darkness of the lower world.
[46] If Theseus has escaped Pluto, Hippolytus has gone to fill his place.

THESEUS. What fury pricks thee on, wild with grief? Why that sword? What mean thine outcries and lamentations over the hated corpse?

PHAEDRA. Me, me, assault, O savage ruler of ocean's depths; against me send forth the blue sea's monsters, whatever in her inmost womb farthest Tethys bears, whatever in his restless waves' embrace Ocean hides in his remotest flood. O Theseus, always harsh, who never without harm unto thy loved ones dost come back, son and father [47] have paid for thy homecomings by their death. Thou art the destroyer of thy home, hurtful ever, whether through love or hatred of thy wives.[48] (*Turning to the mangled corpse.*) O Hippolytus, is it such I see thy face? such have I made it? What savage Sinis, what Procrustes, has scattered thy members so, or what Cretan bull, fierce, two-formed monster, filling the labyrinth of Daedalus with his huge bellowings, has torn thee asunder with his horns? Ah, woe is me! whither is thy glorious beauty fled, and thine eyes, my stars? Dost lie low in death? Come back for a little and hearken to my words—no shameful thing I speak—with this hand will I make amends to thee, in my wicked heart will I thrust the sword and set Phaedra free equally from life and crime. Then through waters, through Tartarean pools, through Styx, through rivers of fire will I madly follow thee. Let me appease thy shade; take the spoils of my head, and accept this lock torn from my wounded forehead. It was not ours to be joined in life, but surely it is ours to be joined in death. (*To herself.*) Now die, if thou art pure, for thy husband's sake; if impure, for thy love. Shall I seek again my husband's couch by so great crime defiled? The one horror lacking was that, as if pure, thou shouldst enjoy his couch claimed as thy right. O death, thou only solace of evil love, O death, thou chiefest grace to damaged honor, I fly to thee; spread wide thy forgiving arms.

Hear me, O Athens, and thou, his father, worse than baleful stepdame: I have lied to you, and the crime which, crazed with passion, I had conceived in my own mad breast, I falsely charged to him. Thou, father, hast punished to no purpose; and the chaste youth, through charge of the unchaste, lies there, all pure and innocent. (*To* HIPPOLYTUS.) Recover now thine honor. My impious breast is bare to the sword of justice, and my blood makes atonement to a guiltless man. (*To* THESEUS.) What

---

[47] Theseus' father leaped to his death when his son returned from Crete with a black sail.

[48] Theseus had slain Antiope in a fit of anger, and now has destroyed Hippolytus through jealous love for Phaedra.

thou, his father, shouldst do, now that thy son is murdered, learn from his stepdame: hide thee in Acheron. (*She falls upon her sword and dies.*)

THESEUS. You jaws of wan Avernus, you Taenarean caves, you waves of Lethe, welcome to the wretched, you sluggish pools, hide my impious self, plunge deep and bury me in unending woes. Come now, savage monsters of the deep, now, vast sea, and whatever Proteus has hidden away in the furthest hollow of his waters, and hurry me off, me who felt triumph in crime so great, to your deep pools. And thou, father, who didst ever give too quick assent to my angry prayer, I am not worthy of an easy death who have brought unheard-of destruction on my son and scattered his mangled limbs throughout the fields; who, while, as stern avenger, I was punishing an unreal crime, have myself fallen into true guilt. Heaven, hell, and ocean have I filled up by my sin; there remains no further lot,[49] three kingdoms know me.

For this have I returned? Was the way opened to the light of heaven that I might look on two funerals and a double murder, that, wifeless and childless, I might with one torch light the funeral pyres of son and wife? O giver of light that is but darkness, Hercules give back his boon [50] to Dis; give me up again to the ghosts whom I escaped. Impiously, I make vain prayers for the death I left behind. Thou bloody man, skilful in deadly arts, who didst contrive unheard-of, barbarous ways of death, now upon thyself inflict fitting punishment. Shall a pine-tree, its top bent down to earth, split me in two, shot back into the air? [51] Shall I be hurled headlong over the Scironian cliffs? More dreadful things have I seen which Phlegethon bids imprisoned sinners suffer, compassing them about with his stream of fire; what punishment waits for me, and what place, I know.

You guilty shades, make room, and on these shoulders, these, let the rock rest, the endless task of the aged son [52] of Aeolus, and weigh down my weary hands; let water, lapping my very lips, mock my thirst; [53] let the fell vulture leave Tityus and fly hither, let my liver constantly grow afresh for punishment; and do thou rest awhile, father [54] of my Pirithoüs—let the wheel that never stops its whirling bear these limbs of mine on its swift-

---

[49] A reference to the three lots by which the sons of Saturn divided the universe among themselves.

[50] Hecules had asked the boon of Dis that he might take Theseus with him out of Hades.

[51] This is how Sinis, a robber whom Theseus slew, dealt with his victims.

[52] Sisyphus.

[53] Referring to the torture of Tantalus.

[54] Ixion.

turning rim. Yawn, earth; take me, dire Chaos, take me; this way
to the shades is more fitting for me—my son I follow. And fear
not, thou who rulest the shades; I come clean-handed; [55] receive
me into thy everlasting home, to go forth no more. My prayers
move not the gods; but if I asked impious things, how would
they bend to answer!

CHORUS. Theseus, time without end awaits thy lamentations.
Now pay the rites due to thy son and bury with speed the
scattered limbs mangled so shamefully.

THESEUS. Hither, hither bring the remains of his dear body
and heap together, as they come, the burden of his limbs. Is this
Hippolytus? Mine is the sin, I do acknowledge it; it is I who
have murdered thee, and, lest once only or alone I might be
guilty, when I his father would dare crime, my own sire I summoned to my aid. Behold, I enjoy my father's boon. O child-
lessness, bitter misfortune for broken years! Come, clasp his limbs
and all that is left thee of thy son, thou wretched man, and, in
thy sad breast fondling, cherish them.

CHORUS. The scattered parts of his torn body set thou, his
sire, in order, and put back in place the random pieces. Here
should be his strong right hand, here we must put his left, skilled
in managing the reins; traces of his left side I recognize. But how
large a part is still lacking to our tears!

THESEUS. Be firm, my trembling hands, for your sad duty; be
dry, my cheeks, stay your flowing tears, while a father is portion-
ing out members to his son and fashioning his body. What is this
shapeless, ugly piece, with many a wound torn on every side?
What part it is of thee, I know not; but it is a part of thee. Here,
here lay it down, not in its own but in an empty place. Is this
that face which once gleamed with fire as of the stars, which
turned his enemy's eyes aside? Has his beauty fallen to this? O
dire fate, O cruel favor of the gods! Thus comes back son to
father in answer to his prayer? (*Placing some ornaments on the
torn body.*) Lo, these are thy sire's last gifts. Take them, O thou
who must oft be borne to burial. Now let the fires consume these
limbs. (*To attendants.*) Open wide my palace, gloomy and foul
with slaughter, and let all Athens with loud laments resound. Do
you make ready the flames of the royal pyre; do you seek through
the fields for his body's parts still wandering. (*Pointing to
PHAEDRA's corpse.*) As for her, let her be buried deep in earth,
and heavy may the soil lie on her unholy head!

[55] *i.e.* with no evil designs on Proserpina, as before.

Oedipus

A TRAGEDY

by
SENECA

❧ ❧ ❧

translated by
Frank Justus Miller

DRAMATIS PERSONAE

OEDIPUS, king of Thebes, the son, as he supposed, of Polybus, king of Corinth, and Merope, his wife, but found to be the son of Laïus and Jocasta

JOCASTA, wife of Oedipus, found to be also his mother

CREON, a Theban prince, brother of Jocasta

TIRESIAS, the prophet of Thebes, now old and blind

MANTO, daughter of Tiresias

OLD MAN, sent from Corinth to announce to Oedipus the death of Polybus

PHORBAS, shepherd in charge of the royal flocks of Thebes

MESSENGER, who announces the self-inflected blindness of Oedipus and the suicide of Jocasta

CHORUS of Theban elders

The scene is laid before the royal palace of Thebes; the play opens in the early morning of the day within which the tragedy is consummated.

ARGUMENT

An oracle once came to Laïus, king of Thebes, that he should perish by his own son's hands. When, therefore, a son was born to him, he gave the infant to his chief shepherd to expose on Mount Cithaeron. But the tender-hearted rustic gave the babe instead to a wandering herdsman of Polybus, the king of Corinth.

Years later a reputed son of Polybus, Oedipus by name, fearing an oracle which doomed him to slay his father and wed his mother, fled from Corinth, that so he might escape this dreadful fate. As he fared northward he met and slew an old man who imperiously disputed the narrow way with him. Upon arriving at the Theban land he read the riddle of the Sphinx, and so destroyed that monster which Juno had sent to harass the land which she hated; and for this service Oedipus was made the husband of Jocasta, the widowed queen of Laïus (recently slain, so said report, by a band of robbers, on the high road), and set upon the vacant throne.

Now other years have passed, and sons and daughters have been born to the royal pair. But now a dreadful pestilence afflicts the State. Oedipus has sent Creon to consult the oracle, to learn the cause and seek the means of deliverance from the scourge. And while he waits his messenger's return the murky dawn still finds him grieving for his kingdom's wretched plight.

OEDIPUS. Now night is driven away; the hesitant sun returns, and rises, sadly veiling his beams in murky cloud; with woeful flame he brings a light of gloom and will look forth upon our homes stricken with ravening plague, and day will reveal the havoc which night has wrought.

Does any man rejoice in royalty? O deceitful good, how many ills dost hide beneath thy smiling face! As lofty peaks do ever catch the winds, and as the cliff, which with its jutting rocks cleaves the vast deep, is beaten by the waves of even a quiet sea, so does exalted empire lie exposed to fate. How happily had I escaped the sceptre of my father, Polybus! An exile freed from cares,[1] fearless, wandering, upon a kingdom (be heaven and the gods my witness) I came by chance. Things unspeakable I fear— that by my hand my father shall be slain. Of this the Delphic laurels warn me, and another, still greater crime they assign to me. Is any wickedness greater than a murdered sire? O hapless filial love!—I am ashamed to tell my doom—Phoebus threatens the son with his father's chamber, with bed made infamous, defiled by unhallowed passion. It was the fear of this that drove me from my father's realm. Not as a fugitive [2] did I leave my home; of my own will, distrustful of myself, O Nature, I made thy laws secure. When thou dreadest some great calamity, though thou thinkst it cannot befall, still do thou fear. I dread all things exceedingly, and I do not trust myself unto myself.

Now, even now the fates are aiming some blow at me; for what am I to think when this pestilence, so deadly to Cadmus' race, so widespread in its destruction, spares me alone? For what evil am I reserved? Midst the ruins of my city, midst funerals to be lamented with tears ever fresh, midst the slaughter of a nation, I stand unscathed—aye! prisoner at Phoebus' bar. Couldst thou hope that to crimes like thine a wholesome kingdom would be granted? I have made heaven pestilent.

No soft breeze with its cool breath relieves our breasts that pant with heat, no gentle Zephyrs blow; but Titan augments the scorching dog-star's fires, close-pressing upon the Nemean Lion's [3] back. Water has fled the streams, and from the herbage verdure. Dirce is dry, scant flows Ismenus' stream, and with its meagre wave scarce wets the naked sands. With paling light glides Phoebus' sister athwart the sky, and the gloomy heavens are wan in the lowering day. No star in clear nights glitters, but a heavy, black fog broods over the lands. The citadels of the heavenly gods and their homes on high are veiled in hellish aspect. The ripened corn withholds its fruitful harvest, and though the golden crop waves high its wheaten ears, the grain dies shrivelled on its parched stalk. No class is free from death; but every age and sex is smitten alike. Young men with old, fathers with sons, are joined by the deadly plague; husband and wife on a single pyre are burned, and funerals lack bitter tears and lamentations. Nay, the persistent bane of our so great a woe has of itself dried our eyes and, as oft in utmost misery, our tears have perished. Here to the final flames a stricken father bears his son; there a

---

[1] i.e. regarding the oracle, whose fulfilment he thought he had escaped.
[2] i.e. to avoid the consequences of some crime already committed.
[3] The sun is in the constellation of Leo in July.

crazed mother carries her child and hastens back to bring another to the selfsame pyre. Nay more, in their very grief new grief arises and midst funeral rites their own rites befall. Anon, with others' fires they burn the bodies of their own; yes, fire is stolen, for the wretched have no shame. No separate mounds cover the hallowed bones. Mere burning is enough; how small a part is turned to ashes! No ground is left for tombs; now woods refuse more pyres. Neither prayers nor any skill avails the stricken. Healers fall victims; the disease drags down those who seek to aid.

Prostrate at the altars, I stretch suppliant hands, begging my fates to hasten, that I may anticipate my country's ruin and not fall after all the rest, and mine become the last funeral of my realm. Oh, divinities too harsh, Oh, heavy fate! To me alone in all this people is death denied, so ready for all others? Come, fly the land thy baleful band has tainted, leave the tears, the deaths, the pest-laden air which thou bringst with thee, ill-omened guest; fly quickly (long since were it well)—even to thy parents! [4]

JOCASTA (*who has entered in time to hear her husband's last words*). What boots it, husband, to make woe heavier by lamentation? This very thing, I think, is regal—to face adversity and, the more dubious thy station and the more the greatness of empire totters to its fall, the more firm to stand, brave with unfaltering foot. It is not a manly thing to turn the back to Fortune.

OEDIPUS. Far from me is the crime and shame of cowardice, and my valor knows not dastard fears. Should swords be drawn against me, should the bristling power of Mars rush on me, against even the fierce Giants would I boldly bear opposing hands. The Sphinx, weaving her words in darkling measures, I fled not; I faced the bloody jaws of the fell prophetess and the ground white with scattered bones. And when from a lofty cliff, already hovering over her prey, she prepared her pinions and, lashing her tail like a savage lion, stirred up her threatening wrath, I asked for her riddle. Thereupon came a sound of dread; her jaws crashed, and her talons, brooking no delay, eager for my vitals, tore at the rocks. The lot's intricate, guile-entangled words, the grim riddle of the winged beast, I solved.

(*To himself.*) Why too late dost thou now in madness pray for death? Thou hadst thy chance to die. This sceptre is thy meed of praise, this thy reward for the Sphinx destroyed. That dust, that cursed dust of the artful monster is warring against me still;

[4] *i.e.* Polybus, king of Corinth, and Merope, his wife, who, he supposed, were his parents and from whom he had fled to Thebes.

that pest which I destroyed is now destroying Thebes. One only salvation is left us now, if any way of salvation Phoebus shows.

CHORUS. Thou art falling, O noble race of Cadmus, with all thy city. Reft of its tillers thou seest thy land, O pitiable Thebes. Destruction feeds, O Bacchus, on the soldiery of thine, thy comrades to farthest Ind, who dared to ride on the Eastern plains and plant thy banners on the world's first edge. The Arabs, blest with their cinnamon groves, they saw, and fleeing horsemen, the backs of the treacherous Parthians,[5] to be feared for their flying shafts; they pierced to the shores of the ruddy sea,[6] whence Phoebus discloses his rising beams, opens the gates of day, and with nearer torch darkens the naked Indians.

We, the offspring of an unconquered stock, are perishing, are falling beneath the fierce onslaught of fate. Each hour a new train moves on to Death; the long array of a mournful band hastes to the shades; the gloomy procession jams, and for the throng that seeks burial the seven gates spread not wide enough. The grievous wrack of carnage halts and funeral crowds funeral in unbroken line.

First the plague struck the slow-moving sheep; to their bane did the woolly flock crop the rich herbage. Ready to smite his victim's neck, the priest had taken his stand; while his upraised hand aimed the unerring blow, the bull, his horn glimmering with gold, sank dully down unstruck. Shattered by the blow of a heavy axe, the neck of another yawned open; but no blood, only foul gore, oozing from the dark wound, stained the steel. The prancing steed, slowing in mid-course, fell down and flung his rider over his sinking shoulder.

The abandoned cattle lie stricken in the fields; the bull pines away amidst his dying kine. The herdsman deserts his dwindling herd, midst his wasting bullocks dying. No more do stags fear ravenous wolves; subsides the mad lion's roar; no fierceness now among the shaggy bears. The lurking serpent has lost its bane; parched and dying he lies, his venom dried.

No more do the woods, crowned with their own foliage, shed dusky shadows on the mountain-sides; the fields no more grow green with fertile soil, no more do the vine's full branches bend beneath the load of its own deity; all things have felt our plague.

They have burst the bars of abysmal Erebus, the throng of sisters with Tartarean torch,[7] and Phlegethon,[8] changing his own

---

[5] A reference to the proverbial "Parthian shot," delivered while in flight or seeming flight.
[6] Referring not to our "Red Sea," but to the Indian Ocean.
[7] The Furies.
[8] Phlegethon was the burning stream of Hades.

course, has mingled Styx with our Sidonian [9] streams. Dark Death opens wide his greedy, gaping jaws and unfolds all his wings, and the boatman [10] who plies the troubled stream with roomy skiff, though hardy in his vigorous old age, can scarce draw back his arms wearied with constant poling, worn out with ferrying the fresh throng over. Nay more, they say that the Cerberus has burst his chains of Taenarian [11] iron, and is wandering through our fields; that the earth has rumbled; that ghosts go stealing through the groves, larger than mortal forms; that twice have Cadmean forests trembled and shed their snows; twice has Dirce welled up with blood; in the silent night Amphion's hounds have bayed.

O dire appearance and new form of death, far heavier than death! Benumbing languor fetters the listless limbs; the sickly cheeks burn red; small spots overspread the face. Then hot vapors scorch the body's very citadel [12] and distend the cheeks with blood, the eyes stand staring, and accursèd fire [13] feeds upon the limbs. There is a ringing in the ears; black blood drips from the strained nostrils and bursts the swelling veins. Full oft does a grating cough rack the inmost frame. Now they strain cold stones close to their breasts; or where new freedom in the house permits, since the watcher has been borne forth, you [14] hasten to the springs, and with full draughts feed your fevered thirst. Prostrate the crowds lie at the altars and pray for death—this alone the compliant gods bestow. They seek the shrines, not that they may appease the divinities with gifts, but joying to glut the very gods.

(CREON is *seen returning from his mission to Delphi.*)

OEDIPUS. Who, pray, is he who seeks the palace with hasty steps? Is Creon at hand, noble in blood and deed, or does my sick fancy see false for true?

CHORUS. He is at hand, Creon, by all our prayers desired.

(*Enter* CREON.)

OEDIPUS. With dread am I shaken, fearing the trend of fate,[15] and my fluttering heart wavers betwixt two moods; where joy with grief commingled lies in doubt, the uncertain soul fears though it longs to know.

O brother of my consort, if to weary hearts thou bringest any aid, quickly declare thy news.

---

[9] *i.e.* Phoenician. Cadmus, son of Agenor, king of Phoenicia, had founded Thebes.
[10] Charon.
[11] Hercules dragged Cerberus from Hades through a cave in Taenarum.
[12] *i.e.* the head.
[13] *Sacer ignis* usually supposed to be erysipelas, "St. Anthony's fire."
[14] He addresses the sick folk who, when the watcher is dead, rush to the water, which only inflames their thirst.
[15] *i.e.* of the oracle which Creon had been sent to consult.

CREON. Doubtful lies the answer and involved the doom.

OEDIPUS. Who grants a doubtful help to sufferers, grants none.

CREON. In mazy riddles is the Delphic god wont to hide his secrets.

OEDIPUS. Speak out, though it be doubtful; to read riddles to Oedipus alone is given.

CREON. The god bids the king's murder be atoned by banishment and the murdered Laïus be avenged. Not sooner shall the bright sun course the heavens, and give wholesome draughts of unpolluted air.

OEDIPUS. And who was the murderer of the illustrious king? Tell whom Phoebus names, that he may pay the penalty.

CREON. May it be safe, I pray, to have told of things to sight and hearing dreadful. Numbness has settled through my limbs; my chill blood freezes. When Phoebus' hallowed shrine I entered with reverent feet and raised pious hands in due supplication to the god, the double peaks of snow-clad Parnassus gave an angry roar; the overhanging laurel of Phoebus trembled and shook its foliage, and suddenly the holy waters of the Castalian spring stood still. The priestess of Leto's son began to fling loose her bristling locks and, deep stirred, to suffer Phoebus. She had not yet reached the cave, when, with a mighty roar, words louder than voice of man leaped forth: [16]

" Kind shall the stars return to the Theban city of Cadmus,

If, O fugitive guest, Ismenian Dirce thou leavest,

Stained with the blood of a king, from infancy known to Apollo.

Brief shall be to thee the joys of thy impious slaughter:

With thee war shalt thou bring, and war to thy sons leave behind thee,

Foully returned once more to the impious womb of thy mother."

OEDIPUS. That which, at Heaven's warning, I am now prepared to do should fittingly have been done in honor of the dead king's dust, that none might treacherously profane the sacred sceptre. Kings have most need to guard the life of kings; none has care for him when dead whom alive he fears.

CREON. Our care for the dead a greater fear dispelled.

OEDIPUS. Did any fear prevent a pious duty?

CREON. Aye, the Sphinx and the dire threats of her accursèd chant.

OEDIPUS. Now at Heaven's command let the crime be expiated.

Whoever of the gods dost look with favor upon kingdoms—

---

[16] The oracles were commonly given out in dactylic hexameters.

thou,[17] thou whose are the laws of the swift-revolving heavens; and thou,[18] greatest glory of the unclouded sky, who presidest over the twelve signs [19] in thy changing course, who dost unroll the slow centuries with swift wheel; and thou, his sister,[20] ever faring opposite to thy brother, Phoebe, night-wanderer; thou [21] whom the winds obey; who over the level deep dost speed thy azure car; and thou [22] who dost allot homes devoid of light—do ye all attend: Him by whose hand Laïus fell may no peaceful dwelling, no friendly household gods, no hospitable land in exile entertain; over shameful nuptials may he lament and impious progeny; may he, too, slay his own father with his own hand and do—can aught heavier be entreated?—whatever I have fled from. There shall be no place for pardon. I swear by the sway which I now, a stranger, bear, and by that which I abandoned; by my household gods; by thee, O father Neptune, who in double stream dost play against my shores on either side [23] with scanty waves. And do thou [24] thyself come as witness to my words, thou who dost inspire the fate-speaking lips of Cirrha's priestess: So may my father spend peaceful age and end his days secure on his lofty throne; so may Merope know the nuptial torches of her Polybus alone, as by no grace shall the guilty one escape my hand.

But tell me, where was the impious crime committed? Did he die in open battle or by treachery?

CREON. Seeking holy Castalia's leafy groves, he trod a way hedged in by close-pressing thickets, where the road, three-forking, branches out upon the plains. One road cuts through Phocis, the land that Bacchus loves, whence lofty Parnassus, leaving the lowlands, by a gentle slope lifts heavenward his two peaks; but one leads off to the land [25] of Sisyphus bathed by two seas; a third into the Olenian fields, through a low valley winding, reaches the vagrant waters and crosses the cool shallows of Elis' stream. Here as he fared, relying on peaceful times, a band of robbers suddenly attacked him with the sword and wrought the crime unwitnessed. (TIRESIAS *is seen approaching.*) But in the nick of time, stirred by Phoebus' oracle, Tiresias, though slow with trembling limbs, comes hurrying, and with him Manto, leading her sightless father.

---

[17] Jupiter.
[18] Phoebus, the sun.
[19] *i.e.* of the Zodiac.
[20] Phoebe, the moon.
[21] Neptune.
[22] Pluto.
[23] He believes that the Isthmus of the Corinth is his native land.
[24] Apollo.
[25] The Isthmus.

(*Enter* TIRESIAS, *old and blind, led by his daughter,* MANTO.)

OEDIPUS. O thou to the gods consecrate, thou next to Phoebus' self, explain the oracle; tell whom the fates demand.

TIRESIAS. That my tongue is slow to speak, that it craves delay, it behooves thee not, O great-souled Oedipus, to wonder; from the blind much of the truth is hidden. But whither my country, whither Phoebus calls me, I will follow. Let us search out the fates; if my blood were fresh and warm, I would receive the god in my own breast.[26] Drive to the altars a pure white bull and a heifer whose neck has never borne the curved yoke. Do thou, my child, who guides thy blind father, report the clear tokens of the prophetic sacrifice.

(*The victims are stationed at the altars as directed.*)

MANTO. A perfect victim stands before the sacred altars.

TIRESIAS. To our vows invoke Heaven's presence with the accustomed prayer, and heap the altars with the Orient's gift of frankincense.

MANTO. Now have I heaped incense on the gods' sacred hearth.

TIRESIAS. What of the flame? Does it already seize upon the generous feast?

MANTO. It flashed up with sudden light, and suddenly died down.

TIRESIAS. Did the fire stand clear and bright? Did it lift a pure, pointed flame straight skyward and, spreading, unfold its topmost crest upon the air, or sidewise does it creep uncertain of its course, and with wavering smoke fall murkily?

MANTO. Not one appearance only had the changeful flame. As when rain-bringing Iris entwines her various colors, who, over a great space of heaven sweeping, by her painted bow proclaims the storm, so wouldst thou be in doubt what color is lacking, what is present in the flame; dark blue, mingled with yellow spots, it hovered, then was blood-red, and at last trailed off in blackness.

But see, the combative flame is separating into two parts and the discordant embers of one sacred pile are rent in two—O father, I tremble as I gaze: Bacchus' gift poured out changes to blood, and dense smoke wreathes the king's head; denser still it settles about his very face and with its thick cloud has hidden light in gloom. O father, tell us what is means.

TIRESIAS. What can I tell, halting mid conflicting voices of a soul amazed? What shall I say? Dire ills they are, but hidden in mystery. It is the gods' wont with clear signs to manifest their

---

[26] *i.e.* he would speak directly by inspiration instead of proceeding by the different methods of divination.

wrath. What is it which they would, and again would not, reveal?
What grim menace are they concealing? Something which shames
the gods. Quick, bring the victims hither, and with salted meal
sprinkle the bullocks' necks. With placid mien do they suffer the
rites and the outstretched hands?

MANTO. Facing the east, the bull, lifting high his head, shrank
from the day and turned in terror from the sun's bright face.

TIRESIAS. With one blow smitten do they fall to earth?

MANTO. The heifer threw herself upon the ready steel and with
one blow fell; but the bull, twice smitten, hither and yon wanders uncertain and feebly drives forth his scarce-resisting life.

TIRESIAS. Does the blood spurt, quick from out a narrow thrust,
or does it but slowly overflood a deep-driven blow?

MANTO. The blood of one through the proper path, where the
breast gapes wide, pours in a stream; the other's grievous wounds
are stained with but scanty drops; nay, backward turning, the
blood flows copiously through mouth and eyes.

TIRESIAS. These ill-omened sacrifices rouse dread forebodings.
But describe to me the sure marks of the entrails.

MANTO. Father, what is this? With no gentle motion, as is
their wont, do the entrails shake and quiver, but my whole hand
do they cause to tremble and blood spurts afresh from the veins.
The heart, diseased through and through, is withered and lies
deep hidden, and the veins are of livid hue. A great part of the
entrails is wanting, and from the rotting liver black gall oozes
forth, and see—ever fatal omen for sole sovereignty—two heads
rise side by side with equal bulge; yet each cloven head is hidden
in but thin membrane, refusing a lurking place to secret things.
The hostile [27] side rises with sturdy strength and shows seven
swelling veins; but all these an intercepting line cuts straight
across, preventing their return. The positions have been changed;
no organ lies in its own place, but all things are reversed: on the
right side lie the lungs all clogged with blood, and with no room
for breath; the left is not the region of the heart; no caul with
soft covering stretches its rich folds over the entrails. Nature is
subverted; even the womb follows not its law. Let us look close
and see whence comes this stiffness in the entrails. What monstrosity is this? A foetus in an unmated heifer! nor does it lie in
accustomed fashion, but fills its mother in an unnatural place.
Moaning it moves its limbs, and its weak members twitch with

[27] The priests, or haruspices, made an imaginary division of the entrails
into two parts; the one, they assigned to friendly influences, the other, to
hostile. According to the appearance of both these parts, they foretold coming
events.

convulsive rigors. Livid gore has stained the entrails black. (*She ceases her inspection as the bodies of the victims suddenly begin to move.*) The sadly mangled forms essay to move, and one disembowelled body strives to rise and menaces the priests with its horns; the entrails flee from my hand. Nor is that sound which strikes thy ears the deep lowing of the herd, nor are frightened cattle bellowing anywhere; it is the lowing of the altar-fires, the affrighted murmurings of the hearth.

OEDIPUS. What do these signs of the terrifying rites portend? Declare; with no timid ear will I drink in thy words. Extremest ills are wont to make men calm.

TIRESIAS. Thou wilt look with envy upon these ills for which thou seekest aid.

OEDIPUS. Tell me the one thing the gods would have me know: who has defiled his hands with the murder of the king?

TIRESIAS. Neither the birds which on light pinion cut the depths of heaven, nor vitals plucked from still living breasts, can summon up the name. We must essay some other path: the king himself must be recalled from the regions of perpetual night, that, released from Erebus, he may point out his murderer. We must unseal the earth, must implore the implacable divinity of Dis, must draw forth hither the people of infernal Styx. Say to whom thou wilt assign the awful mission; for it is not right for thee, whose are the highest powers of state, to look upon the shades.

OEDIPUS. Thee, Creon, this task demands, to whom as next in succession my kingdom looks.

TIRESIAS. While we are loosing the bars of abysmal Styx let the people's hymn sound with the praise of Bacchus.

(*Exeunt* CREON, TIRESIAS, *and* MANTO.)

CHORUS. Bind your streaming locks with the nodding ivy, Bacchantes, and in your soft hands grasp the Nysaean thyrsus!

Bright glory of the sky, come hither to the prayers which thine own illustrious Thebes, O Bacchus, offers to thee with suppliant hands. Hither turn with favor thy virginal face; with thy star-bright countenance drive away the clouds, the grim threats of Erebus, and greedy fate. Thee it becomes to circle thy locks with flowers of the springtime, thee to cover thy head with Tyrian turban, or thy smooth brow to wreathe with the ivy's clustering berries; now to fling loose thy lawless-streaming locks, again to bind them in a knot close-drawn; in such guise as when, fearing thy stepdame's [28] wrath, thou didst grow to manhood with false-

---

[28] Juno's.

seeming limbs, a pretended maiden with golden ringlets, with saffron girdle binding thy garments. So thereafter this soft vesture has pleased thee, folds loose hanging and the long-trailing mantle. Seated in thy golden chariot, thy lions with long trappings covered, all the vast coast of the Orient saw thee, both he who drinks of the Ganges and whoever breaks the ice of snowy Araxes.

On an unseemly ass old Silenus attends thee, his swollen temples bound with ivy garlands; while thy wanton initiates lead the mystic revels. Along with thee a troop of Bassarids in Edonian dance beat the ground, now on Mount Pangaeus' peak, now on the top of Thracian Pindus; now midst Cadmean dames has come a maenad, the impious comrade of Ogygian Bacchus, with sacred fawn-skins girt about her loins, her hand a light thyrsus brandishing. Their hearts maddened by thee, the matrons have set their hair a-flowing; and at length, after the rending of Pentheus' limbs, the Bacchanals, their bodies now freed from the frenzy, looked on their infamous deed as though they knew it not.

Cadmean Ino, foster-mother of shining Bacchus, holds the realms of the deep, encircled by hands of Nereids dancing; over the waves of the mighty deep a boy holds sway, new come, the kinsman of Bacchus, no common god, Palaemon.

Thee, O boy,[29] a Tyrrhenian band once captured and Nereus allayed the swollen sea; the dark blue waters he changes to meadows. Thence flourish the plane-tree with vernal foliage and the laurel-grove dear to Phoebus; the chatter of birds sounds loud through the branches. Fast-growing ivy clings to the oars, and grape-vines twine at the mast-head. On the prow an Idaean lion roars; at the stern crouches a tiger of Ganges. Then the frightened pirates swim in the sea, and plunged in the water their bodies assume new forms: the robbers' arms first fall away; their breasts smite their bellies and are joined in one; a tiny hand comes down at the side; with curving back they dive into the waves, and with crescent-shaped tail they cleave the sea; and now as curved dolphins they follow the fleeing sails.

On its rich stream has Lydian Pactolus borne thee, leading along its burning banks the golden waters; the Massagetan who mingles blood with milk in his goblets has unstrung his vanquished bow and given up his Getan arrows; the realms of axe-wielding Lycurgus have felt the dominion of Bacchus; the fierce lands of the Zalaces have felt it, and those wandering tribes whom neighboring Boreas smites, and the nations which Maeotis' cold

---

[29] When Bacchus, still a boy, was kidnapped by Tyrrhenian pirates, he made their mast sprout vines and lions and tigers to walk the deck. The pirates jumped overboard and were turned to dolphins.

water washes, and they on whom the Arcadian [30] constellation looks down from the zenith and the two wagons. He has subdued the scattered Gelonians; he has wrested their arms from the warrior maidens; [31] with downcast face they fell to earth, those Thermodontian hordes, gave up at length their light arrows, and became maenads. Sacred Cithaeron has flowed with the blood of Ophionian [32] slaughter; the Proetides fled to the woods, and Argos, in his stepdame's very presence, paid homage to Bacchus.

Naxos, girt by the Aegean sea, gave him in marriage a deserted maiden,[33] compensating her loss with a better husband. Out of the dry rock there gushed Nyctelian liquor; [34] babbling rivulets divided the grassy meadows; deep the earth drank in the sweet juices, white fountains of snowy milk and Lesbian wine mingled with fragrant thyme. The new-made bride is led to the lofty heavens; Phoebus a stately anthem sings, with his locks flowing down his shoulders, and twin Cupids brandish their torches. Jupiter lays aside his fiery weapons and, when Bacchus comes, abhors his thunderbolt.

While the bright stars of the ancient heavens shall run in their courses; while the ocean shall encircle the imprisoned earth with its waters; while the full moon shall gather again her lost radiance; while the Day Star shall herald the dawn of the morning and while the lofty Bears shall know naught of caerulean Nereus; [35] so long shall we worship the shining face of beauteous Lyaeus.[36]

(*Enter* CREON, *returned from the rites of necromancy.*)

OEDIPUS. Although thy very face displays signs of woe, declare by whose life we are to appease the gods.

CREON. Thou bidst me speak what fear would leave unsaid.

OEDIPUS. If falling Thebes is not enough to move thee, at least be moved by the tottering sceptre of a kindred house.

CREON. Thou wilt long not to have known what thou desirest overmuch to know.

OEDIPUS. An idle remedy for ills is ignorance. What! wilt even bury revelations of the public weal?

---

[30] The two phrases refer to the same constellation, conceived first as bears and second as wagons or wains.
[31] The Amazons.
[32] Referring to Pentheus' death.
[33] Ariadne, deserted by Theseus.
[34] *i.e.* wine. The following lines describe the wonders of nature's bounty in honor of Bacchus' nuptials.
[35] Nereus, a sea-god, is here used for the sea itself, and the description "sea-blue" is literally applied.
[36] Bacchus.

CREON. Where foul the medicine, it is loathsome to be healed.

OEDIPUS. Speak out thy tidings, or, by severe suffering broken, thou shalt know what the power of an angered king can do.

CREON. Kings hate the words whose speaking they compel.

OEDIPUS. To Erebus shalt thou be sent, a cheap sacrifice for all, unless by thy speech thou disclose the secrets which the rites reveal.

CREON. Let me be silent. Can any less liberty be sought from kings?

OEDIPUS. Often, even more than speech, to king and kingdom dumb liberty brings bane.

CREON. When silence is not allowed, what is allowed?

OEDIPUS. He weakens power who is silent when bidden to speak.

CREON. Words forced from me I pray thee hear with calm.

OEDIPUS. Was any ever punished for speech compelled?

CREON. Far from the city is a grove dusky with ilex-trees near the well-watered vale of Dirce's fount. A cypress, lifting its head above the lofty wood, with mighty stem holds the whole grove in its evergreen embrace; and an ancient oak spreads its gnarled branches crumbling in decay. The side of one devouring time has torn away; the other, falling, its roots rent in twain, hangs propped against a neighboring trunk. Here are the laurel with bitter berries, slender linden-trees, Paphian myrtle, and the alder, destined to sweep its oarage over the boundless sea; and here, mounting to meet the sun, a pine-tree lifts its knotless bole to front the winds. Midmost stands a tree of mighty girth, and with its heavy shade overwhelms the lesser trees and, spreading its branches with a mighty reach, it stands, the solitary guardian of the wood. Beneath this tree a gloomy spring overflows, that knows nor light nor sun, numb with perpetual chill; an oozy swamp surrounds the sluggish pool.

Hither when the aged priest came, there was no delay; the place furnished night.[37] Then a ditch is dug and into it are thrown brands plucked from funeral pyres. The priest shrouds his body in a mournful pall and waves a branch.[38] His gloomy robe sweeps over his feet; in the squalid garb of mourning the old man advances, his hoary hair bound with a wreath of death-dealing yew. Black-fleeced [39] sheep and oxen of sable hue are backward dragged. The flame devours the feast, and the living victims writhe in the deathly fire. Then he summons the spirits

[37] The proposed rites were ordinarily performed only at night.

[38] i.e. of some funereal tree, as the yew or cypress.

[39] These features are characteristic of the rites of necromancy which are here described.

of the dead, and thee who rulest the spirits, and him [40] who blocks the entrance to the Lethaean stream; over and over he repeats a magic rune, and fiercely, with frenzied lips, he chants a charm which either appeases or compels the flitting ghosts. He makes libation of blood upon the altars, burns the victims whole, and soaks the trench with plenteous blood. Of snowy milk likewise he makes libation, pours wine with his left [41] hand, repeats his chants, and, with gaze on ground, summons the ghosts with deeper tone and wild.

Loud bayed the pack of Hecate; thrice the deep valley gave out a mournful noise; the whole place was shaken and the ground was stricken from below. "My prayers are heard," says the priest; "prevailing words I uttered; blind Chaos is burst open, and for the tribes of Dis a way is given to the upper world." All the wood shrank down, its foliage bristling; the stout oaks were split and the whole grove shook with horror; the earth also shrank back, and from her depths gave forth a groan—whether Hell brooked it ill that its deep abyss was assailed, or Earth of herself, that she might give passage to the dead, with crashing noise burst her close barriers; or else in mad rage three-headed Cerberus shook his heavy chains.

Suddenly the earth yawned and opened wide with gulf immeasurable. Myself, I saw the numb pools amidst the shadows; myself, the wan gods and night in very truth. My frozen blood stood still and clogged my veins. Forth leaped a savage cohort and stood full-armed, the whole viper brood, the troop of brothers sprung from Dircaean [42] teeth. Then grim Erinys shrieked, and blind Fury and Horror, and all the forms which spawn and lurk midst the eternal shades: Grief, tearing her hair; Disease, scarce holding up her wearied head; Age, burdened with herself; impending Fear, and greedy Pestilence, the Ogygian people's curse. Our spirits died within us. Even she [43] who knew the rites and the arts of her aged sire stood amazed. But he, undaunted and bold from his lost sight, summons the bloodless throng of cruel Dis.

Straightway, like clouds, the shadowy forms flit forth and snuff the air of open heaven. Not as many falling leaves does Eryx show; nor does Hybla in mid-spring as many flowers produce, when in close masses cling the swarming bees; as many waves

[40] Cerberus.
[41] Because offered to the malignant infernal powers.
[42] A far-fetched epithet from the fact that it was in Dirce's cave that the dragon was found which Cadmus slew and from whose teeth the warriors sprang.
[43] Manto.

break not on the Ionian sea; as many birds, fleeing cold Strymon's threats, leave not the wintry lands and, cleaving the sky, change Arctic snows for the warm valley of the Nile; as were the throngs which the priest's call summoned forth. Eagerly the shivering ghosts seek the shelter of the shady grove. First from the ground, his right hand grasping a wild bull by the horns, Zethus emerges, and Amphion, in his left holding the shell [44] which by its sweet music drew the rocks. And midst her children Niobe, at last safe in her pride, holds up her head with insolent arrogance, and numbers over her shades. A mother worse than she, Agave comes, still raging; her the whole band follows who rent their king in pieces, and after the Bacchanals mangled Pentheus comes, even now savage and holding to his threats.

At length, when often called, one lifts his shame-stricken head and, shrinking afar from all the throng, seeks to hide himself. The seer presses hard after him and redoubles his Stygian prayers, until he bring out to open view the features that fain would hide—Laius! I shudder as I tell it. There he stood, a sight of horror, his limbs streaming over with blood, his ragged locks matted with foul filth; and with raving lips he spoke: "O savage house of Cadmus, rejoicing ever in kindred blood, brandish the thyrsus, with frenzied hands rend thy sons—it were better so; for Thebes' crowning crime is—the love of mother. O fatherland, not by the wrath of Heaven, but by sin art thou despoiled. It is not the plague-fraught south wind with its destructive blast, nor yet the earth, too little watered by the rain from heaven, that with its dry breath is harming thee; but thy blood-stained king, who as the price of cruel murder has seized the sceptre and the incestuous chamber of his sire, detested son!—but worse the mother than the son, again pregnant in her unhallowed womb; and to his own origin he returned and brought his mother impious progeny, and (a thing the beasts scarce do) himself begot brothers to himself—entanglement of evil, a monster more confused than his own Sphinx. Thee, thee, who in thy blood-stained hand dost hold the sceptre, thee and thy whole city will I, thy father, still unavenged, pursue; and with me Erinys as bridesmaid of thy nuptials will I bring, yea, I will bring her sounding with her lash; thine incestuous house will I overturn and thy household with unnatural strife will I destroy.

"Wherefore speedily expel ye the king from out your borders, in exile drive him to any place soever with his baleful step. Let him leave the land; then, blooming with flowers of spring, shall it renew its verdure, the life-giving air shall give pure breath

[44] Lyre.

again, and their beauty shall come back to the woods; Ruin and Pestilence, Death, Suffering, Corruption and Distress, fit company for him, shall all depart together. And he himself with hastening steps shall long to flee our kingdom, but I will set wearisome delays before his feet and hold him back. He shall creep, uncertain of his way, with the staff of age groping out his gloomy way. Rob ye him of the earth; his father will take from him the sky." [45]

OEDIPUS. An icy chill has crept through my bones and limbs; all that I feared to do I am accused of having done. But Merope, still wed to Polybus, refutes the charge of incest; and Polybus, alive and well, cleanses my hands. Each parent clears me from the charge of blood and incest: what room is left for crime? As for Laïus, Thebes mourned his loss long ere I set foot on Boeotian soil. Is the old priest lying, or is some god oppressing Thebes? [46] —Now, now I hold the confederates of a crafty plot: the priest invents these charges, using the gods as a screen for trickery and to thee he promises my sceptre.

CREON. I, should I wish my sister driven from the throne? If sacred fealty to my kindred house held me not fixed in my present station, yet that high estate itself, ever overfraught with care, would frighten me. Let it be thine in safety to lay off this burden, nor let it overwhelm thee when thou wouldst withdraw. Now more safely wilt thou set thyself in humbler place.

OEDIPUS. Dost even urge me of free will to lay down the heavy cares of state?

CREON. Thus would I counsel those to whom the way even yet is open to either choice; but as for thee it is necessary now to bear thy lot.

OEDIPUS. Whoso longs to reign, his surest way is to praise humble life and prate of ease and sleep. Calm is oft counterfeited by a restless soul.

CREON. Does not my long loyalty plead enough for me?

OEDIPUS. To traitors loyalty gives opening for treason.

CREON. Free from a king's burdens, I enjoy a king's advantages; my home is honored by throngs of citizens, and no day rises to dawning from the night on which my royal kinsman's bounty does not overflow my house; apparel, rich food, deliverance, all are granted to many through my favor. What should I think still lacking to a lot so blest?

OEDIPUS. What still is lacking; [47] prosperity has no bounds.

CREON. Shall I then, my cause unheard, fall like a criminal?

---

[45] Both passages point to Oedipus' self-inflicted blindness.
[46] i.e. bringing sedition as well as pestilence.
[47] i.e. royal power.

OEDIPUS. Did ye show due regard for my life? Did Tiresias hear my cause? And yet ye hold me guilty. Ye set the example; I but follow it.

CREON. What if I am innocent?

OEDIPUS. Doubts as if certainties kings are wont to fear.

CREON. Who trembles with vain fear, true fear deserves.

OEDIPUS. Set free the guilty, and he hates; let all that's doubtful perish.

CREON. Thus is hatred bred.

OEDIPUS. He who fears hatred overmuch, knows not to rule; fear is the guard of kingdoms.

CREON. Who harshly wields the sceptre with tyrannic sway, fears those who fear; terror recoils upon its author's head.

OEDIPUS (to attendants). Shut up the guilty man in a rocky dungeon and guard him well. I to the royal palace will return.

(CREON is led away by attendants. Exit OEDIPUS.)

CHORUS. Not thou [48] the cause of our great perils, not on thy account do the fates assail the house of Labdacus; nay, it is the ancient wrath of the gods that follows us. Castalia's grove lent its shade to the Sidonian wanderer and Dirce bathed the colonists from Tyre, when great Agenor's son, [49] weary with tracking Jove's thefts [50] over all the world, in fear halted beneath our trees, worshipping his sister's ravisher; and, by the advice of Phoebus, bidden to follow a straying heifer which had never bent beneath the plough or the slow wagon's curving yoke, he gave up his quest [51] and named a nation [52] from that ill-omened heifer.

From that time on, our land has ever produced strange monsters; either a serpent, rising from the valley's depths, hisses on high above the ancient oaks and overtops the pines; ever higher, above the Chaonian trees he lifts his dark-blue head, although his greater part still lies upon the ground; or else the earth, teeming with impious birth, brings forth armed men: loud resounded the battle-call from the curving horn, and the brazen trumpet sent forth its piercing notes. Their tongues and lips, never nimble before, were first employed in the battle-cry of their unfamiliar voice.

The kindred bands filled the plains, and this offspring, worthy of the seed that had been sown, measured their life by a single day; born after the passing of the Morning Star, they perished

48 Oedipus.
49 Cadmus.
50 Europa, whom Jove, in bull form, had stolen away. Agenor had sent Cadmus to find her, with instructions not to return unless successful.
51 i.e. the quest enjoined upon him by his father.
52 Boeotia, from Greek *bous*, cow.

ere Hesperus arose. The wanderer [53] quaked at prodigies so strange, and fearfully awaited the assault of the new-born folk; until the savage youths [54] fell in death, and their mother [55] beheld the children she had but now brought forth returned to her own bosom. With this may the horror of civil strife have passed! May the Thebes of Hercules [56] know those fratricidal struggles only!

What of the doom of Cadmus' grandson, when the antlers of a long-lived stag covered his brow with their strange branches, and his own hounds pursued their master? Headlong from the woods and mountains the swift Actaeon fled, and with feet more nimble, scouring glades and rocky places, shuddered at the feathers [57] fluttering in the breeze, and avoided the snares he himself had set; at length he gazed into the still pond's water and saw his horns and his beast-like countenance. It was in that same pool the goddess [58] of too stern chastity had bathed her virgin limbs!

OEDIPUS. My soul broods over its cares and renews its fears. That by my crime Laïus fell, gods both of heaven and hell affirm; and yet my soul, conscious of innocence and known to itself better than to the gods, makes denial. Retracing the dim path of memory, I see one met on the way fallen beneath the blow of my stout staff and given over to Dis; but first the old man arrogantly from his car thrust the younger from the way. Yet that was far from Thebes, where Phocis' land parts the three-forked roads. (*Enter* JOCASTA.) O then, my soul's own mate, resolve my doubts, I pray thee; what span of life had Laïus at his death? In the fresh prime of life died he, or in broken age?

JOCASTA. Midway between age and youth, but nearer age.

OEDIPUS. Did a great throng gird the king about?

JOCASTA. The most mistook the uncertain path and strayed; a few by faithful toil kept near his car.

OEDIPUS. Did any companion share the royal fate?

JOCASTA. One did faith and valor cause to share his fate.

OEDIPUS (*aside*). I have the guilty man; the number tallies, and the place. (*To* JOCASTA.) But add the time.

JOSCATA. Now is the tenth harvest being reaped.

[53] *i.e.* Cadmus, exiled by his father.
[54] The monsters sprung from the dragon's teeth.
[55] The earth.
[56] Hercules was born at Thebes.
[57] Tied to bushes along deer-runs in order to frighten the animals in the desired direction.
[58] Diana.

(*Enter an old Corinthian messenger.*)

OLD MAN (*to* OEDIPUS). The Corinthians summon thee to thy father's throne. Polybus has gained his everlasting rest.

OEDIPUS. How heartless Fortune assails me on every hand! But tell me by what fate my sire is fallen.

OLD MAN. Soft slumber set his aged spirit free.

OEDIPUS. My father lies dead, and by no violence. I call to witness that now I may lift clean hands to heaven, hands that need fear no charge of crime. But the more fearful part of my fates remains.

OLD MAN. All fears thy father's kingdom will dispel.

OEDIPUS. I would seek my father's kingdom, but from my mother do I shrink.

OLD MAN. Dost fear thy mother, who, in anxious suspense, longs for thy coming?

OEDIPUS. It is love itself bids me flee.

OLD MAN. Wilt leave her widowed?

OEDIPUS. There dost thou touch on the very thing I fear!

OLD MAN. Speak out; what hidden fear weighs on thy soul? It is my wont to offer kings a loyal silence.

OEDIPUS. Warned by the Delphic oracle, I dread my mother's bed.

OLD MAN. Then cease thy empty fears, thy horrible forebodings; Merope was not in truth thy mother.

OEDIPUS. What did she hope to gain by a changeling son?

OLD MAN. Kings' children hold rude loyalty in check.[59]

OEDIPUS. The secrets of the chamber—tell how thou knowest them.

OLD MAN. It was these hands gave thee, a tiny babe, unto thy mother.

OEDIPUS. Thou gav'st me to my mother; but who gave me to thee?

OLD MAN. A shepherd, beneath Cithaeron's snowy peak.

OEDIPUS. What chance brought thee within that wood?

OLD MAN. On that mountain-side was I tending my horned flocks.

OEDIPUS. Now name also the sure marks upon my body.

OLD MAN. Thy soles had been pierced with iron, and thou hast thy name [60] from thy swollen and crippled feet.

OEDIPUS. Who was he who gave thee my body as a gift? I seek to know.

[59] Royal offspring (and hence the insurance of succession) is the strongest hold upon lagging loyalty which threatens to fall away.
[60] Oedipus means "swollen-footed" in Greek.

OLD MAN. He fed the royal flocks; there was a humbler band of shepherds under him.

OEDIPUS. Tell me his name.

OLD MAN. An old man's early memory grows faint, failing through weakness and long disuse.

OEDIPUS. Couldst recognize the man by face and feature?

OLD MAN. Perchance I might; some trifling mark oft-times calls back the memory of things that time has buried and made dim.

OEDIPUS. Let all the flocks be driven hither to the sacred altars, their guides with them; go, slaves, and quickly summon those with whom is the herds' chief control.

(*The slaves depart on the errand.*)

OLD MAN. Whether design or chance conceals these things, suffer to lie hid for ever what has lain hid so long; truth often is made clear to the discoverer's bane.

OEDIPUS. Can any bane greater than all this be feared?

OLD MAN. Great, be thou sure, is that bane which thou seekst with toil so great. Here meet, from that side and from this, the public weal and the king's, and both are in equal balance. Keep thy hand from both; challenge thou nothing; let the fates unfold themselves.[61]

OEDIPUS. It is not expedient to disturb a happy state; that is with safety changed which is at its worst.

OLD MAN. Dost seek for a nobler thing than royal lineage? Beware lest thou rue the finding of thy parentage.

OEDIPUS. I will seek certainty even of rueful birth; so resolved am I to know. (*Enter* PHORBAS. OEDIPUS *to himself.*) Behold the ancient, heavy with years, once keeper of the royal flocks, Phorbas. (*To* OLD MAN.) Dost recall the old man's name or features?

OLD MAN. His form comes easily to my memory; but that face, while not well known, again is not unknown to me. (*To* PHORBAS.) While Laïus held the throne, didst ever as a slave drive rich flocks on Cithaeron's tracts?

PHORBAS. Cithaeron, abounding ever in fresh pasturage, in summer-time gave feeding-ground for my flocks.

OLD MAN. Dost thou know me?

PHORBAS. My memory falters and is in doubt.

OEDIPUS. Didst thou once give a boy to this man here? Speak

61 *i.e.* let well enough alone. The condition of the state is critical, and Oedipus' personal problem is acute; but wisdom bids keep hands off and let the fates unfold themselves.

out. Thou falterest? Why do thy cheeks change color? Why seekst for words? Truth scorns delay.

PHORBAS. Thou stirrest matters overclouded by long lapse of time.

OEDIPUS. Speak, lest pain force thee to the truth.

PHORBAS. I did give him an infant, a worthless gift; never could he have enjoyed the light or sky.

OLD MAN. Far be the omen! He lives and I pray may live.

OEDIPUS. Why dost thou say that the child thou gavest did not survive?

PHORBAS. Through both his feet a slender iron rod was driven, binding his legs together. A swelling engendered in the wound, galled the child's body, a loathsome plague.

OEDIPUS (*to himself*). Why seekest further? Now doth fate draw near. (*To* PHORBAS.) Who was the babe? Speak out.

PHORBAS. My loyalty forbids.

OEDIPUS. Hither with fire, someone! Now shall flames banish loyalty.

PHORBAS. Is truth to be sought along such cruel ways? Pardon I beg.

OEDIPUS. If I seem harsh to thee, and headstrong, vengeance is in thy hands; speak thou the truth. Who was he? Of what sire begot? Of what mother born?

PHORBAS. *Born of thy—wife.*

OEDIPUS. Yawn, earth! And do thou, king of the dark world, ruler of shades, to lowest Tartarus hurl this unnatural interchange betwixt brood and stock. Citizens, heap stones upon my accursed head; slay me with weapons. Let father, let son assail me with the sword; let husbands and brothers arm hands against me, and let the sick populace snatch brands from the pyres and hurl them at me. The crime of the age I wander, hate of the gods, destruction of holy law, the very day I drew the untried air already worthy of death. (*To himself.*) Now be stout of soul, now dare some deed worthy of thy crimes. Go, get thee to the palace with hurrying feet; congratulate thy mother on her house enriched by children. (*Exit.*)

CHORUS. Were it mine to shape fate at my will, I would trim my sails to gentle winds, lest my yards tremble, bent beneath a heavy blast. May soft breezes, gently blowing, unvarying, carry my untroubled barque along; may life bear me on safely, running in middle course.

While, in fear of the Cretan king, madly the lad Icarus sought the stars, in strange devices trusting, and strove to vanquish true birds in flight, and laid his commands on pinions all too false, his name robbed the sea of its own name.[62] But shrewd old Daedalus, balancing a middle path, stopped midway of the clouds, awaiting his winged son (as a bird flees the threatening hawk and gathers her scattered and frightened brood), until the boy in the sea plied hands enmeshed in the shackles of his daring flight. Whatsoever exceeds the allotted bounds, hangs in a place unsure. (*Enter a messenger from within the palace.*) But what is this? The doors creak open; behold, a servant of the king, stricken with woe, beats with his hand upon his head. Tell us what news thou bringst.

MESSENGER. When Oedipus grasped his foretold fate, and his breed unspeakable, he condemned himself as convicted of the crime and, seeking the palace with deadly purpose, he entered within that hateful roof with hurried step. As over the fields a Libyan lion rages, with threatening front and shaking his tawny mane; so he, his face fierce with passion, with eyes wild staring, with groans and deep mutterings, limbs with cold sweat streaming, froths and threatens, and his mighty, deep-buried anguish overflows. He, raging in soul, plans some monstrous deed to match his destiny.

"Why do I delay punishment?" he cries; "let someone with the sword assail this guilty breast, or overwhelm me with burning fire or stones. What tigress, what ravening bird will pounce upon my vitals? Do thou thyself, thou all-holding haunt of crime, O curst Cithaeron, send thy wild beasts against me from thy forests, send thy maddened dogs—once more send Agave.[63] O soul, why shrinkst from death? Death alone saves innocence from fortune."

With this he lays impious hand on hilt and draws his sword. "So then? With brief suffering like this canst atone for so great crimes, and with one blow wilt pay all debts? Thy death—for thy father it is enough; what then to thy mother, what to thy children shamefully begot, what to her who with utter ruin is atoning for thy crime, thy mourning country, wilt thou give? Thou canst not pay![64] Let that same Nature who in Oedipus alone reverses established laws, devising strange births, be changed anew for my punishment. Be it thine to live again, to die again, ever to be reborn, that at each birth thou mayst pay new penalties. Now use thy wit, poor wretch; let that which may not oft befall, befall thee long—choose thou a lasting death. Search out a way whereon to wander, not mingling with the dead and

---

62 The sea was subsequently called after him the Icarian sea.
63 Agave in her madness had helped tear Pentheus in pieces.
64 *i.e.* by mere death.

yet removed from the living; die thou, but reaching not thy sire. Dost hesitate, O soul?"

Lo, with sudden shower a flood overwhelms his face and waters his cheeks with weeping. "And is it enough to weep? Only thus far shall mine eyes overflow with some few drops? Nay, driven from their sockets, let them follow the tears they shed. Ye gods of wedlock, is it enough? These eyes must be dug out!" He speaks and raves with wrath; his cheeks burn threatening with ferocious fire, and his eyeballs scarce hold themselves in their place; his face is full of reckless daring and mad savagery, as of one in boundless rage; with groans and dreadful cries, his hands into his eyes he thrusts. But his starting eyes stand forth to meet them and, eagerly following their kindred hands rush upon their wound. With hooked fingers he greedily searches out his eyes and, torn from their very roots, he drags both eyeballs out; still stay his hands in the empty sockets and, deep fixed, tear with their nails the deep-set hollows of his eyes and empty cavities; vainly he rages, and with excessive fury raves.

The hazard of light is over; he lifts his head, surveys the regions of the sky with his empty sockets, and makes trial of the night. The shreds which still hang from eyes unskilfully plucked out he breaks away, and in triumph cries aloud to all the gods: "Spare now my land, I pray you; now have I done justice, I have paid the debt I owed; at last have I found night worthy of my wedlock." A hideous shower drenches his face and his mangled brow spouts streams of blood from his bursting veins.

CHORUS. By fate are we driven; yield ye to fate. No anxious cares can change the threads of its inevitable spindle. Whatever we mortals bear, whatever we do, comes from on high; [65] and Lachesis [66] maintains the decrees of her distaff which by no hand may be reversed. All things move on in an appointed path, and our first day fixed our last. Those things God may not change which speed on their way, close woven with their causes. To each his established life goes on, unmovable by any prayer. To many their very fear is bane; for many have come upon their doom while shunning doom.

The gates have sounded, and he himself, with none to guide and sightless, gropes his way.

(*Enter* OEDIPUS.)

OEDIPUS. All's well, it is finished; to my father have I paid my debt. How sweet the darkness! What god, at length appeased, has shrouded my head in this dark veil? Who has forgiven my

[65] A Stoic doctrine.
[66] One of the three Fates.

crimes? I have escaped the conscious eye of day. Nothing, thou parricide, dost owe to thy right hand; the light hath fled from thee. This is the face befitting Oedipus.

(*Enter* JOCASTA.)

CHORUS. See, there, with hurried step, frantic, beside herself, Jocasta rushes forth, just as, in frenzied rage, the Cadmean mother [67] tore her son's head away and realized her deed. She hesitates, longs and yet fears to speak to the afflicted one. Now shame has given way to grief; but her first words falter on her lips.

JOCASTA. What shall I call thee? Son? Dost question it? Thou art my son; does "son" shame thee? Though thou wouldst not, speak, my son—why dost thou turn away thy head, thy sightless face?

OEDIPUS. Who wills not that I enjoy my darkness? Who restores my eyes? My mother's, lo, my mother's voice! I have worked in vain. It is unlawful that we meet again. Let the vast sea roll between our impious selves, let remote lands separate, and if beneath this world there hangs another, facing other stars and a straying sun, let it take one of us.

JOCASTA. Fate's is that fault of thine: by fate no one is made guilty.

OEDIPUS. Now spare thy words, mother, spare my ears, by these remnants of my mangled body, I beseech thee, by the unhallowed offspring of my blood, by all that in our names is right and wrong. [68]

JOCASTA (*aside*). Why art benumbed, my soul? Since thou hast shared his guilt, why dost refuse to share his punishment? Through thee, incestuous one, all grace of human law has been confused and lost. Die then, and let out thy impious spirit with the sword. Not if the father of the gods himself, shaking the universe, with deadly hand should hurl his glittering bolts at me, could I ever pay penalty equal to my crimes—I, a mother accurst. Death is my darling wish; let the way of death be sought.

(*To* OEDIPUS.) Come, lend thy hand against thy mother, if thou art parricide; this lacks to crown thy work.

(*To herself.*) Nay, let me seize his sword; by this blade lies slain my husband—nay, why not call him by his true name?— my husband's father. Shall I pierce my breast with this, or thrust it deep into my bared throat? Thou knowest not to choose a place? Strike here, my hand, through this capacious womb, which

67 Agave.
68 He prays her in the name both of their proper (mother and son) and improper (husband and wife) relations.

bore my husband and my sons! (*She stabs herself and falls dead.*)

CHORUS. There lies she slain. Her hand dies on the wound, and the sword is driven out by strong streams of blood.

OEDIPUS. Thee, O fate-revealer, thee, guardian and god of truth, do I upbraid. My father only did I owe the fates; twice parricide and more guilty than I feared, I have slain my mother; for by my sin is she done to death. O lying Phoebus, I have outdone the impious fates.

With quaking step pursue thy darkling ways; with faltering feet grope through blind night with apprehensive hand. Make haste, planting uncertain steps, go, speed thee, fly!—but stop, lest thou stumble and fall upon thy mother.

All ye who are weary in body and burdened with disease, whose hearts are faint within you, see, I fly, I leave you; lift your heads. Milder skies come when I am gone. He who, though near to death, still keeps some feeble life, may freely now draw deep, life-giving draughts of air. Go, bear ye aid to those given up to death; all pestilential humors of the land I take with me. Ye blasting Fates, thou quaking terror of Disease, Wasting, and black Pestilence, and mad Despair, come ye with me, with me. It is sweet to have such guides.   (*Exit.*)

Medea

A TRAGEDY

by
SENECA

⚜ ⚜ ⚜

translated by
Frank Justus Miller

DRAMATIS PERSONAE

MEDEA, daughter of Aeëtes, king of Colchis, and wife of Jason.

JASON, son of Aeson, and nephew of Pelias, the usurping king of Thessaly; organizer and leader of the Argonautic expedition to Colchis in quest of the Golden Fleece.

CREON, king of Corinth, who had received into his hospitable kingdom Medea and Jason, fugitives from Thessaly, after Medea had plotted the death of Pelias.

NURSE of Medea.

MESSENGER.

TWO SONS of Medea and Jason (personae mutae).

CHORUS OF CORINTHIANS, friendly to Jason and hostile to Medea.

The time of the play is confined to the single day of the culmination of the tragedy, the day proposed by Creon for the banishment of Medea and the marriage of Jason to Creusa, daughter of Creon.

The scene is in Corinth, in the court of the house of Jason.

ARGUMENT

Although *the play is confined in time to the final day of catastrophe at Corinth, the background is the whole romantic story of the Argonauts: how Jason and his hero-comrades, at the instigation of Pelias, the usurping king of Thessalian Iolchos, undertook the first voyage in quest of the Golden Fleece; how, after many adventures, these first sailors reached the kingdom of Aeëtes, who jealously guarded the fleece, since upon its possession depended his own kingship; how the three deadly labors were imposed upon Jason before the fleece could be won—the yoking of the fiery bulls, the contest with the giants that sprang from the sown serpent's teeth, and the overcoming of the sleepless dragon that ever guarded the fleece; how, smitten by love of him, the beautiful barbaric Medea, daughter of the king, by the help of her magic aided Jason in all these labors and accompanied him in his flight; how to retard her father's pursuit she slew her brother and scattered his mangled remains in the path as they fled; how again, for love of Jason, she restored his father to youth and tricked Pelias' own daughters into slaying their aged sire; how, for this act, Medea with her husband were exiled from Thessalia and dwelt in Corinth; how, for ten happy years, she lived with her husband and two sons in this alien land, her wild past almost forgotten, her magic untouched.*

But now Jason has been won away from his wife, and is about to wed Creusa, the daughter of Creon, king of Corinth. The wedding festivities have already begun when the play opens and reveals Medea invoking all the powers of heaven and hell in punishment of her false lord.

Medea. Ye gods of wedlock, and thou, Lucina, guardian of the nuptial couch, and thou [1] who didst teach Tiphys to guide his new barque to the conquest of the seas, and thou, grim ruler of the deeps of Ocean, and Titan, who dost portion out bright day

[1] Minerva.

351

unto the world, and thou who dost show thy bright face as witness of the silent mysteries, O three-formed Hecate, and ye gods by whose divinity Jason swore to me, to whom Medea may more lawfully appeal—thou chaos of endless night, ye realms remote from heaven, ye unhallowed ghosts, thou lord [2] of the realm of gloom, and thou, his queen,[3] won by violence but with better faith than I, with ill-omened speech I make my prayer to you. Be present, be present, ye goddesses [4] who avenge crime, your hair foul with writhing snakes, grasping the smoking torch with your bloody hands, be present now, such as once ye stood in dread array beside my marriage couch; upon this new wife destruction bring, destruction on this father-in-law and the whole royal stock.

I have yet curse more dire to call down on the bridegroom—may he live. Through unknown cities may he wander, in want, in exile, in fear of life, hated and homeless; may he seek hospitality at strange doors, by now a familiar applicant; may he desire me for wife, and, than which I can pray nothing worse, may his children be like their father and like their mother.—Already borne, borne is my vengeance! I have borne children! But why frame complaints and idle words? Shall I not go against my enemies? I'll snatch the bridal-torches from their hands and the light from heaven. Does he behold this, the Sun, father of my race, and do men still behold him [5] as, sitting in his chariot, he courses over bright heaven's accustomed spaces? Why does he not return to his rising and measure back the day? Grant, oh, grant that I ride through the air in my father's car; give me the reins, O sire, give me the right to guide thy fire-bearing steeds with the flaming reins; then let Corinth, with her twin shores cause of delay [6] to ships, be consumed by flames and bring the two seas together.

This course alone remains, that I myself bear the wedding torch unto the chamber and, after sacrificial prayers, slay victims on the consecrated altars. Amid the very entrails seek thou a way for punishment, if thou livest, O soul, if there remains to thee aught of thy old-time strength. Away with womanish fears, clothe thy heart with unfeeling Caucasus. Whatever horror the Black Sea has beheld, or the Phasis River, the Corinthian Isthmus shall behold. Wild deeds, unheard-of, horrible, calamities at which heaven and earth alike shall tremble, my heart deep within is planning—wounds, slaughter, death, creeping from limb to limb. Ah, too trivial the deeds I have rehearsed; these things I did in

2 Pluto.
3 Proserpina.
4 The Furies.
5 He should be darkened at sight of such wickedness.
6 i.e. by requiring ships to sail around the Peloponnesus.

girlhood. Let my grief rise to more deadly strength; greater crimes become me, now that I am a mother. Gird thyself with wrath, and prepare thee for deadly deeds with the full force of madness. Let the story of thy rejection match the story of thy marriage. How wilt thou leave thy husband? Even as thou didst follow him. Break off now dull delay; the home which by crime was gained, by crime must be abandoned.

CHORUS (*chanting the wedding hymn for* JASON *and* CREUSA).
May the gods above who rule over heaven, and they who rule the sea, with gracious divinity attend on our prince's marriage, amid the people's ritual silence. First to the sceptre-bearing Thunderer let the bull with white-shining hide offer his high-raised neck. Juno Lucina let a heifer appease, snow-white, untouched by the yoke; and let Pax who restrains the bloody hands of rough Mars, who brings peace to warring nations and holds plenty in her rich horn, mild goddess, be given a tender victim. And do thou, O Hymen, who attendest the torches of lawful marriage, dissipating the night with propitious hand, hither come, reeling with drunken footstep, binding thy temples with garlands of roses. And thou star of evening, forerunner of twilight, who returnest ever slowly for lovers—thee, mothers, thee, brides eagerly await, to see thee full soon thy bright beams scattering.

Our maiden in beauty far excels the Cecropian brides of Athens, and those who on Taÿgetus' ridges are trained after the manner of men by the unwalled city of Sparta, and those who bathe in Boeotian waters and Alpheus' sacred stream.

Should he wish to be judged in beauty, all will yield to the son of Aeson, our leader—the ruthless lightning's son, Bacchus, who yokes the wild tigers, and he [7] who makes tremble the tripod, the stern virgin's [8] brother; with his twin, Castor, Pollux will yield, more skilful in boxing.

So, so, ye heaven-dwellers, I pray you, let this bride surpass brides, this husband far excel husbands.

When she has taken her stand midst her train of maidens, her one beauty shines more brightly than all. So does starlight splendor wane with the coming of the sun, and the huddled flock of the Pleiades vanish away when Phoebe, shining with borrowed light, with encircling horns encloses her full-orbed disk.

While on such beauty the young lover gazes, see, her cheeks are suddenly covered with rosy blushes. So snowy wool, dipped in purple dye, does redden; so shines the sun when the shepherd at dawn, wet with the dew, beholds it.

[7] Apollo.
[8] Diana.

Do thou, O bridegroom, rescued from the marriage bonds of barbarous Phasis, wont with fear and reluctant hand to caress an unruly wife, joyfully take to thy arms the Aeolian maid [9]—now at last 'tis with the parents' will.

Sport, youths, with free banter and jesting; let your songs ring out, O youths, in responsive cadence; rarely against our lords is unrebuked licence given.

Comely, noble scion [10] of Lyaeus, the thyrsus-bearer, now is the time to light thy torch of frayed pinewood; toss on high the ritual fire with tipsy fingers. Let saucy, sharp wit pour forth festive banterings and let the throng be free with jesting.—Let *her* pass in silent gloom who steals away to wed with a foreign husband.

MEDEA. We are undone! Upon my ears has sounded the marriage-hymn. So great a calamity scarce I myself, scarce even yet can comprehend? Had Jason the heart to do this; having robbed me of my father, native land, and kingdom, could he cruelly leave me alone in a foreign land? Has he scorned my deservings, who saw flames and sea conquered by my crime? Does he think that all my powers of evil are so exhausted? Perplexed, witless, with mind scarce sane, I am tossed to every side. Whence can I get vengeance? I would that he had a brother! [11] A wife he has; into her heart let the sword be driven. Is this enough to offset my woes? All monstrous deeds which Pelasgian, which barbaric cities know, all that thy own hands do not know, must be made ready now. Let thine own crimes urge thee on, and let them all return in memory—the bright ornament of the kingdom stolen away, and the wicked girl's little comrade [12] hewn in pieces with the sword, his murder forced upon his father's sight, his body scattered over the deep, and the limbs of aged Pelias seethed in a brazen pot. Murder and impious bloodshed how often have I wrought!—and yet no crime have I done in wrath; it was ill-omened love that stirred me.

But what else could Jason have done, once made subject to another's will and power? He should have bared his breast unto the sword—nay, ah, nay, mad grief, say not so! If possible, may he live, my Jason, as once he was: if not, still may he live and, mindful of me, keep unharmed the gift I gave, his life. The fault is Creon's, all, who with unbridled sway dissolves marriages, tears mothers from their children, and breaks pledges bound by

9 Creusa, a descendant of Aeolus.
10 Hymen, son of Bacchus and Venus.
11 That he might be slain as her own had been.
12 Absyrtus, whom Medea killed to delay her father's pursuit.

straitest oath; on him be my attack, let him alone pay the penalties which he owes. I will pile his home high with ashes; its dark pinnacles wrapt in flames Medea shall see, where, jutting out, it holds ships in tedious delay.

NURSE. Be silent, I pray thee, and confide to secret grief thy hidden plaints. Whoever has dumbly borne hard blows with patient and calm soul, has been able to repay them; it is hidden wrath that harms; hatred proclaimed loses its chance for vengeance.

MEDEA. Light is the grief which can take counsel and hide itself; great ills lie not in hiding. It is pleasing to face the foe.

NURSE. Stay this frenzied outburst, my child; even silent calm can scarce defend thee.

MEDEA. Fortune fears the brave, the cowardly overwhelms.

NURSE. If there is place for courage, then should it be approved.

MEDEA. It can never be that for courage there is no place.

NURSE. No hope points out a way for our broken fortunes.

MEDEA. Whoso has naught to hope, let him despair of naught.

NURSE. The Colchians are no longer on thy side, thy husband's vows have failed, and there is nothing left of all thy wealth.

MEDEA. Medea is left—in her thou beholdest sea and land, and sword and fire and gods and thunderbolts.

NURSE. The king is to be feared.

MEDEA.   My father was a king.

NURSE. Fearst thou not arms?

MEDEA.   Not though they were sprung from earth.[13]

NURSE. Thou'lt die.

MEDEA.   I wish it.

NURSE.   Flee!

MEDEA.   Of flight I have repented.

NURSE. Medea,

MEDEA.   Will I be.

NURSE.   Thou art a mother.

MEDEA.   By whom, thou seest.

NURSE. Dost delay flight?

MEDEA.   Flee I shall, but I'll take vengeance first.

NURSE. The avenger will pursue.

MEDEA.   Perchance I shall find means to stay him.

NURSE. Check thy words, spare now thy threats, foolish one, and thy proud spirit humble; 'tis well to fit thee to the times.

MEDEA. Fortune can take away my wealth, but not my spirit.—

[13] As when armed warriors sprang from the dragon's teeth sowed in the earth by Jason.

But under whose blows does the king's door upon its hinges creak? It is Creon himself, puffed with Pelasgian power.

(MEDEA *has retired to the back of the stage. Exit* NURSE. *Enter* CREON.)

CREON. Medea, Colchian Aeëtes' baleful child, has she not yet taken herself from my realm? She is plotting mischief; I know her guile, I know her power. Whom will she spare? Whom will she let live in peace? I was making ready to rid me of this outrageous pest by the sword's means and with all speed; but the prayers of my daughter's husband have prevailed. I have granted her life; let her free my boundaries from fear, and depart in safety. (*He sees* MEDEA *approaching.*) Boldly she moves to meet me, and with threatening mien seeks closer speech. Keep her off, ye slaves, from touch and approach far off; bid her keep silence; let her learn at last to obey a king's commands. (*To* MEDEA.) Hence in swift flight! remove at once thine abominable presence, dire, horrible!

MEDEA. What crime, what fault is punished by my exile?

CREON. What cause expels her—that may an innocent woman ask.

MEDEA. If thou'rt my judge, then hear me; if my king, command.

CREON. A king's commands, just and unjust, thou must obey.

MEDEA. Unjust rule never abides continually.

CREON. Go, complain to the Colchians.

MEDEA. I go; but let him take me who brought me thence.

CREON. Thy prayer comes too late; my resolve is fixed.

MEDEA. He who has judged aught, with the other side unheard, may have judged righteously, but was himself unrighteous.

CREON. Didst thou hear Pelias ere he suffered punishment? But say on; let a hearing be granted to thine excellent case.

MEDEA. How hard it is to turn away from wrath the spirit when once aroused, and how royal it seems to him who has grasped the sceptre in his proud hands to go on as he has begun, I have learned in my own royal home. For, although I am overwhelmed by piteous disaster, an exile, suppliant, lonely, forsaken, buffeted on all sides, once I had glory from my noble father, and from my grandsire, the Sun, traced illustrious descent. All the land that Phasis waters with its calm, winding stream, all that Scythian Pontus sees behind it, where the sea grows sweet with marshy waters, all that the unwedded hordes,[14] crescent-shielded, hemmed by Thermodon's banks, fill with alarm—over all this my father rules. High-born, blest of heaven, in royal power and

14 The Amazons.

splendor then I shone; then princes sued for marriage with me, whom now I must sue. Swift and fickle is fortune and, swooping down, has torn me from royalty and given me over to exile.

Put thy trust in royalty, although light chance hither and thither tosses even mighty wealth! This is the glorious, great privilege of kings, which time can never snatch away—to succor the afflicted, on a safe hearth to shelter suppliants. This only have I brought from my Colchian realm, that by my own self I saved that great glory and illustrious flower of Greece, bulwark of the Achaeans, offspring of gods.[15] Orpheus is my gift, who softens the rocks by his singing and draws trees after him; mine, too, are the twins, Castor and Pollux, and the sons of Boreas [16] and Lynceus, who with far-flung gaze sees things removed even beyond Pontus,—and all the Minyans. For of the leader [17] of the leaders I say no word; for him naught is owing; I count none debtor for his sake. For you Greeks I brought back the rest; him only for myself.

Come on now, and heap all kinds of shameful deeds upon me. I will confess them; but as for crimes, this only can be charged, the rescue of the Argo. Suppose modesty should please the maiden, suppose her filial duty should please her; then will the whole Pelasgian land perish with its leaders, and this thy son-in-law will first fall before the fiery breath of the fierce bull.[18] Let what fortune will, oppress me; I repent not the glorious salvation of so many kings. Whatever reward I have won by all my crimes, it is in thy hands. Arraign and condemn me, if it is thy pleasure; but give me back my sin.[19] I am guilty, I confess it, Creon; such didst thou know me when I clasped thy knees and as suppliant sought the loyalty of thy protecting hand. Once more, some corner, some abiding-place for my woes I beg, some paltry hiding-place; if from thy city thou art pleased to drive me, let some remote nook in thy realm be given me.

CREON. That I am not one to wield the sceptre with violence nor to trample upon misery with haughty foot, methinks I have not unclearly shown by choosing for son-in-law an exile, crushed and stricken with heavy fear—aye, one whom Acastus, lord of Thessaly, demands for punishment and death. He complains that his father,[20] palsied and weak with age, burdened with years,

15 The Argonauts.
16 Zetes and Calaïs.
17 Jason.
18 In vivid memory she puts herself back at the parting of the ways, where she was debating in her heart as to her course, and from this standpoint she speaks.
19 *i.e.* Jason, for whom she sinned.
20 Pelias.

was taken off, and the murdered old man's limbs torn asunder, when, deceived by thy guile, his [21] pious sisters dared an impious crime. Jason can defend his own cause if it is separate from thine; no blood has stained his innocence, his hand wielded no sword, and he has kept far off and free from company of such as thou. Thou, thou contriver of wickedness, who combinest woman's wanton recklessness and man's strength, with no thought of reputation, away! Purge my kingdom and take thy deadly herbs with thee; free the citizens from fear; abiding in some other land, harry [22] the gods.

MEDEA. Dost force me to flee? Give back then to the fugitive her ship, yea, give back her comrade.[23] Why dost thou bid me flee alone? I did not come alone. If it is war [24] thou fearest, drive us both from thy kingdom. Why make distinction between two culprits? It is for him Pelias lies dead, and not for me. Add flight, theft, a deserted father, a mangled brother, any crime which even now the bridegroom is teaching his new wives [25]—it is no crime of mine. Full oft have I been made guilty, but never for myself.

CREON. Thy going is already overdue. Why dost contrive delay with words?

MEDEA. Suppliant I make this last prayer to thee as I depart: let not the mother's guilt drag down her guiltless sons.

CREON. Go then; these will I take as father to my fatherly embrace.

MEDEA. By the blest bed of this royal marriage, by thy hopes for the future, and by the estate of thrones, which fickle Fortune disturbs with changeful lot, I pray thee be bountiful of a brief stay of my flight, while I, their mother, imprint on my sons the latest kiss, perchance my dying act.

CREON. For treachery thou art seeking time.

MEDEA. What treachery can be feared in time so scant?

CREON. No time is too brief for harm to those on evil bent.

MEDEA. Dost refuse a poor mother just a little time for tears?

CREON. Though my ingrained fear bids me refuse thy plea, one day shall be given to prepare for banishment.

MEDEA. 'Tis more than enough, though thou retrench it somewhat. I also am in haste.

CREON. With thy life shalt thou pay penalty if before Phoebus brings the bright day thou art not gone from Isthmus.

21 *i.e.* Acastus'.
22 *i.e.* by the power of her witchcraft.
23 Jason.
24 *i.e.* with Acastus.
25 She uses the plural with a sneer.

But the marriage rites summon me, summons the festal day to pray to Hymen.   (*Exeunt*.)

CHORUS. Too venturesome the man who in frail barque first cleft the treacherous seas and, with one last look behind him at the well-known shore, trusted his life to the fickle winds; who, ploughing the waters on an unknown course, could trust to a slender plank, stretching too slight a boundary between the ways of life and death.

Unsullied the ages our fathers saw, with crime banished afar. Then every man inactive kept to his own shores and lived to old age on ancestral fields, rich with but little, knowing no wealth save what his home soil had yielded. Not yet could any read the sky and use the stars with which the heavens are spangled; not yet could ships avoid the rainy Hyades; not yet did the fires of the Olemian Goat nor the Attic Wain which slow old Boötes follows and controls, not yet did Boreas, not yet Zephyrus have names.

Tiphys made bold to spread his canvas on the vasty deep and to write new laws for the winds: now to spread full-bellied sail, now to set the sail sideways and catch cross-breezes, now to set the yards in safety midway of the mast, now to bind them at the top, when the too eager sailor prays for winds and aloft the ruddy topsails flutter. The lands, well separated before by nature's laws, the Thessalian ship [26] made one, bade the deep suffer blows of oars, and the sequestered sea become a part of our human fear.

Heavy the penalties which that bold ship paid, brought through long terrors, when two mountains, barriers of the deep, from either side quick rushing, roared as with sound of thunder, and the sea, caught between, sprinkled their peaks and the clouds themselves. Bold Tiphys paled with fear and let the helm slip wholly from his faltering hand; Orpheus was still, his lyre mute with amaze, and the Argo herself lost voice.[27] What of the time the maid of Sicilian Pelorus, Scylla, her waist begirt with ravenous dogs, opened all her gaping throats together? Who did not shudder in every limb when that one monster howled with so many tongues? What of the time when the deadly pests [28] soothed the Ausonian sea with their tuneful songs, when, sounding back on his Pierian lyre, Thracian Orpheus well-nigh forced the Siren to follow, though wont to hold ships spell-bound by her song? Of

26 The Argo.
27 The Argo's figurehead was made of wood from the talking oaks of Dodona and had itself power to speak and give timely warnings.
28 The Sirens.

this voyage what was the prize? The golden fleece and Medea,
worse evil than the sea, worthy to be the first ship's merchandise.

Now, in our time, the deep has ceased resistance and submits
utterly to law; no famous Argo, framed by a Pallas' hand, with
princes to man its oars, is sought for; any little craft now wanders
at will upon the deep. All bounds have been removed, cities have
set their walls in new lands, and the world, now passable throughout, has left nothing where it once had place: the Indian drinks
of the cold Araxes, the Persians quaff the Elbe and the Rhine.
There will come an age in the far-off years when Ocean shall
unloose the bonds of things, when the whole broad earth shall be
revealed, when Tethys shall disclose new worlds and Thule not be
the limit of the lands.

NURSE (*sees* MEDEA *hurrying out of the house*). Dear child,
whither hurriest thou abroad? Stay, curb thy passion, check thy
impetuous haste. (MEDEA *goes on without heeding*.)   As a
maenad uncertainly directs her frenzied steps when now she raves
at the oncoming of the god, on snowy Pindus' top or on Nysa's
ridges, so she runs now here, now there, with frantic rush, marks
of distracted passion in her face. Her cheeks aflame, she pants
with deep sobs for breath, shouts aloud, weeps floods of tears,
beams with joy; she assumes the proof of every passion. Whither
the weight of her wrath inclines, where it aims its threats, hangs
still in doubt; she threatens, seethes with rage, complains, groans
aloud. Where will this wave break itself? Madness overflows its
bounds. No simple or half-way crime does she ponder in her
heart; she will outdo herself. I recognize the marks of her old-
time rage. Something great is impending, wild, monstrous, impious. (MEDEA *now approaches*.) I see madness in her face. May
Heaven avert my fears!

MEDEA (*aside*). If thou seekst, poor soul, what limit thou
shouldst set to hate, copy thy love. Can it be that unavenged I
should endure this royal wedding? Shall this day go idly by so
anxiously besought, so anxiously bestowed? While the central
earth shall bear up the balanced heavens, while the bright universe shall pursue its unchanging rounds, while sands lack number, while day attends the sun and stars the night, while the
dry [29] Bears revolve about the pole, and rivers fall to the sea,
my madness shall never cease its quest of vengeance and shall
grow on for ever. What ferocity of beasts, what Scylla, what
Charybdis, sucking up the Ausonian and Sicilian waters, or what
Aetna, resting heavily on panting Titan, shall burn with such
threats as I? No whirling river, no storm-tossed sea, no Pontus,

[29] Because these constellations never set beneath the ocean.

raging beneath the north-west wind, no violence of fire, fanned by the gale, could imitate the onrush of my wrath. I shall lay prostrate and destroy all things.

Did he [30] fear Creon and the threats of Thessaly's king? [31] True love can fear no man. But grant that under compulsion he yielded and made surrender; he could at least have come to me, could have spoken some last words to his wife. This also, though bold of heart, he feared to do. Surely it was in the power of the king's son-in-law to put off the time of my cruel banishment— one day was given for my two children. But I complain not that the time is short; it shall stretch far. This day shall do, shall do that whereof no day shall ever be dumb. I will storm the gods, and shake the universe.

NURSE. Win back thy woe-troubled heart, my mistress; calm thy soul.

MEDEA. The only calm for me—if with me I see the universe overwhelmed in ruins; with me let all things pass away. It is sweet to drag others down when thou art perishing. (*Exit.*)

NURSE (*calling after* MEDEA). Beware how many perils are to be feared if thou persist; no one may safely assail the strong.

(*Enter* JASON.)

JASON. O fate, ever hard, and fortune, cruel—when she rages and when she spares, equally malign! How often does God find cures for us worse than our perils; should I resolve to be faithful to my wife according to her deserts, my life would be forfeited to death; should I refuse to die, alas! I must be faithless. It is not fear, but fearful father-love that has conquered faith; surely my children would share their parents' death. O holy Justice, if in heaven thou dwellest, I call thy divinity to witness: the sons have prevailed upon the sire. Nay, even she herself, though she is fierce of heart and ill brooks the yoke, would rather, methinks, take thought for her sons than for her marriage rights. My mind is fixed to assail her wrath with prayers. (*Enter* MEDEA.) And see, at sight of me she starts up, bursts into a passion, displays her hate; all her anguish is in her face.

MEDEA. We are fleeing, Jason, fleeing. It is no new thing to change our abode; but the cause of flight is new—it was *for* thee I was wont to flee. I withdraw, I go away, whom thou art forcing to flee forth from thy home; but whither dost thou send me back? Shall I seek Phasis and the Colchians, my father's kingdom, the fields drenched with my brother's blood? What lands dost thou bid me seek? What waters dost show to me? The jaws

30 Jason.
31 Acastus.

of the Pontic sea through which I brought back the noble band
of princes, following thee, thou adulterer, through the Clashing
Rocks? Is it little Iolcos or Thessalian Tempe I shall seek? All
the ways which I have opened for thee I have closed upon myself. Whither dost send me back? Thou imposest exile on an
exile, but givest no place. But let me go. A king's son-in-law has
commanded it; I'll not refuse. Heap dire penalties upon me;
them have I deserved. Let the angry king crush thy mistress with
cruel punishments, load her hands with chains, shut her up and
bury her in dungeons of eternal darkness; I shall suffer less than
I deserve.

O ungrateful man, let thy heart recall the bull's fiery breath,
and, midst the savage terrors of an unconquered race, the fire-
breathing herd on Aeëtes' arm-bearing [32] plain, the weapons of
the suddenly appearing foe, when, at my order, the earth-born
soldiery fell in mutual slaughter. Think, too, on the long-sought
spoil of the ram of Phrixus, the sleepless dragon, bidden to close
his eyes in unknown slumber, my brother given up to death,
crime not done once alone in one act of crime; think on the
daughters [33] who, lured by my guile, dared dismember the old
man who was never to return to life. By the hopes of thy children, thine established house, by the monsters conquered, by
these hands which I have never spared in thy service, by the
perils we have undergone, by heaven and sea, witnesses of my
marriage, have mercy on me; happy thyself, give thy suppliant
her turn at happiness. Seeking a kingdom for another, I have
given up my own; of all that wealth which, plundered even from
the distant swart tribes of India, the Scythians heap up, that
golden treasure which, since the packed palace can scarce con-
tain it, we hang upon the trees,[34] I brought away nothing in my
exile save only my brother's limbs. Those also I squandered upon
thee; for thee my country has given place, for thee father,
brother, maidenhood—with this dower did I wed thee. Give back
to the fugitive her own.

JASON. When angry Creon was bent on thy destruction, it was
by my tears he was prevailed upon to grant thee banishment.

MEDEA. A punishment I deemed it; now, as I see, exile is a
boon.

JASON. Depart while still thou mayst; take thyself hence;
grievous ever is the wrath of kings.

[32] Where the dragon's teeth sowed by Jason sprang up into full-armed
warriors.
[33] Of Pelias.
[34] Referring to the golden fleece.

MEDEA. In urging this upon me, thou art Creusa's advocate; thou wouldst remove the rival whom she hates.

JASON. What! Medea charge me with love?

MEDEA. Yes, murder, too, and treachery.

JASON. What crime, pray, canst thou charge to me?

MEDEA. Whatever I have done.

JASON. This one thing remains still for me, to become guilty of thy sins as well.

MEDEA. They are, they are thine own; who profits by a sin has done the sin. Though all should hold thy wife infamous, do thou alone protect her, do thou alone call her innocent; let her be guiltless in thy sight, who for thy sake is guilty.

JASON. Unwelcome is life which one is ashamed to have accepted.

MEDEA. Then one should not keep a life which he is ashamed to have accepted.

JASON. Nay, calm thy wrath-stirred heart; for thy sons' sake be reconciled.

MEDEA. I reject, forswear, disown them! Shall Creusa bear brothers to my children?

JASON. Yes, a queen, to the sons of exiles; a royal lady to the fallen.

MEDEA. Never may such ill day come to the wretched, as shall mingle a base breed with illustrious stock Phoebus' sons with the sons of Sisyphus.

JASON. Why, wretched woman, dost thou drag both me and thee to ruin? Begone, I pray thee.

MEDEA. Creon has heard my prayer.

JASON. What can I do? Tell me.

MEDEA. For me? Crime.

JASON. A king on this side and on that——

MEDEA. There is (and this more fearsome still) Medea. Let us [35] strive together, and let the prize be Jason.

JASON. I yield, worn with trouble. And do thou thyself beware lest thou tempt fate too often.

MEDEA. Always has every fortune stood beneath my feet.

JASON. Acastus is hard after us.

MEDEA. Nearer foe is Creon; flee them both. That thou arm thy hand against thy father-in-law, and stain thyself with kindred [36] blood, Medea does not compel thee; remain guiltless and escape with me.

[35] i.e. Creon and me.
[36] Acastus was Jason's cousin.

Jason. And who will resist if double war assail us, if Creon and Acastus unite their arms?

Medea. Add the Colchians to these, add Aeëtes, too, to lead them, join Scythians with Pelasgians; to destruction will I give them all.

Jason. I tremble at lofty sceptres.

Medea. See that thou lust not after them.

Jason. Cut short this long discourse, lest it arouse suspicion.

Medea. Now, O most high Jupiter, thunder throughout thy heavens, stretch forth thy hand, thine avenging flames prepare, rend the clouds and make the whole world quake. Let thy bolts be poised with hand that chooseth neither me nor him; whichever of us falls will perish guilty; against us thy bolt can make no error.

Jason. Begin to think with reason, and speak with calm. If any solace from my father-in-law's house can soothe thy flight, request it.

Medea. To scorn the wealth of kings, my soul, as well thou knowest, hath strength and wont. I ask but this: that I may have my children as comrades of my flight, that in their bosoms I may pour forth my tears. Thee new sons await.

Jason. I confess that right gladly would I yield unto thy prayer, but a father's love forbids; for that I should permit this thing, not Creon himself, my king and father-in-law, could force me. This is my reason for living, this, my heart's comfort, consumed as it is with cares. Sooner could I part with breath, with limbs, with light.

Medea (aside). Thus does he love his sons? 'Tis well! I have him! The place to wound him is laid bare. (To Jason.) As I depart, my final message, at least, grant me to speak; grant me to give the last embrace; even that will be a boon. With my latest utterance I beg thee now; let not any words my distracted grief has poured forth remain within thy mind; let the memory of my better self stay with thee, and let these words spoken in wrath be quite forgot.

Jason. All have I driven from my mind, and I also make prayer to thee that thou curb thy hot passion and be calm; peace soothes the soul's distresses.   (Exit.)

Medea. He has gone! Can it be so? Goest thou, forgetful of me and of all the deeds I wrought? Have we fallen from thy memory? Nay, we shall never fall therefrom. (To herself.) To thy task; summon up all thy powers and arts. The fruit of thy crimes is to count nothing crime. There is scant room for fraud;

we are held in fear. There make attack where no one can fear aught. Haste thee now, dare, begin whatever Medea can—and cannot—do. (*To the* NURSE.) Do thou, faithful nurse, comrade of my grief and of my shifting fortunes, help my unhappy plannings. I have a robe, a gift from heaven, the glory of our house and kingdom, given by the Sun to Aeetes as a pledge of fatherhood; there is also a gleaming necklace of woven gold and a golden band which the sparkle of gems adorns, with which the hair is encircled. Let my sons bring these as gifts unto the bride, but let them first be anointed and imbued with baneful poisons. Now call on Hecate. Prepare the death-dealing rites; let altars be erected, and let now their fires resound within the palace.

CHORUS. No violence of fire or of swelling gale, no fearful force of hurtling spear, is as great as when a wife, robbed of her love, burns hot with hate; not when cloudy Auster has brought the winter's rains, and Hister's floods speeds on, wrecking bridges in its course, and wanders afield; not when the Rhone beats back the sea, or when the snows melt into streams beneath the sun's strong rays and in mid-spring Haemus has dissolved. Blind is the fire of love when fanned by rage, cares not to be controlled, brooks no restraint, has no fear of death; 'tis eager to advance even against the sword.

Have mercy, O gods, be gracious, we beseech you, that he [37] may live in safety who tamed the sea; but the lord of the deep is enraged that the second realm is conquered. The youth [38] who dared drive the everlasting chariot, heedless of his father's goal, himself caught the fire which in his madness he scattered over the sky. The familiar path has cost no mortal dear; walk thou where it was safe for folk aforetime, nor break, rash man, the inviolable covenants of the universe.

Whoever handled that daring ship's famous oars and despoiled Pelion of his sacred grove's thick shade, whoever entered between the roaming rocks [39] and, having passed the perils of the deep, moored his vessel on a savage shore, to return captor of foreign gold—all by a dreadful end atoned for the sea's outraged laws.

Punishment the challenged ocean claims. First of all, Tiphys, the tamer of the deep, gave up control to an untrained helmsman; dying on a foreign shore, far from his ancestral realm, in a paltry tomb he lies midst unfamiliar shades. For this, Aulis,

[37] Jason, who first ventured on the sea in the Argo.
[38] Phaëthon.
[39] The Symplegades.

remembering her lost king, in her becalmed harbor holds ships chafing at delay.[40]

That son [41] of the tuneful Muse, at whose sweet melodies the swift stream stood still and the winds were hushed, when the bird, leaving off its own singing, came near him, the whole wood following after—he lay scattered over the Thracian fields, but his head floated down mournful Hebrus; he came to the famil- iar [42] Styx and Tartarus, never to return.

Hercules laid low the sons [43] of Aquilo, he slew Neptune's son [44] wont to take upon him countless shapes; but he himself, after establishing peace on land and sea, after opening up the kingdoms of savage Dis, laid him down, living, on burning Oeta, and gave his body to the devouring flames, consumed by the wasting of the double blood,[45] his wife's offering.

The bristling boar,[46] irresistible in his thrust, laid Ancaeus low; thou, Meleager, dost impiously slay thy mother's brother and diest by thine enraged mother's hand. All these deserved the charge [47] for which that tender boy,[48] sought vainly by mighty Hercules, atoned by death—the boy snatched away, alas, midst peaceful waters. Go now, ye brave, plough up the sea, whose streams ye ought to dread.

Idmon, though he well knew his fate, was slain [49] by a serpent on Libya's sands; true to all, but false to himself alone, Mopsus fell and saw not Thebes again. If he [50] told truth as to the future, Thetis' husband [51] shall in exile wander. Nauplius, while striving to wreck the Argives by false beacon fires, shall fall headlong into the deep; his son [52] shall perish and pay the penalty of his father's sin; [53] Ajax, too, dying midst flame and flood; redeeming from death her lord [54] of Pherae, the wife [55] shall perish, giving up her life for her husband's sake. Pelias himself, who bade the prize of the golden spoil be brought away in the first ship, seeth-

40 *i.e.* Aulis, long after this event, keeps the Greek fleet back from Troy, as if thus taking vengeance on that first fleet which robbed her of her king.
41 Orpheus.
42 Orpheus had visited the lower world once before.
43 Zetes and Calaïs.
44 Periclymenus.
45 *i.e.* the commingled blood of the hydra and of Nessus.
46 The Calydonian boar.
47 *i.e.* of violating the sea.
48 Hylas.
49 He could foresee the fate of others, as of Peleus, but could not foresee and guard against his own.
50 Mopsus.
51 Peleus.
52 Palamedes.
53 *i.e.* of joining in the Argonautic expedition.
54 Admetus.
55 Alcestis.

ing in boiling pot, wandering midst waters close confined, perished by fire. Enough now, ye gods, have ye avenged the sea; spare him [56] who was ordered to the task.

NURSE (*alone*). My spirit quakes with horror; some great disaster is at hand. Monstrously grows her grief, feeds its own fires and renews its former strength. Often have I seen her in frenzy and assailing the gods,[57] drawing down the sky; but greater than such deeds, greater is the monstrous thing Medea is preparing. For now that with maddened steps she has gone out and come to her baleful shrine, she lavishes all her stores and brings forth whatever even she herself long has dreaded, and marshals her whole train of evil powers, things occult, mysterious, hidden; and, supplicating the grim altar with her left hand, she summons destructive agencies, whatever burning Libya's sands produce, what Taurus, stiff with Arctic cold, holds fast in his everlasting snows, and all monstrous things. Drawn by her magic incantations, the scaly brood leave their lairs and come to her. Here a savage serpent drags its huge length along, darts out its forked tongue, and seeks against whom it is to come death-dealing; hearing her incantation, it stops in amaze, knots its swollen body into writhing folds, and settles them into coils. "Petty are the evils," she cries, "and cheap is the weapon which deepest earth begets; from heaven will I seek my poisons. Now, now is the time to set in motion some plan deeper than common guile. Hither let that serpent [58] descend which lies like a vast rushing stream, whose huge folds the two beasts [59] feel, the greater and the less (the greater used [60] by Pelasgians; by Sidonians, the less); let Ophiuchus at length relax his choking grip and give the poison vent; in answer to my incantations let Python come, who dared to attack the twin divinities.[61] Let Hydra return and every serpent cut off by the hand of Hercules, restoring itself by its own destruction. Thou, too, ever-watchful dragon,[62] quitting the Colchians, come thou to my aid, thou who through my incantations wast first lulled to slumber."

When she had summoned forth the whole tribe of serpents, she assembled her evil store of baleful herbs. Whatever trackless Eryx produces on his rocky slopes; plants that grow on heights clothed in unbroken winter, the heights of Caucasus, spattered

---

[56] Jason.
[57] *i.e.* the sun and moon.
[58] The constellation Draco, winding between the two Bears.
[59] The Bears.
[60] *i.e.* as a fixed point in sailing.
[61] Apollo and Diana.
[62] Which guarded the golden fleece.

with Prometheus' gore; plants wherewith the rich Arabians smear their arrows, and the bold Mede, girt with his quiver, or the light-armed Parthians; or those juices which, under the cold pole, high-born Sueban women gather in Hyrcanian groves; whatever the earth produces in the nest-building springtime or when frozen winter has stripped the woods of their glory and bound all things with icy fetters; all plants that bloom with deadly flower, and all whose juices breed cause of death in their twisted roots—all these she handles. Haemonian Athos contributed those baneful herbs, these, mighty Pindus; on the ridges of Pangaeus that plant was lopped of its tender foliage with a bloody sickle; these Tigris fed, checking his deep flood the while; the Danube, those; these, gem-studded Hydaspes, flowing with warm waters, through thirsty tracts, and the Baetis, which gave its name to its own country,[63] pushing into the western sea with languorous flood. These plants felt the knife while Phoebus was making ready the day; the shoot of that was clipped at midnight; while this was severed by finger-nail with muttered charm.

She seizes death-dealing herbs, squeezes out serpents' venom, and with these mingles unclean birds, the heart of a boding owl, and a hoarse screech-owl's vitals cut out alive. Other objects the mistress of evil arts lays out, arranged in separate heaps; in some is the ravening power of fire; in others numbing frost's icy cold. She adds to her poisons words, no less fearsome than they.— But listen, her frenzied step has sounded, and she chants her incantations. All nature shudders as she begins her song.

(*Enter* MEDEA, *singing an incantation.*)

MEDEA. I supplicate the throng of the silent, and you, funereal gods, murky Chaos and shadowy Dis' dark dwelling-place, the abysses of dismal Death, girt by the banks of Tartarus. Leaving your punishments, ye ghosts, haste to the new nuptials; let the wheel stop that is whirling his body, and Ixion stand on earth; let Tantalus in peace drink his fill of the Pirenian spring. You, too, whom a fruitless toil mocks with urns full of holes, ye Danaids, come hither; this day needs your hands. On one alone, my lord's new father, let a penalty rest heavier—let the slippery stone roll Sisyphus [64] backward over the rocks.

Now, summoned by my sacred rites, do thou,[65] orb of the night, put on thy most evil face and come, threatening in all thy forms.[66]

[63] Provincia Baetica, in Spain.
[64] Sisyphus was father of Creon, and he alone is not to be relieved of his toil. This toil is even to be increased, and so bring greater anguish to Creon.
[65] Hecate as the moon-goddess.
[66] Hecate is *triformis, triceps.*

For thee, loosing my hair from its bands after the manner of my people, with bare feet have I trod the secret groves and called forth rain from the dry clouds; I have driven the seas back to their lowest depths, and the Ocean, his tides outdone, has sent his crushing waves farther into the land; and in like manner, with heaven's law confounded, the world has seen both sun and stars together, and you, ye bears, have bathed in the forbidden sea.[67] The order of the seasons have I changed: the summer land has blossomed beneath my magic song, and by my compelling Ceres has seen harvest in winter-time; Phasis has turned his swift waters backward to their source, and Hister, divided into many mouths, has checked his boisterous streams and flowed sluggishly in all his beds. The waves have roared, the mad sea swelled, though the winds were still; the heart of the ancient woods has lost its shadows, when the bright day has come back to them at commandment of my voice; Phoebus has halted in mid-heaven, and the Hyades, moved by my incantations, totter to their fall. The hour is at hand, O Phoebe, for thy sacred rites. (*She offers various gifts to* HECATE.)

To thee I offer these wreaths wrought with bloody hands, each entwined with nine serpent coils; to thee, these serpent limbs which rebellious Typhoeus wore, who caused Jove's throne to tremble. In this is the blood which Nessus, that traitor ferryman, bestowed as he expired. With these ashes the pyre on Oeta sank down which drank in the poisoned blood of Hercules. Here thou seest the billet [68] of a pious sister but impious mother, Althaea, the avenger. These feathers the Harpy left in her trackless lair when she fled from Zetes. Add to these the quills of the wounded Stymphalian bird which felt the darts of Lerna.[69]—You have given forth your voice, ye altars; I see my tripods shaken by the favouring deity.

I see Trivia's swift gliding car, not as when, radiant, with full face, she drives the livelong night, but as when, ghastly, with mournful aspect, harried by Thessalian threats, she skirts with nearer rein the edge of heaven. So do thou wanly shed from thy torch a gloomy light through air; terrify the peoples with new dread, and let precious Corinthian bronzes resound, Dictynna, to

---

67 The Great Bear and the Little Bear never set, or sink into the sea.

68 When her son Meleager had slain her brothers at the hunt, Althaea caused his death by burning the piece of firewood upon which his life depended as long as it was unburned.

69 *i.e.* the arrows of Hercules, poisoned with the gall of the Lernaean hydra.

thy aid.[70] To thee on the altar's bloody turf we perform thy solemn rites; to thee a torch caught up from the midst of a funeral pyre has illumed the night; to thee, tossing my head and with bended neck, I have uttered my magic words; for thee a fillet, lying in funeral fashion, binds my flowing locks; to thee is brandished the gloomy branch of cypress from the Stygian stream; to thee with bared breast will I as a maenad smite my arms with the sacrificial knife. Let my blood flow upon the altars; accustom thyself, my hand, to draw the sword and endure the sight of beloved blood. (*She slashes her arm and lets the blood flow upon the altar.*) Self-smitten have I poured forth the sacred stream.

But if thou complainest that too often thou art called on by my prayers, pardon, I pray; the cause, O Perses' daughter,[71] of my too oft calling on thy bows is one and the same ever, Jason.

Do thou now (*she takes a phial*) poison Creusa's robe that, when she has donned it, the creeping flame may consume her inmost marrow. Within this tawny gold (*she takes a casket*) lurks fire, darkly hid; Prometheus gave it me, even he who expiates with ever-growing liver his theft from heaven, and taught me by his art how to store up its powers. Vulcan has also given me fires which subtly lurk in sulphur; and bolts of living flame I took from my kinsman,[72] Phaëthon. I have gifts from Chimaera's middle part,[73] I have flames caught from the bull's scorched throat, which, well mixed with Medusa's gall, I have bidden to guard their bane in silence.

Give sting to my poisons, Hecate, and in my gifts keep hidden the seeds of fire. Let them cheat the sight, let them endure the touch; let burning fire penetrate to heart and veins; let her limbs melt and her bones consume in smoke, and with her blazing locks let the bride outshine her wedding torches.

My prayers are heard: thrice has bold Hecate bayed loud, and has raised her accursèd fire with its baleful light.

Now all my power is marshalled; hither call my sons that by their hands thou mayst send these costly gifts unto the bride. (MEDEA's *sons are brought in.*) Go, go, my sons, born of an ill-starred mother, win to yourselves by means of gifts and much beseeching your mistress and stepmother. Begone and quickly come you home again, that I may enjoy one last embrace.

---

[70] The moon in eclipse was supposed to be suffering under the spell of magic, which spell might be removed by beating on brazen vessels and by making other loud noises.

[71] *i.e.* Hecate; the bow is typical of her aid in magic.

[72] Both Medea and Phaëthon were descended from Phoebus.

[73] *i.e.* the goat part, which vomited fire.

(*Exeunt sons towards the palace;* MEDEA *in the opposite direction.*)

CHORUS. Whither is this blood-stained maenad borne headlong by mad passion? What crime with reckless fury is she preparing? Her distraught face is hard set in anger, and with fierce tossings of her head she haughtily threatens even the king. Who would think her an exile?

Her cheeks blaze red, pallor puts red to flight; no color in her changing aspect does she keep long. Hither and thither she wanders, as a tigress, robbed of her cubs, ranges in mad course through the jungles of Ganges.

How to curb her anger Medea knows not, nor yet her love; now that anger and love have joined cause, what will the outcome be? When will the wicked Colchian be gone from the Pelasgian borders and free from terror at once our kingdom and our kings? Now, O Phoebus, speed thy chariot with no check of rein; let friendly darkness veil the light, and let Hesperus, vanguard of the night, plunge deep this fearful day.

(*Enter* MESSENGER, *running from the direction of the palace.*)

MESSENGER. All is lost! The kingdom's props have fallen. Daughter and father in commingled ashes lie.

CHORUS. By what snare taken?

MESSENGER. By the common snare of kings—by gifts.

CHORUS. What snare could have been in them?

MESSENGER. Myself, I also marvel, and, though the woeful thing is done, can scarce believe it could be done. What stay is there to ruin? The greedy fire rages through the palace's every part as if it were bidden so. Already the whole house has fallen, the city is in peril.

CHORUS. Let water put out the flames.

MESSENGER. Nay, in this disaster this marvel, too, has happened: water feeds the flames, and the more it is checked, the more fiercely burns the fire; the very defences [74] does it seize upon.

(*Enter* MEDEA, *in time to hear the last words.*)

NURSE (*to* MEDEA). Quickly begone, Medea, from the land of Pelops; seek headlong any land thou wilt!

MEDEA. What I—shall I give ground? Nay, had I fled already, for this I should return. Strange nuptials see I here. (*She becomes absorbed in her own thoughts.*) Why, soul, dost falter? Follow up the attack so well begun. How small a part of thy vengeance is that in which thou art rejoicing! Thou dost love him still, mad one, if it is enough for thee that Jason wifeless be. Seek thou some unaccustomed form of chastisement, and now

[74] Water, the natural defence against fire.

thus prepare thyself: let all right give way; let honor begone, defeated; light is the rod which innocent hands uplift. Bend to thine anger, rouse up thy halting purpose, and with all thy strength drain from thy heart's very depths its old-time violence. Let all that has yet been done be called but piety. To the task; let them know how petty, of what common stamp, were the crimes I wrought to serve him. In them my grief was but practicing; what great deed had prentice hands the power to do? What, a girl's rage? Now I am Medea; my wit has grown through suffering.

Glad am I, glad, that I tore off my brother's head, glad that I carved his limbs, that I robbed my father of his guarded treasure,[75] glad that I armed daughters [76] for an old man's death. Seek thou fresh fields, my grief; no untrained hand wilt thou bring to any crime.

Whither, then, wrath, art tending, or what weapons art thou aiming at the forsworn foe? [77] A dark purpose my fierce spirit has resolved within me, and dares not yet acknowledge to itself. Fool! fool! I have gone too fast—would that mine enemy had children by his paramour! (*She pauses and then addresses herself.*) All offspring that thou hast by him are Creusa's brood. Resolved is this way of vengeance, rightly resolved; for a last deed of guilt, I see it now, must my soul make ready. Children that once were mine, do you pay penalty for your father's crimes.

Horror has smit my heart! My limbs are numb with cold and my heart with terror flutters. Wrath has given place; the mother has all come back, the wife is banished. Can I shed my children's, my own offspring's blood? Ah, mad rage, say not so! Far, even from me, be that unheard-of deed, that accursed guilt! What sin will the poor boys atone? Their sin is that Jason is their father, and, greater sin, that Medea is their mother. (*She pauses.*) Let them die, they are none of mine; let them be lost—they are my own. They are without crime and guilt, yea, they are innocent—I acknowledge it; so, too, was my brother. Why, soul, dost hesitate? Why are my cheeks wet with tears? Why do anger and love now hither, now thither draw my changeful heart? A double tide tosses me, uncertain of my course; as when rushing winds wage mad warfare, and from both sides conflicting floods lash the seas and the fluctuating waters boil, even so is my heart tossed. Anger puts love to flight, and love, anger. O wrath, yield thee to love.

Hither, dear children, sole comfort of my fallen house, come hither and link your entwining limbs with mine. Let your father

75 The golden fleece.
76 *i.e.* of Pelias.
77 Jason.

have you unharmed, so but your mother may have you too. But exile and flight press hard upon me; now, now will they be torn from my bosom and carried away from me, midst tears and sighs and kisses.—Let them be lost to their father; they are lost to me. My grief grows again and my hate burns hot; Erinys, as of old, claims my unwilling hand. O wrath, where thou dost lead I follow. I would that from my womb the throng of proud Niobe had sprung, and that I had been the mother of twice seven sons! Too barren have I been for vengeance—yet for my brother and my father there is enough, for I have borne two sons.

Whither hastes that headlong horde of Furies? Whom seek they? Against whom are they preparing their flaming blows? Whom does the hellish host threaten with its bloody brands? A huge snake hisses, whirled with the writhing lash. Whom does Megaera seek with her deadly torch? Whose shade comes there dimly seen, its limbs all scattered? It is my brother, and it is punishment he seeks. We'll pay, yes, all the debt. Plunge your brands into my eyes, tear, burns; see, my breast is open to the Furies.

O brother, bid the avenging goddesses depart from me, and go in peace to the deep-buried ghosts; to myself leave me and use this hand, brother, which has drawn the sword—(*She slays the first son.*) With this victim I appease thy ghost.—What means that sudden noise? 'Tis arms they are making ready, and they seek me for my slaying. To the lofty roof of our palace will I mount, now the bloody work has been begun. (*To her remaining son.*) Do thou come with me. (*To her dead son.*) Thy corpse also will I take hence with me. Now to the task, O soul; not in secrecy must thy great deed be lost; to the people approve thy handiwork. (*Exit* MEDEA, *carrying the body of her dead son and leading the living. Enter* JASON *in the street below shouting to the citizens.*)

JASON. Ye faithful souls, who mourn your prince's doom, rally to me that we may take the author herself of this dread crime. Here, here, my brave band of warriors, bring weapons, raze this house to the very ground.

MEDEA (*appearing on the house top.*) Now, now have I regained my regal state, my brother, my sire; and the Colchians have once more the spoil of the golden fleece; restored is my kingdom, my ravished virginity is restored. Oh, divinities, at last propitious, oh, festal day, oh, nuptial day! On! the crime is accomplished; but vengeance is not yet complete; be done with it while thy hands are still about it. Why dost thou delay now, O soul? Why hesitate, though thou canst do it? Now has my wrath died within me. I am sorry for my act, ashamed. What, wretched woman, have I done?—wretched, say I? Though I repent, yet have I done it! Great joy steals on me 'gainst my will, and lo, it is increasing. (*She catches sight of* JASON *in the crowd below.*) This one thing I lacked, that yon man should behold. Naught have I done as yet; whatever crime I've done is lost unless he see it.

JASON (*discovering her*). See, there she is herself, leaning over the sheer battlement! Someone bring fire that she may fall consumed by her own flames.

MEDEA. Nay, Jason, heap up for thy sons their last funeral pyre; build them a tomb. Thy wife and father have already the services due the dead, buried by me; this son has met his doom, and this shall suffer like fate before thy eyes.

JASON. By all the gods, by our flight together, by our marriage couch, to which I have not been faithless, spare the boy. If there is any guilt, 'tis mine. I give myself up to death; destroy my guilty head.

MEDEA. Here (*Pointing to the living son.*) where thou dost forbid it, where it will grieve thee, will I plunge the sword. Go now, haughty man, take thee maids for wives, abandon mothers.

JASON. One is enough for punishment.

MEDEA. If this hand could be satisfied with the death of one, it would have sought no death at all. Though I slay two, still is the count too small to appease my grief. If in my womb there still lurk any pledge of thee, I'll search my very vitals with the sword and hale it forth.

JASON. Now end what thou hast begun—I make no more entreaty—and at least spare my sufferings this suspense.

MEDEA. Enjoy a slow revenge, hasten not, my grief; mine is the day; we are but using the allotted [78] time.

JASON. O heartless one, slay me.

MEDEA. Thou biddst me pity—(*She slays the second son.*) It is well, it's done. I had no more atonement to offer thee, O grief. Lift thy tear-swollen eyes hither, ungrateful Jason. Dost recognize thy wife? It is thus [79] I am wont to flee. A way through the air has opened for me; two serpents offer their scaly necks bending to the yoke. Now, father, take back thy sons. (*She throws the bodies down to him.*) I through the air on my winged car shall ride. (*She mounts the car and is borne away.*)

JASON (*calling after her*). Go on through the lofty spaces of high heaven and bear witness, where thou ridest, that there are no gods.

[78] *i.e.* Creon had granted Medea this whole day for her own in Corinth.
[79] By means of a dragon-drawn car which now appears in the air.

Selected Bibliography

PLAUTUS
Best editions of the complete plays, in Latin text are by: F. Ritschl (Leipzig, 1884–1890); W. M. Lindsay (Oxford, 1903); A. Ernout (Paris, 1932–1938).

Best editions of individual plays, with Latin text and notes and commentary in English or German:
J. Brix and M. Niemayer, *Menaechmi*. Leipzig, 1891.
———, *Captivi*. Leipzig, 1897.
W. M. Lindsay, *Captivi*. London, 1900.
E. A. Sonnenschein, *Rudens*. London, 1903.
F. Marx, *Rudens*. Leipzig, 1928.

Books about Plautus:
G. Michaut, *Plaute*. Paris, 1920.
E. Fraenckel, *Plautinisches im Plautus*. Berlin, 1922.
P. Lejay, *Plaute*. Paris, 1925.
T. Frank, *Life and Literature in the Roman Republic*. Berkeley (Calif.), 1930.
G. Jachmann, *Plautinisches und Attisches*. Berlin, 1931.
G. Norwood, *Plautus and Terence*. New York, 1932.
F. A. Wright, *Three Roman Poets*. London, 1932.

TERENCE
Best Latin editions:
R. Kauer and W. M. Lindsay, *Text of Terence*. Oxford, 1926.
S. G. Ashmore, *The Comedies of Terence*. New York, 1908. Has notes and commentary.

Books about Terence:
P. Fabia, *Les Prologues de Térence*. Paris, 1888.
G. Norwood, *The Art of Terence*. Oxford, 1923.
———, *Plautus and Terence*. New York, 1923.
T. Frank, *Life and Literature in the Roman Republic*. Berkeley (Calif.), 1930.

SENECA

Best Latin text:
R. Peiper, *L. Annaei Senecae Tragoediae*. Leipzig, 1902.

Selected plays with Latin texts, and notes and commentary in English:
H. M. Kingery, *Hercules Furens, Troades, Medea*. New York, 1908.

Books about Seneca:
F. Holland, *Seneca*. London, 1920.
F. L. Lucas, *Seneca and Elizabethan Tragedy*. Cambridge, 1922.
C. W. Mendell, *Our Seneca*. New Haven (Conn.), 1941.

ROMAN THEATER

M. Bieber, *The History of Greek and Roman Theater*. Princeton, 1939.
P. W. Harsh, *A Handbook of Classical Drama*. Stanford, 1944.
W. Beare, *The Roman Stage*. London, 1950.

HISTORIES OF LATIN LITERATURE

J. W. Duff, *A Literary History of Rome, from the Origins to the Close of the Golden Age*. London, 1909.
———, *A Literary History of Rome in the Silver Age*. London, 1927.
H. J. Rose, *A Handbook of Latin Literature*. New York, 1960; reprint of 1936 edition.
M. Hadas, *A History of Latin Literature*. New York, 1952.

INFLUENCES

G. Highet, *The Classical Tradition*. Oxford, 1949.

BANTAM CLASSICS

are chosen from the whole span
of living literature. They
comprise a balanced selection
of the best novels, poems, plays
and stories by writers whose
works and thoughts have made
an indelible impact on
Western culture.

BANTAM CLASSICS